W9-CAB-184

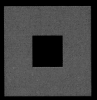

THE WILD STORM
※ VOLUME 1

WARREN ELLIS
※ WRITER

JON DAVIS-HUNT
※ ARTIST

STEVE BUCCELLATO
IVAN PLASCENCIA
JOHN KALISZ
※ COLORISTS

SIMON BOWLAND
※ LETTERER

JIM LEE,
SCOTT WILLIAMS
AND ALEX SINCLAIR
※ COLLECTION
COVER ARTISTS

MARIE JAVINS	Editor – Original Series
BRITTANY HOLZHERR	Assistant Editor – Original Series
JEB WOODARD	Group Editor – Collected Editions
STEVE COOK	Design Director – Books and Publication Design
BOB HARRAS	Senior VP – Editor-in-Chief, DC Comics
PAT McCALLUM	Executive Editor, DC Comics
DIANE NELSON	President
DAN DiDIO	Publisher
JIM LEE	Publisher
GEOFF JOHNS	President & Chief Creative Officer
AMIT DESAI	Executive VP – Business & Marketing Strategy, Direct to Consumer & Global Franchise Management
SAM ADES	Senior VP & General Manager, Digital Services
BOBBIE CHASE	VP & Executive Editor, Young Reader & Talent Development
MARK CHIARELLO	Senior VP – Art, Design & Collected Editions
JOHN CUNNINGHAM	Senior VP – Sales & Trade Marketing
ANNE DePIES	Senior VP – Business Strategy, Finance & Administration
DON FALLETTI	VP – Manufacturing Operations
LAWRENCE GANEM	VP – Editorial Administration & Talent Relations
ALISON GILL	Senior VP – Manufacturing & Operations
HANK KANALZ	Senior VP – Editorial Strategy & Administration
JAY KOGAN	VP – Legal Affairs
JACK MAHAN	VP – Business Affairs
NICK J. NAPOLITANO	VP – Manufacturing Administration
EDDIE SCANNELL	VP – Consumer Marketing
COURTNEY SIMMONS	Senior VP – Publicity & Communications
JIM (SKI) SOKOLOWSKI	VP – Comic Book Specialty Sales & Trade Marketing
NANCY SPEARS	VP – Mass, Book, Digital Sales & Trade Marketing
MICHELE R. WELLS	VP - Content Strategy

THE WILD STORM VOLUME 1

Published by DC Comics. Compilation and all new material Copyright © 2017 DC Comics. All Rights Reserved. Originally published in single magazine form in THE WILD STORM 1-6. Copyright © 2017 DC Comics. All Rights Reserved. All characters, their distinctive likenesses and related elements featured in this publication are trademarks of DC Comics. The stories, characters and incidents featured in this publication are entirely fictional. DC Comics does not read or accept unsolicited submissions of ideas, stories or artwork.

DC Comics, 2900 West Alameda Ave., Burbank, CA 91505
Printed by Solisco Printers, Scott, QC, Canada. 9/15/17. First Printing.
ISBN: 978-1-4012-7418-4

Library of Congress Cataloging-in-Publication Data is available.

PEFC Certified

This product is from sustainably managed forests, recycled and controlled sources

PEFC/26-31-02   www.pefc.org

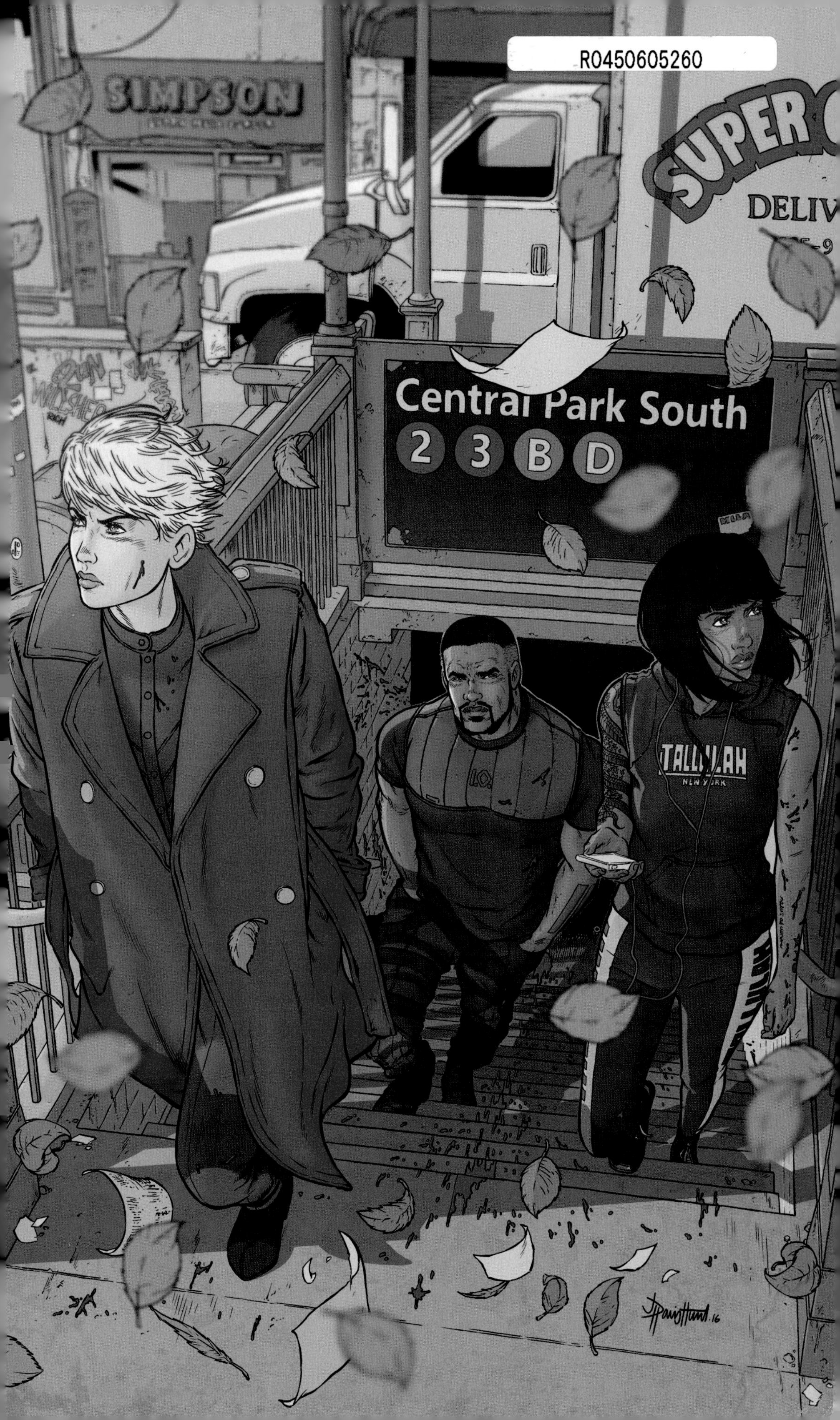
SIMPSON
SUPER
Central Park South
2 3 B D
TALLULAH
NEW YORK

1

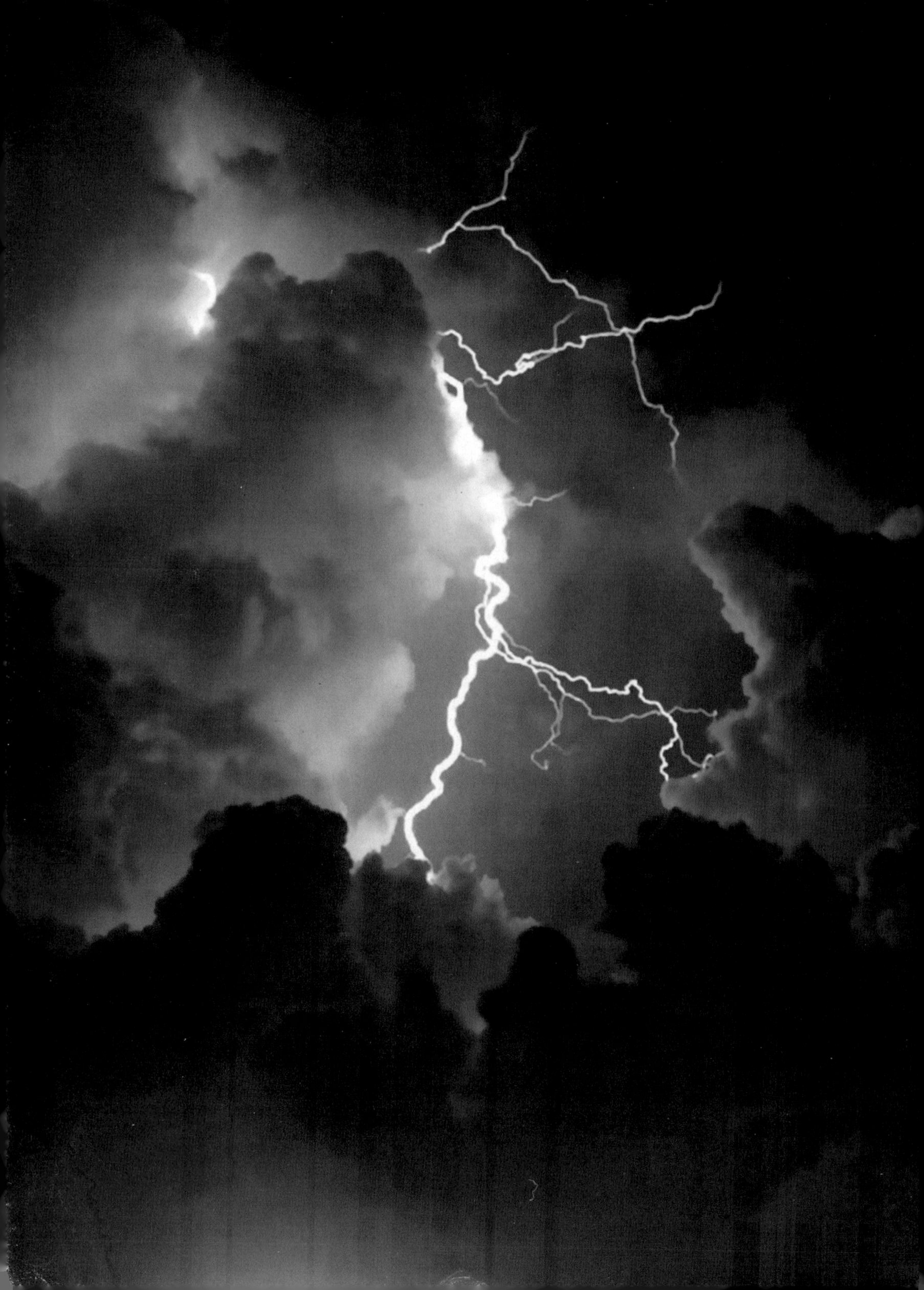

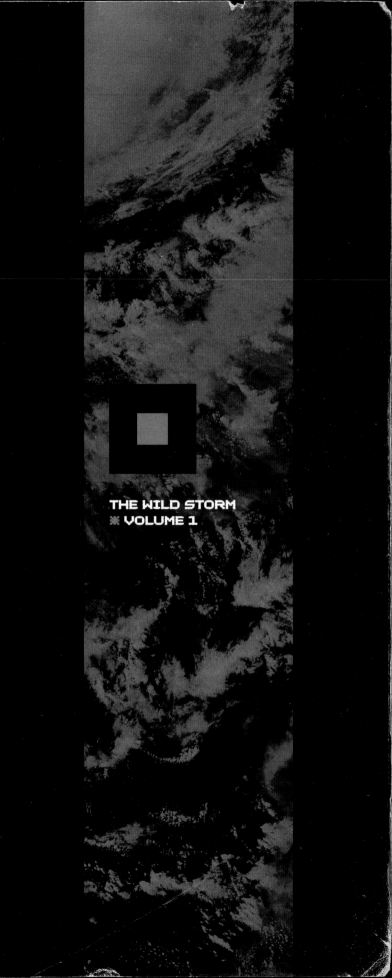

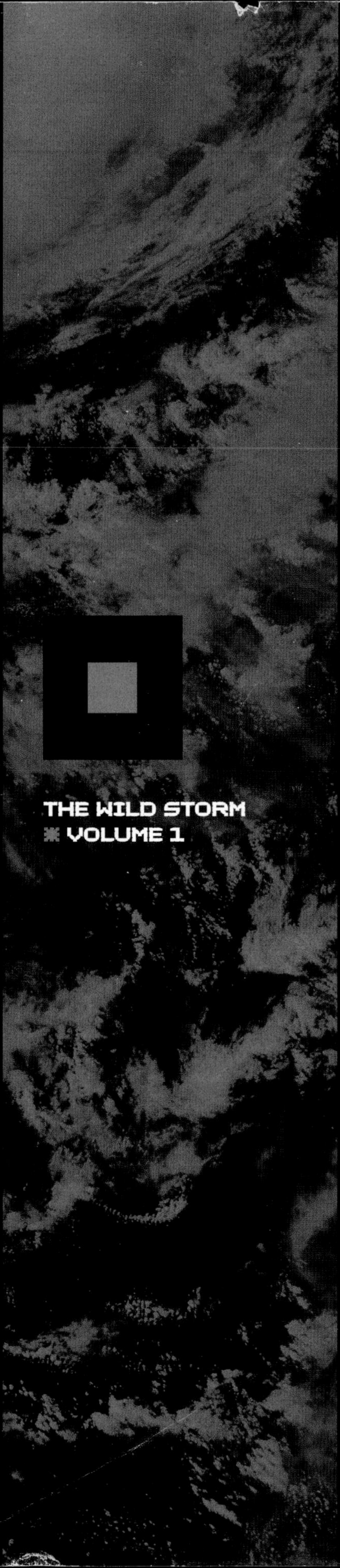
THE WILD STORM
VOLUME 1

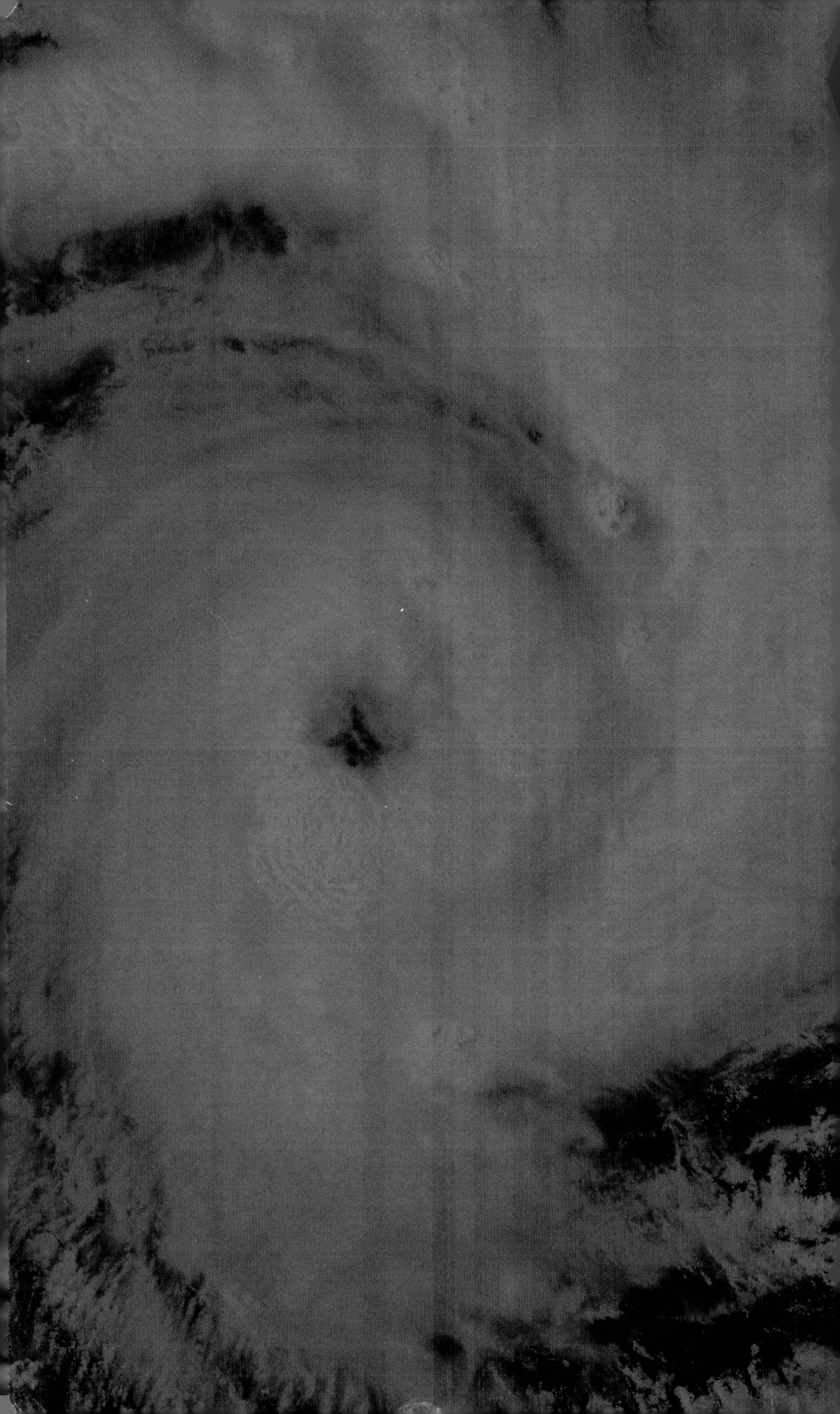

Zealot to Division.

The interview went badly. Send in the cleaning team.

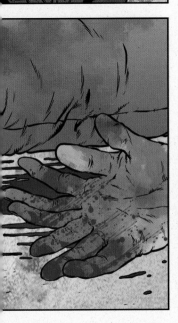

The intel was correct. Home-brew gene editing and some contraband software.

The interviewee was difficult.

Sorry.

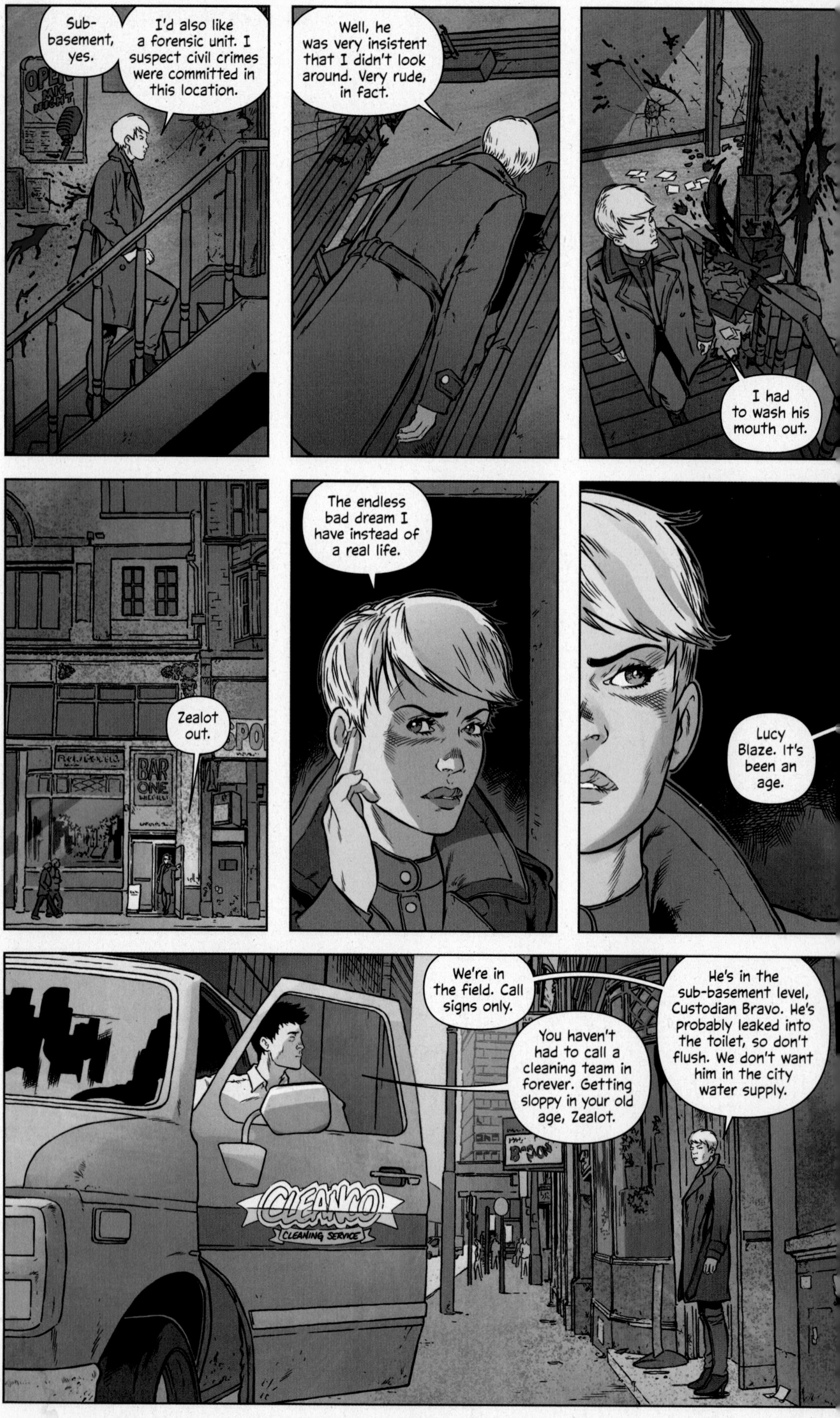
OPEN MIC NIGHT
Sub-basement, yes.
I'd also like a forensic unit. I suspect civil crimes were committed in this location.
Well, he was very insistent that I didn't look around. Very rude, in fact.
I had to wash his mouth out.
BAR ONE
Zealot out.
The endless bad dream I have instead of a real life.
Lucy Blaze. It's been an age.
We're in the field. Call signs only.
He's in the sub-basement level, Custodian Bravo. He's probably leaked into the toilet, so don't flush. We don't want him in the city water supply.
You haven't had to call a cleaning team in forever. Getting sloppy in your old age, Zealot.
CLEANCO
CLEANING SERVICE

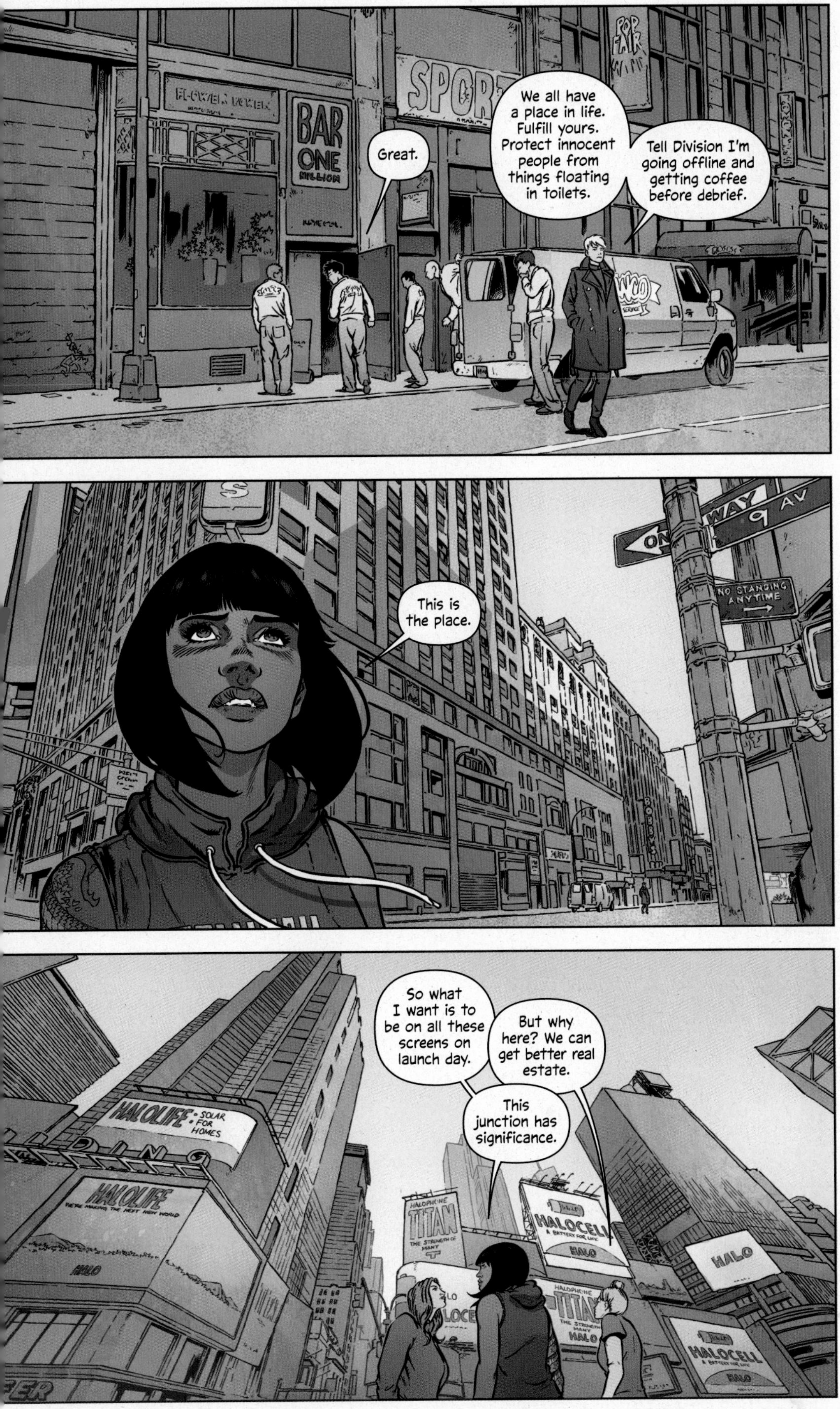
FLOWER POWER
BAR ONE MILLION
SPORT
POP FAIR
Great.
We all have a place in life. Fulfill yours. Protect innocent people from things floating in toilets.
Tell Division I'm going offline and getting coffee before debrief.
ONE WAY
9 AV
NO STANDING ANYTIME
This is the place.
So what I want is to be on all these screens on launch day.
But why here? We can get better real estate.
This junction has significance.
HALOLIFE • SOLAR FOR HOMES
HALOLIFE
WE'RE MAKING THE NEXT NEW WORLD
HALO
HALOPHONE TITAN THE STRENGTH OF MANY
HALOCELL A BATTERY FOR LIFE
HALO

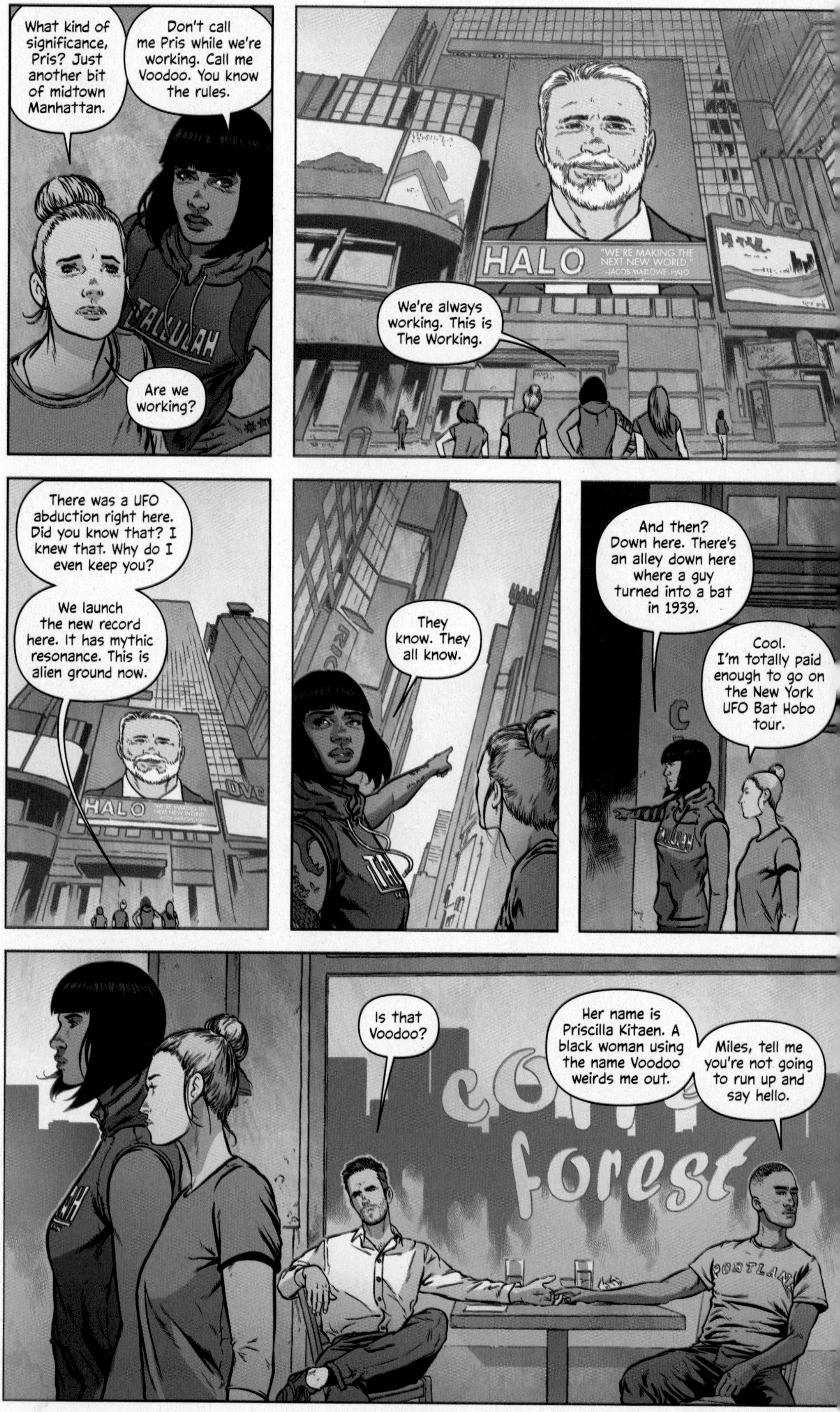
What kind of significance, Pris? Just another bit of midtown Manhattan.
Don't call me Pris while we're working. Call me Voodoo. You know the rules.
Are we working?
TALLULAH
HALO
"WE'RE MAKING THE NEXT NEW WORLD." -JACOB MARLOWE, HALO
DVC
We're always working. This is The Working.
There was a UFO abduction right here. Did you know that? I knew that. Why do I even keep you?
We launch the new record here. It has mythic resonance. This is alien ground now.
They know. They all know.
And then? Down here. There's an alley down here where a guy turned into a bat in 1939.
Cool. I'm totally paid enough to go on the New York UFO Bat Hobo tour.
Is that Voodoo?
Her name is Priscilla Kitaen. A black woman using the name Voodoo weirds me out.
Miles, tell me you're not going to run up and say hello.
forest

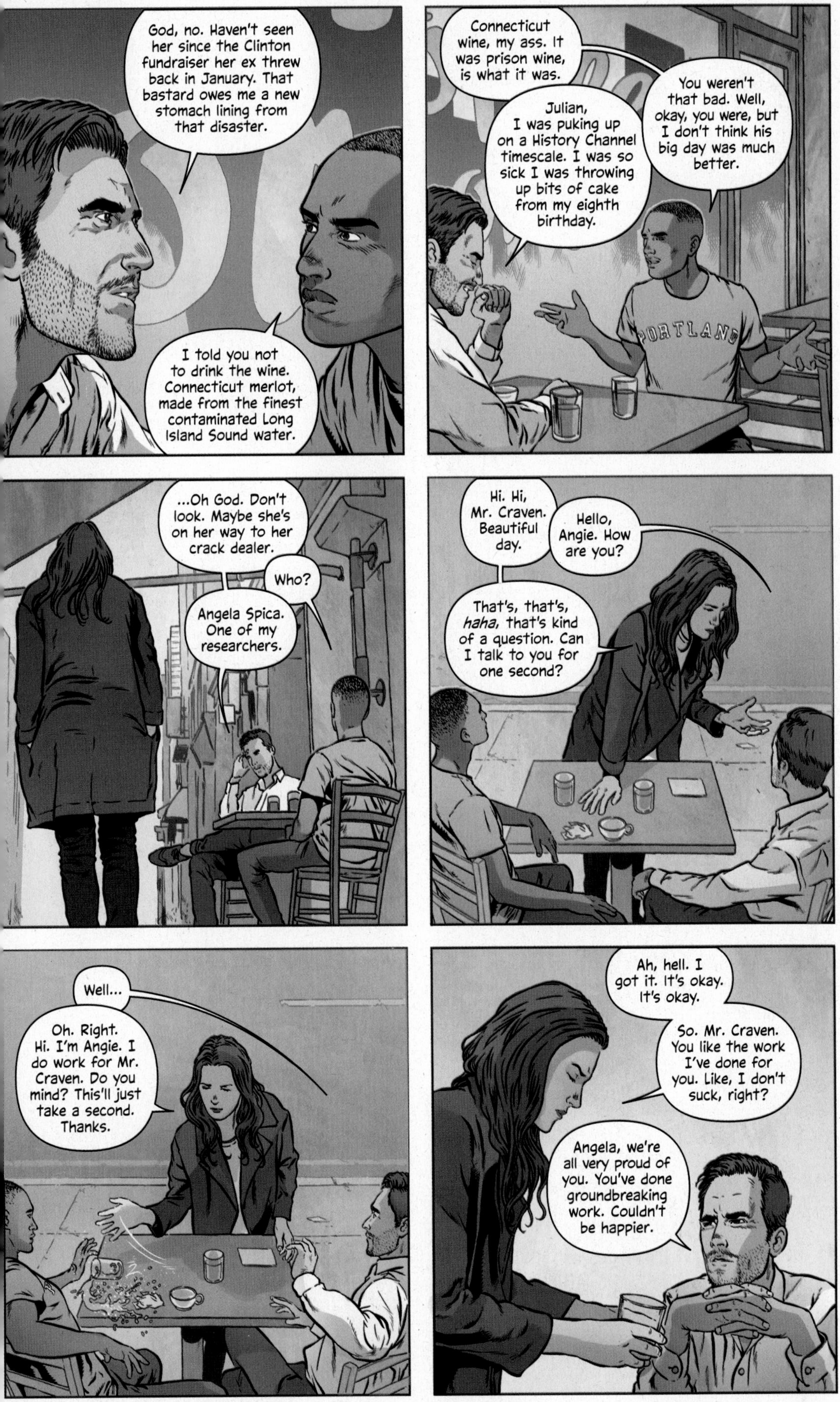
God, no. Haven't seen her since the Clinton fundraiser her ex threw back in January. That bastard owes me a new stomach lining from that disaster.
I told you not to drink the wine. Connecticut merlot, made from the finest contaminated Long Island Sound water.
Connecticut wine, my ass. It was prison wine, is what it was.
Julian, I was puking up on a History Channel timescale. I was so sick I was throwing up bits of cake from my eighth birthday.
You weren't that bad. Well, okay, you were, but I don't think his big day was much better.
PORTLAND
...Oh God. Don't look. Maybe she's on her way to her crack dealer.
Who?
Angela Spica. One of my researchers.
Hi. Hi, Mr. Craven. Beautiful day.
Hello, Angie. How are you?
That's, that's, *haha*, that's kind of a question. Can I talk to you for one second?
Well...
Oh. Right. Hi. I'm Angie. I do work for Mr. Craven. Do you mind? This'll just take a second. Thanks.
Ah, hell. I got it. It's okay. It's okay.
So. Mr. Craven. You like the work I've done for you. Like, I don't suck, right?
Angela, we're all very proud of you. You've done groundbreaking work. Couldn't be happier.

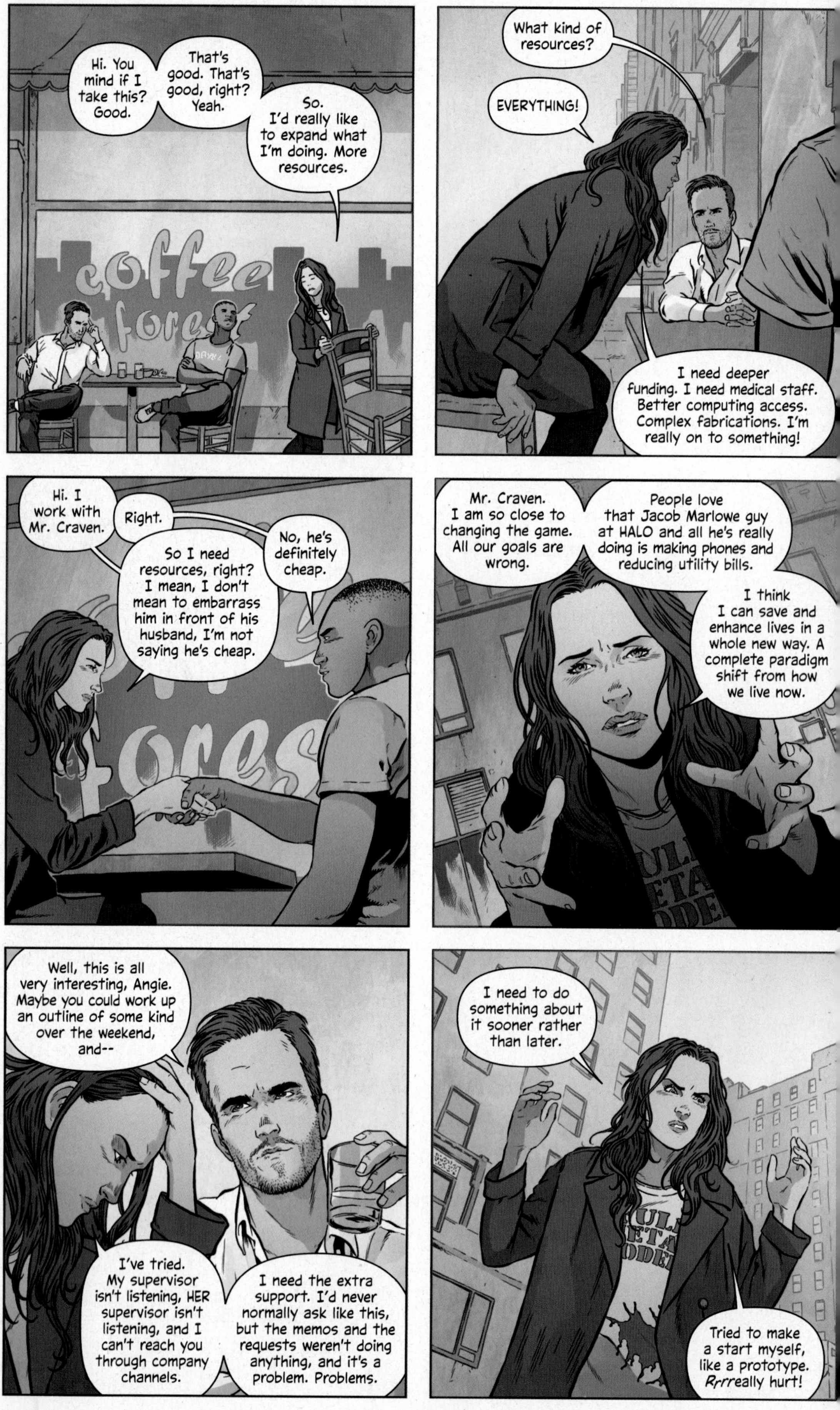
Hi. You mind if I take this? Good.
That's good. That's good, right? Yeah.
So. I'd really like to expand what I'm doing. More resources.
What kind of resources?
EVERYTHING!
I need deeper funding. I need medical staff. Better computing access. Complex fabrications. I'm really on to something!
Hi. I work with Mr. Craven.
Right.
No, he's definitely cheap.
So I need resources, right? I mean, I don't mean to embarrass him in front of his husband, I'm not saying he's cheap.
Mr. Craven. I am so close to changing the game. All our goals are wrong.
People love that Jacob Marlowe guy at HALO and all he's really doing is making phones and reducing utility bills.
I think I can save and enhance lives in a whole new way. A complete paradigm shift from how we live now.
Well, this is all very interesting, Angie. Maybe you could work up an outline of some kind over the weekend, and--
I've tried. My supervisor isn't listening, HER supervisor isn't listening, and I can't reach you through company channels.
I need the extra support. I'd never normally ask like this, but the memos and the requests weren't doing anything, and it's a problem. Problems.
I need to do something about it sooner rather than later.
Tried to make a start myself, like a prototype. *Rrrr*eally hurt!

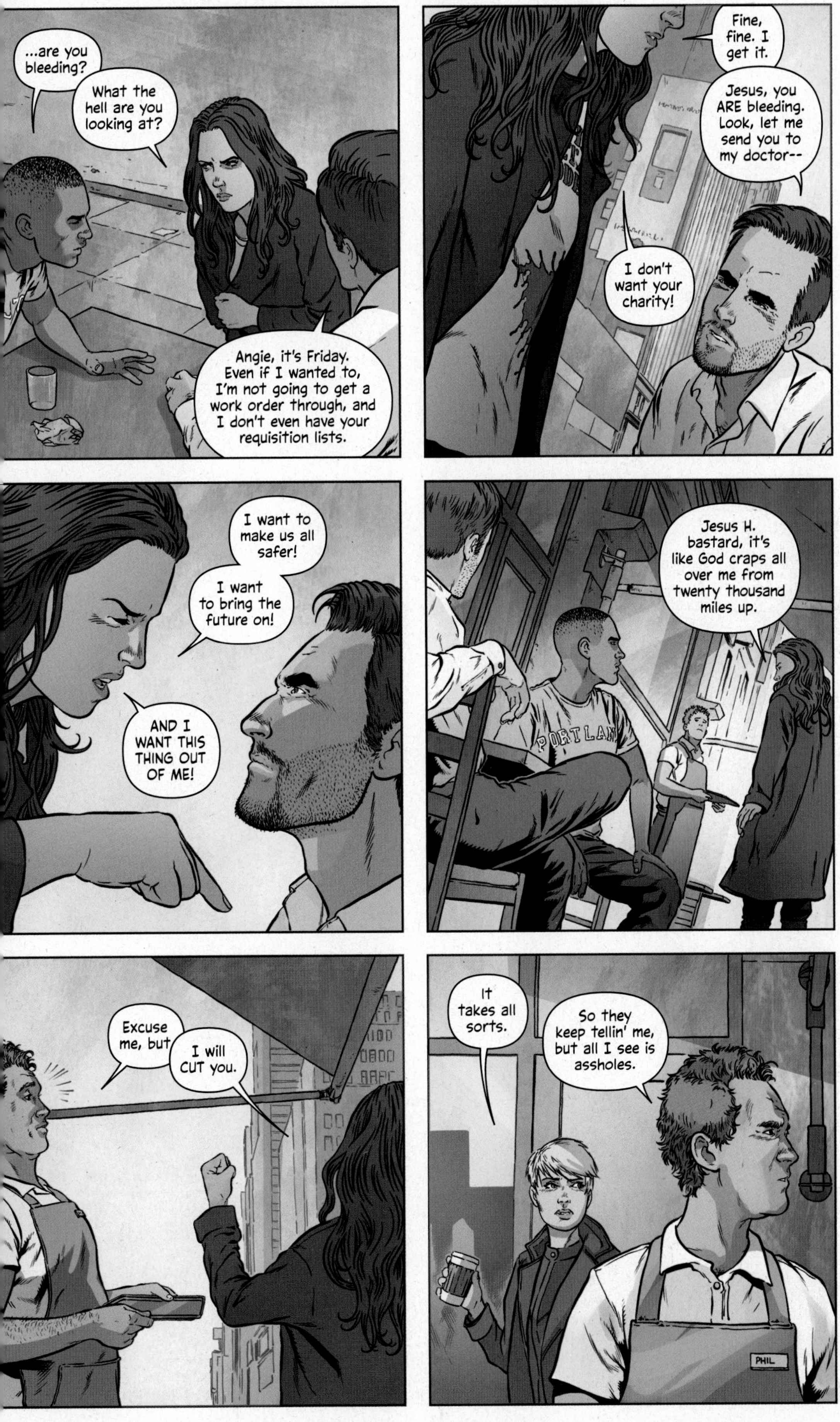
...are you bleeding?
What the hell are you looking at?
Angie, it's Friday. Even if I wanted to, I'm not going to get a work order through, and I don't even have your requisition lists.
Fine, fine. I get it.
Jesus, you ARE bleeding. Look, let me send you to my doctor--
I don't want your charity!
I want to make us all safer!
I want to bring the future on!
AND I WANT THIS THING OUT OF ME!
Jesus H. bastard, it's like God craps all over me from twenty thousand miles up.
Excuse me, but
I will CUT you.
It takes all sorts.
So they keep tellin' me, but all I see is assholes.
PHIL

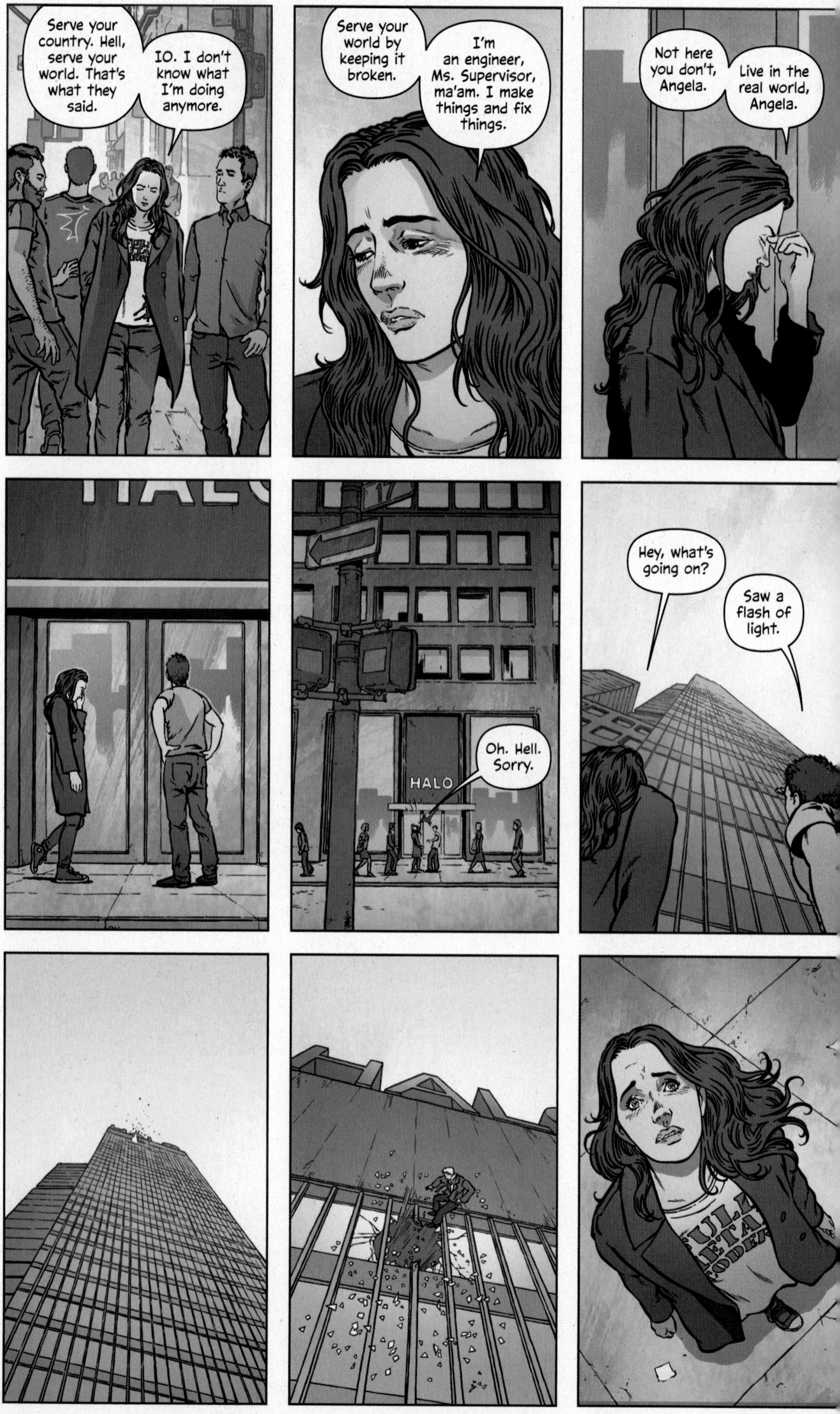

Serve your country. Hell, serve your world. That's what they said.
IO. I don't know what I'm doing anymore.
Serve your world by keeping it broken.
I'm an engineer, Ms. Supervisor, ma'am. I make things and fix things.
Not here you don't, Angela.
Live in the real world, Angela.
HALO
HALO
Oh. Hell. Sorry.
Hey, what's going on?
Saw a flash of light.

Is anybody--

--can anybody--

Main engine start.

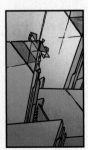

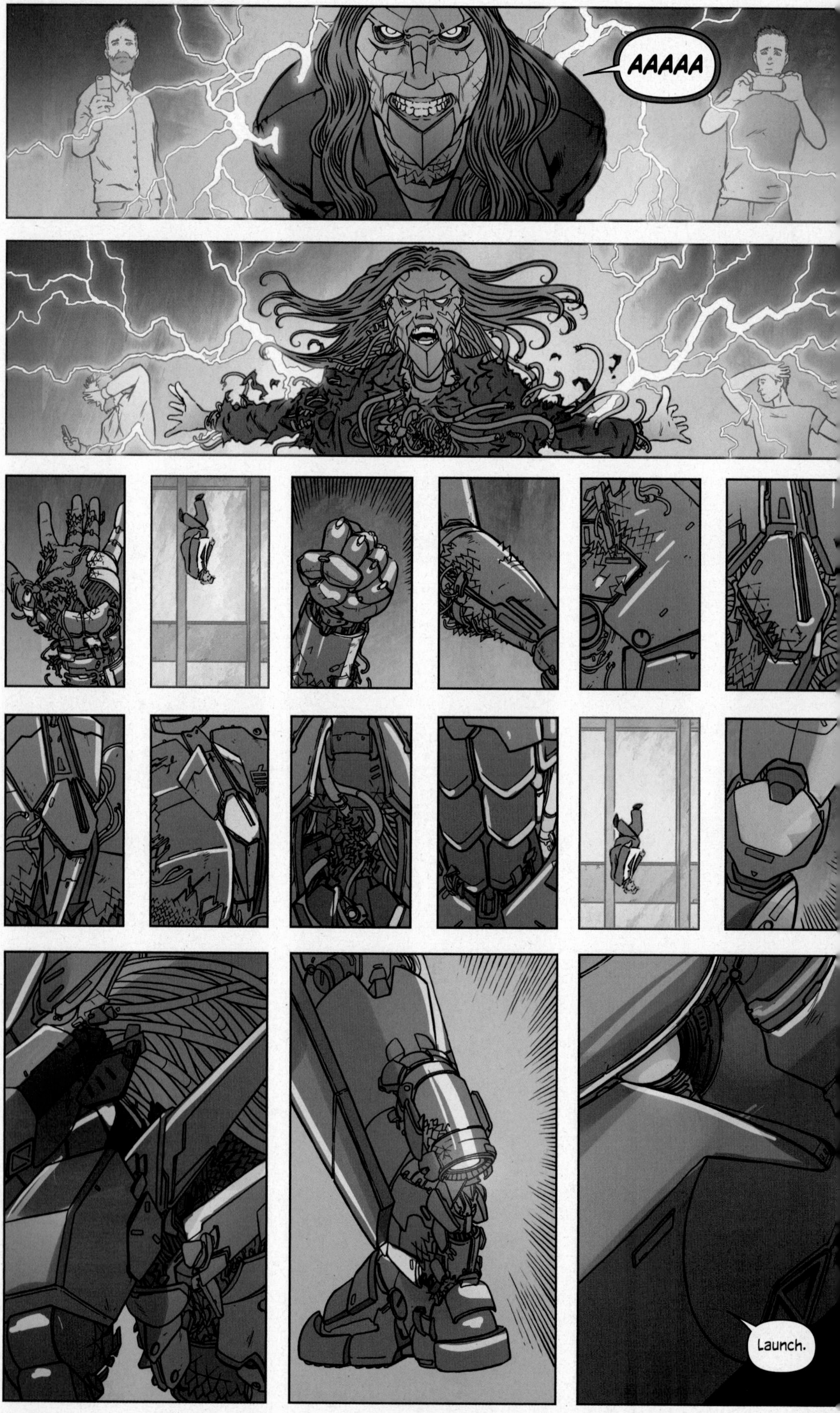
AAAAA
Launch.

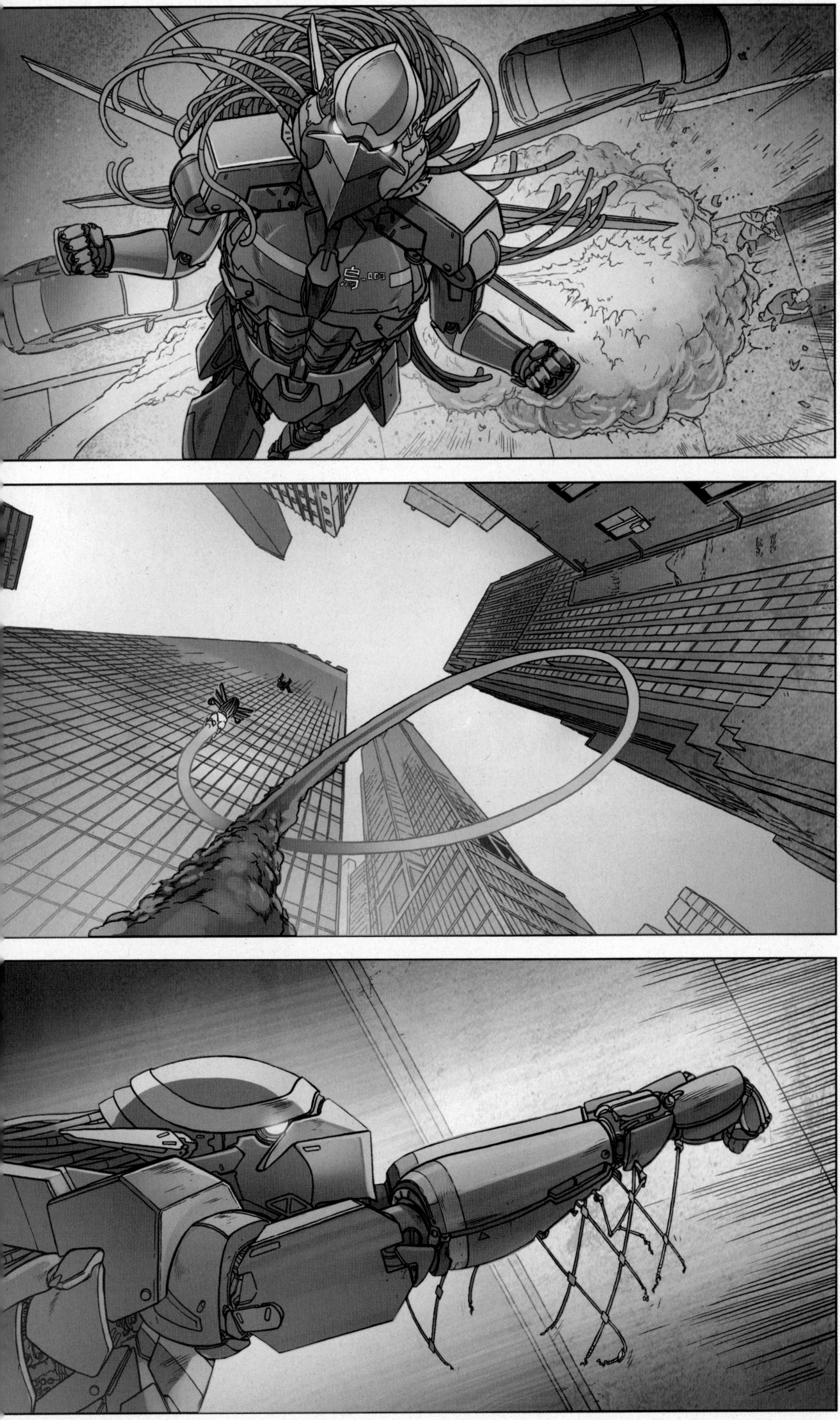

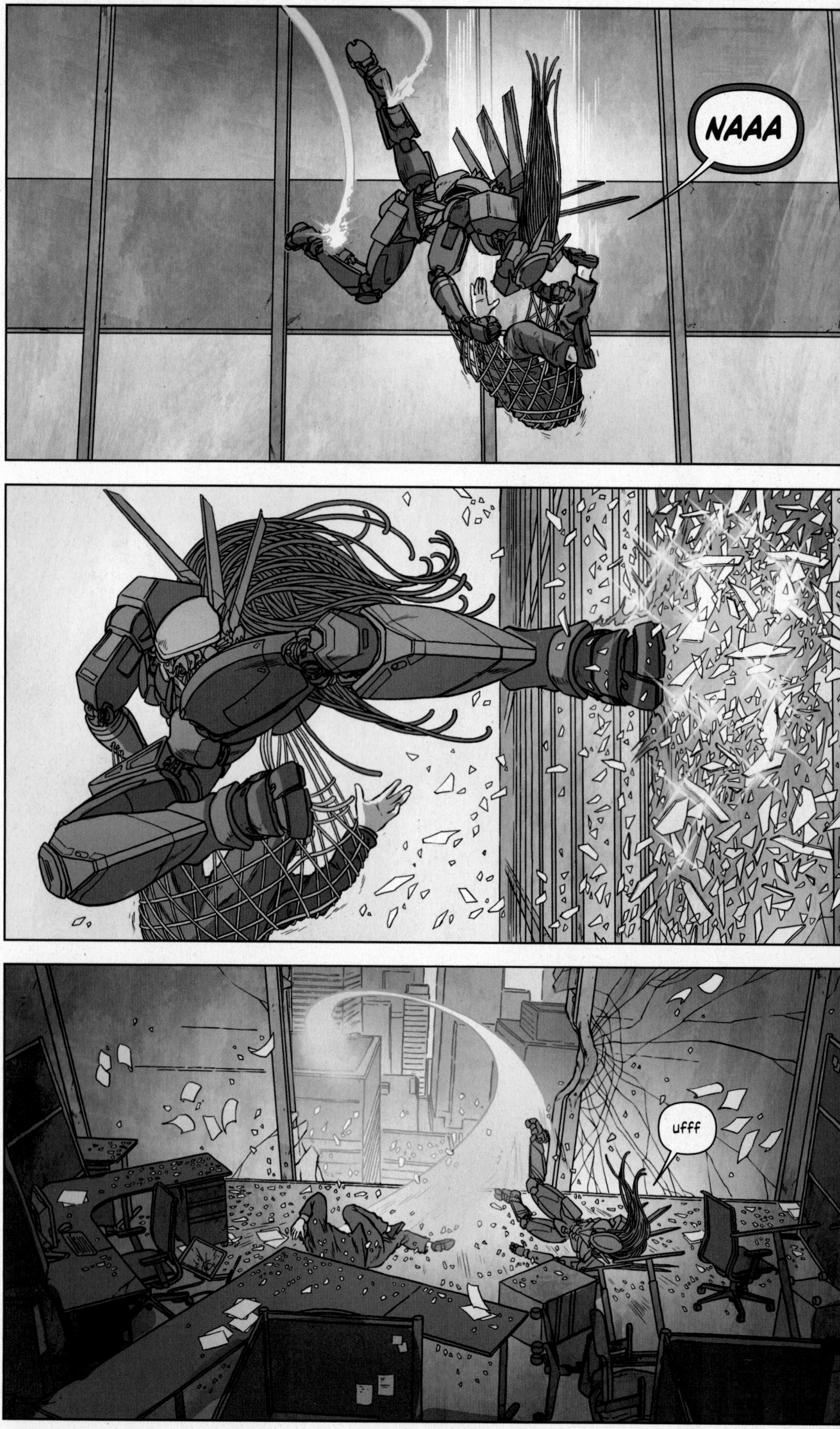
NAAA
ufff

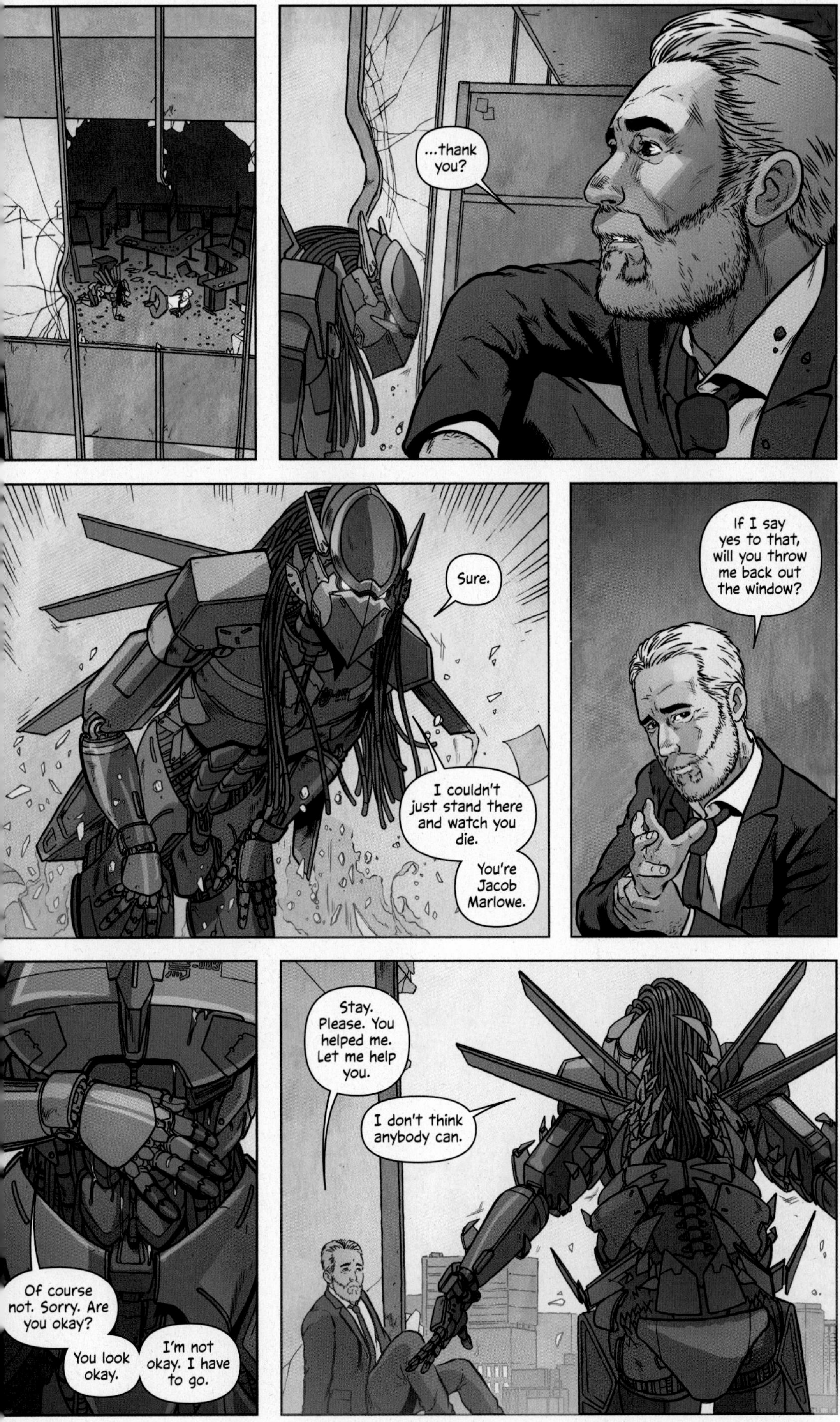
...thank you?
Sure.
I couldn't just stand there and watch you die.
You're Jacob Marlowe.
If I say yes to that, will you throw me back out the window?
Of course not. Sorry. Are you okay?
You look okay.
I'm not okay. I have to go.
Stay. Please. You helped me. Let me help you.
I don't think anybody can.

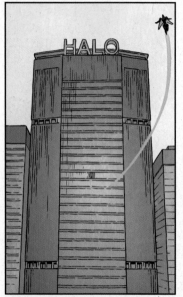

Adrianna?

Michael Cray from IO just tried to kill me. And there's something new in the world.

Wake up the CAT.

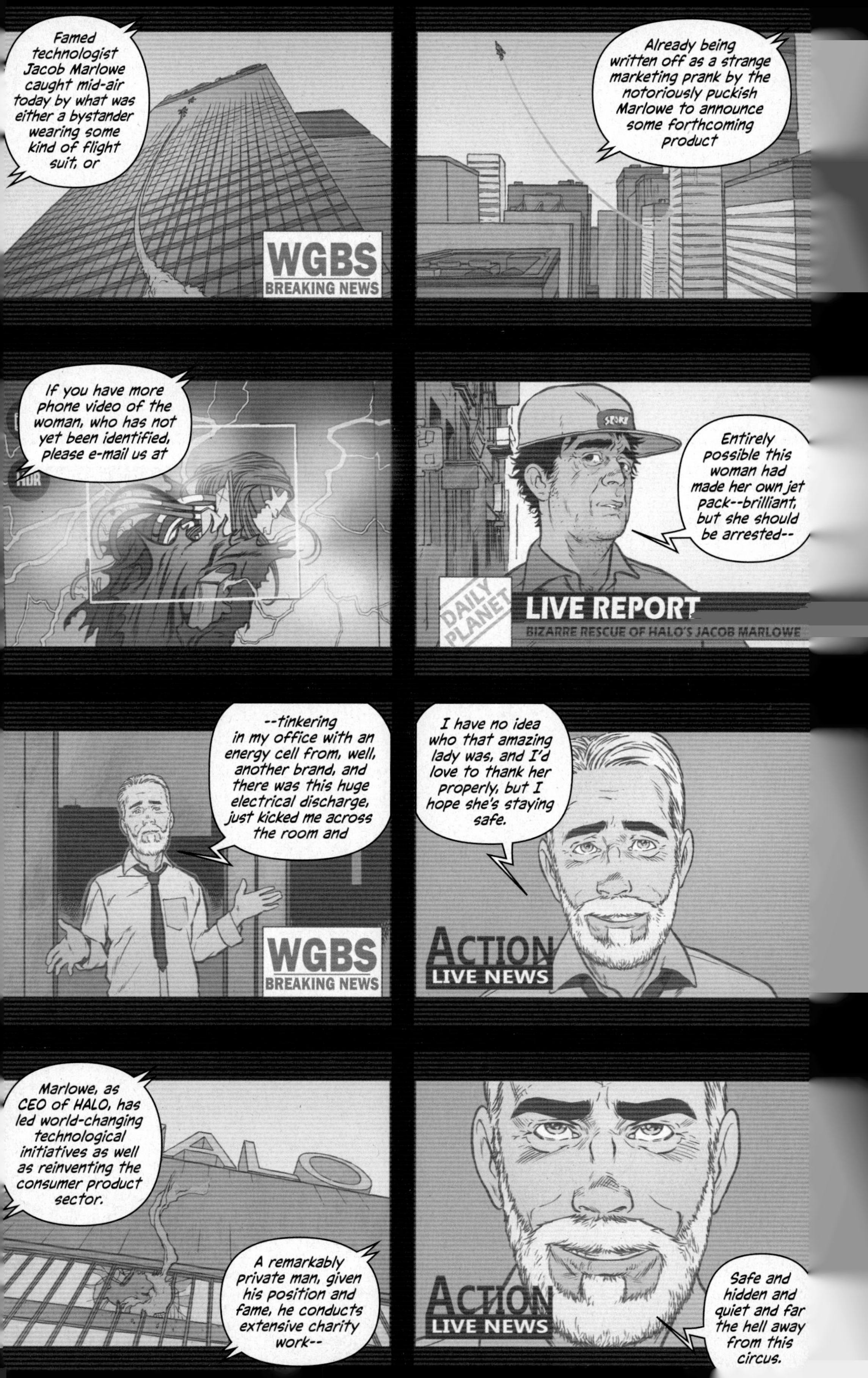
Famed technologist Jacob Marlowe caught mid-air today by what was either a bystander wearing some kind of flight suit, or
WGBS
BREAKING NEWS
Already being written off as a strange marketing prank by the notoriously puckish Marlowe to announce some forthcoming product
If you have more phone video of the woman, who has not yet been identified, please e-mail us at
Entirely possible this woman had made her own jet pack--brilliant, but she should be arrested--
DAILY PLANET
LIVE REPORT
BIZARRE RESCUE OF HALO'S JACOB MARLOWE
--tinkering in my office with an energy cell from, well, another brand, and there was this huge electrical discharge, just kicked me across the room and
WGBS
BREAKING NEWS
I have no idea who that amazing lady was, and I'd love to thank her properly, but I hope she's staying safe.
ACTION
LIVE NEWS
Marlowe, as CEO of HALO, has led world-changing technological initiatives as well as reinventing the consumer product sector.
A remarkably private man, given his position and fame, he conducts extensive charity work--
ACTION
LIVE NEWS
Safe and hidden and quiet and far the hell away from this circus.

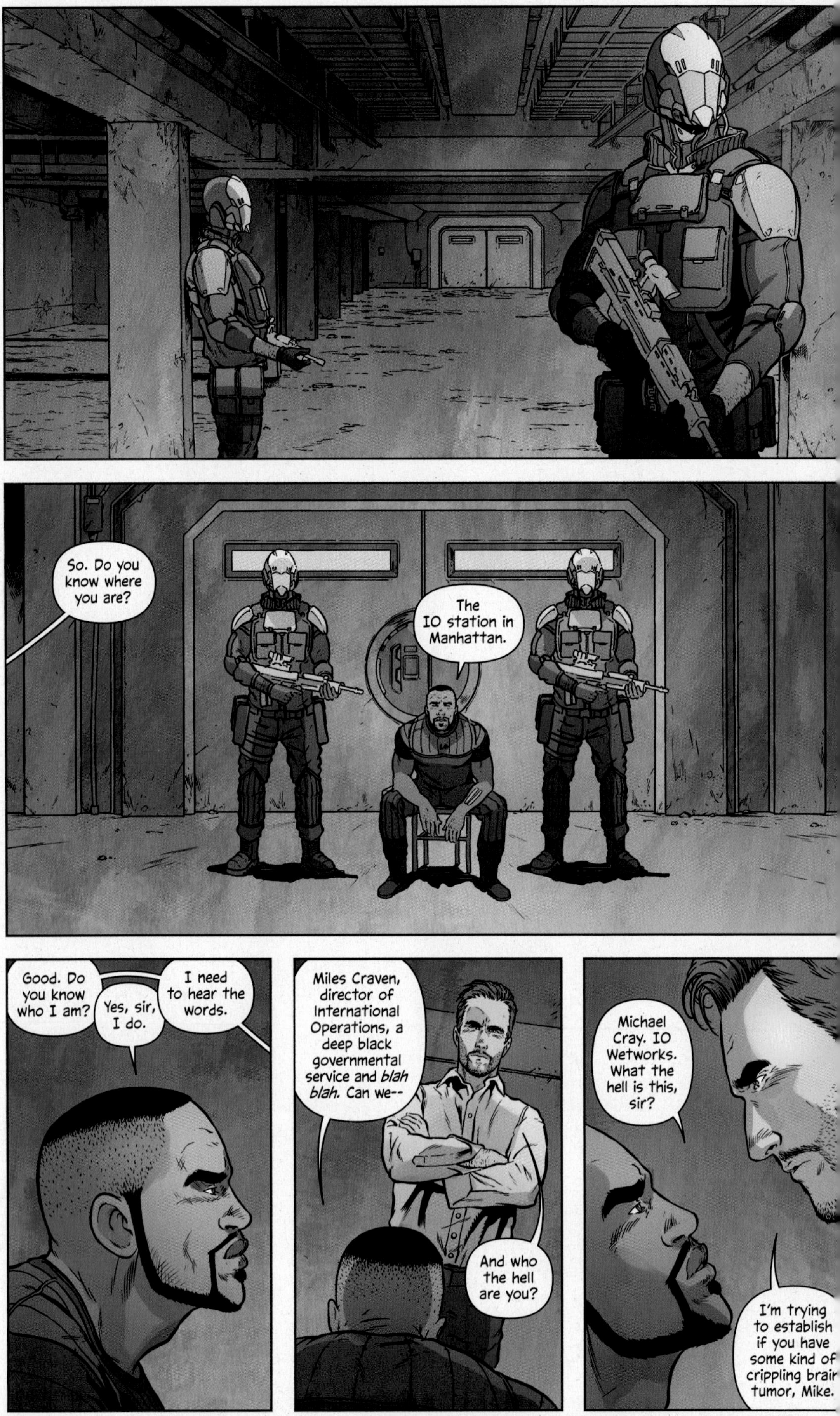
So. Do you know where you are?
The IO station in Manhattan.
Good. Do you know who I am?
Yes, sir, I do.
I need to hear the words.
Miles Craven, director of International Operations, a deep black governmental service and *blah blah*. Can we--
And who the hell are you?
Michael Cray. IO Wetworks. What the hell is this, sir?
I'm trying to establish if you have some kind of crippling brair tumor, Mike.

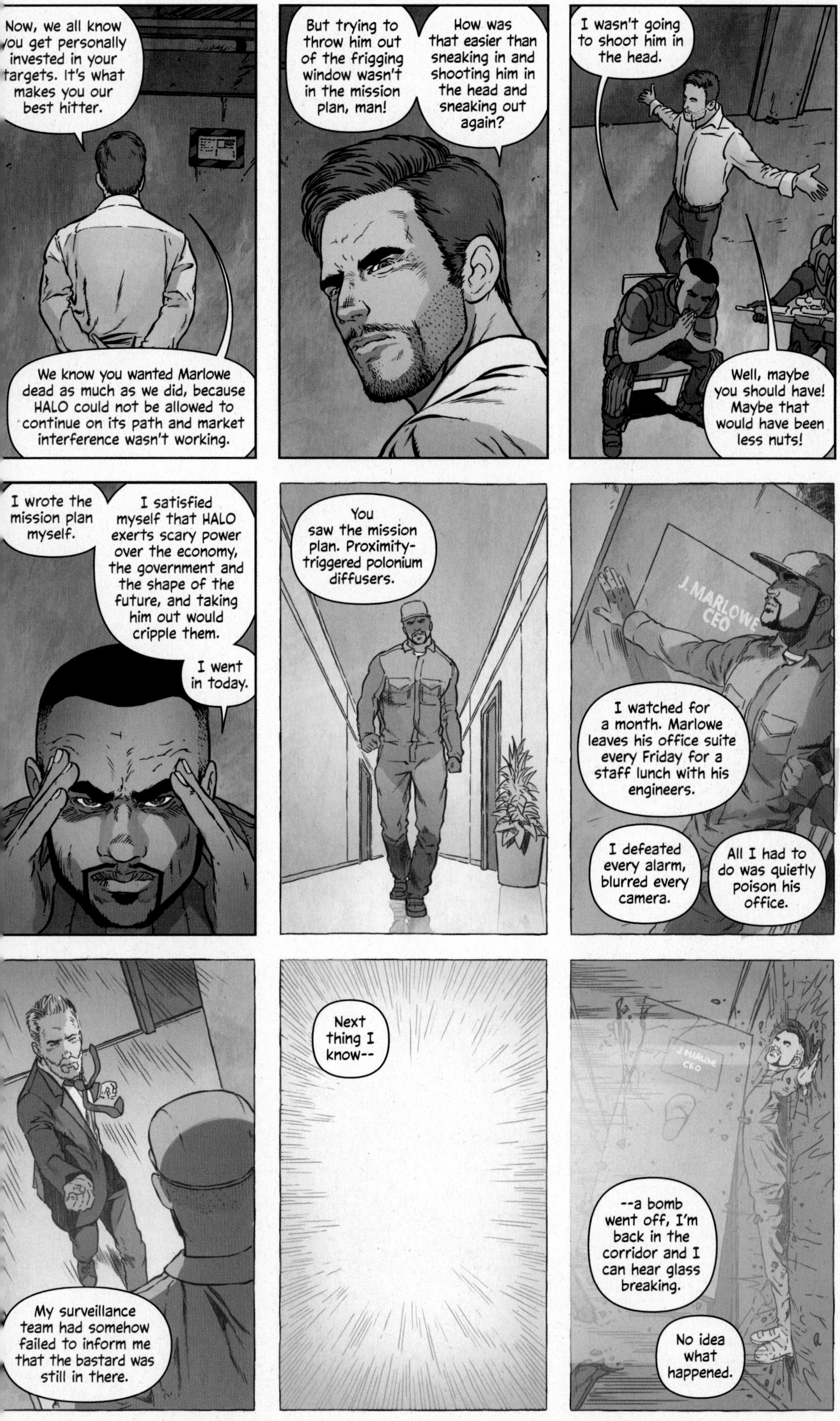
Now, we all know you get personally invested in your targets. It's what makes you our best hitter.
We know you wanted Marlowe dead as much as we did, because HALO could not be allowed to continue on its path and market interference wasn't working.
But trying to throw him out of the frigging window wasn't in the mission plan, man!
How was that easier than sneaking in and shooting him in the head and sneaking out again?
I wasn't going to shoot him in the head.
Well, maybe you should have! Maybe that would have been less nuts!
I wrote the mission plan myself.
I satisfied myself that HALO exerts scary power over the economy, the government and the shape of the future, and taking him out would cripple them.
I went in today.
You saw the mission plan. Proximity-triggered polonium diffusers.
J. MARLOWE CEO
I watched for a month. Marlowe leaves his office suite every Friday for a staff lunch with his engineers.
I defeated every alarm, blurred every camera.
All I had to do was quietly poison his office.
My surveillance team had somehow failed to inform me that the bastard was still in there.
Next thing I know--
J. MARLOWE CEO
--a bomb went off, I'm back in the corridor and I can hear glass breaking.
No idea what happened.

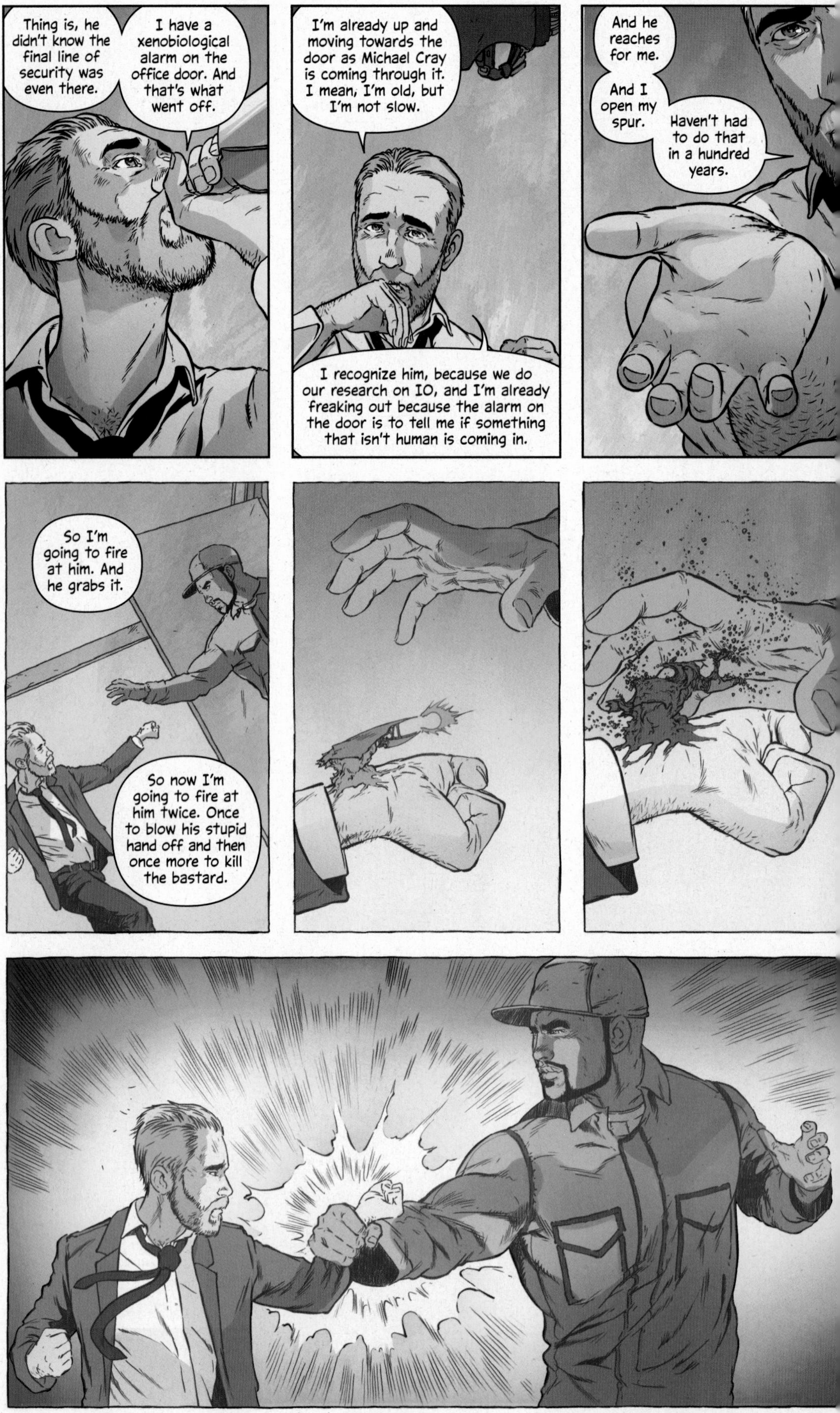
Thing is, he didn't know the final line of security was even there.
I have a xenobiological alarm on the office door. And that's what went off.
I'm already up and moving towards the door as Michael Cray is coming through it. I mean, I'm old, but I'm not slow.
I recognize him, because we do our research on IO, and I'm already freaking out because the alarm on the door is to tell me if something that isn't human is coming in.
And he reaches for me.
And I open my spur.
Haven't had to do that in a hundred years.
So I'm going to fire at him. And he grabs it.
So now I'm going to fire at him twice. Once to blow his stupid hand off and then once more to kill the bastard.

And the whole spur deflagrates. Like he killed the energy cells just by touching them and they exploded.

Throws him through the wall. Throws me through the window.

At this point, I know that IO have finally figured out what I really am and have sent their top killer to murder me.

What I don't know is how he can compromise non-human biology by touching it, and how he's even visible to a xenobiological anyway.

Going through the window, I figure that's all the surprises today has for me.

And then a metal lady flies up from the street, catches me, kicks in another window, tosses me in and leaves.

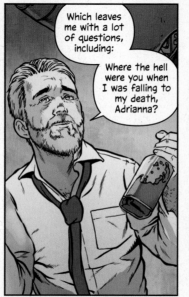

Which leaves me with a lot of questions, including:

Where the hell were you when I was falling to my death, Adrianna?

Oh. I was wondering when you were going to--

Ask where the hell you were?

--take a breath.

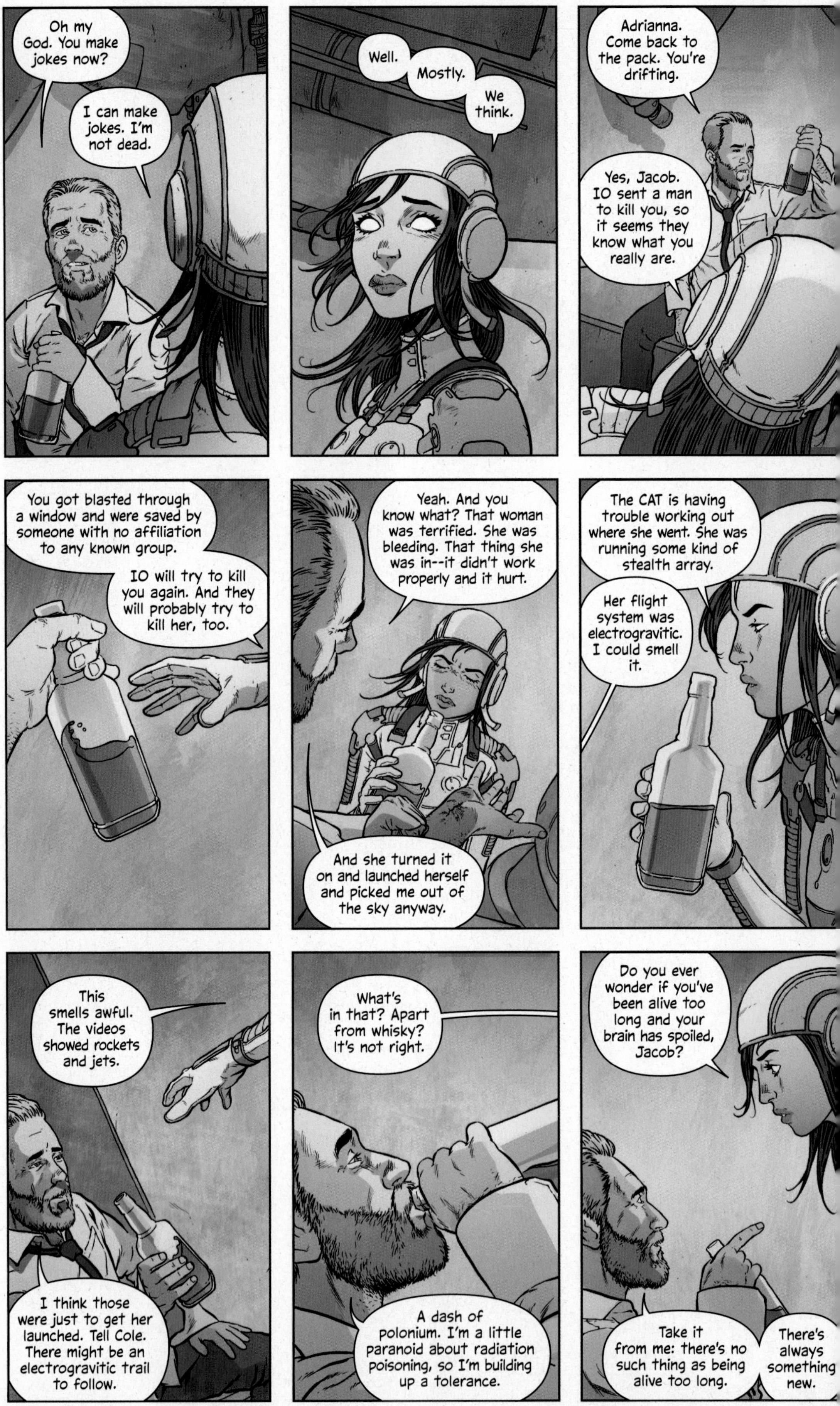
Oh my God. You make jokes now?
I can make jokes. I'm not dead.
Well.
Mostly.
We think.
Adrianna. Come back to the pack. You're drifting.
Yes, Jacob. IO sent a man to kill you, so it seems they know what you really are.
You got blasted through a window and were saved by someone with no affiliation to any known group.
IO will try to kill you again. And they will probably try to kill her, too.
Yeah. And you know what? That woman was terrified. She was bleeding. That thing she was in--it didn't work properly and it hurt.
And she turned it on and launched herself and picked me out of the sky anyway.
The CAT is having trouble working out where she went. She was running some kind of stealth array.
Her flight system was electrogravitic. I could smell it.
This smells awful. The videos showed rockets and jets.
I think those were just to get her launched. Tell Cole. There might be an electrogravitic trail to follow.
What's in that? Apart from whisky? It's not right.
A dash of polonium. I'm a little paranoid about radiation poisoning, so I'm building up a tolerance.
Do you ever wonder if you've been alive too long and your brain has spoiled, Jacob?
Take it from me: there's no such thing as being alive too long.
There's always something new.

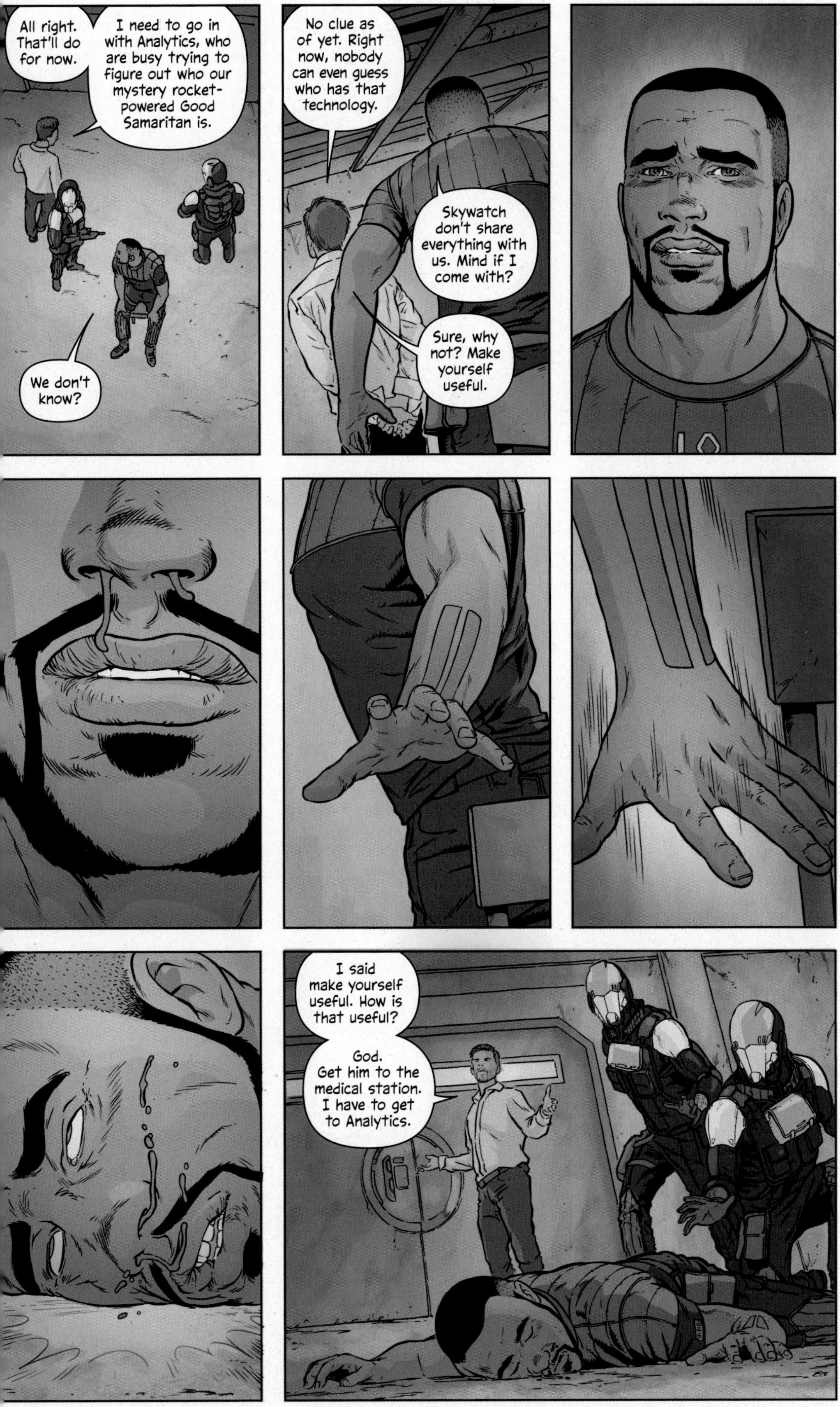
All right. That'll do for now.
I need to go in with Analytics, who are busy trying to figure out who our mystery rocket-powered Good Samaritan is.
We don't know?
No clue as of yet. Right now, nobody can even guess who has that technology.
Skywatch don't share everything with us. Mind if I come with?
Sure, why not? Make yourself useful.
I said make yourself useful. How is that useful?
God. Get him to the medical station. I have to get to Analytics.

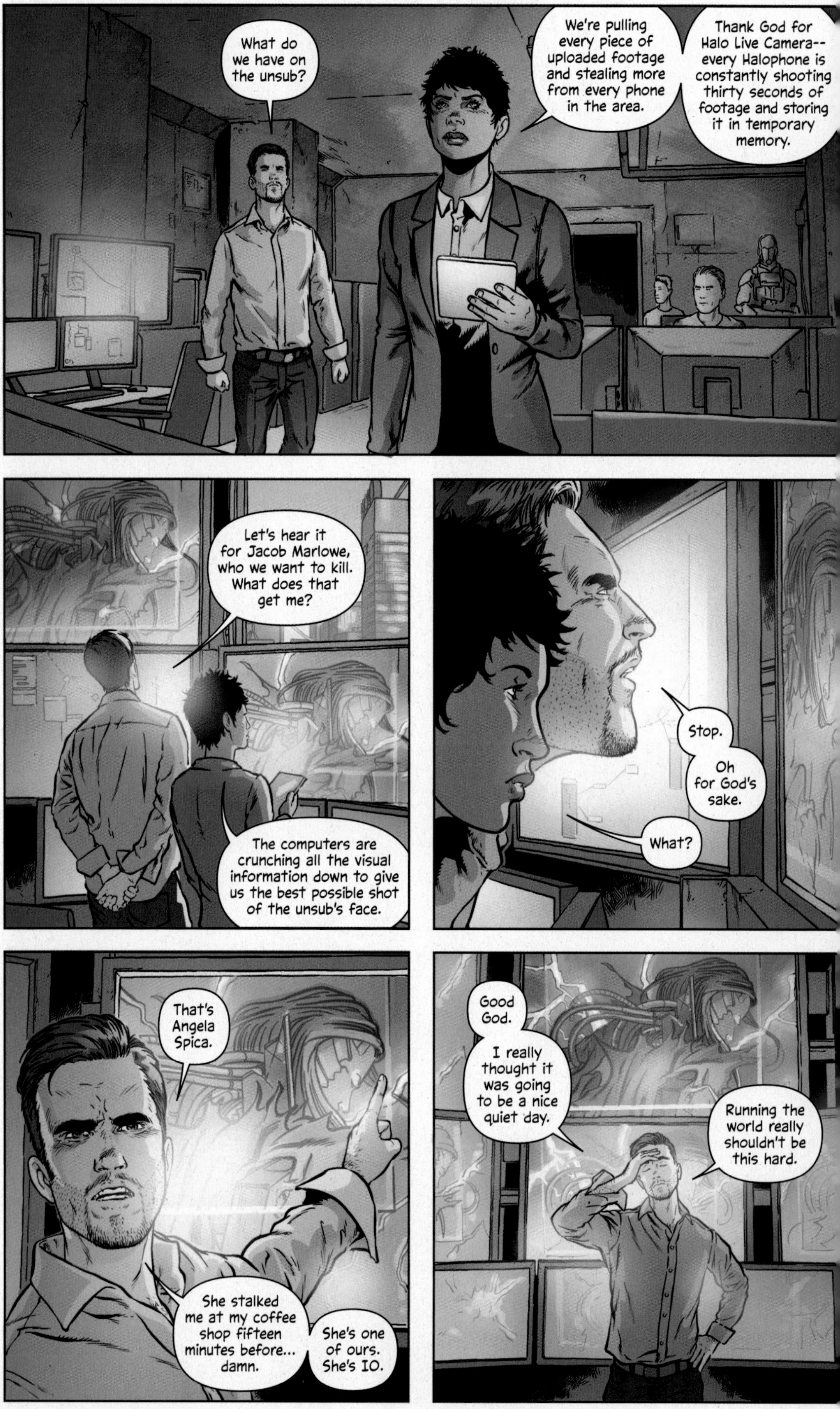
What do we have on the unsub?
We're pulling every piece of uploaded footage and stealing more from every phone in the area.
Thank God for Halo Live Camera--every Halophone is constantly shooting thirty seconds of footage and storing it in temporary memory.
Let's hear it for Jacob Marlowe, who we want to kill. What does that get me?
The computers are crunching all the visual information down to give us the best possible shot of the unsub's face.
Stop.
Oh for God's sake.
What?
That's Angela Spica.
She stalked me at my coffee shop fifteen minutes before... damn.
She's one of ours. She's IO.
Good God.
I really thought it was going to be a nice quiet day.
Running the world really shouldn't be this hard.

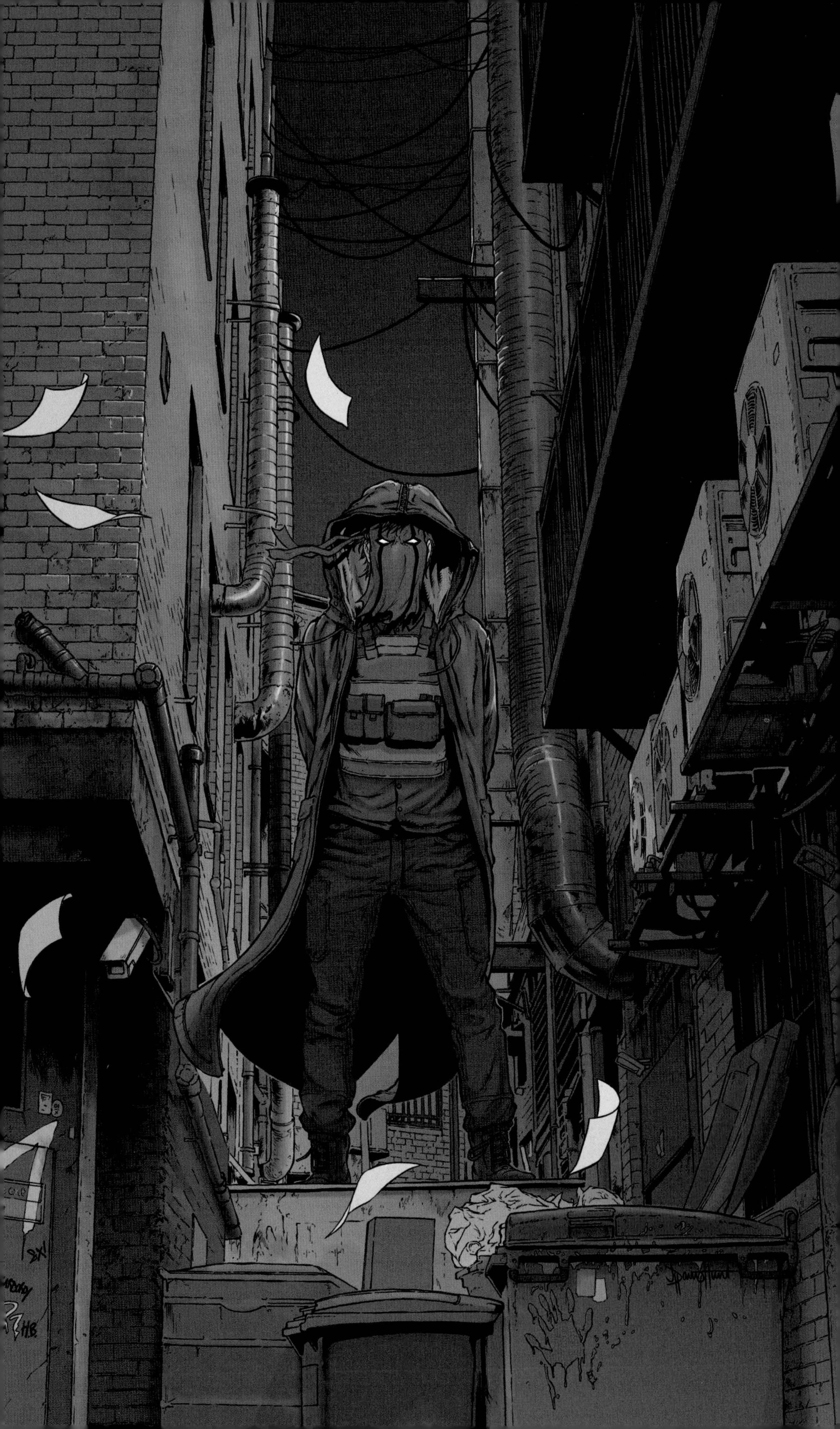

2

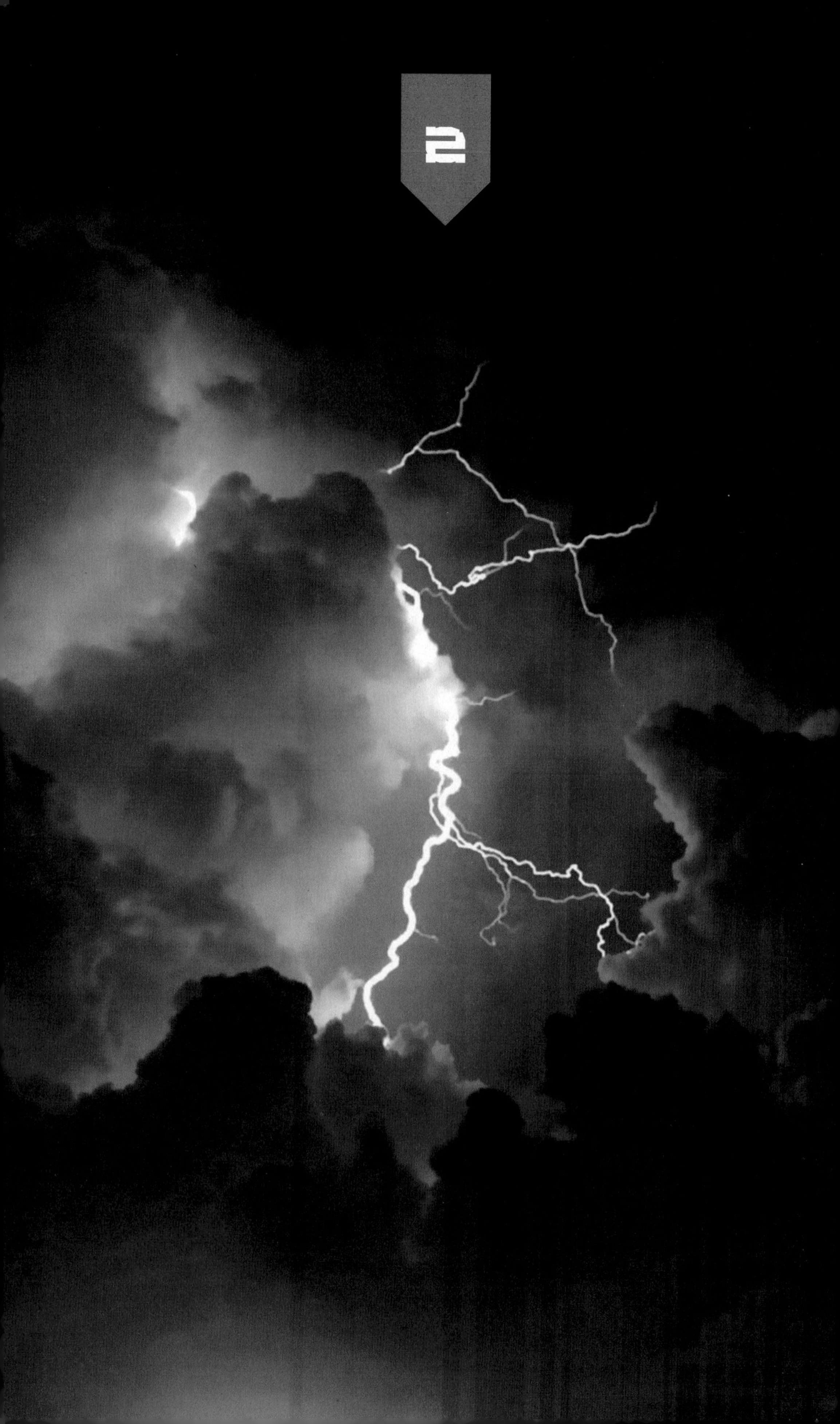

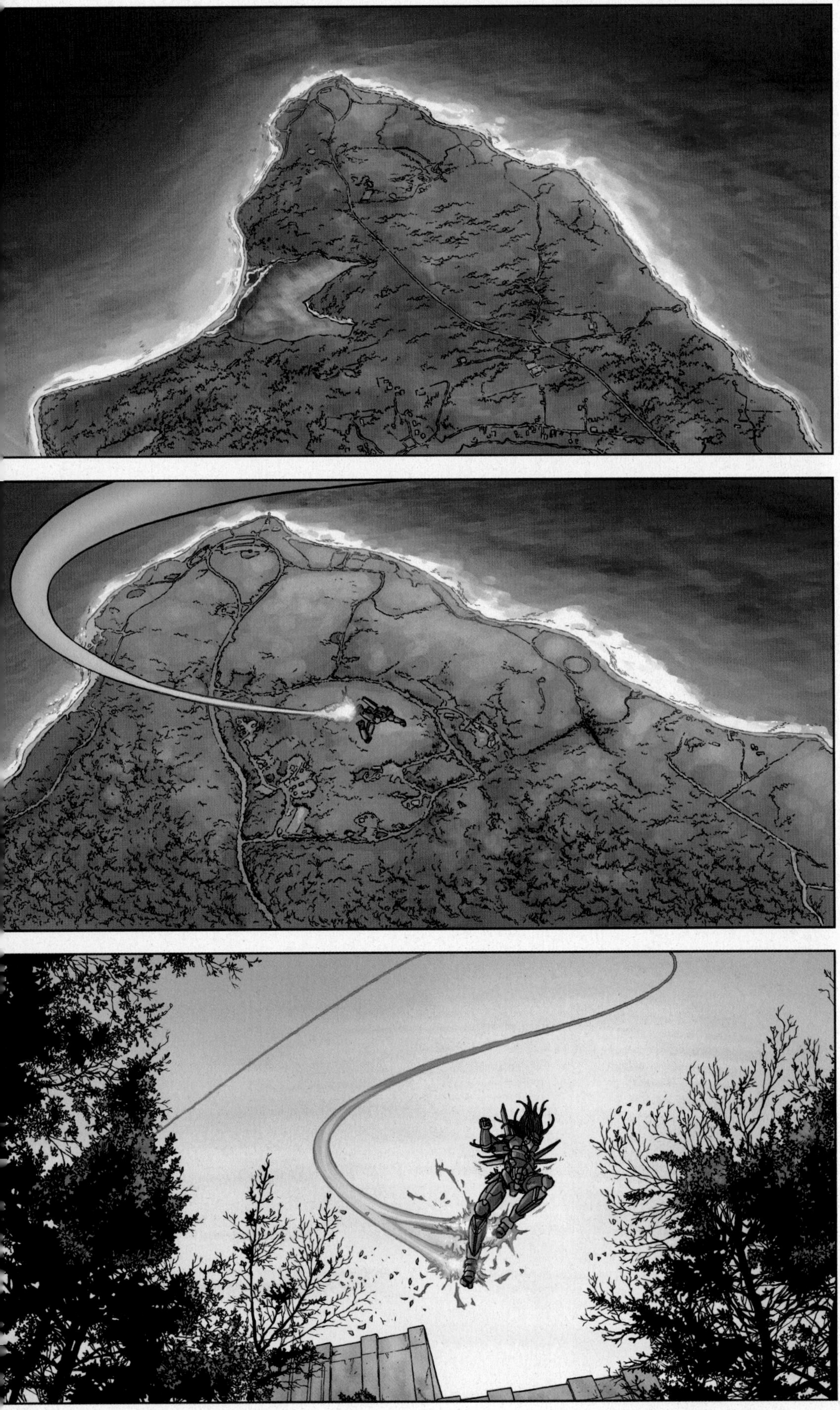

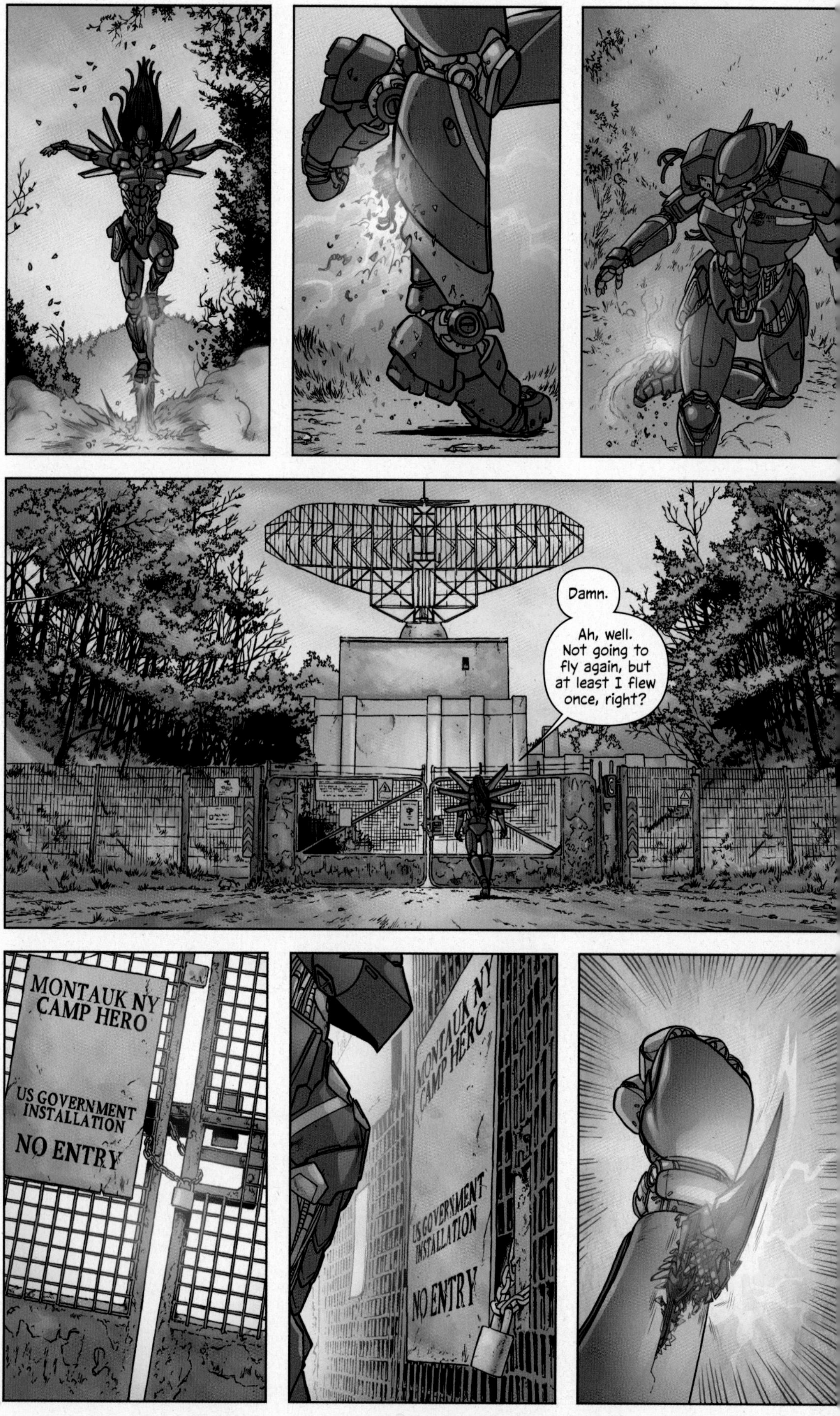
Damn.
Ah, well. Not going to fly again, but at least I flew once, right?
MONTAUK NY CAMP HERO
US GOVERNMENT INSTALLATION
NO ENTRY
MONTAUK NY CAMP HERO
US GOVERNMENT INSTALLATION
NO ENTRY

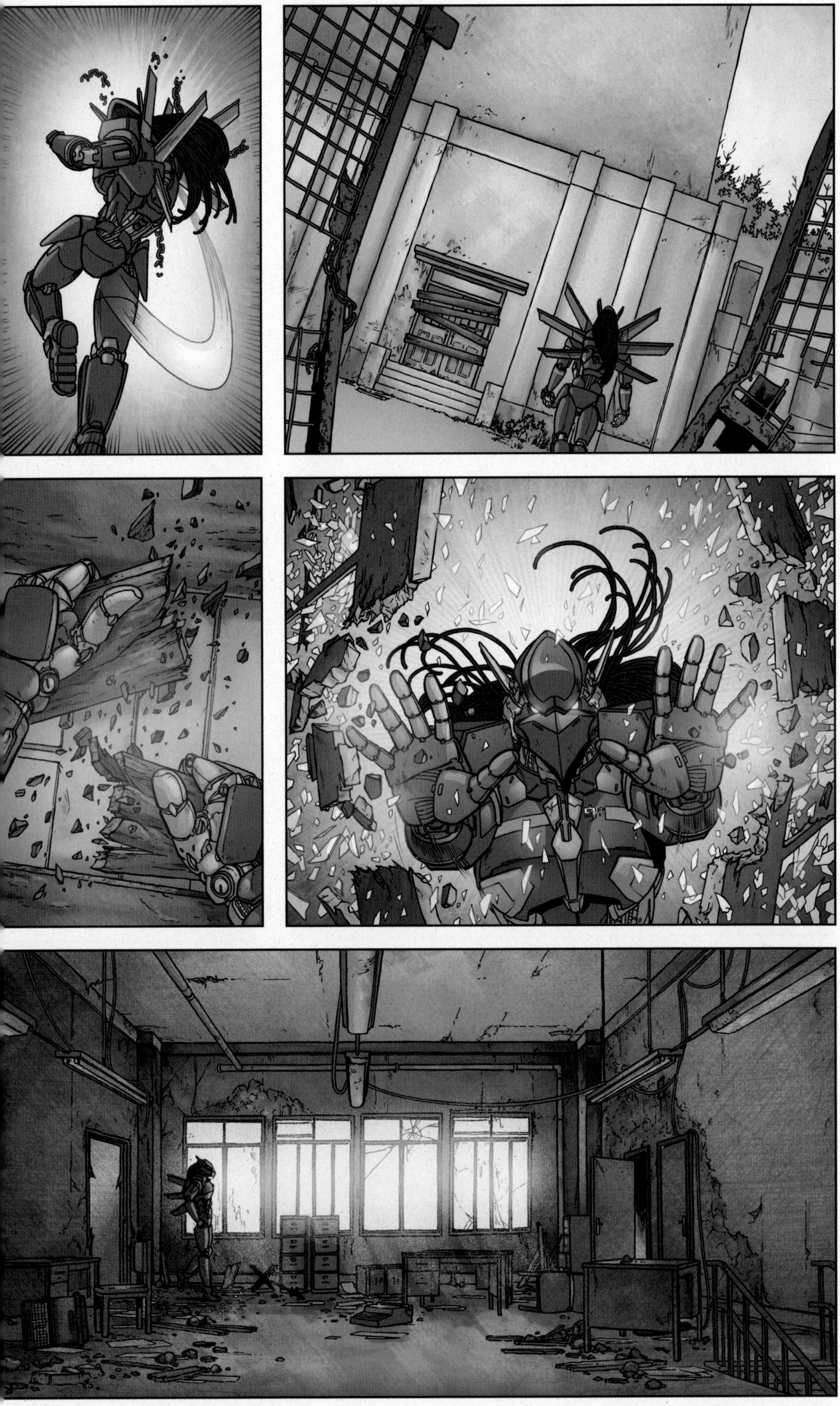

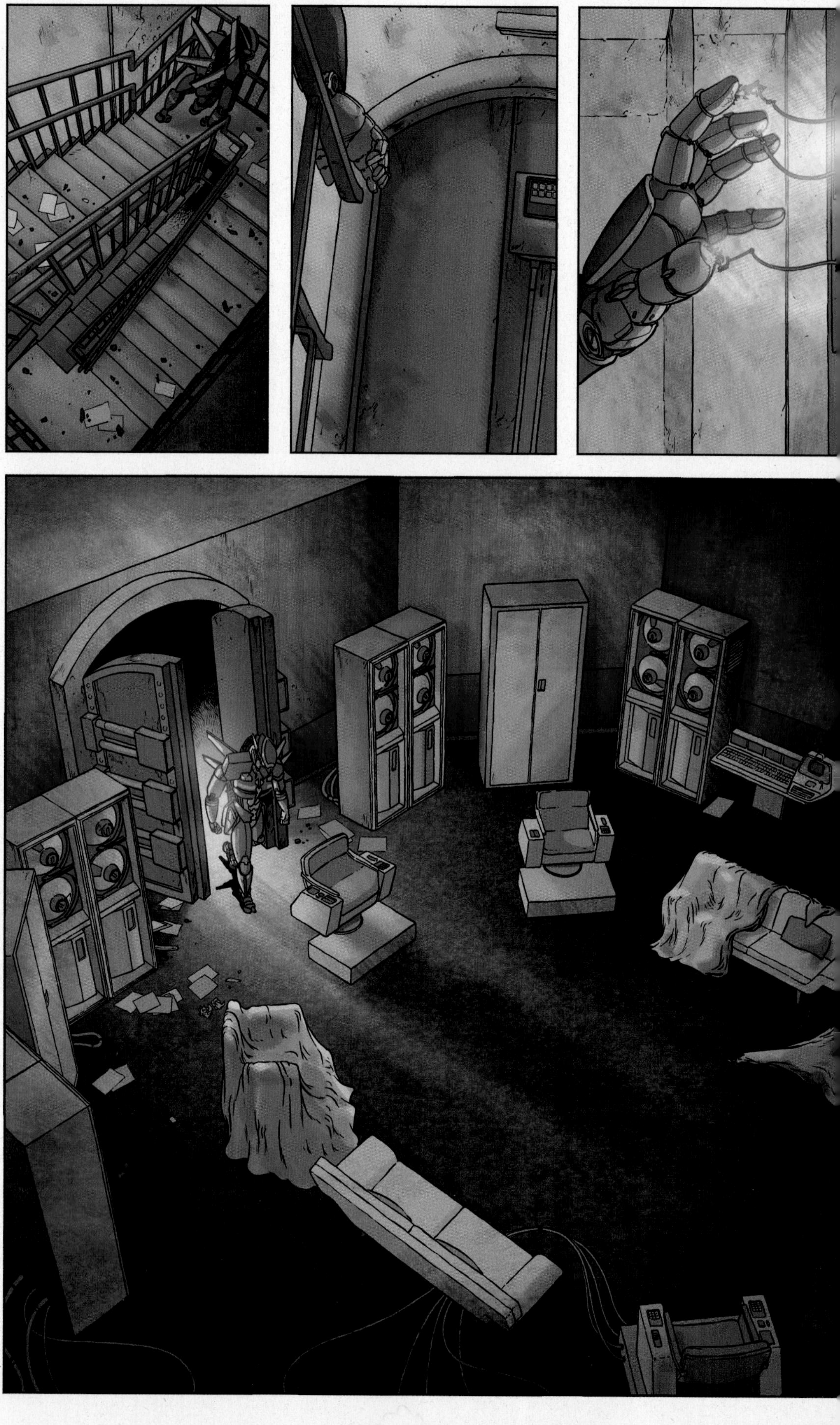

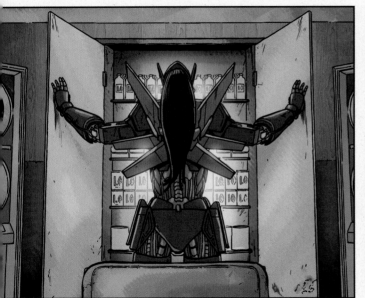

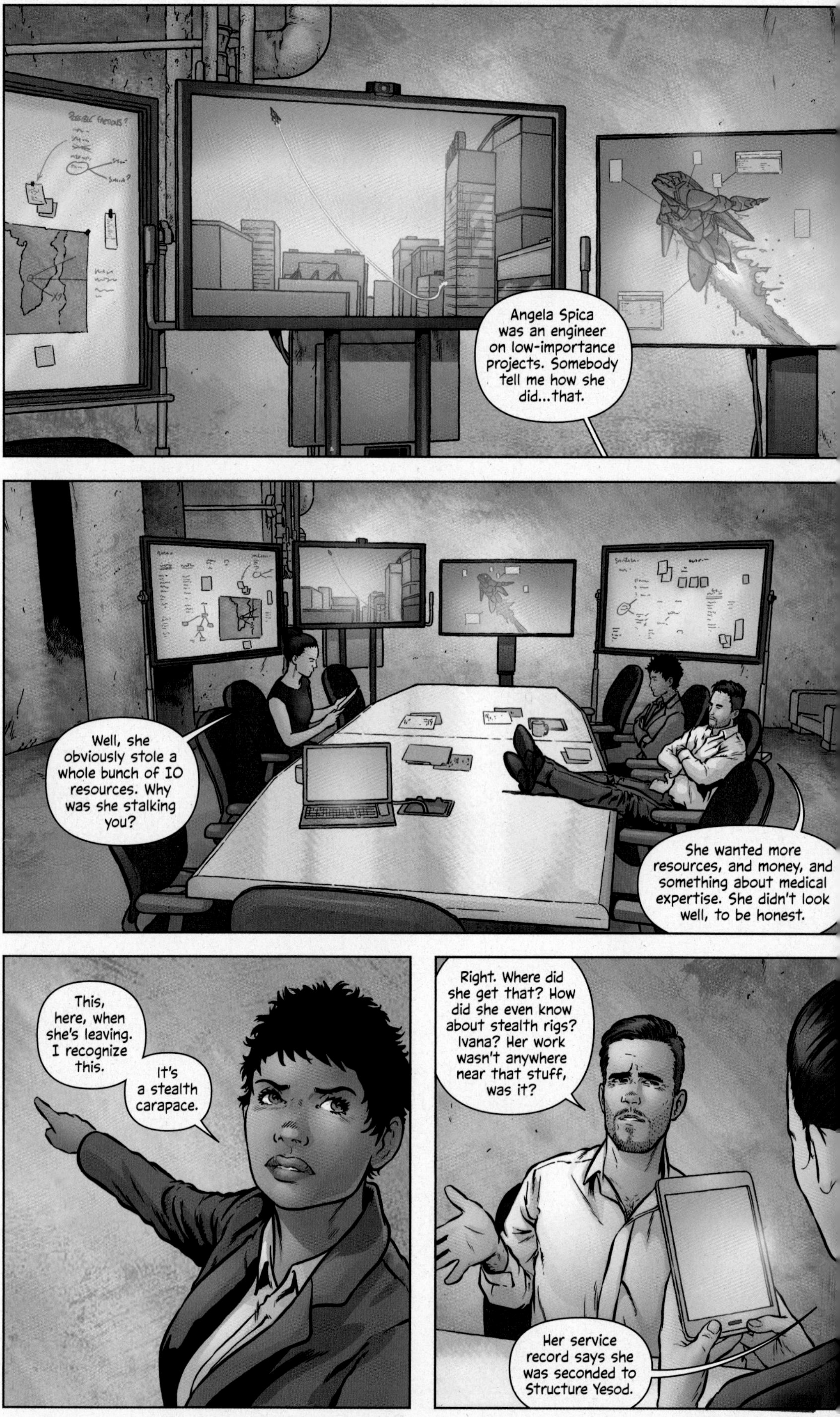

Angela Spica was an engineer on low-importance projects. Somebody tell me how she did...that.
Well, she obviously stole a whole bunch of IO resources. Why was she stalking you?
She wanted more resources, and money, and something about medical expertise. She didn't look well, to be honest.
This, here, when she's leaving. I recognize this.
It's a stealth carapace.
Right. Where did she get that? How did she even know about stealth rigs? Ivana? Her work wasn't anywhere near that stuff, was it?
Her service record says she was seconded to Structure Yesod.

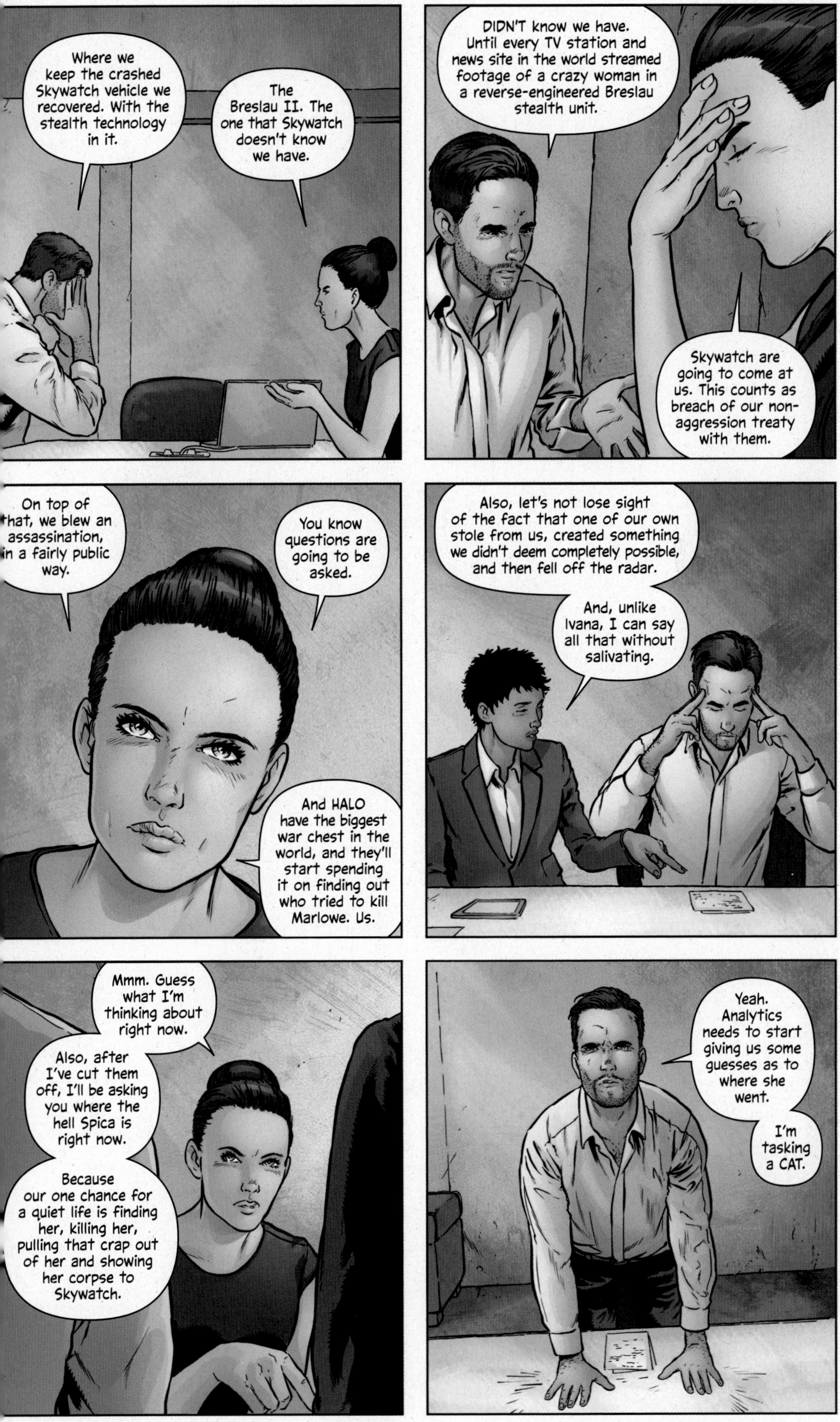
Where we keep the crashed Skywatch vehicle we recovered. With the stealth technology in it.
The Breslau II. The one that Skywatch doesn't know we have.
DIDN'T know we have. Until every TV station and news site in the world streamed footage of a crazy woman in a reverse-engineered Breslau stealth unit.
Skywatch are going to come at us. This counts as breach of our non-aggression treaty with them.
On top of that, we blew an assassination, in a fairly public way.
You know questions are going to be asked.
And HALO have the biggest war chest in the world, and they'll start spending it on finding out who tried to kill Marlowe. Us.
Also, let's not lose sight of the fact that one of our own stole from us, created something we didn't deem completely possible, and then fell off the radar.
And, unlike Ivana, I can say all that without salivating.
Mmm. Guess what I'm thinking about right now.
Also, after I've cut them off, I'll be asking you where the hell Spica is right now.
Because our one chance for a quiet life is finding her, killing her, pulling that crap out of her and showing her corpse to Skywatch.
Yeah. Analytics needs to start giving us some guesses as to where she went.
I'm tasking a CAT.

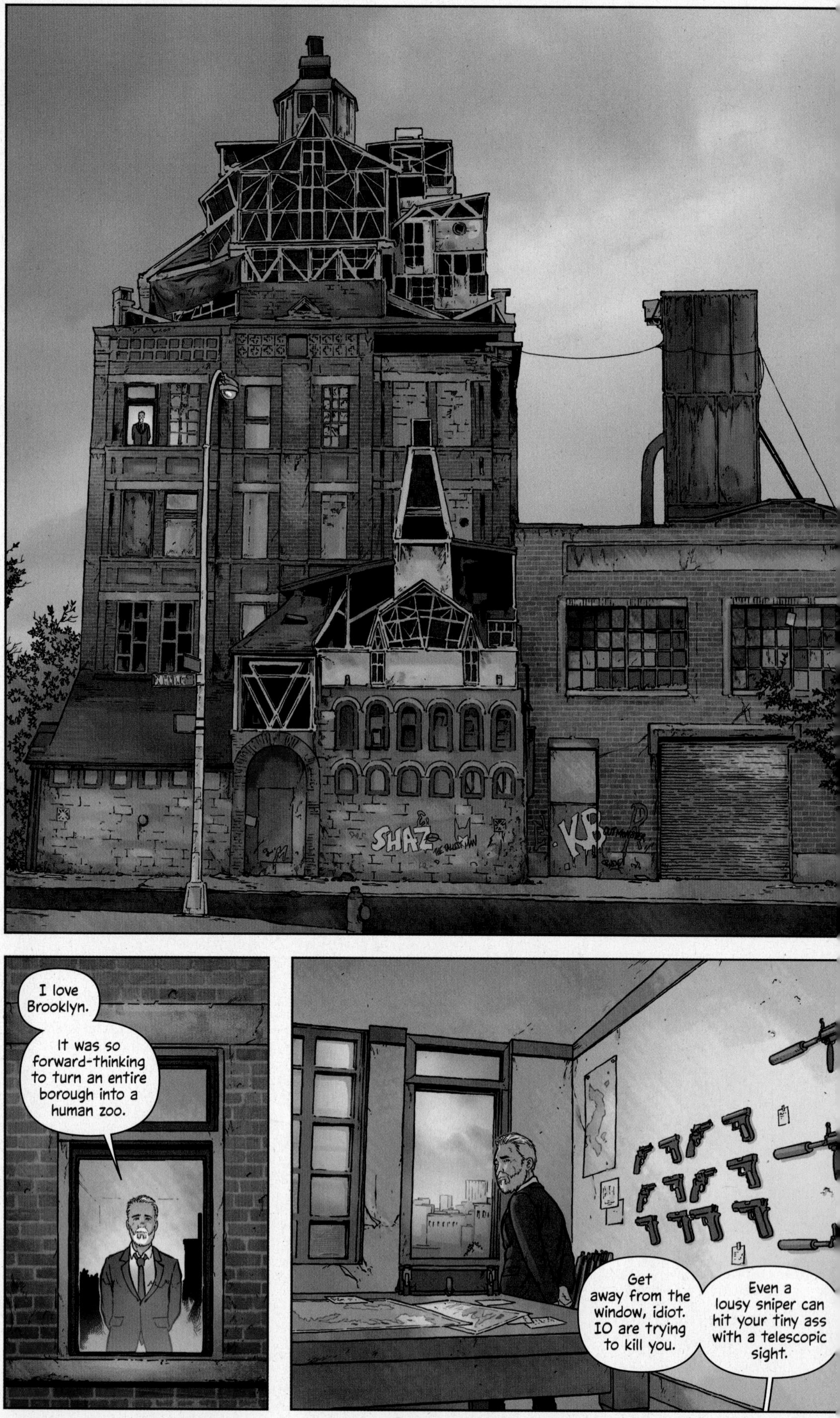
SHAZ
I love Brooklyn.
It was so forward-thinking to turn an entire borough into a human zoo.
Get away from the window, idiot. IO are trying to kill you.
Even a lousy sniper can hit your tiny ass with a telescopic sight.

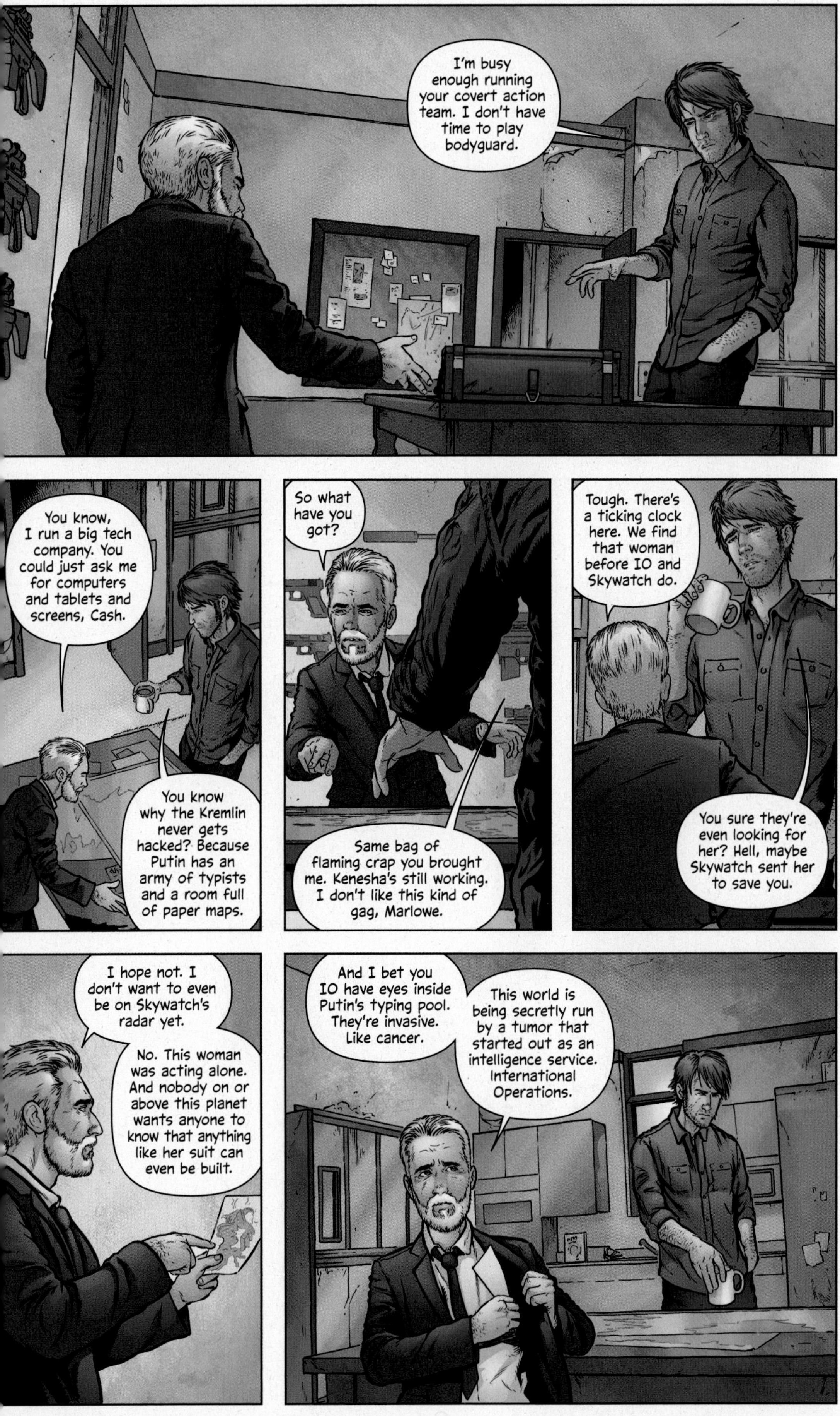
I'm busy enough running your covert action team. I don't have time to play bodyguard.
You know, I run a big tech company. You could just ask me for computers and tablets and screens, Cash.
You know why the Kremlin never gets hacked? Because Putin has an army of typists and a room full of paper maps.
So what have you got?
Same bag of flaming crap you brought me. Kenesha's still working. I don't like this kind of gag, Marlowe.
Tough. There's a ticking clock here. We find that woman before IO and Skywatch do.
You sure they're even looking for her? Hell, maybe Skywatch sent her to save you.
I hope not. I don't want to even be on Skywatch's radar yet.
No. This woman was acting alone. And nobody on or above this planet wants anyone to know that anything like her suit can even be built.
And I bet you IO have eyes inside Putin's typing pool. They're invasive. Like cancer.
This world is being secretly run by a tumor that started out as an intelligence service. International Operations.

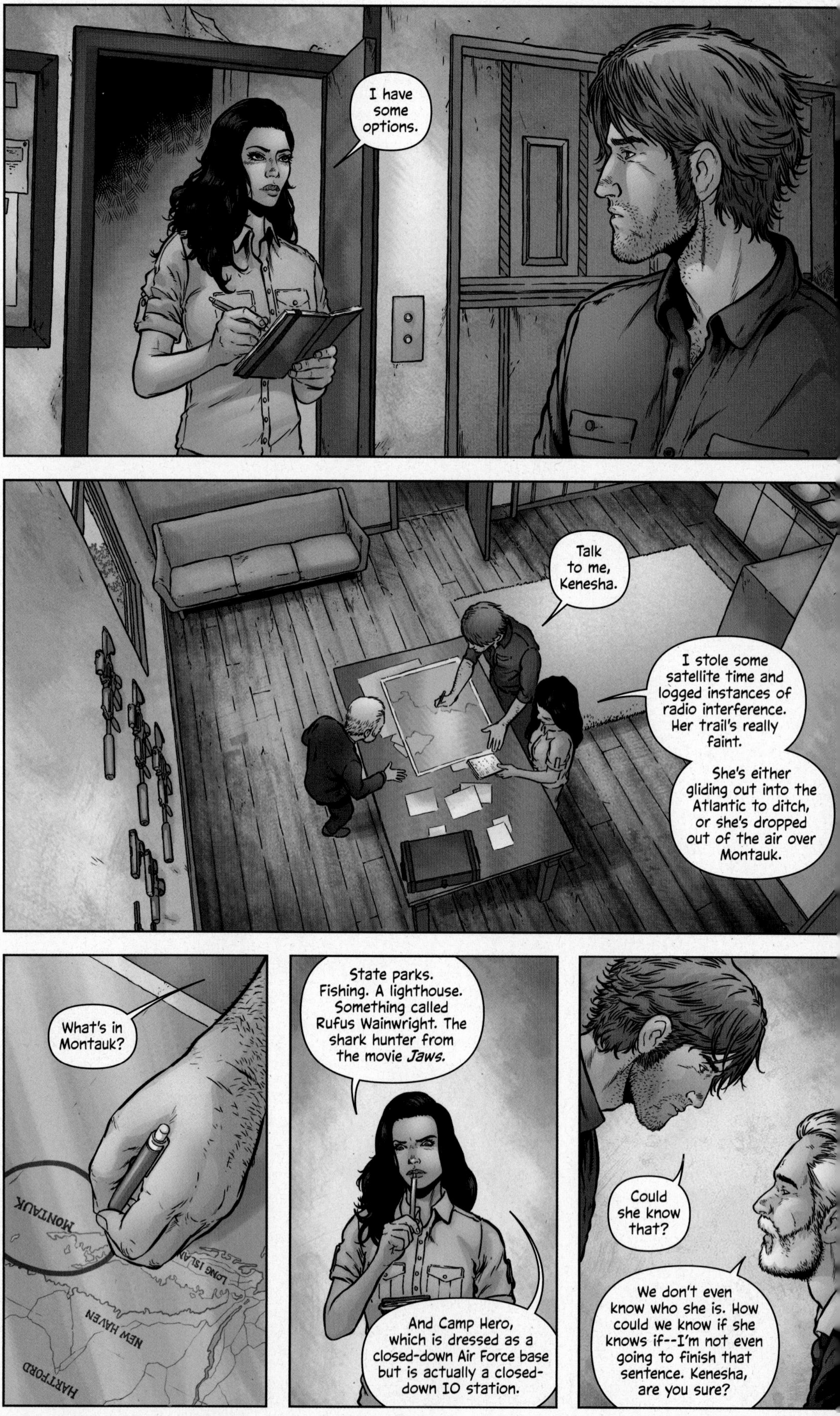
I have some options.
Talk to me, Kenesha.
I stole some satellite time and logged instances of radio interference. Her trail's really faint.
She's either gliding out into the Atlantic to ditch, or she's dropped out of the air over Montauk.
What's in Montauk?
MONTAUK
LONG ISLAN
NEW HAVEN
HARTFORD
State parks. Fishing. A lighthouse. Something called Rufus Wainwright. The shark hunter from the movie *Jaws.*
And Camp Hero, which is dressed as a closed-down Air Force base but is actually a closed-down IO station.
Could she know that?
We don't even know who she is. How could we know if she knows if--I'm not even going to finish that sentence. Kenesha, are you sure?

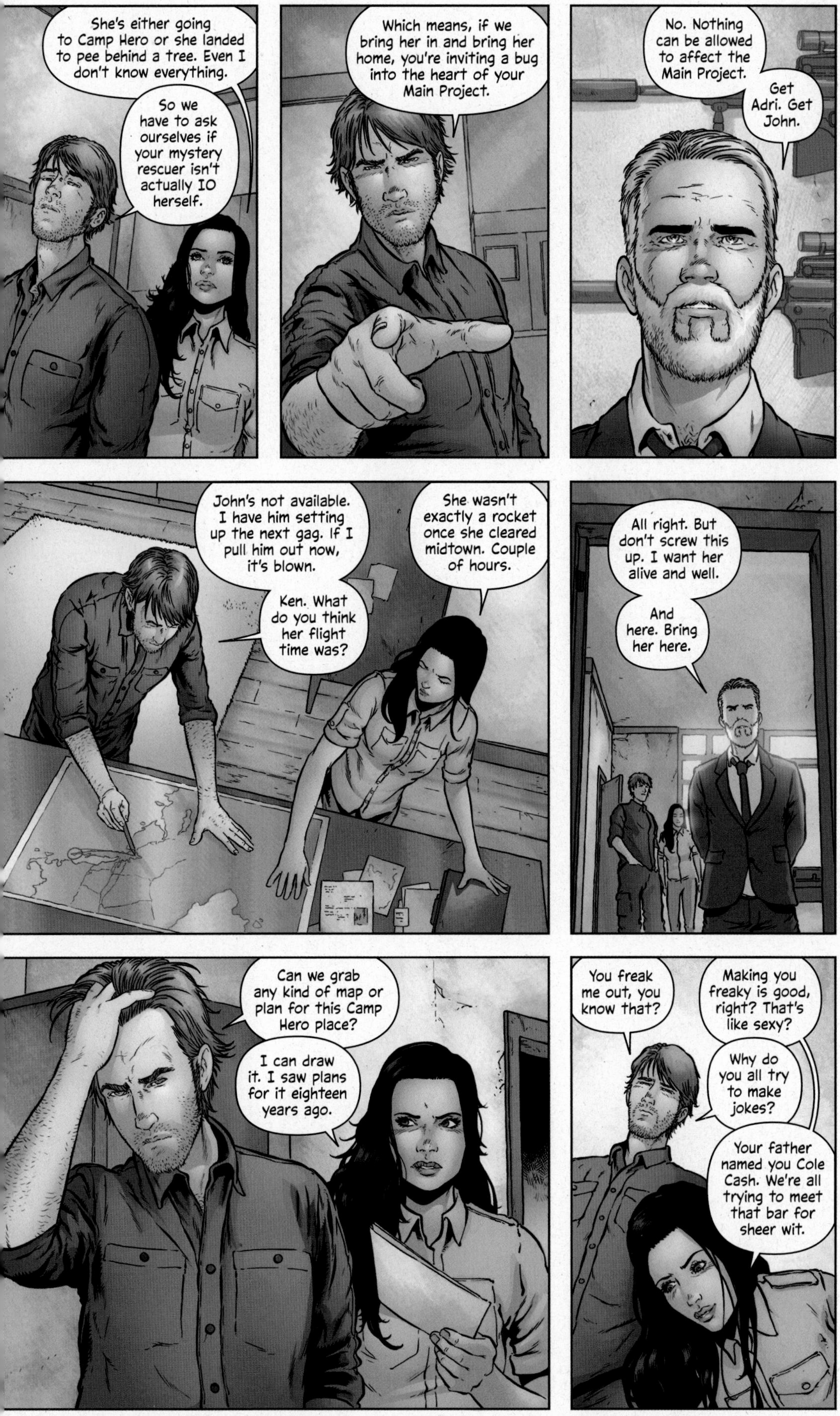
She's either going to Camp Hero or she landed to pee behind a tree. Even I don't know everything.
So we have to ask ourselves if your mystery rescuer isn't actually IO herself.
Which means, if we bring her in and bring her home, you're inviting a bug into the heart of your Main Project.
No. Nothing can be allowed to affect the Main Project.
Get Adri. Get John.
John's not available. I have him setting up the next gag. If I pull him out now, it's blown.
Ken. What do you think her flight time was?
She wasn't exactly a rocket once she cleared midtown. Couple of hours.
All right. But don't screw this up. I want her alive and well.
And here. Bring her here.
Can we grab any kind of map or plan for this Camp Hero place?
I can draw it. I saw plans for it eighteen years ago.
You freak me out, you know that?
Making you freaky is good, right? That's like sexy?
Why do you all try to make jokes?
Your father named you Cole Cash. We're all trying to meet that bar for sheer wit.

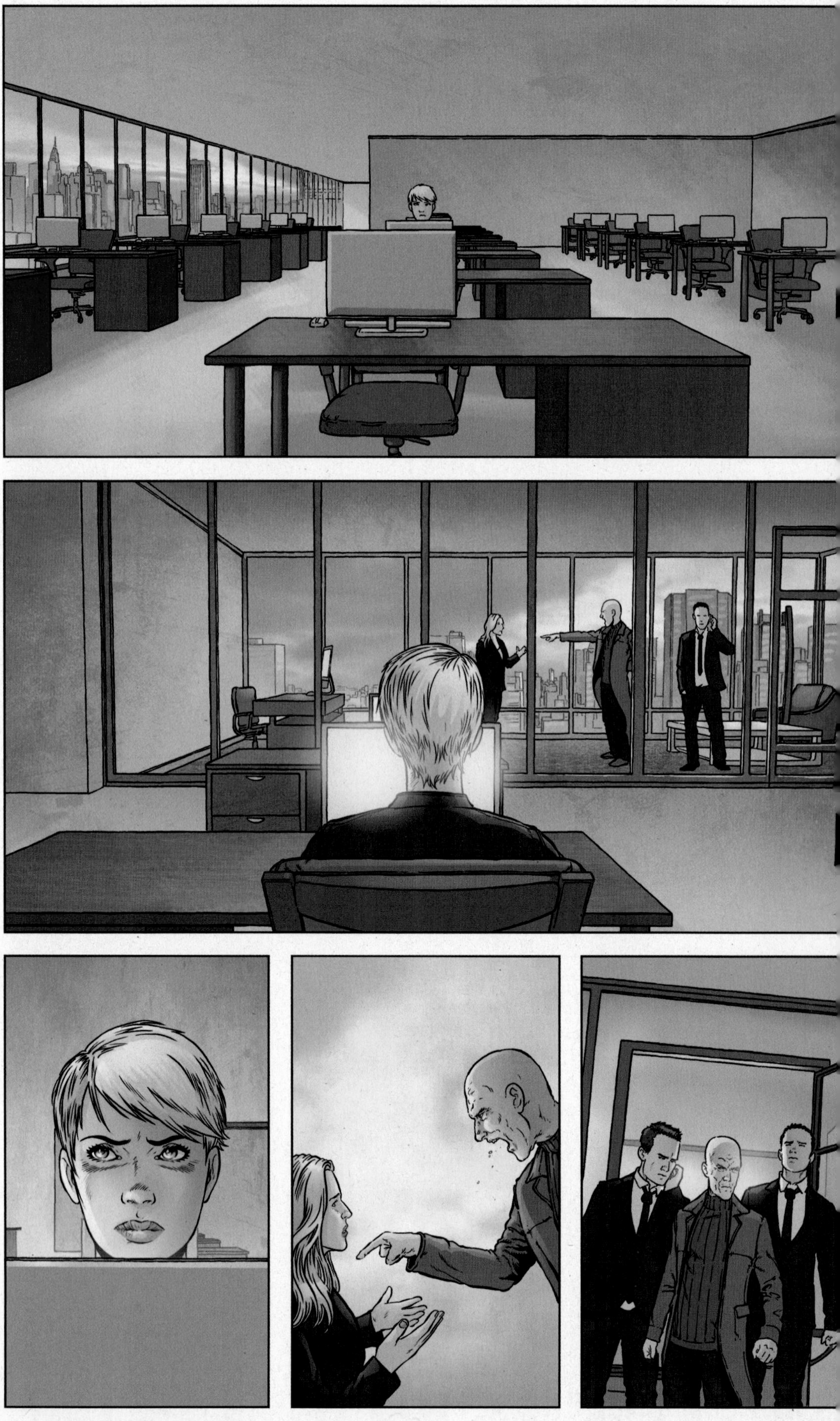

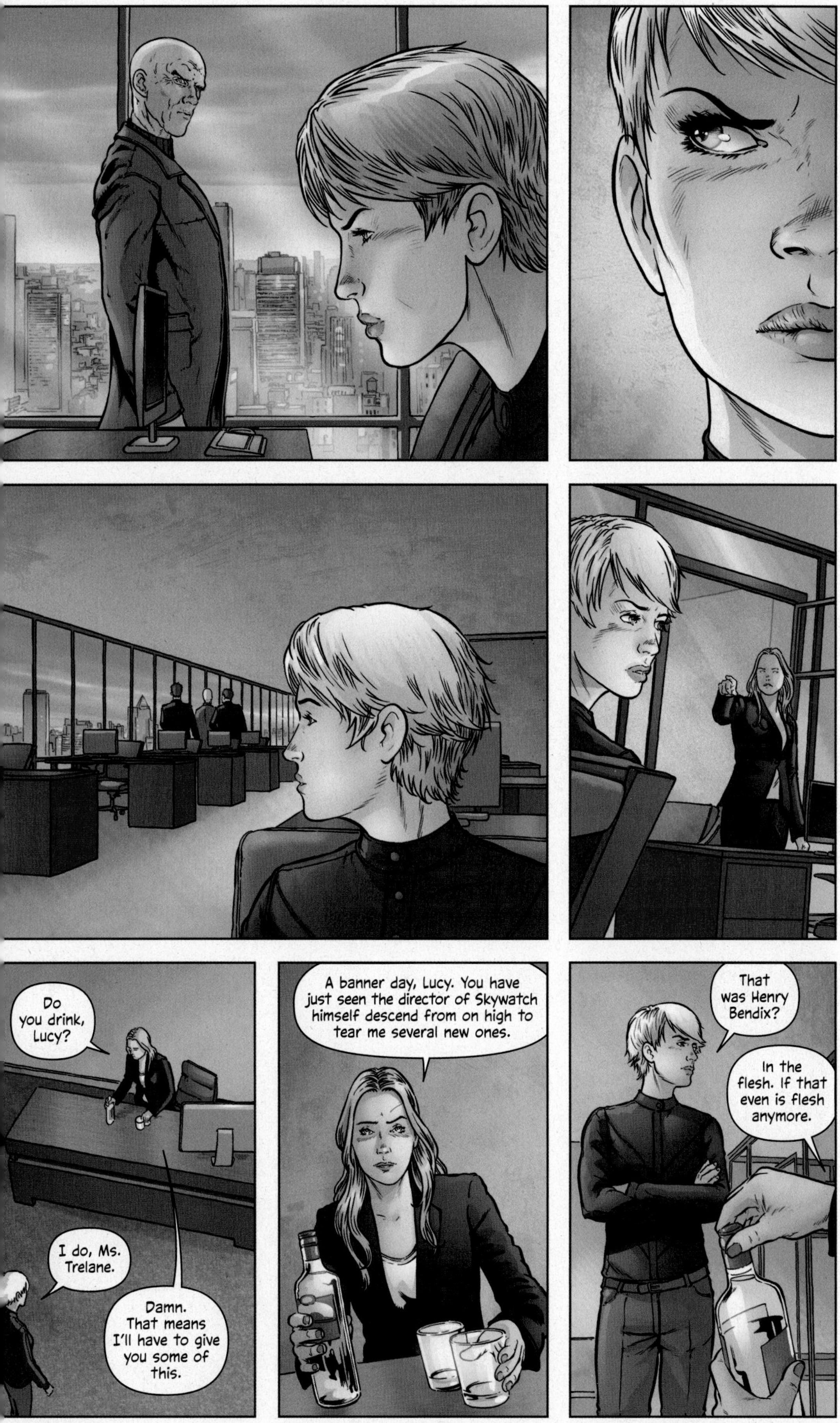
Do you drink, Lucy?
I do, Ms. Trelane.
Damn. That means I'll have to give you some of this.
A banner day, Lucy. You have just seen the director of Skywatch himself descend from on high to tear me several new ones.
That was Henry Bendix?
In the flesh. If that even is flesh anymore.

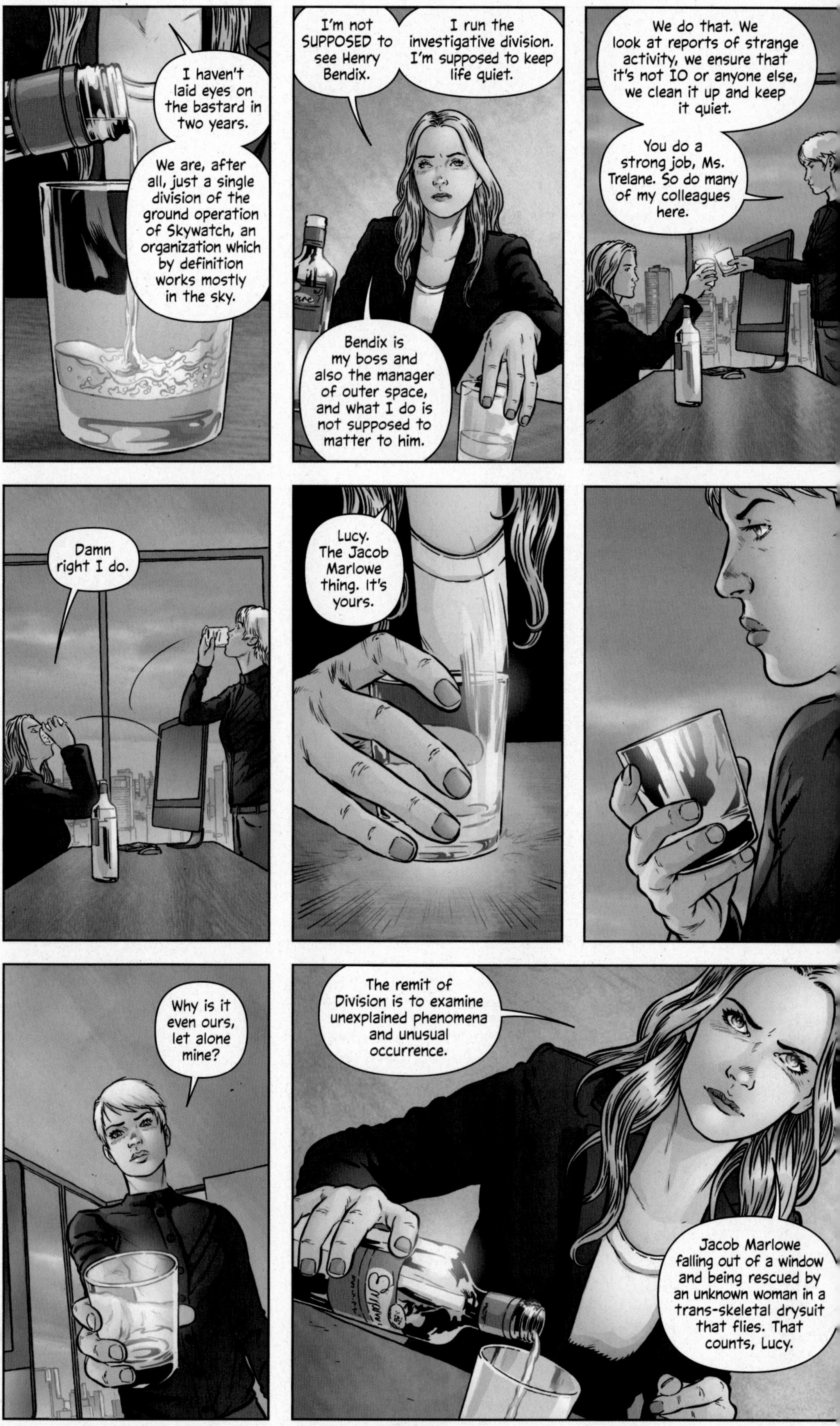
I haven't laid eyes on the bastard in two years.
We are, after all, just a single division of the ground operation of Skywatch, an organization which by definition works mostly in the sky.
I'm not SUPPOSED to see Henry Bendix.
I run the investigative division. I'm supposed to keep life quiet.
Bendix is my boss and also the manager of outer space, and what I do is not supposed to matter to him.
We do that. We look at reports of strange activity, we ensure that it's not IO or anyone else, we clean it up and keep it quiet.
You do a strong job, Ms. Trelane. So do many of my colleagues here.
Damn right I do.
Lucy. The Jacob Marlowe thing. It's yours.
Why is it even ours, let alone mine?
The remit of Division is to examine unexplained phenomena and unusual occurrence.
Jacob Marlowe falling out of a window and being rescued by an unknown woman in a trans-skeletal drysuit that flies. That counts, Lucy.

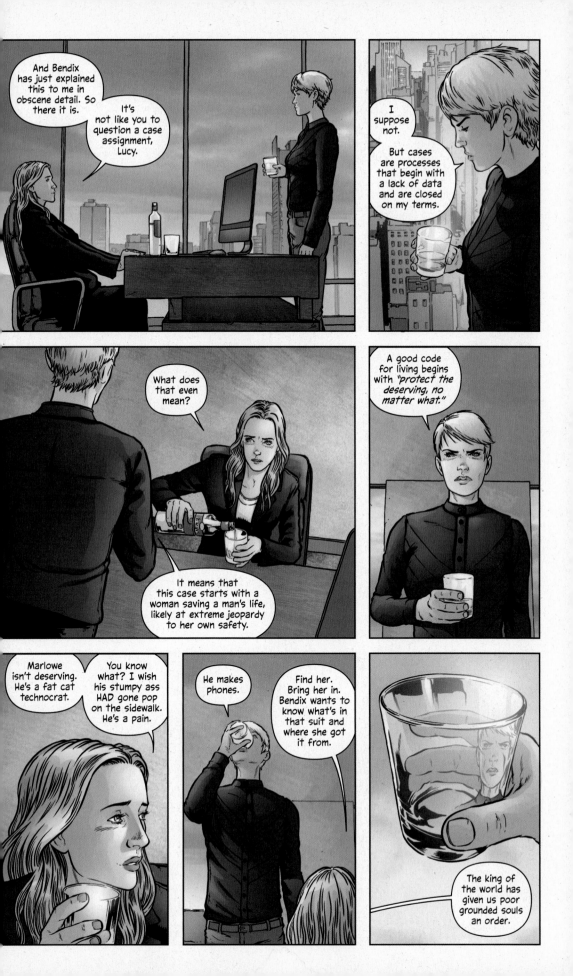

And Bendix has just explained this to me in obscene detail. So there it is.

It's not like you to question a case assignment, Lucy.

I suppose not.

But cases are processes that begin with a lack of data and are closed on my terms.

What does that even mean?

A good code for living begins with *"protect the deserving, no matter what."*

It means that this case starts with a woman saving a man's life, likely at extreme jeopardy to her own safety.

Marlowe isn't deserving. He's a fat cat technocrat.

You know what? I wish his stumpy ass HAD gone pop on the sidewalk. He's a pain.

He makes phones.

Find her. Bring her in. Bendix wants to know what's in that suit and where she got it from.

The king of the world has given us poor grounded souls an order.

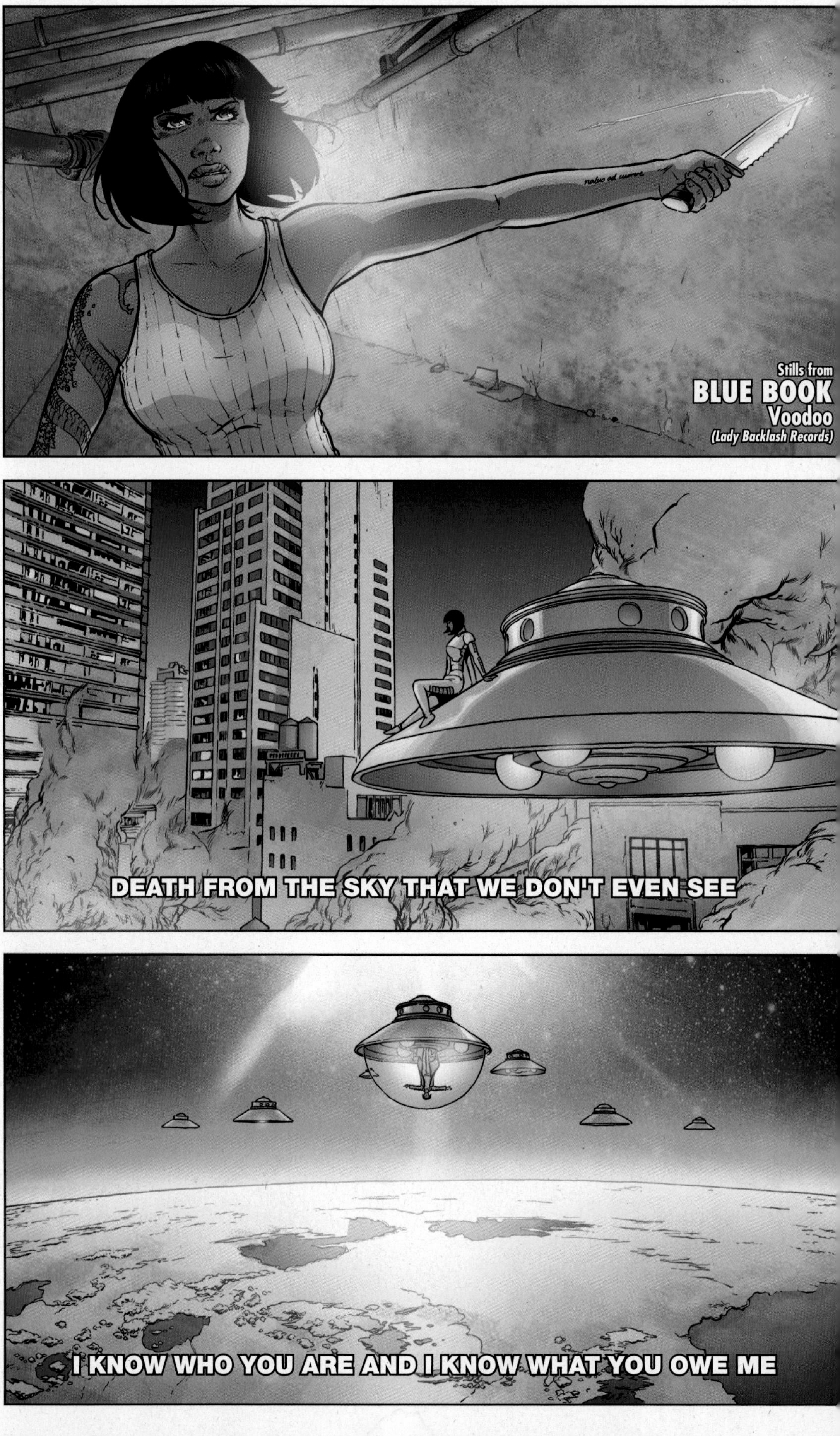
Stills from
BLUE BOOK
Voodoo
(Lady Backlash Records)
DEATH FROM THE SKY THAT WE DON'T EVEN SEE
I KNOW WHO YOU ARE AND I KNOW WHAT YOU OWE ME

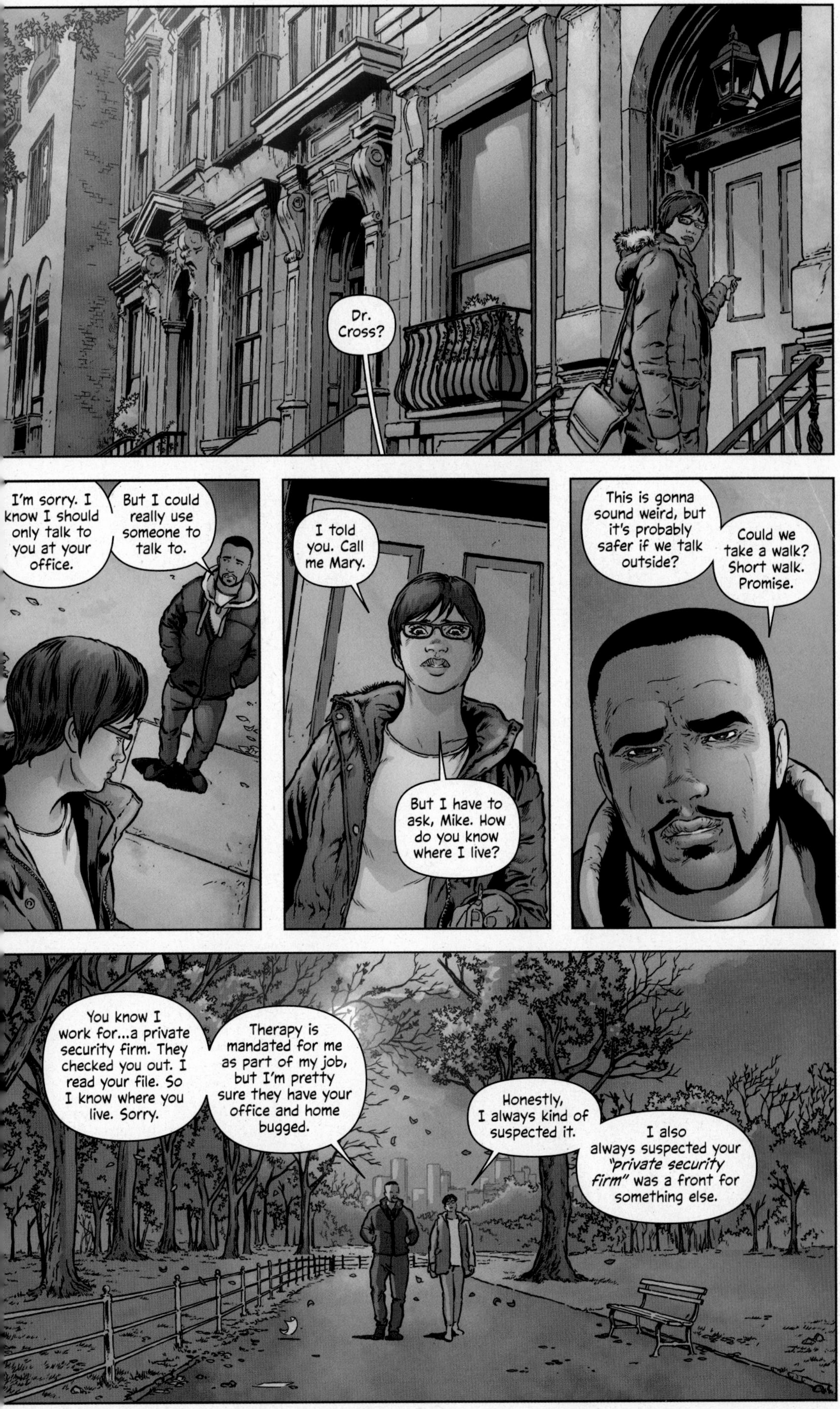
Dr. Cross?
I'm sorry. I know I should only talk to you at your office.
But I could really use someone to talk to.
I told you. Call me Mary.
But I have to ask, Mike. How do you know where I live?
This is gonna sound weird, but it's probably safer if we talk outside?
Could we take a walk? Short walk. Promise.
You know I work for...a private security firm. They checked you out. I read your file. So I know where you live. Sorry.
Therapy is mandated for me as part of my job, but I'm pretty sure they have your office and home bugged.
Honestly, I always kind of suspected it.
I also always suspected your *"private security firm"* was a front for something else.

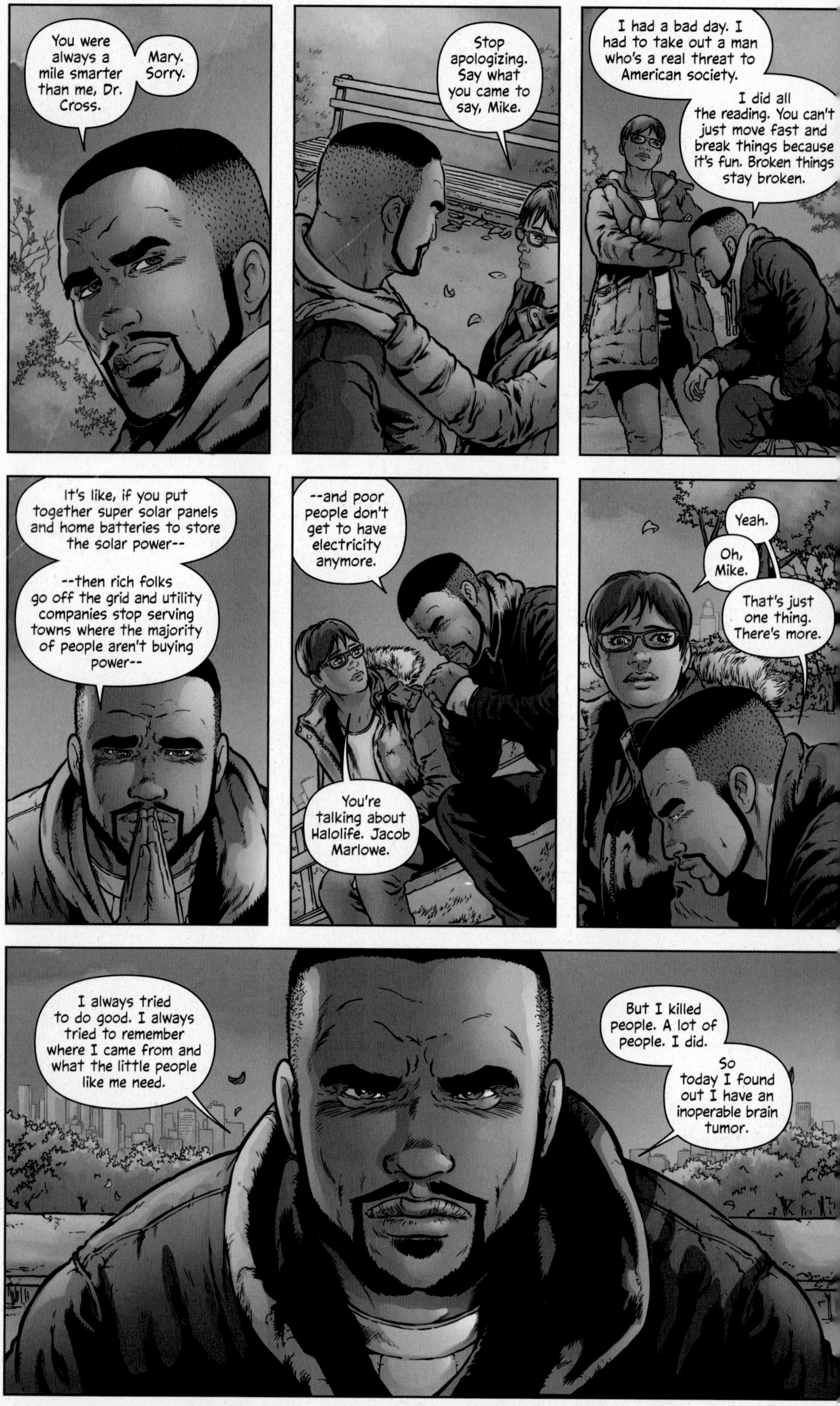
You were always a mile smarter than me, Dr. Cross.
Mary. Sorry.
Stop apologizing. Say what you came to say, Mike.
I had a bad day. I had to take out a man who's a real threat to American society.
I did all the reading. You can't just move fast and break things because it's fun. Broken things stay broken.
It's like, if you put together super solar panels and home batteries to store the solar power--
--then rich folks go off the grid and utility companies stop serving towns where the majority of people aren't buying power--
--and poor people don't get to have electricity anymore.
You're talking about Halolife. Jacob Marlowe.
Yeah.
Oh, Mike.
That's just one thing. There's more.
I always tried to do good. I always tried to remember where I came from and what the little people like me need.
But I killed people. A lot of people. I did.
So today I found out I have an inoperable brain tumor.

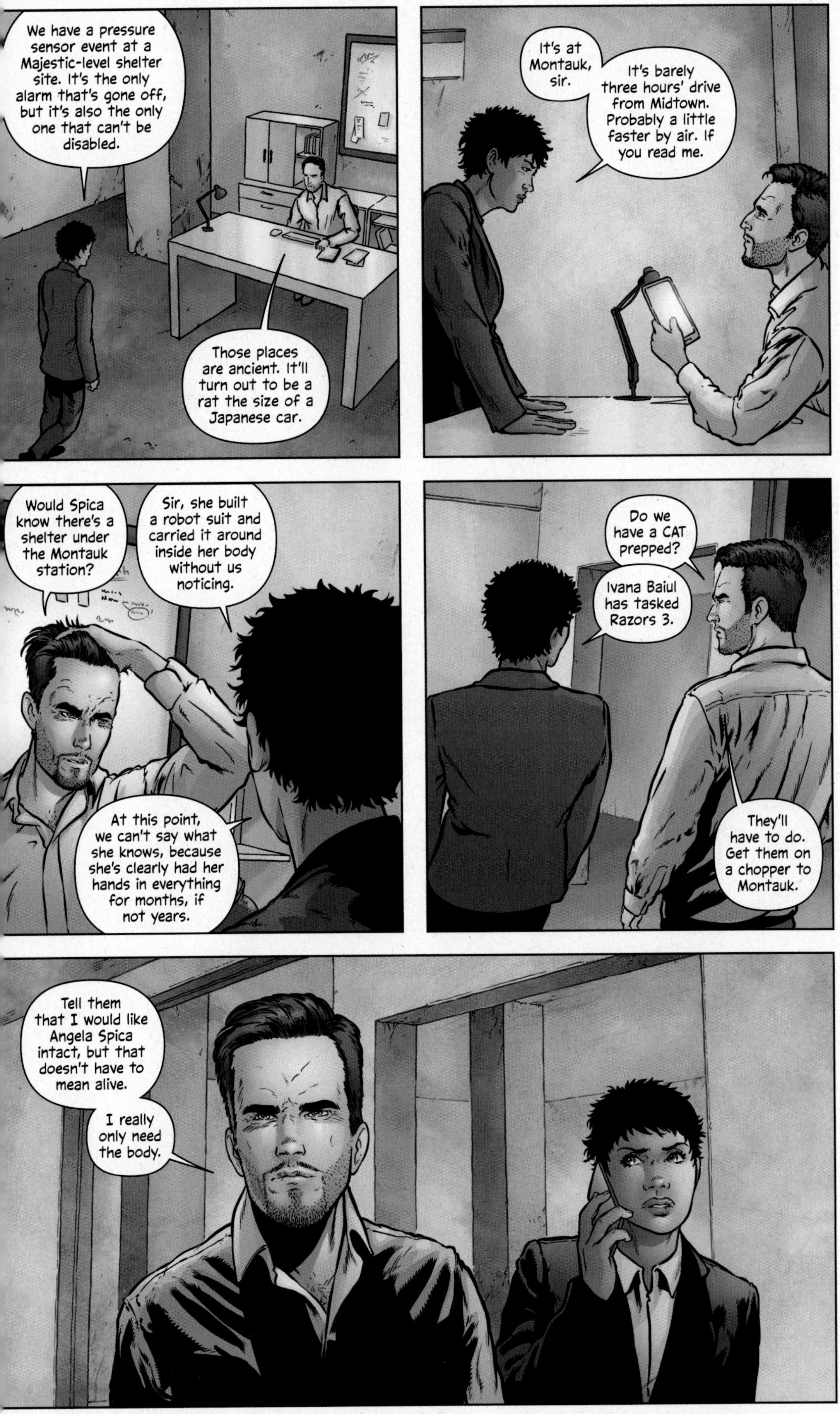
We have a pressure sensor event at a Majestic-level shelter site. It's the only alarm that's gone off, but it's also the only one that can't be disabled.
Those places are ancient. It'll turn out to be a rat the size of a Japanese car.
It's at Montauk, sir.
It's barely three hours' drive from Midtown. Probably a little faster by air. If you read me.
Would Spica know there's a shelter under the Montauk station?
Sir, she built a robot suit and carried it around inside her body without us noticing.
At this point, we can't say what she knows, because she's clearly had her hands in everything for months, if not years.
Do we have a CAT prepped?
Ivana Baiul has tasked Razors 3.
They'll have to do. Get them on a chopper to Montauk.
Tell them that I would like Angela Spica intact, but that doesn't have to mean alive.
I really only need the body.

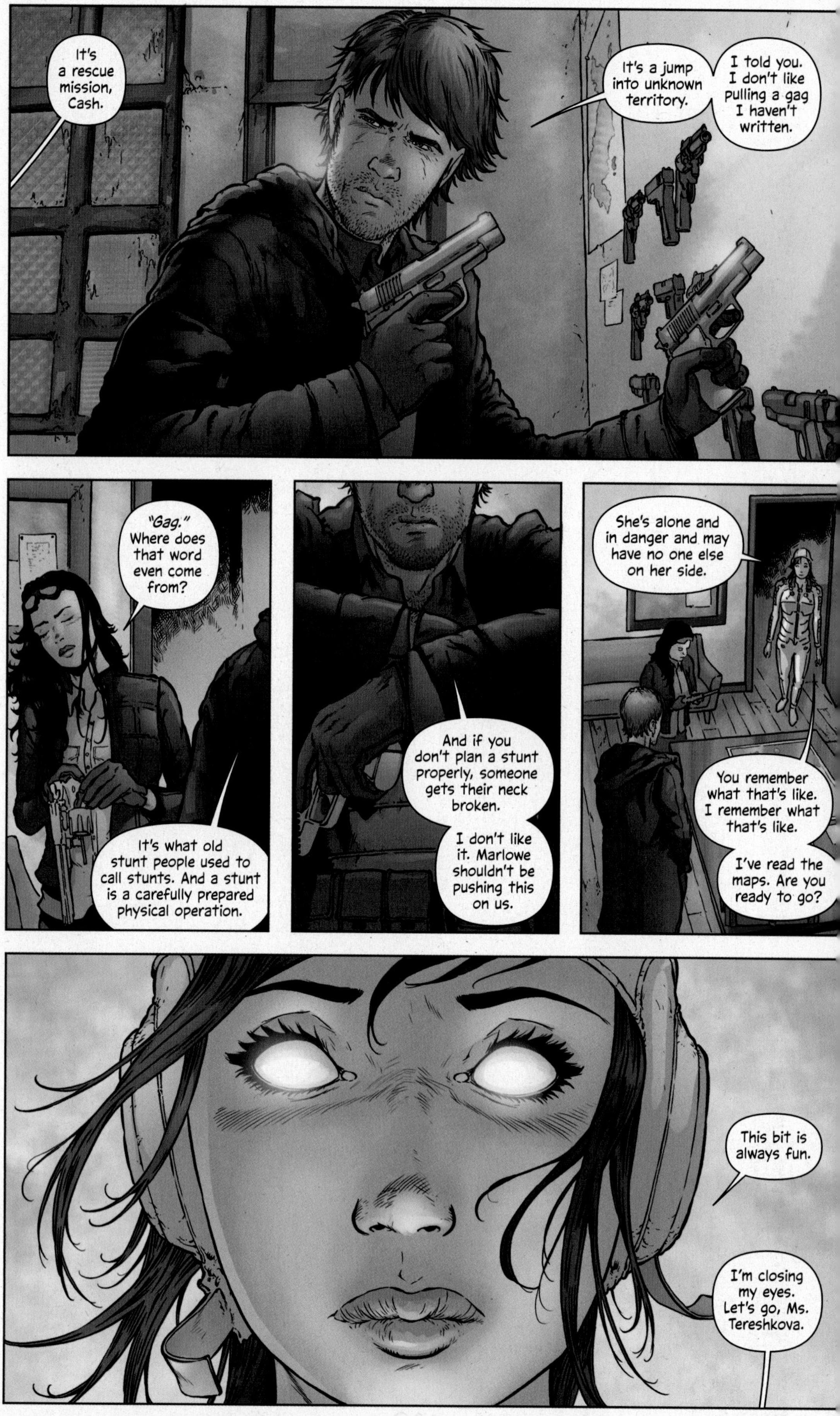
It's a rescue mission, Cash.
It's a jump into unknown territory.
I told you. I don't like pulling a gag I haven't written.
"Gag." Where does that word even come from?
It's what old stunt people used to call stunts. And a stunt is a carefully prepared physical operation.
And if you don't plan a stunt properly, someone gets their neck broken.
I don't like it. Marlowe shouldn't be pushing this on us.
She's alone and in danger and may have no one else on her side.
You remember what that's like. I remember what that's like.
I've read the maps. Are you ready to go?
This bit is always fun.
I'm closing my eyes. Let's go, Ms. Tereshkova.

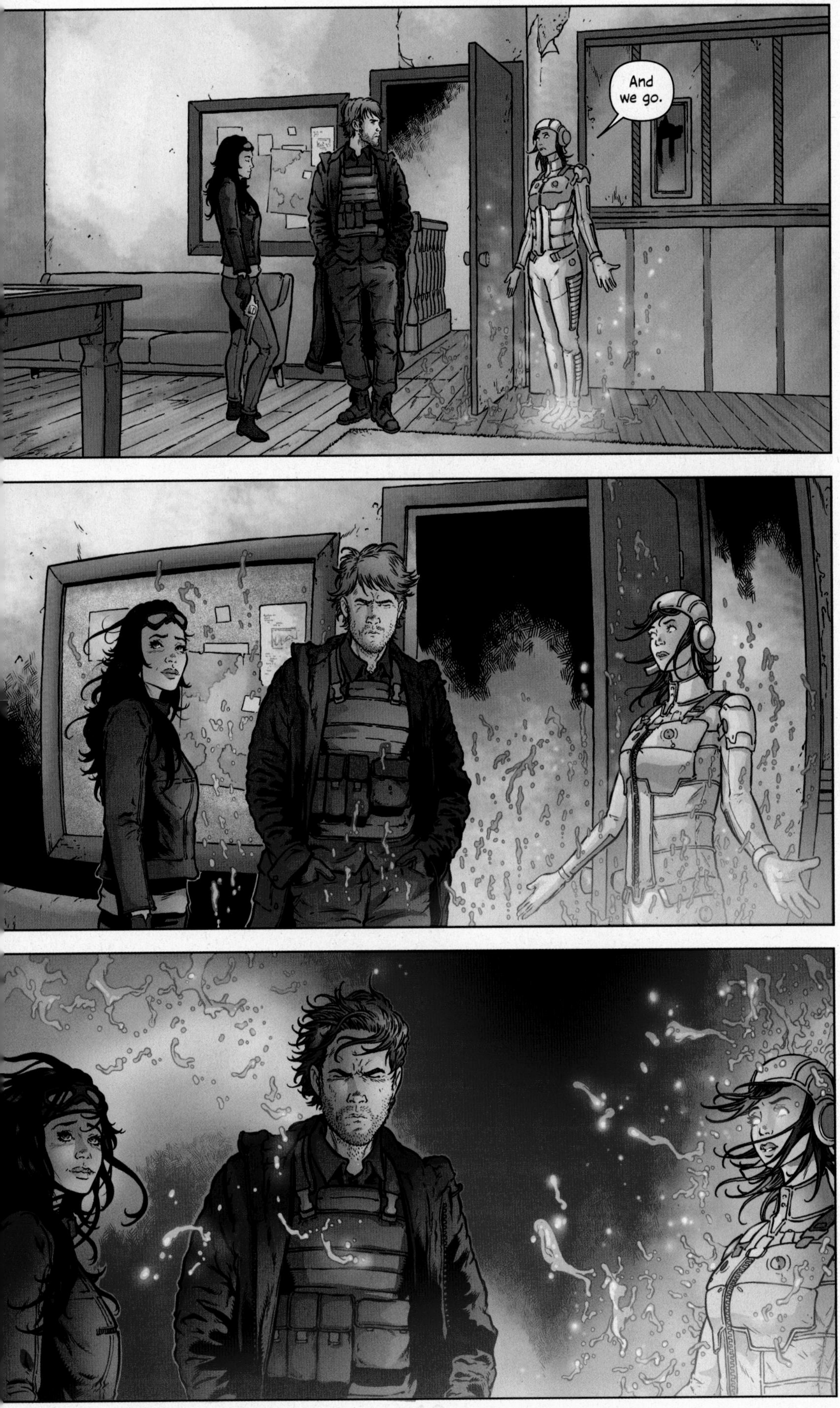
And we go.

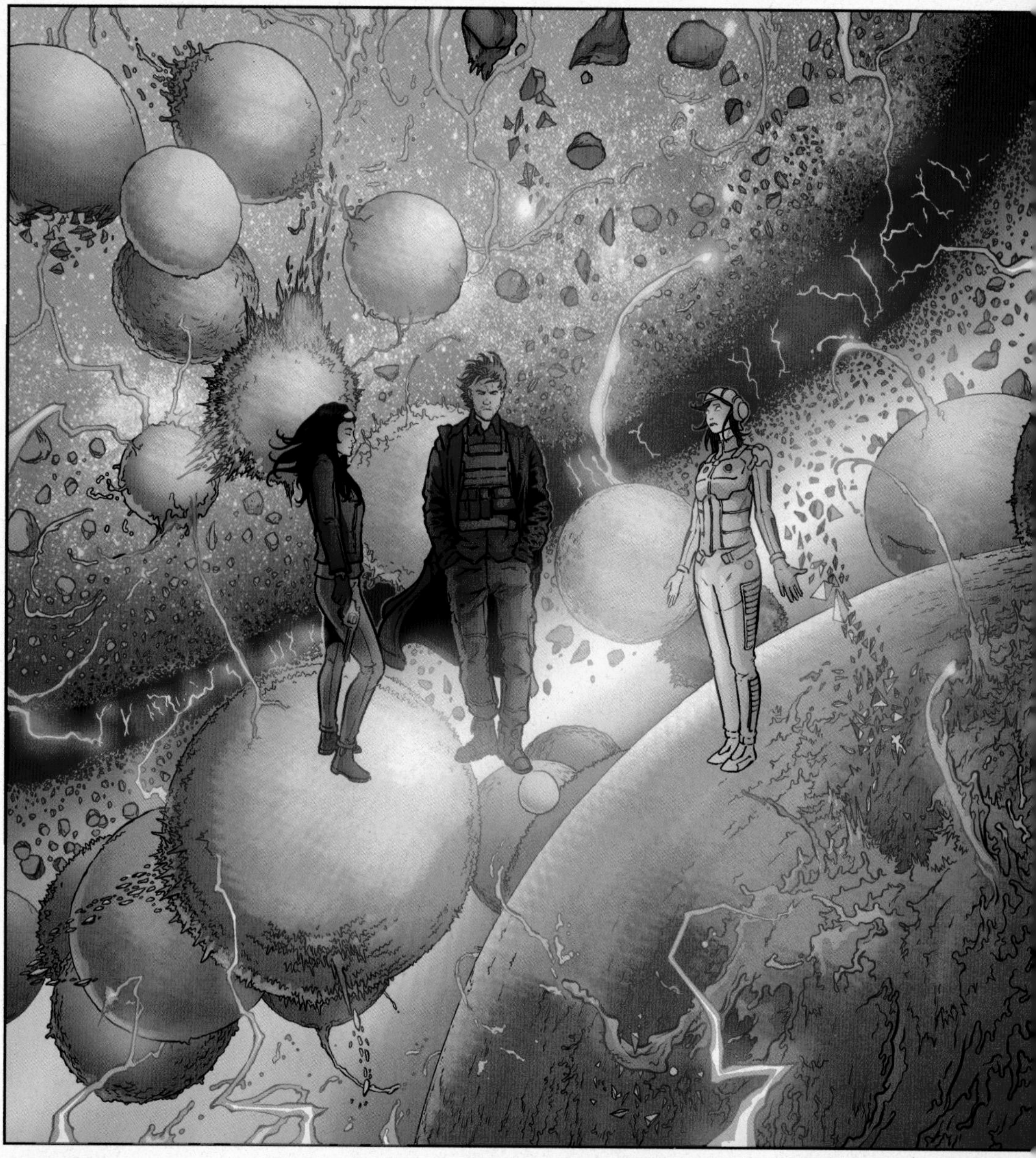
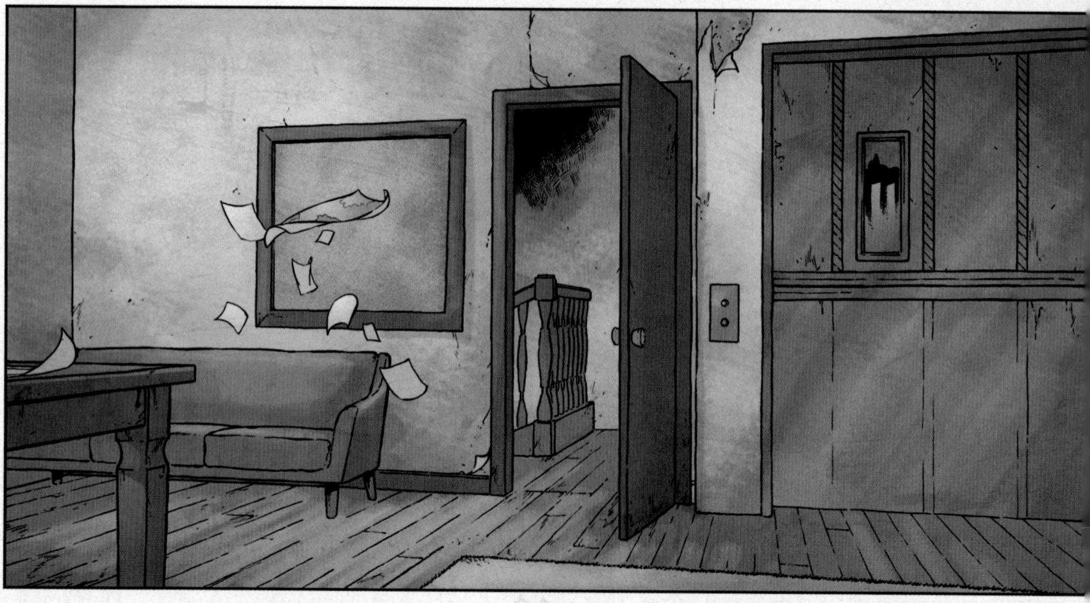

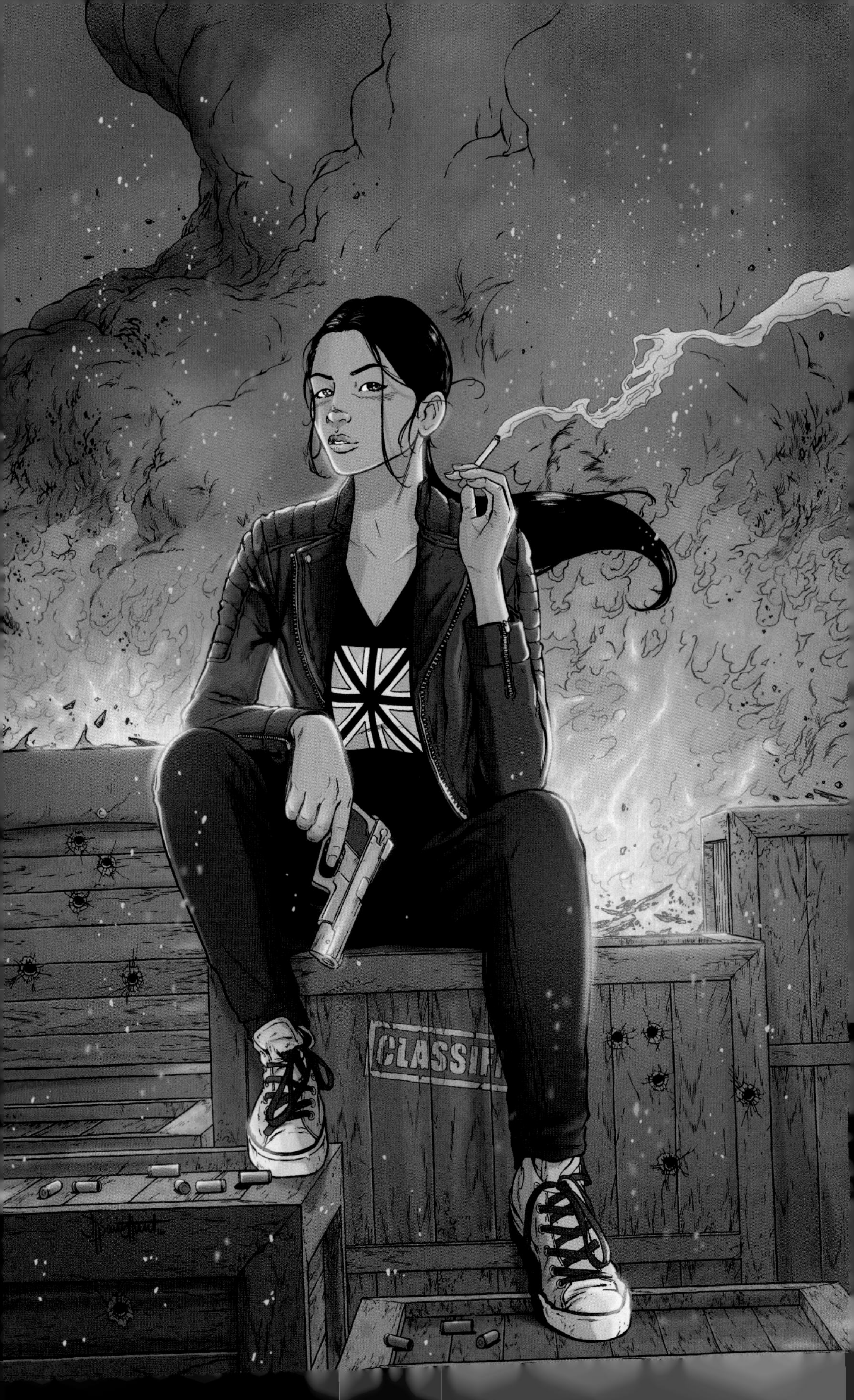

3

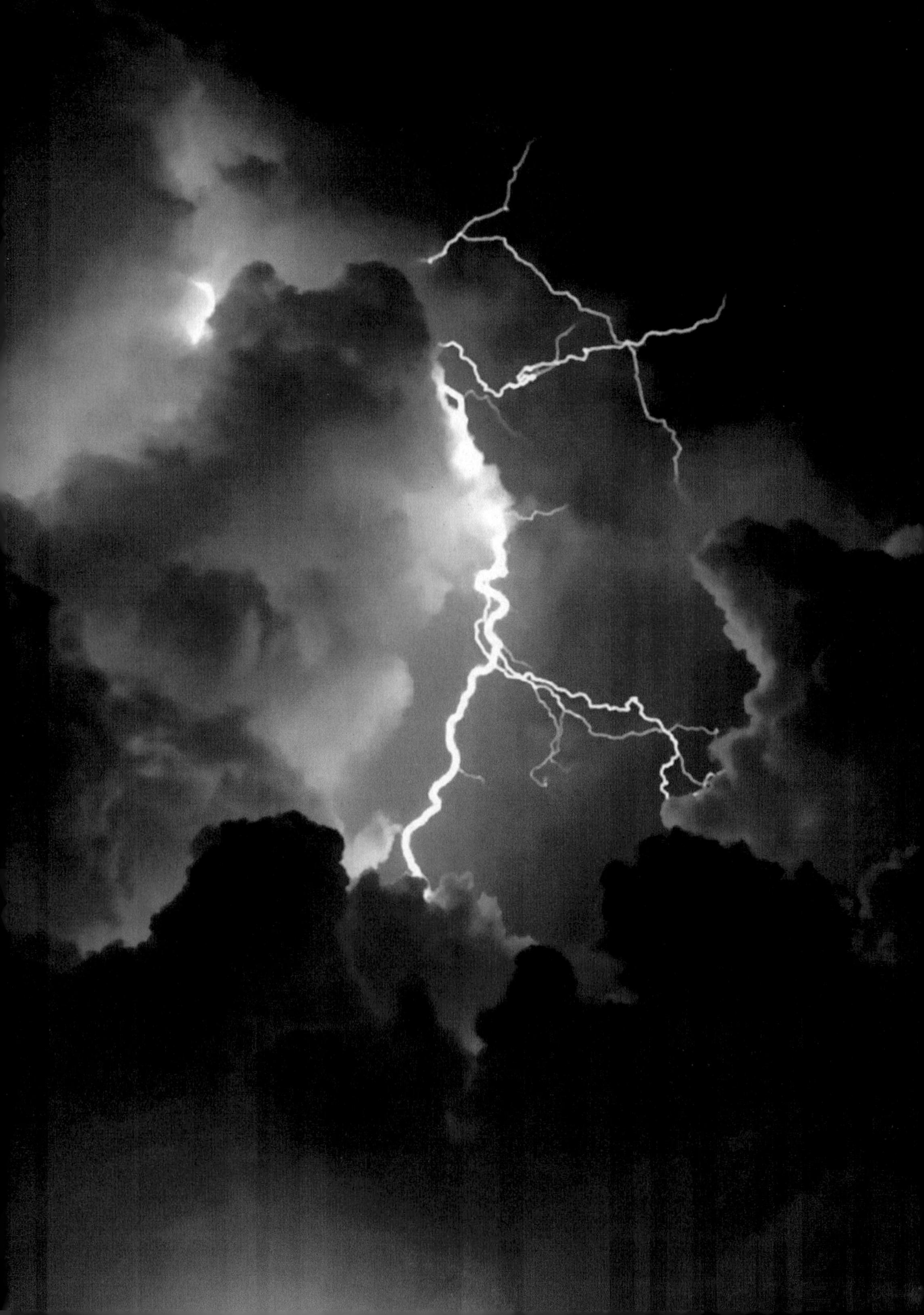

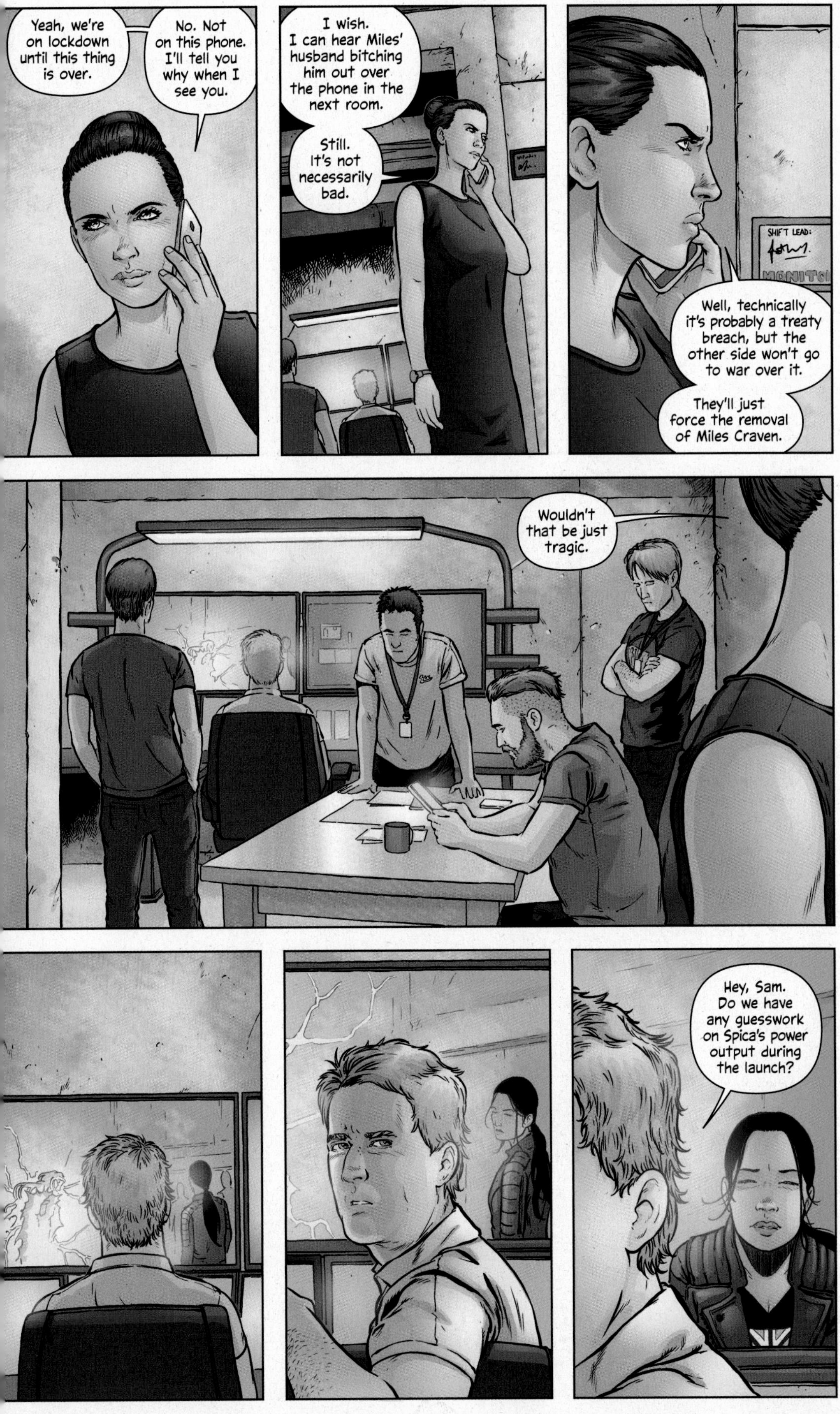

Yeah, we're on lockdown until this thing is over.
No. Not on this phone. I'll tell you why when I see you.
I wish. I can hear Miles' husband bitching him out over the phone in the next room.
Still. It's not necessarily bad.
SHIFT LEAD:
Well, technically it's probably a treaty breach, but the other side won't go to war over it.
They'll just force the removal of Miles Craven.
Wouldn't that be just tragic.
Hey, Sam. Do we have any guesswork on Spica's power output during the launch?

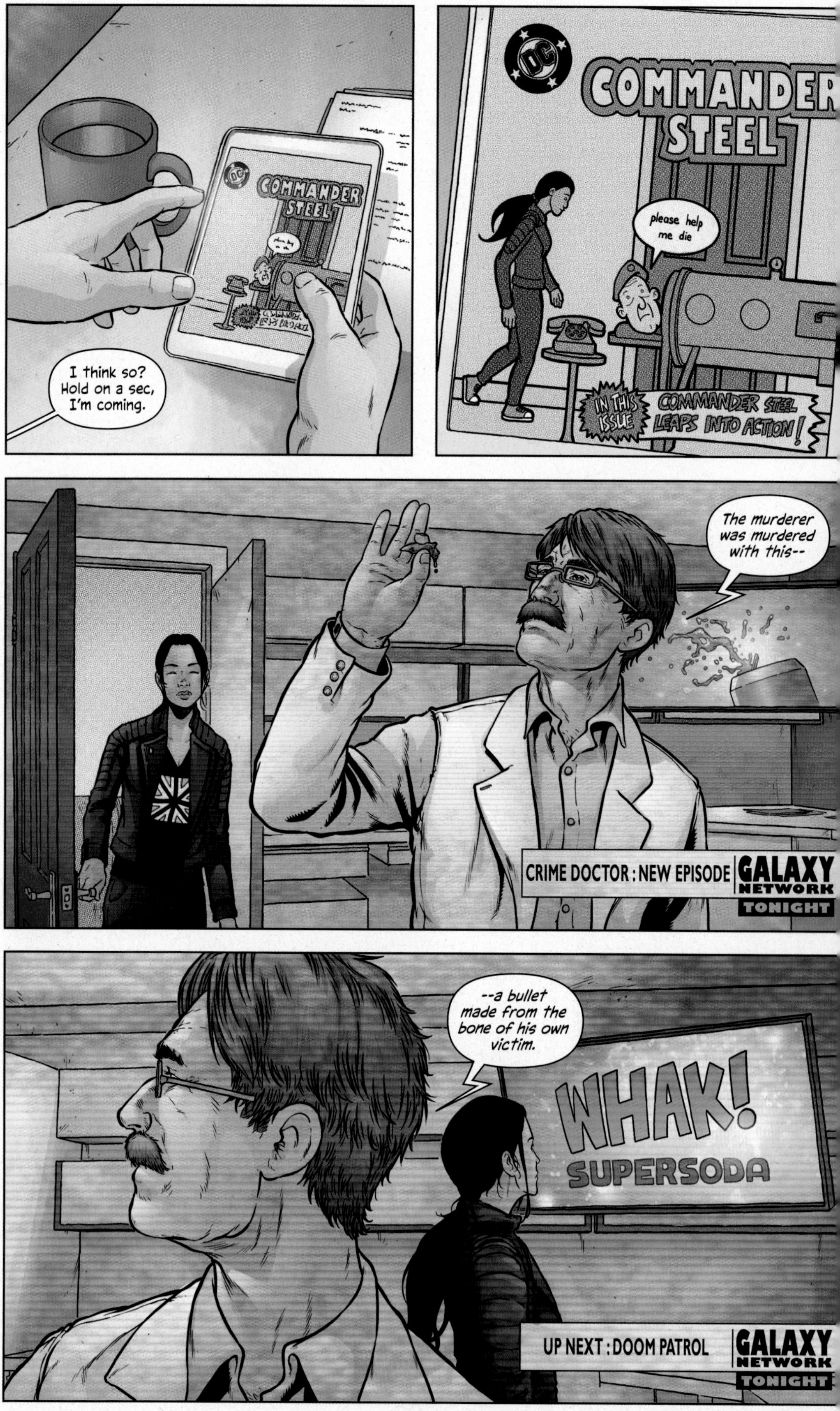
I think so? Hold on a sec, I'm coming.
COMMANDER STEEL
please help me die
IN THIS ISSUE
COMMANDER STEEL LEAPS INTO ACTION!
The murderer was murdered with this--
CRIME DOCTOR : NEW EPISODE
GALAXY NETWORK
TONIGHT
--a bullet made from the bone of his own victim.
WHAK!
SUPERSODA
UP NEXT : DOOM PATROL
GALAXY NETWORK
TONIGHT

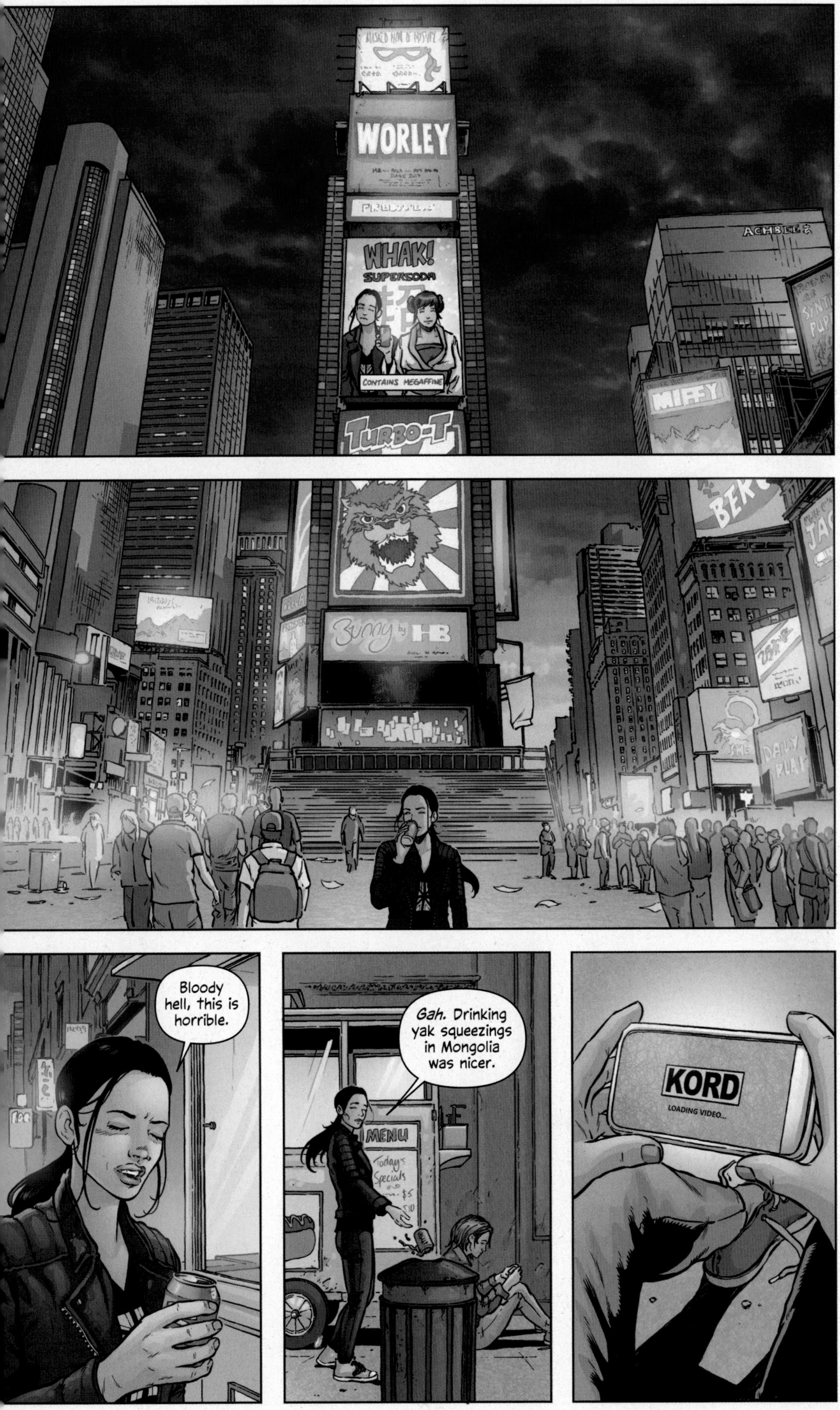
WORLEY
WHAK!
SUPERSODA
CONTAINS MEGAFFINE
TURBO-T
MIFFY
Bunny by HB
Bloody hell, this is horrible.
Gah. Drinking yak squeezings in Mongolia was nicer.
MENU
Today's Specials
KORD
LOADING VIDEO...

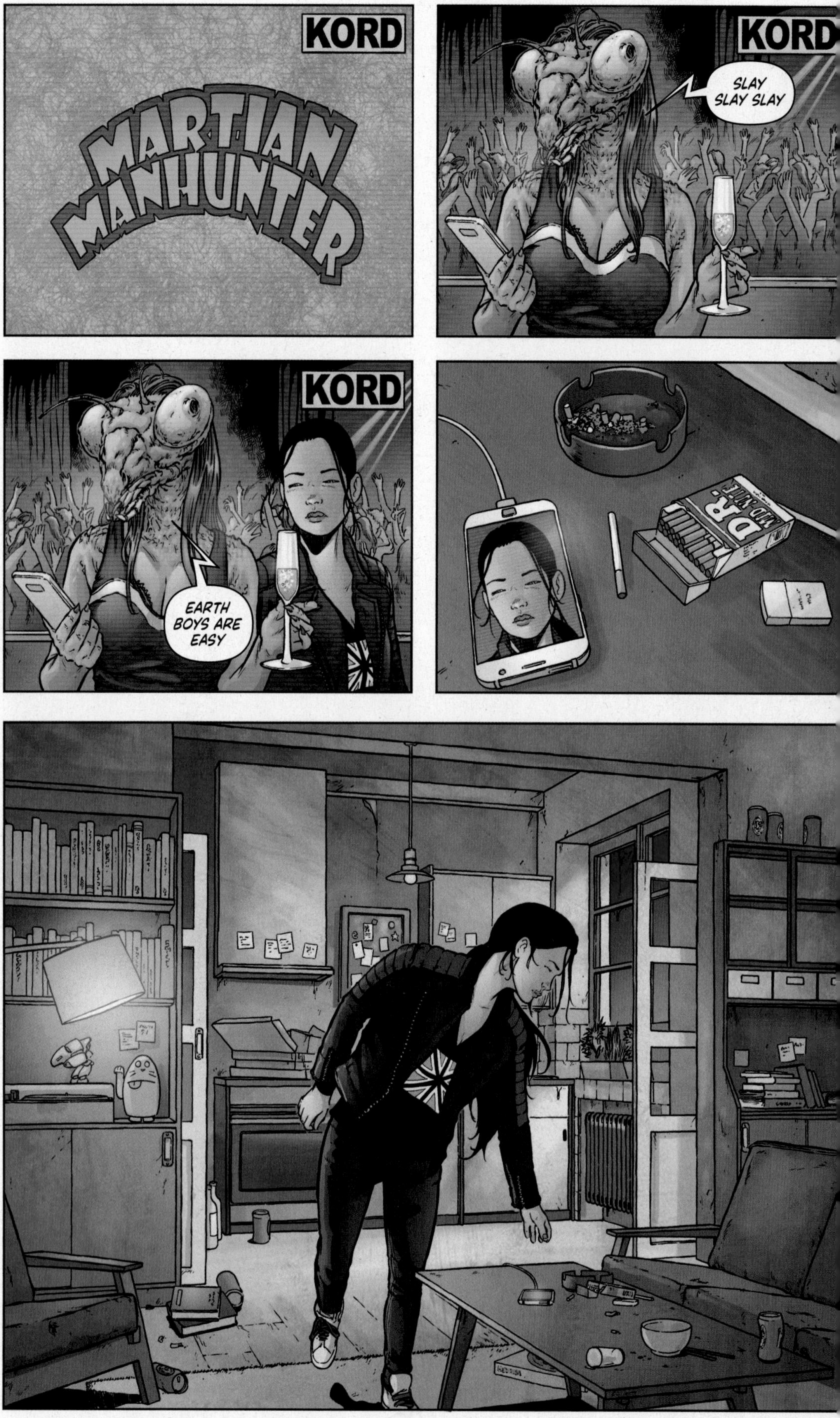
KORD
MARTIAN MANHUNTER
KORD
SLAY SLAY SLAY
KORD
EARTH BOYS ARE EASY

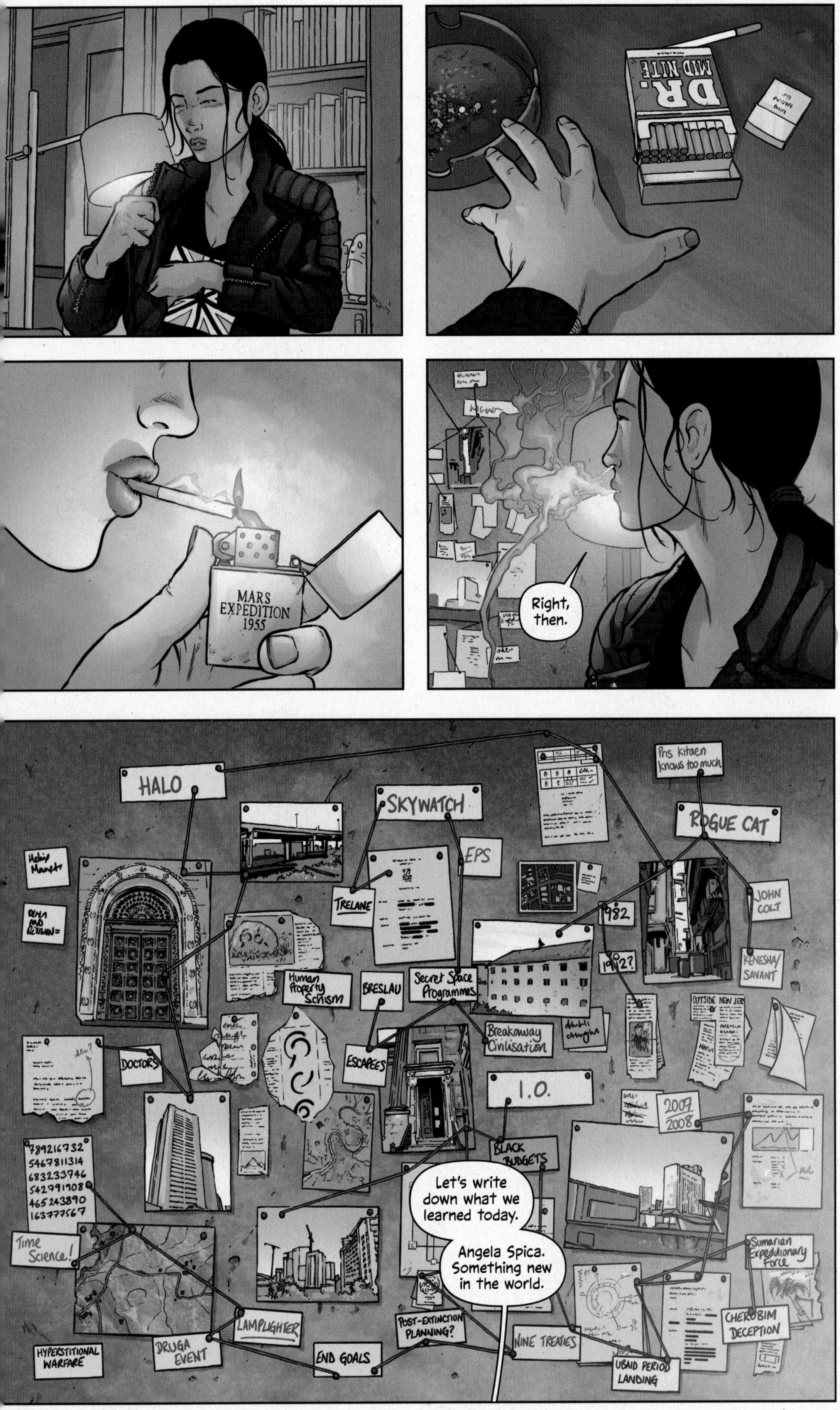
MARS
EXPEDITION
1955
Right, then.
HALO
SKYWATCH
ROGUE CAT
Pris Kitaen knows too much
EPS
TRELANE
JOHN COLT
KENESHA/SAVANT
Human Property Schism
BRESLAU
Secret Space Programmes
Breakaway Civilisation
DOCTORS
ESCAPEES
I.O.
2007
2008
BLACK BUDGETS
789216732
5467811314
683233746
542791908
465243890
163777567
Time Science!
Sumarian Expeditionary Force
CHERUBIM DECEPTION
LAMPLIGHTER
HYPERSTITIONAL WARFARE
DRUGA EVENT
END GOALS
POST-EXTINCTION PLANNING?
NINE TREATIES
UBAID PERIOD LANDING
Let's write down what we learned today.
Angela Spica. Something new in the world.

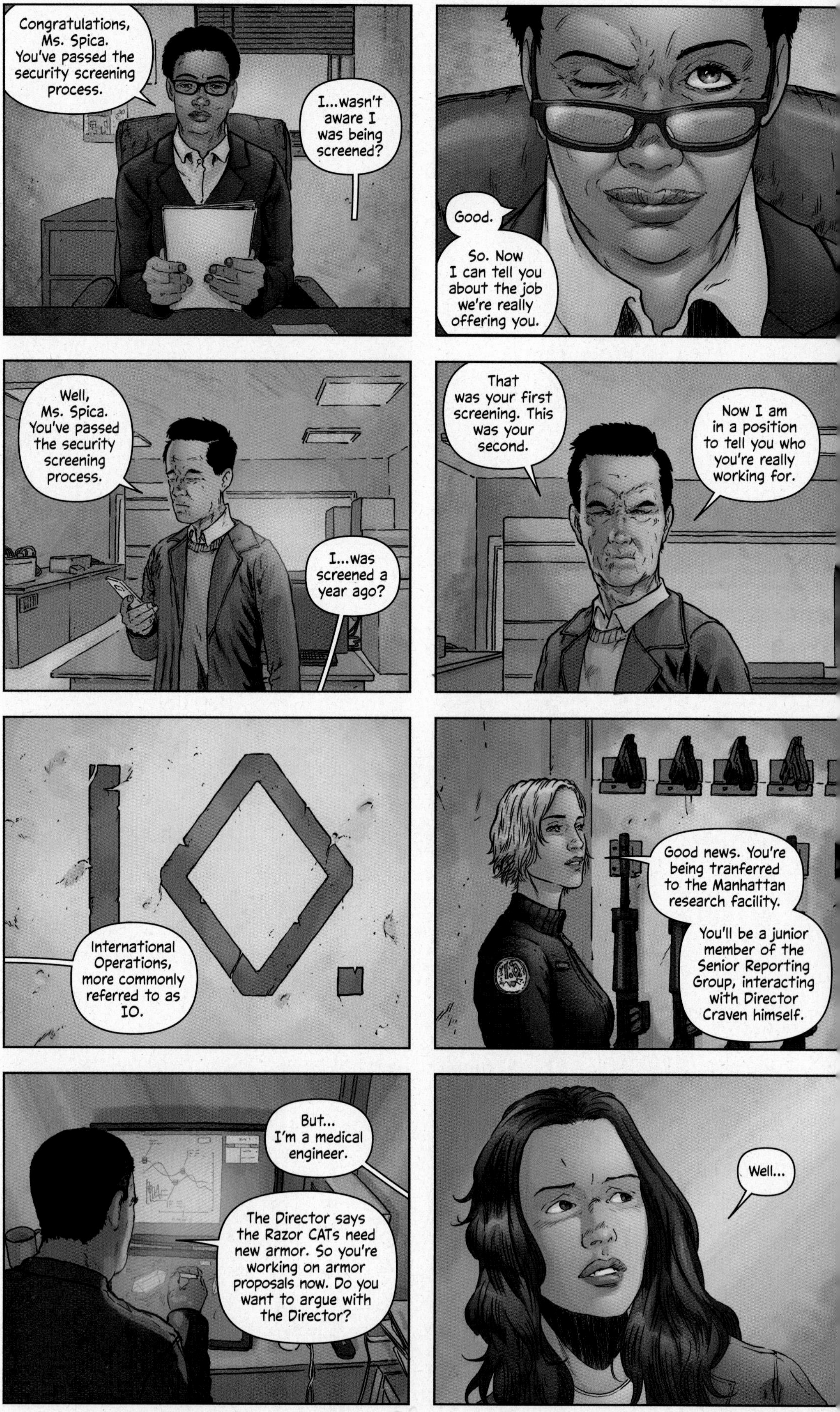

Congratulations, Ms. Spica. You've passed the security screening process.
I...wasn't aware I was being screened?
Good.
So. Now I can tell you about the job we're really offering you.
Well, Ms. Spica. You've passed the security screening process.
I...was screened a year ago?
That was your first screening. This was your second.
Now I am in a position to tell you who you're really working for.
International Operations, more commonly referred to as IO.
Good news. You're being tranferred to the Manhattan research facility.
You'll be a junior member of the Senior Reporting Group, interacting with Director Craven himself.
But... I'm a medical engineer.
The Director says the Razor CATs need new armor. So you're working on armor proposals now. Do you want to argue with the Director?
Well...

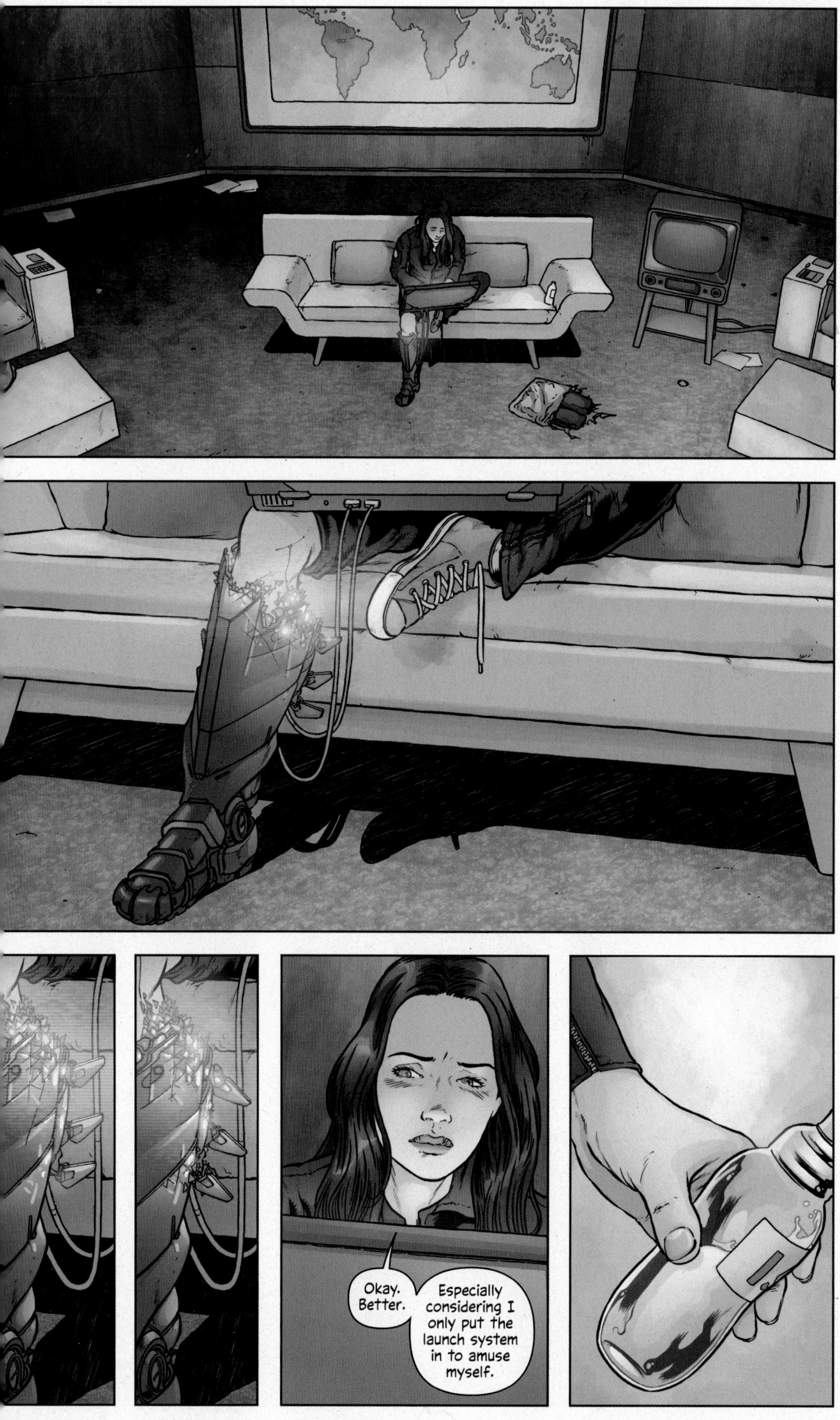
Okay. Better.
Especially considering I only put the launch system in to amuse myself.

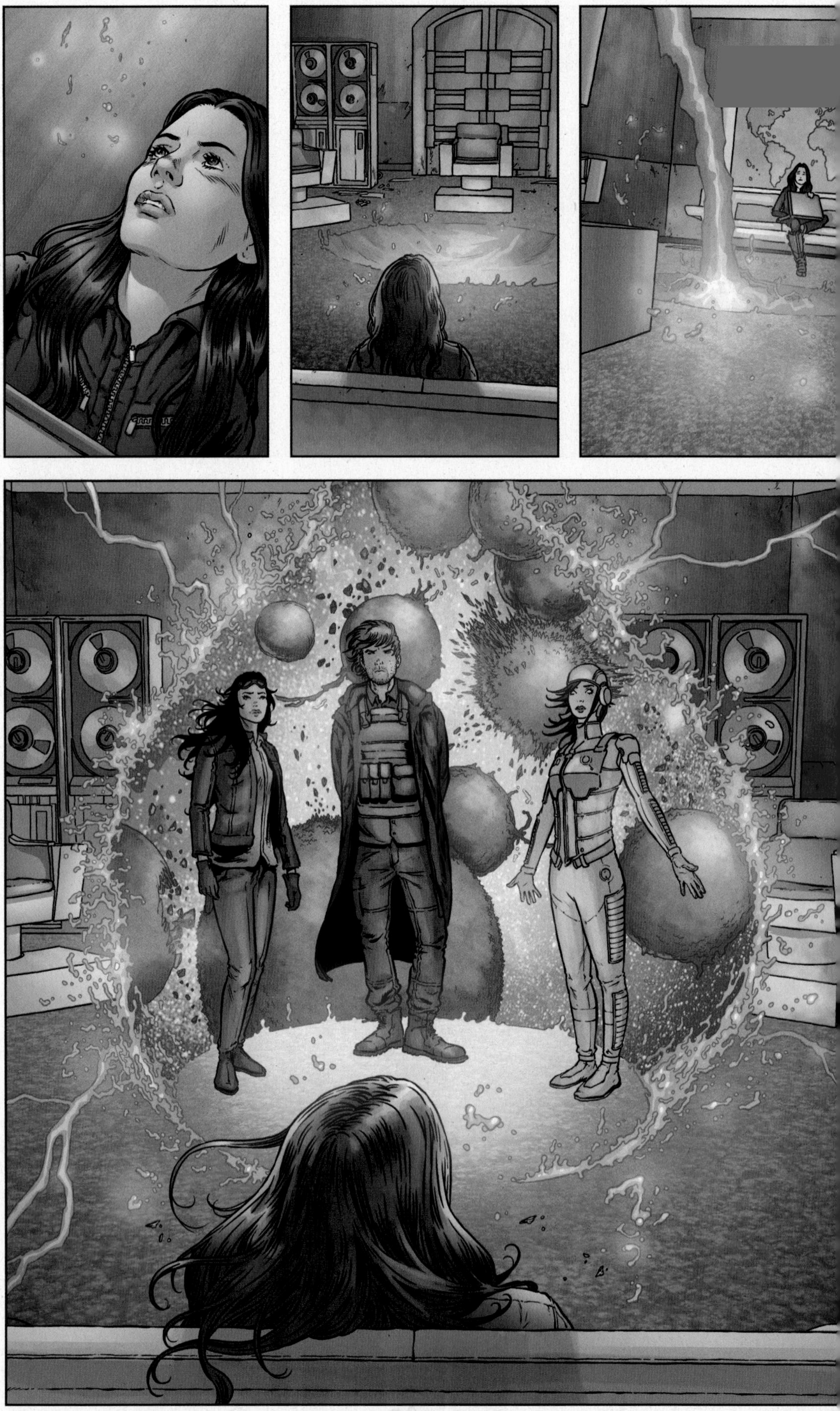

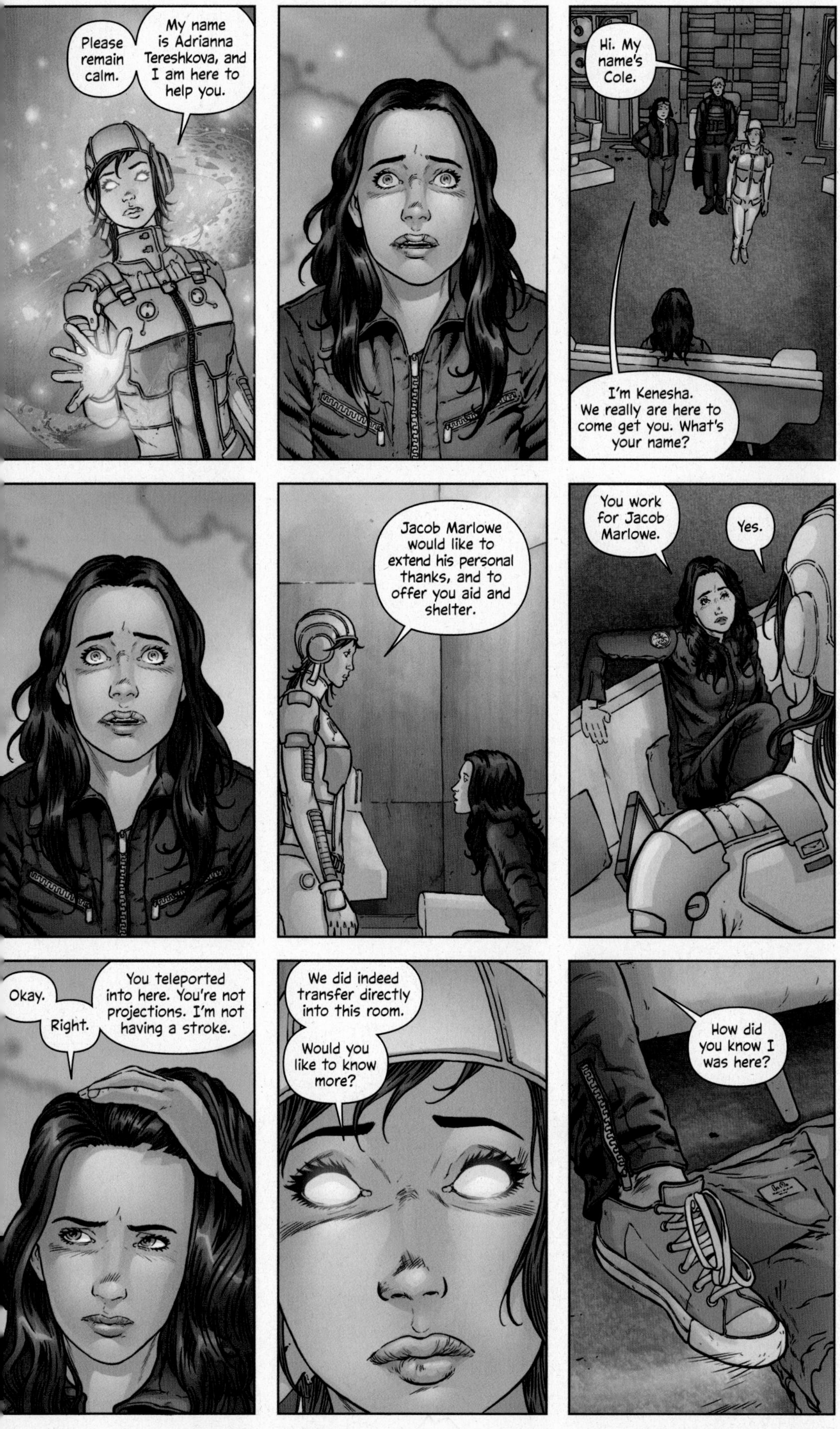

Please remain calm.
My name is Adrianna Tereshkova, and I am here to help you.
Hi. My name's Cole.
I'm Kenesha. We really are here to come get you. What's your name?
Jacob Marlowe would like to extend his personal thanks, and to offer you aid and shelter.
You work for Jacob Marlowe.
Yes.
Okay.
Right.
You teleported into here. You're not projections. I'm not having a stroke.
We did indeed transfer directly into this room.
Would you like to know more?
How did you know I was here?

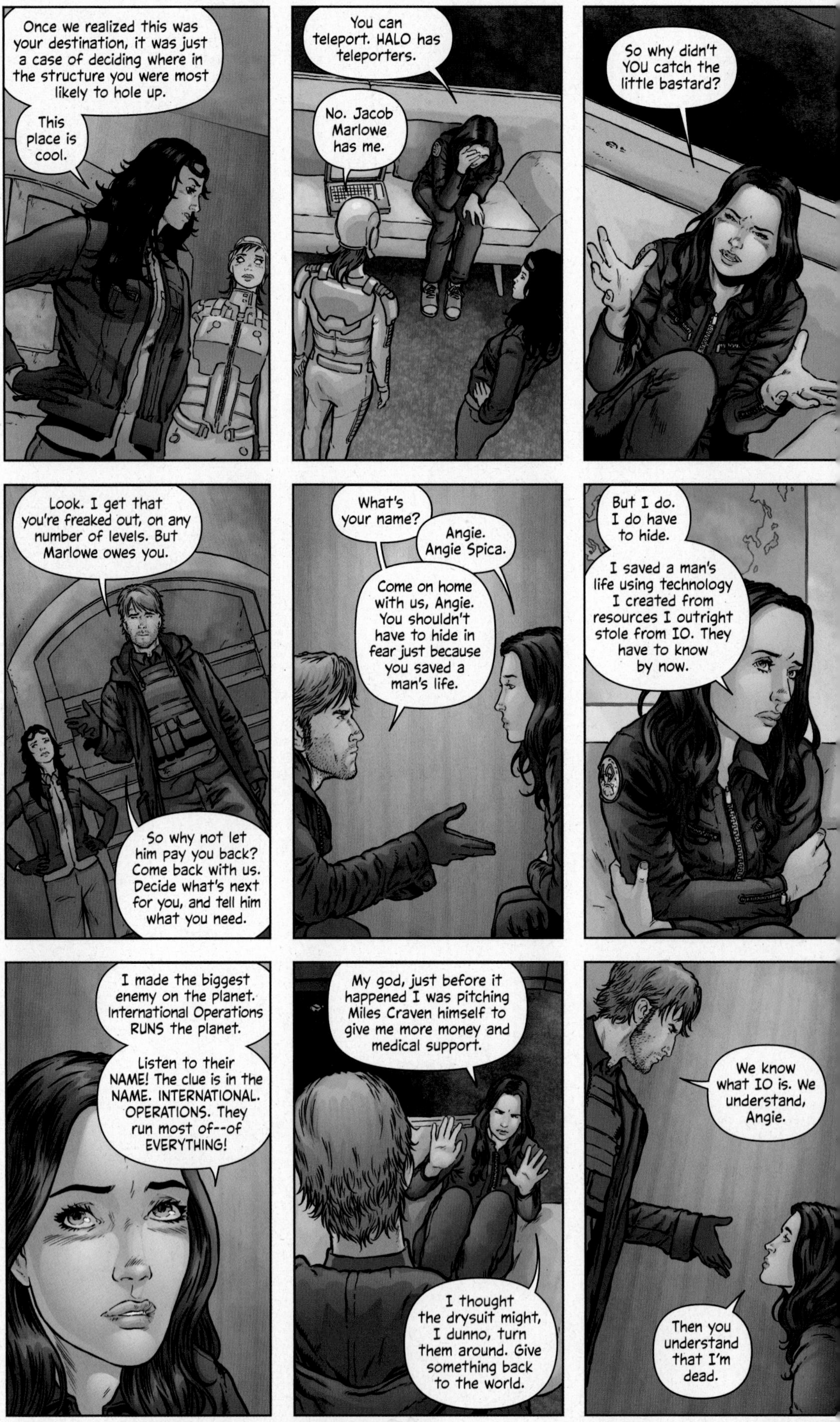
Once we realized this was your destination, it was just a case of deciding where in the structure you were most likely to hole up.
This place is cool.
You can teleport. HALO has teleporters.
No. Jacob Marlowe has me.
So why didn't YOU catch the little bastard?
Look. I get that you're freaked out, on any number of levels. But Marlowe owes you.
So why not let him pay you back? Come back with us. Decide what's next for you, and tell him what you need.
What's your name?
Angie. Angie Spica.
Come on home with us, Angie. You shouldn't have to hide in fear just because you saved a man's life.
But I do. I do have to hide.
I saved a man's life using technology I created from resources I outright stole from IO. They have to know by now.
I made the biggest enemy on the planet. International Operations RUNS the planet.
Listen to their NAME! The clue is in the NAME. INTERNATIONAL. OPERATIONS. They run most of--of EVERYTHING!
My god, just before it happened I was pitching Miles Craven himself to give me more money and medical support.
I thought the drysuit might, I dunno, turn them around. Give something back to the world.
We know what IO is. We understand, Angie.
Then you understand that I'm dead.

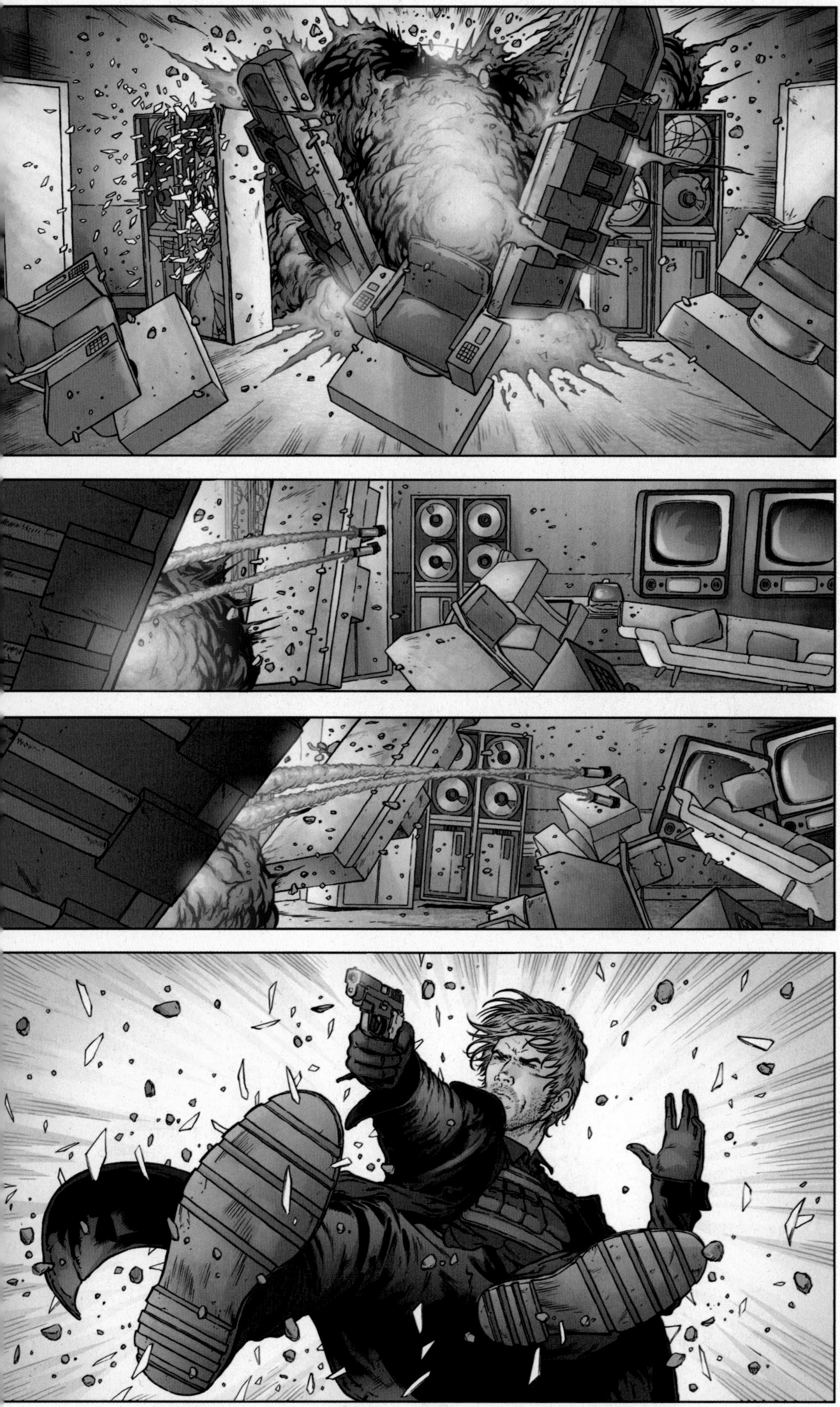

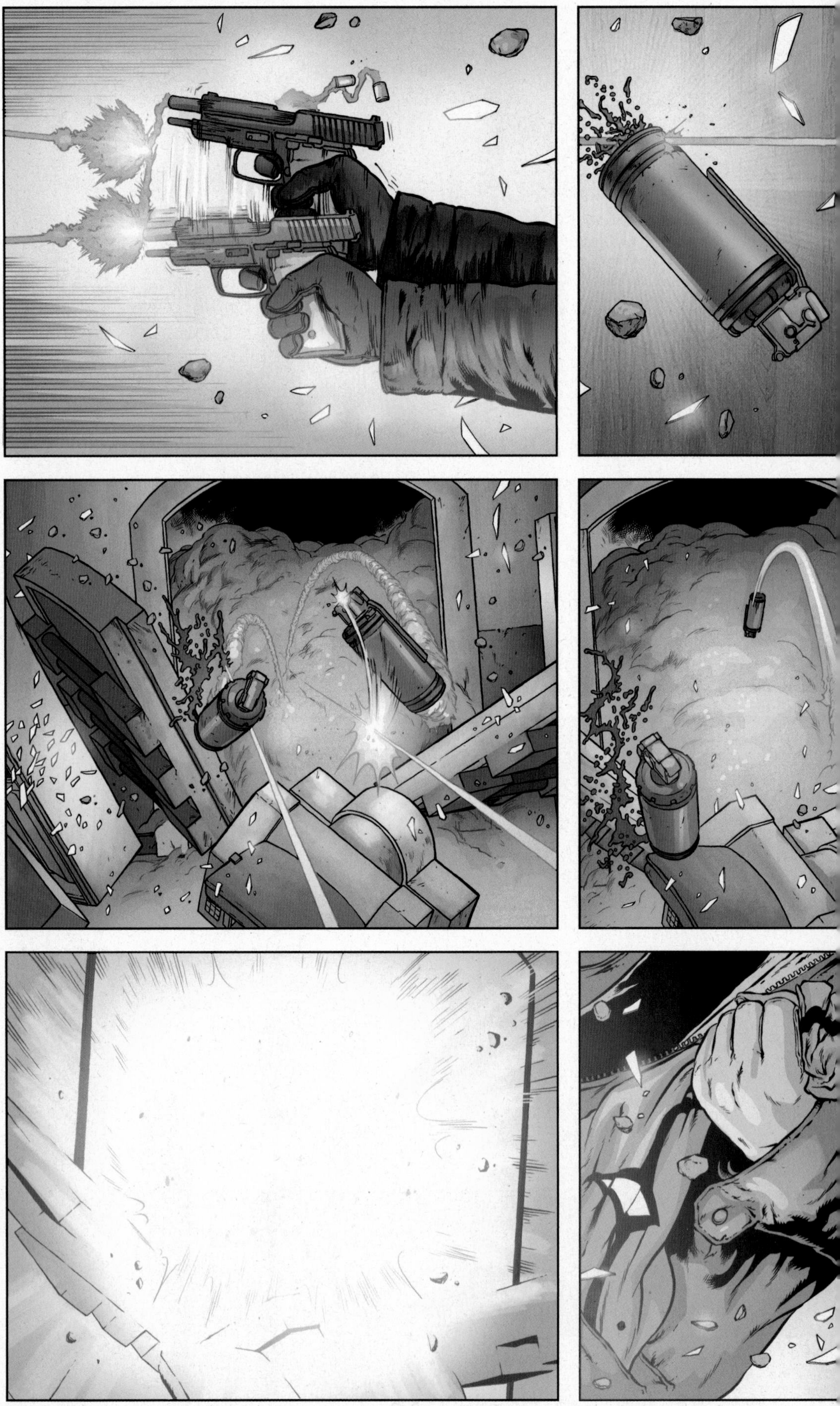

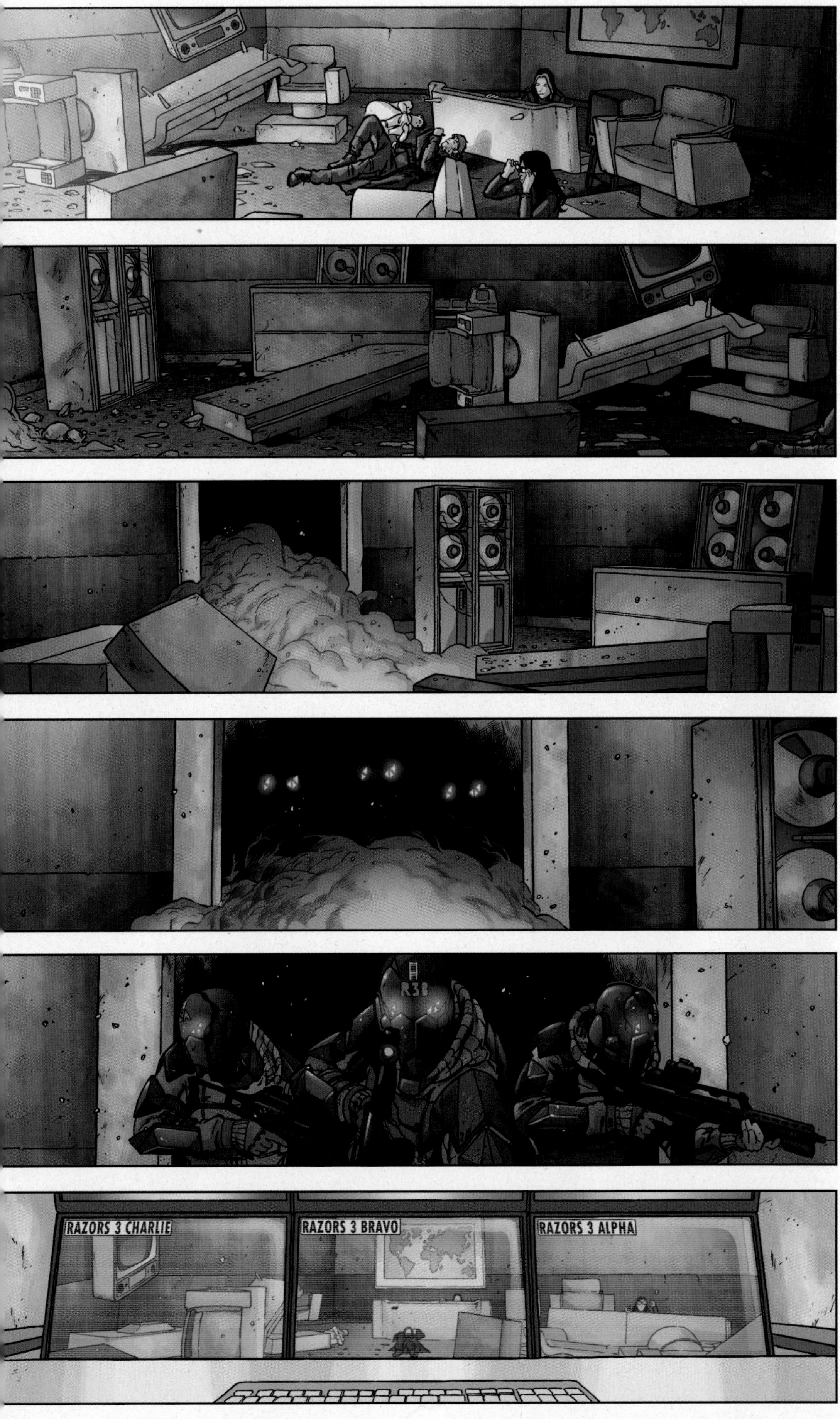
R3B
RAZORS 3 CHARLIE
RAZORS 3 BRAVO
RAZORS 3 ALPHA

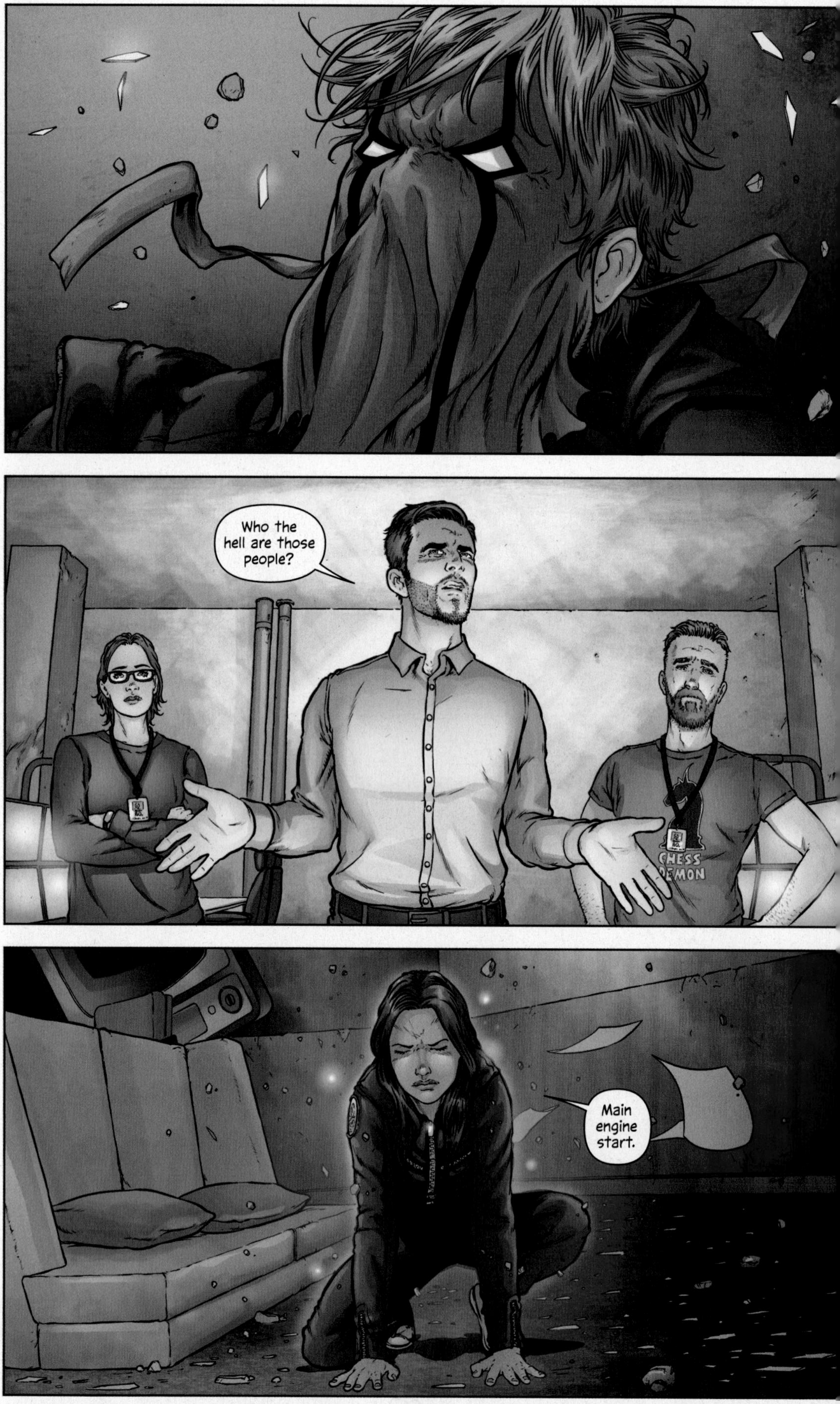
Who the hell are those people?
CHESS DEMON
Main engine start.

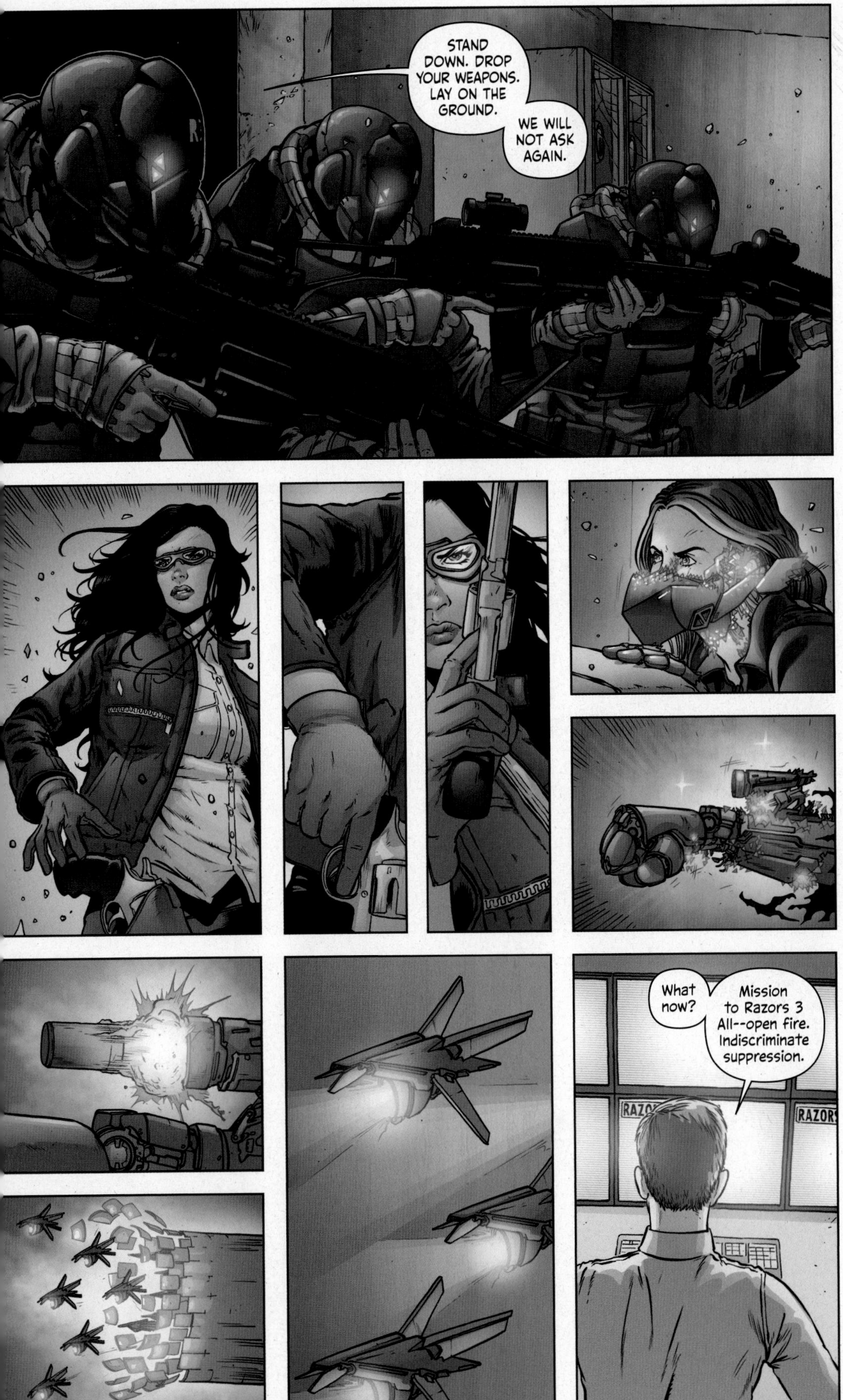

STAND DOWN. DROP YOUR WEAPONS. LAY ON THE GROUND.
WE WILL NOT ASK AGAIN.
What now?
Mission to Razors 3 All--open fire. Indiscriminate suppression.
RAZORS

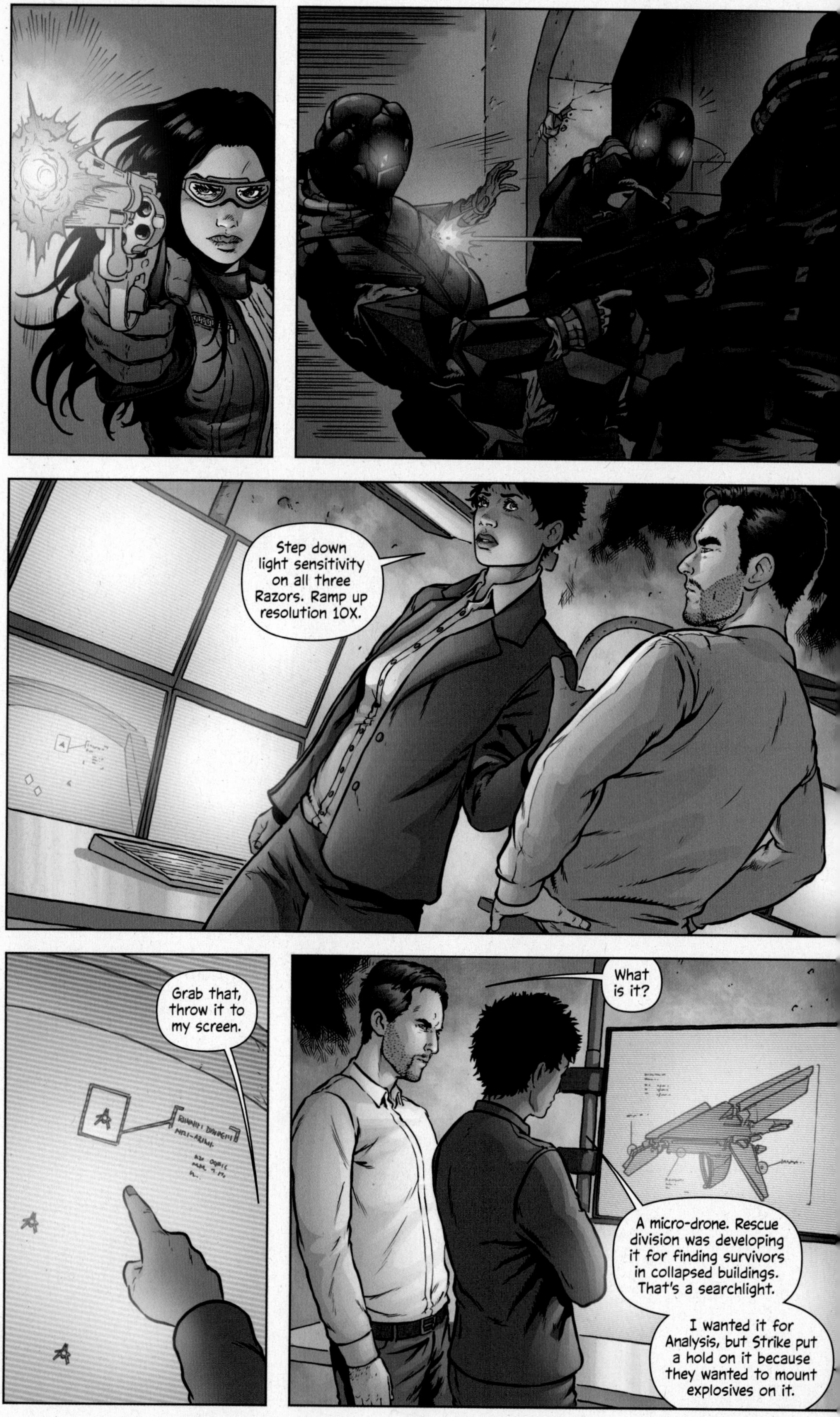
Step down light sensitivity on all three Razors. Ramp up resolution 10X.
Grab that, throw it to my screen.
What is it?
A micro-drone. Rescue division was developing it for finding survivors in collapsed buildings. That's a searchlight.
I wanted it for Analysis, but Strike put a hold on it because they wanted to mount explosives on it.

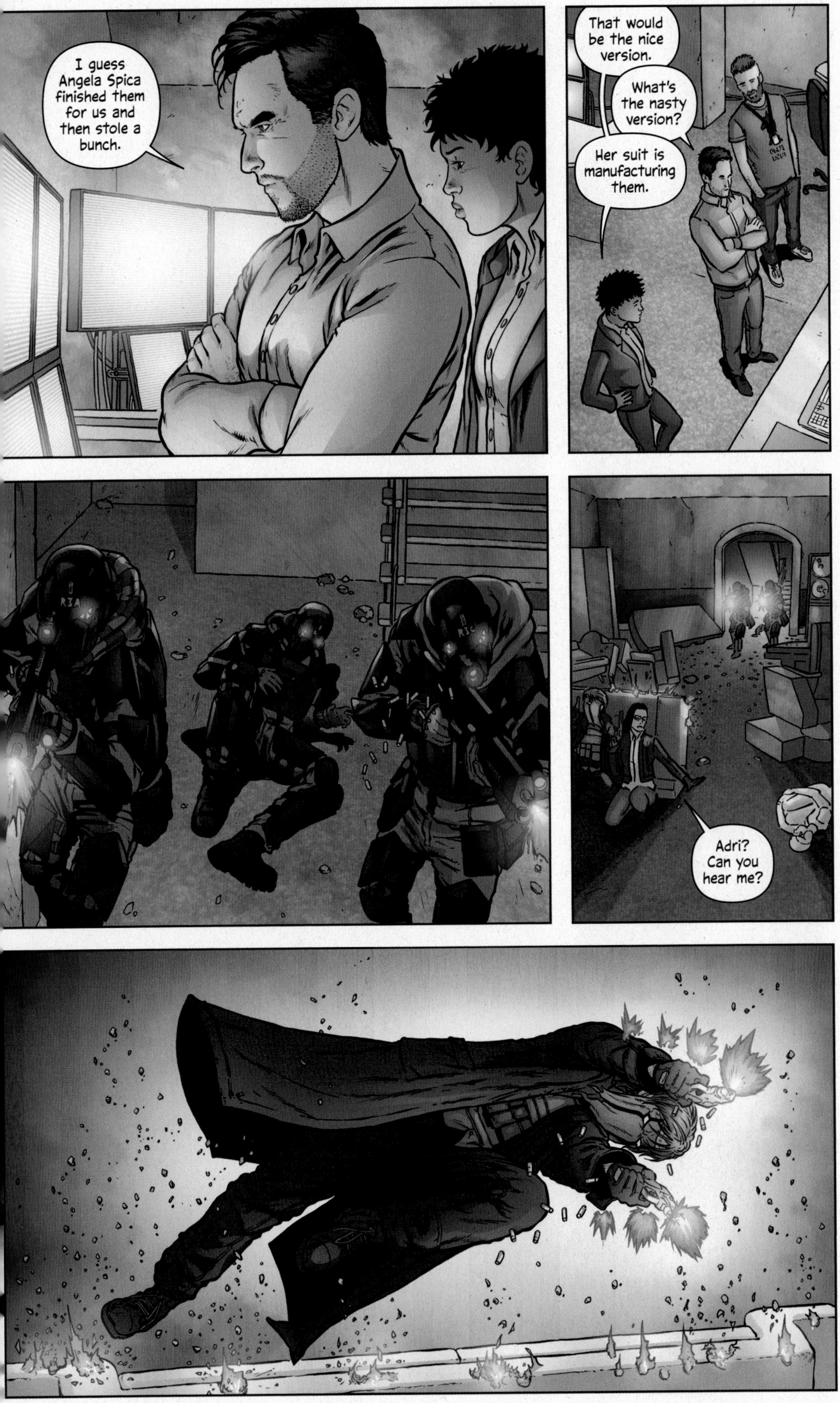
I guess Angela Spica finished them for us and then stole a bunch.
That would be the nice version.
What's the nasty version?
Her suit is manufacturing them.
Adri? Can you hear me?

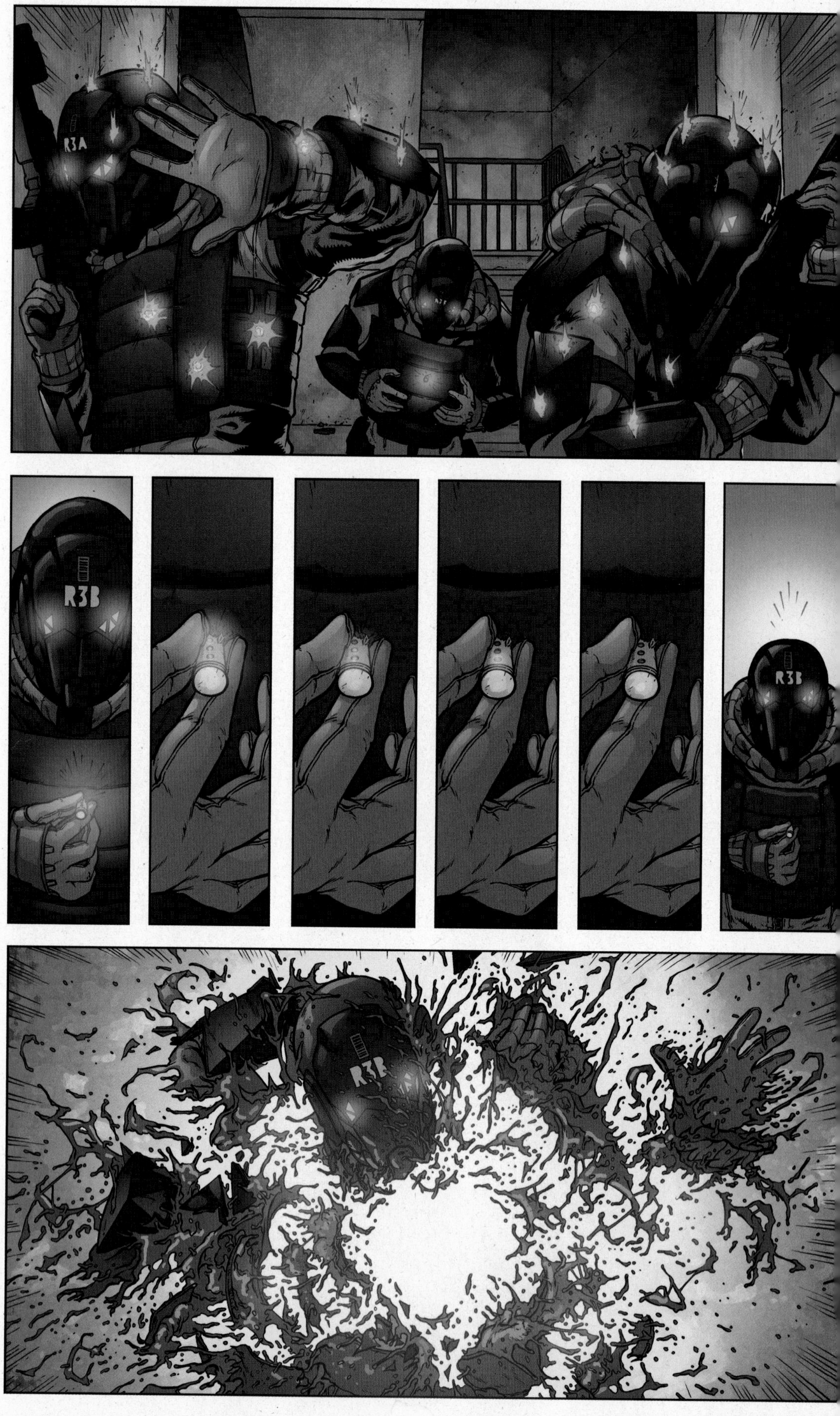
R3A
R3B
R3B
R3B

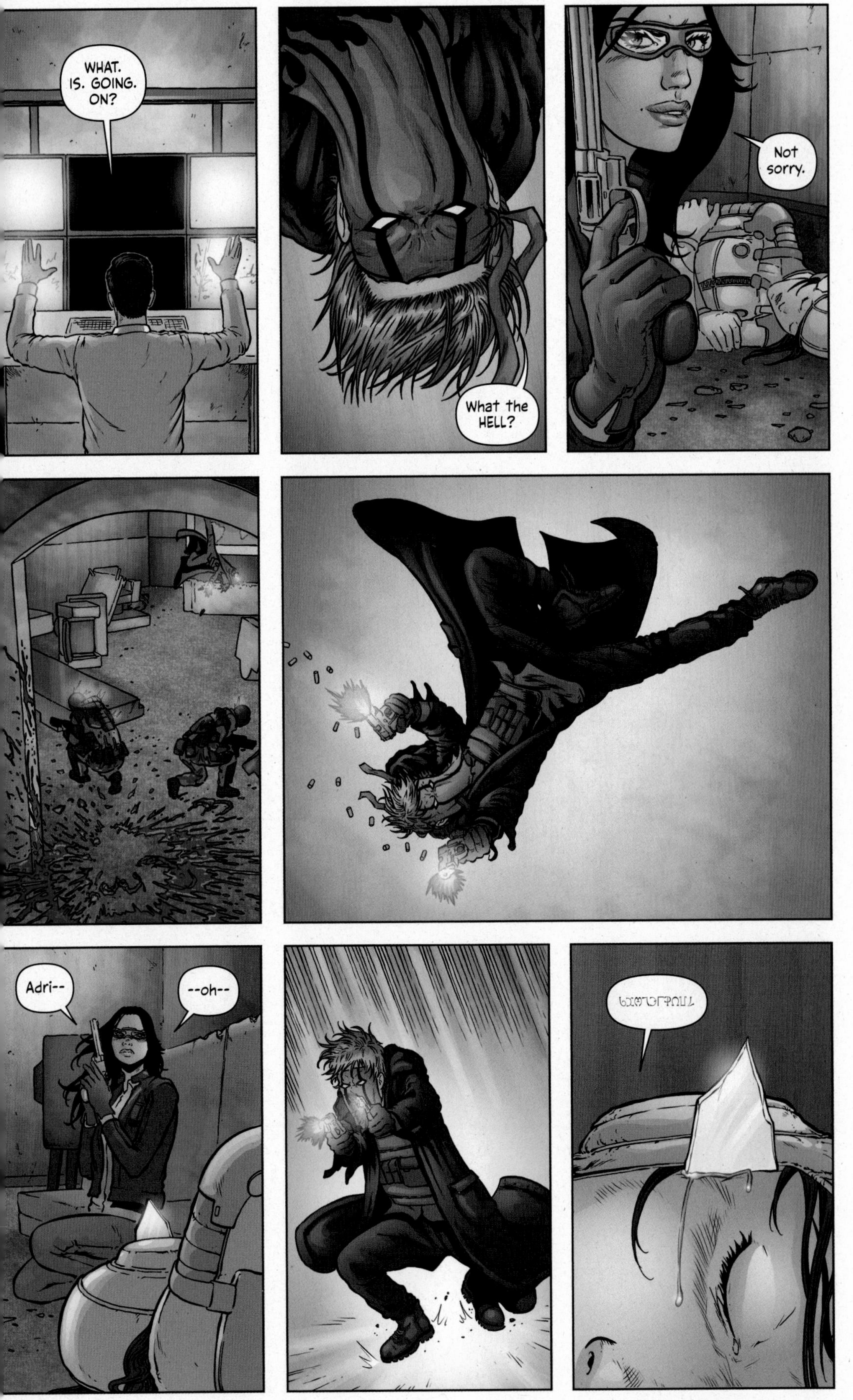
WHAT. IS. GOING. ON?
What the HELL?
Not sorry.
Adri--
--oh--

Mission to Razors 3 Alpha-- fire countermeasures and withdraw to deploy explosives. I want that room demolished.

Analysis.

You don't need it. You know what you're looking at.

We've theorized their existence for years.

Look at them. No mission patches, no I.D. Look at their tactics.

You're looking at an unaffiliated covert action team, Miles. Just as we always feared.

A wild CAT.

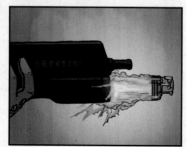

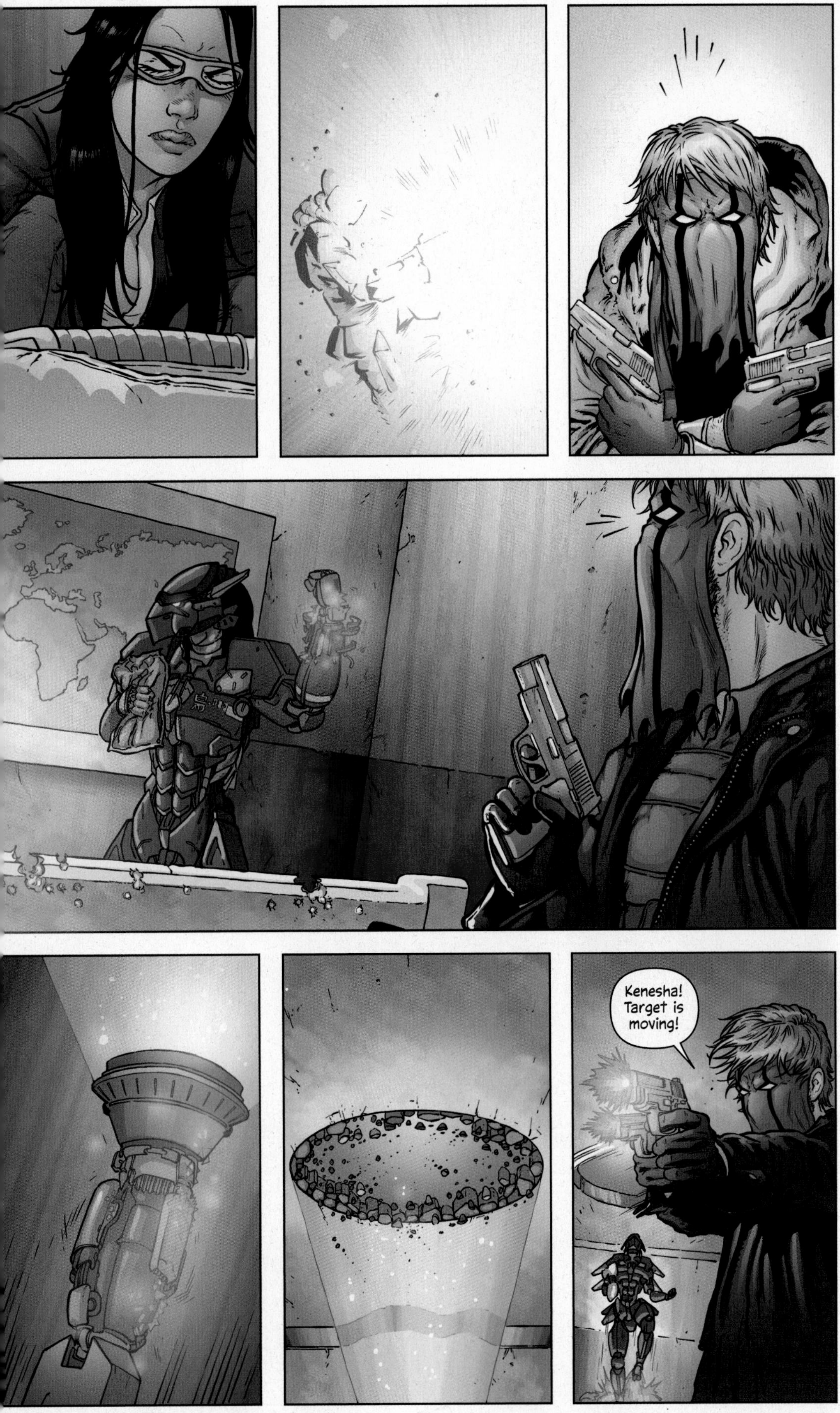
Kenesha! Target is moving!

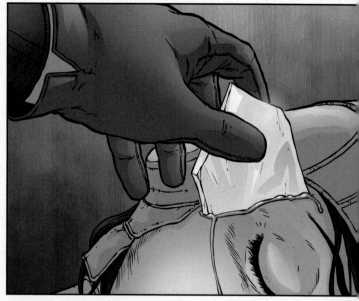

Oh god. We're going to lose Razors 3.

Who are these people and why and how are they murdering my people?

Razors 3 All: immediate demolition. No survivors.

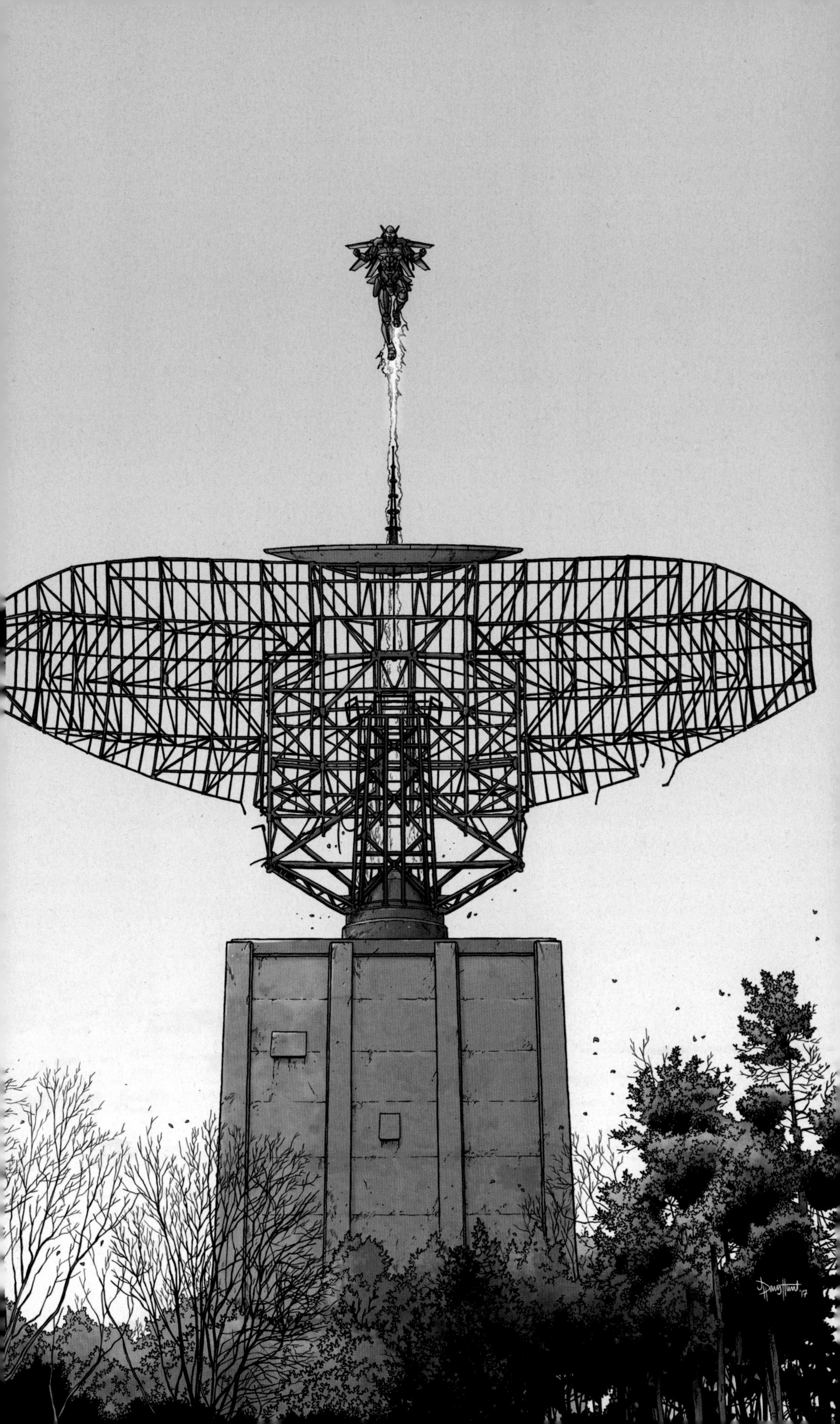

4

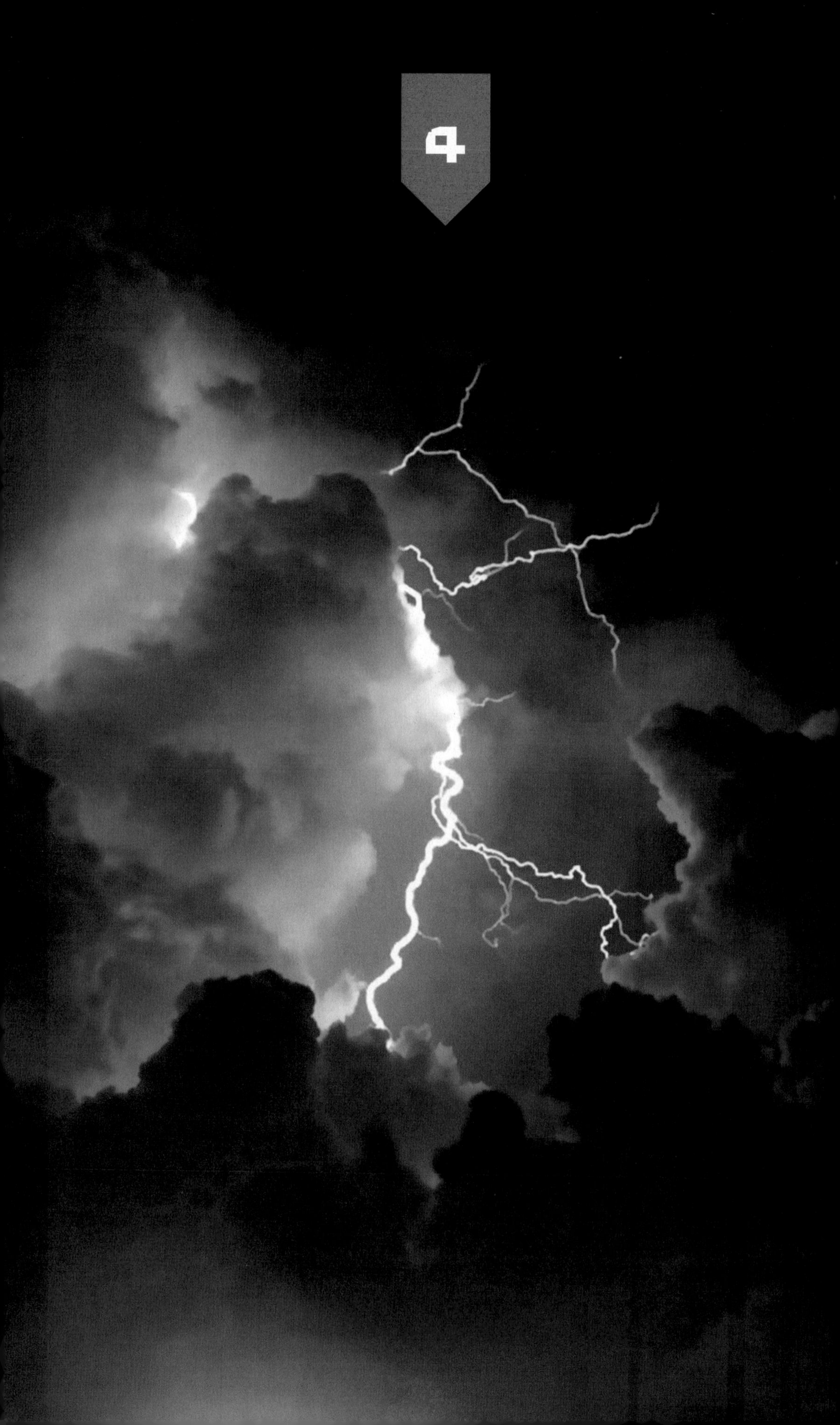

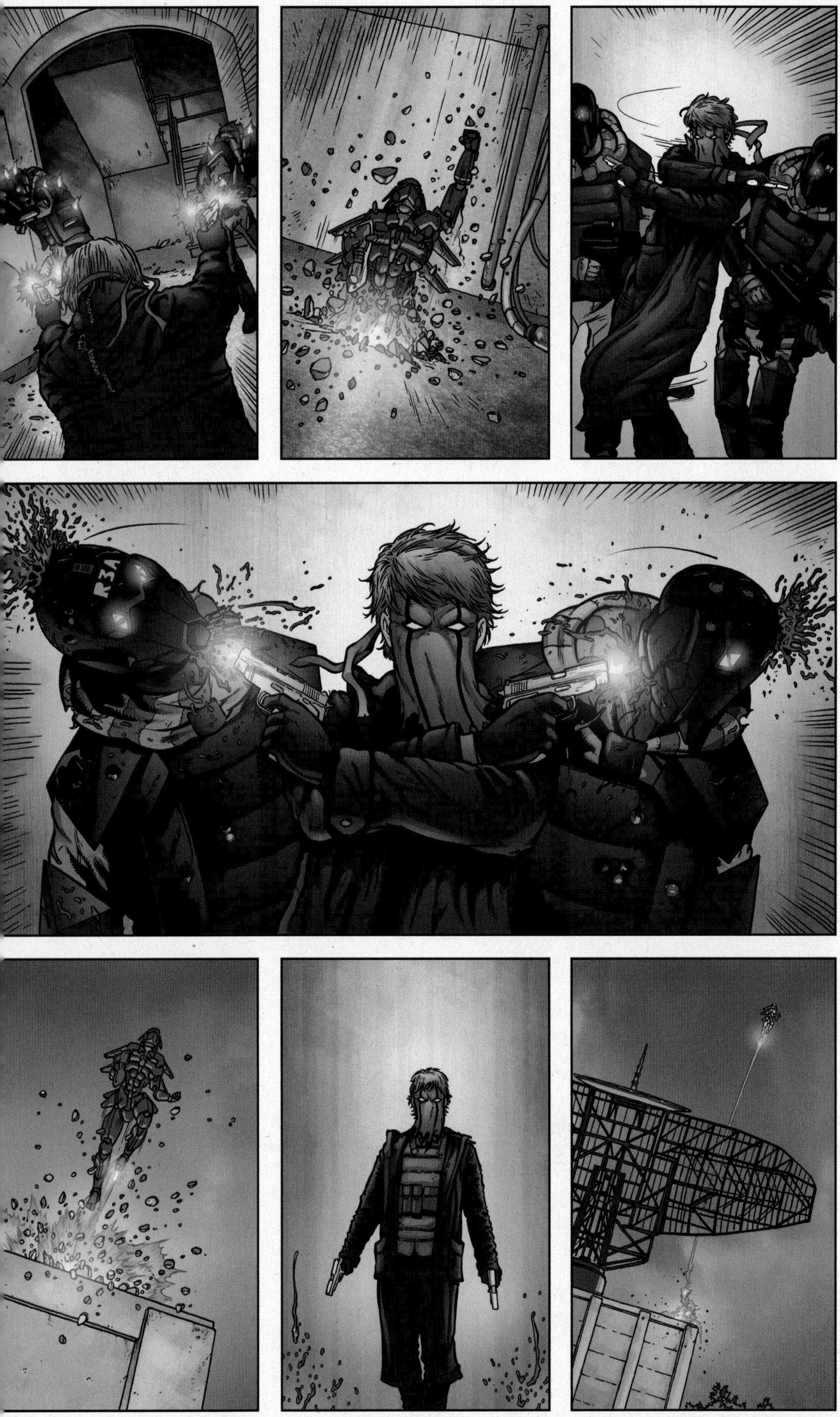
R3A

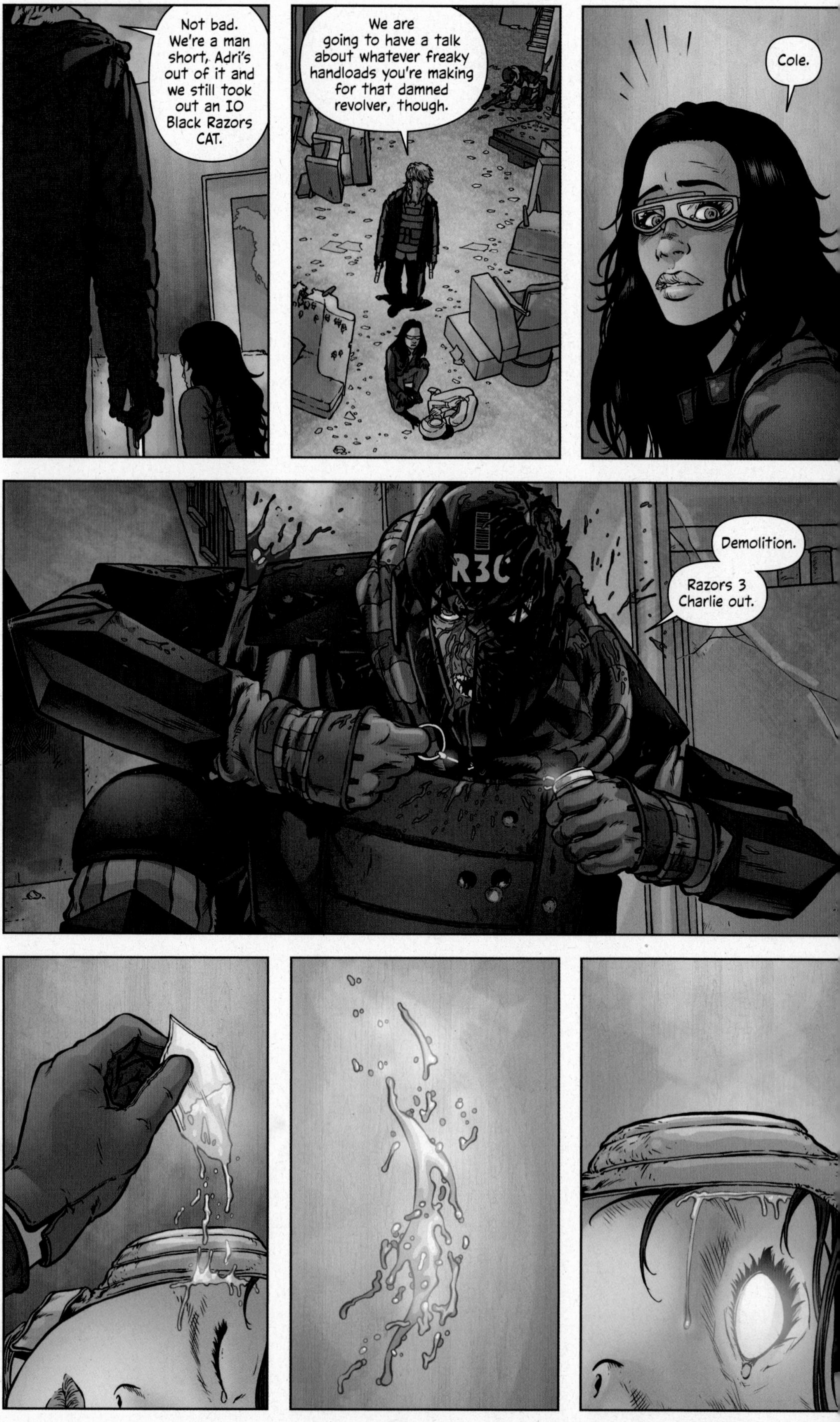
Not bad. We're a man short, Adri's out of it and we still took out an IO Black Razors CAT.
We are going to have a talk about whatever freaky handloads you're making for that damned revolver, though.
Cole.
Demolition.
Razors 3 Charlie out.
R3C

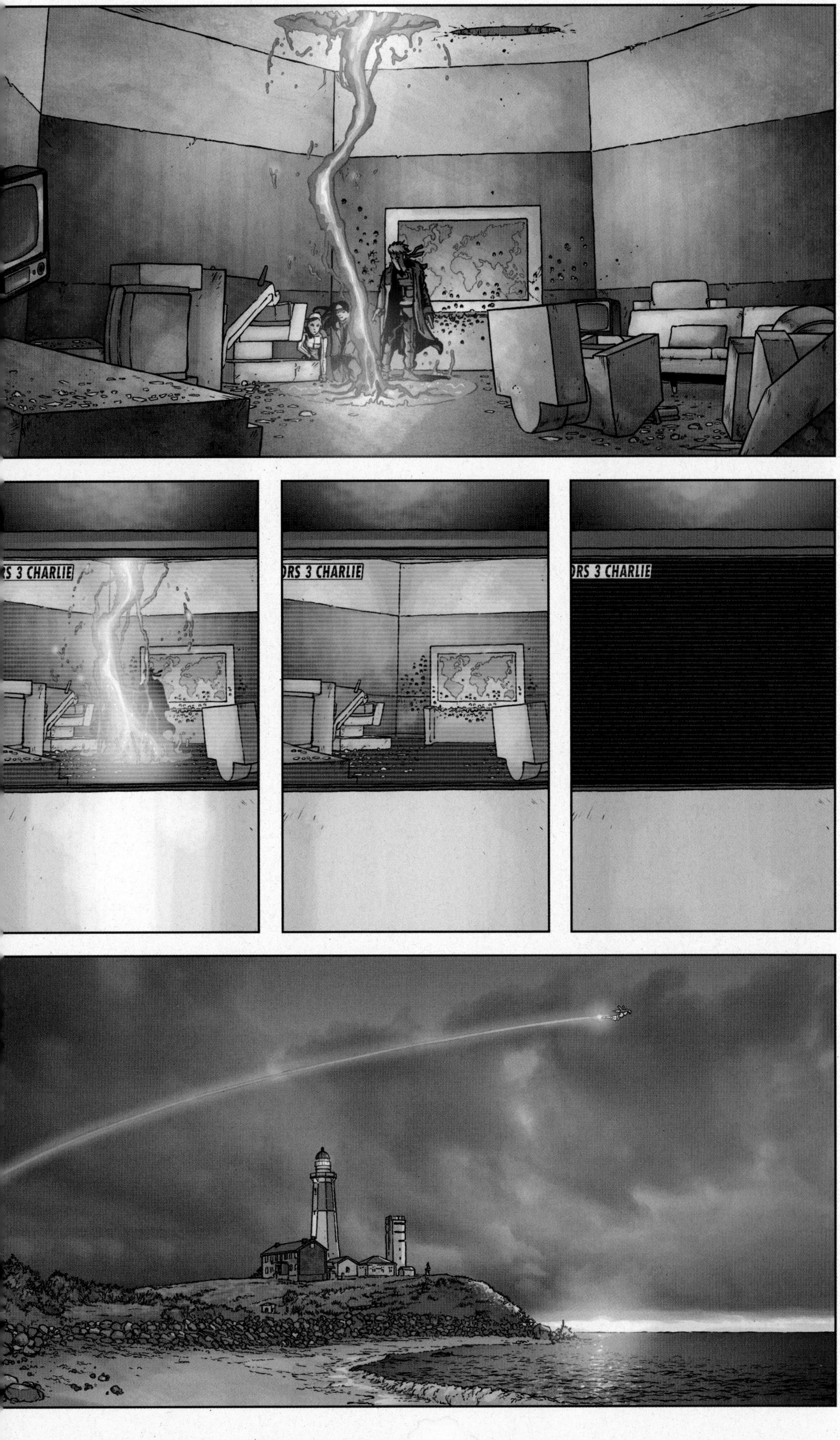
RS 3 CHARLIE
DRS 3 CHARLIE
DRS 3 CHARLIE

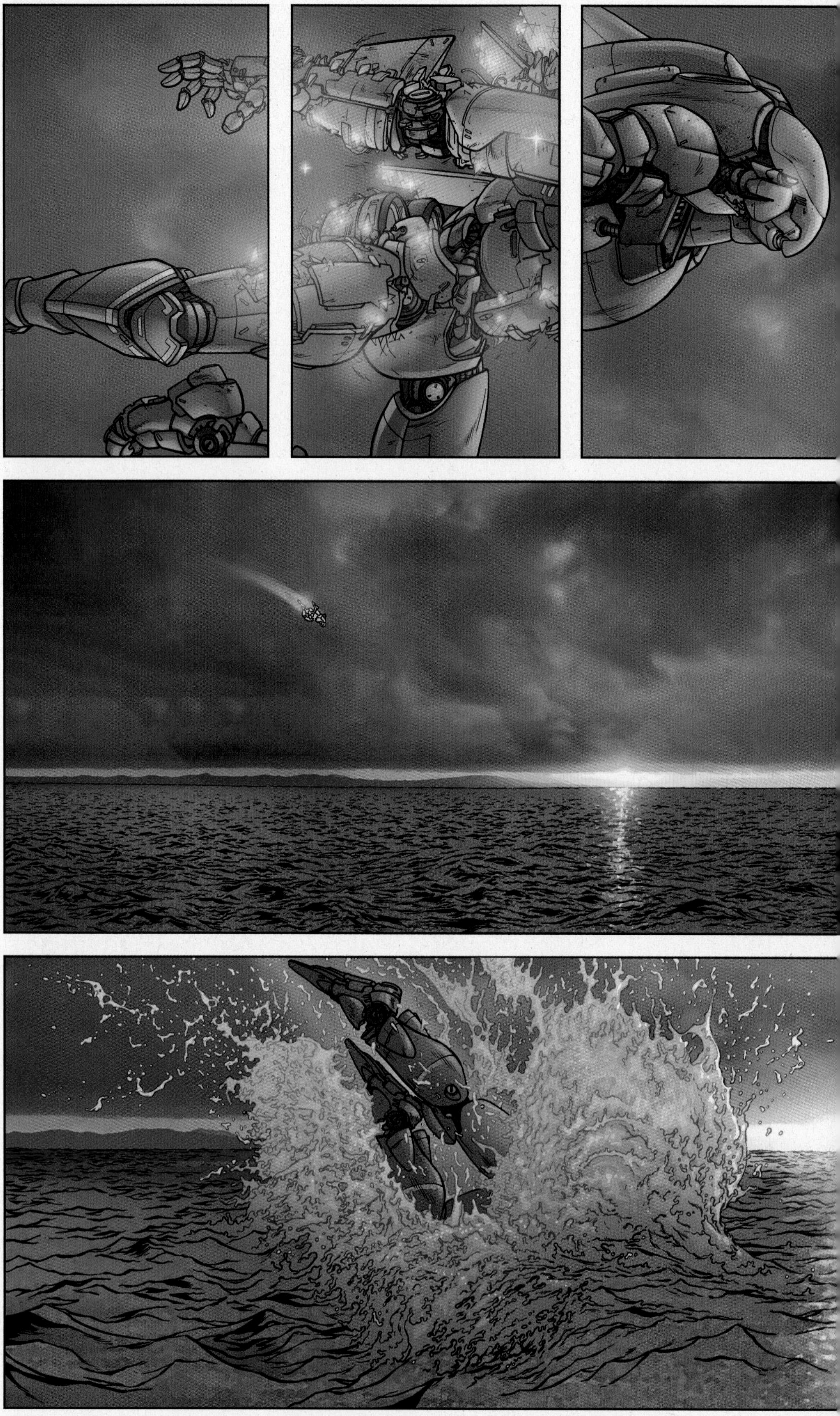

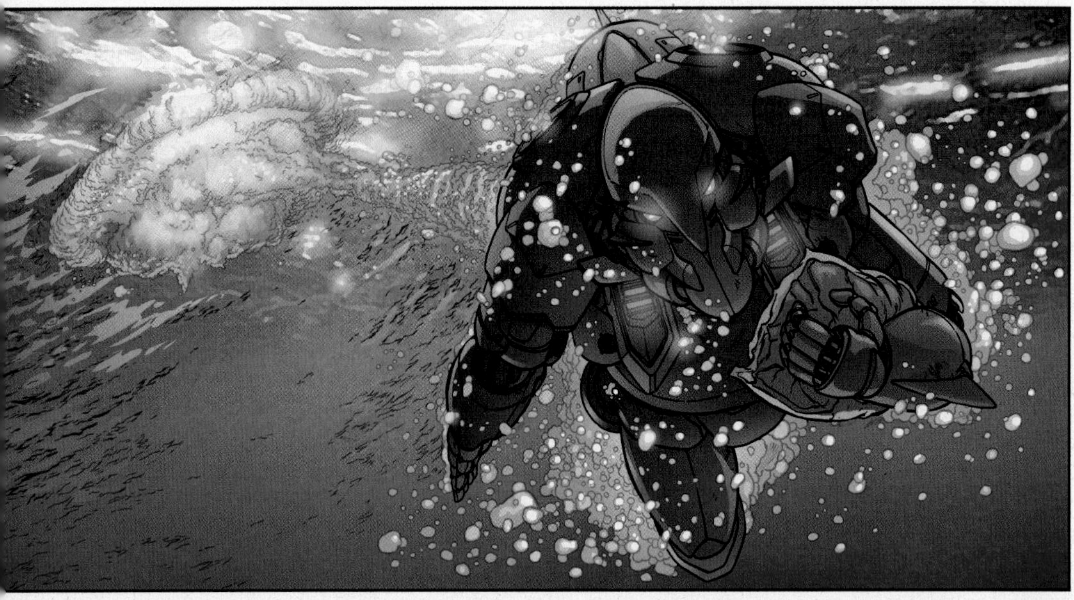

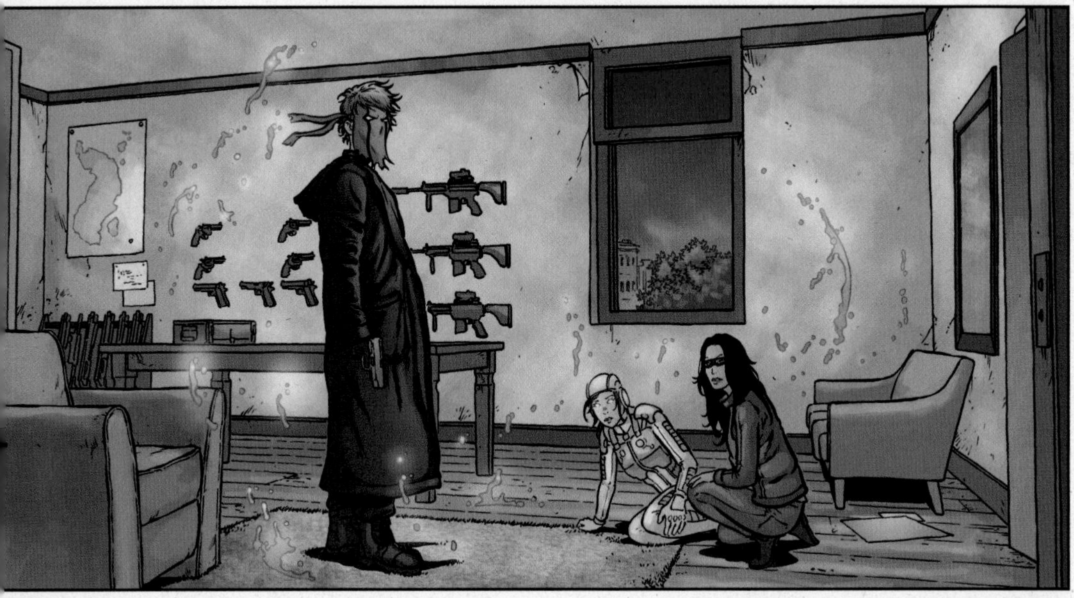

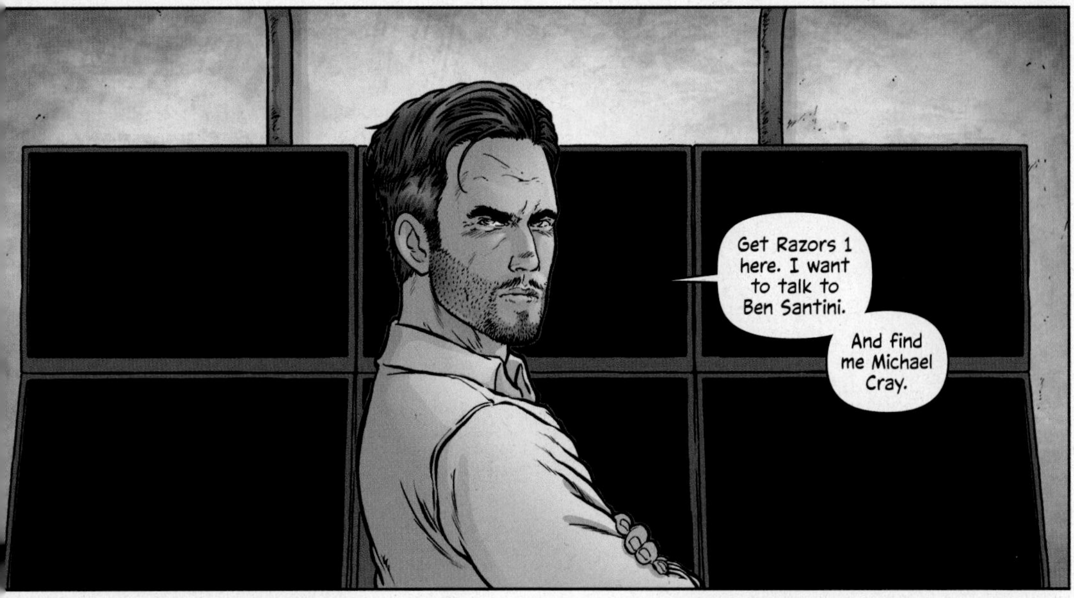
Get Razors 1 here. I want to talk to Ben Santini.
And find me Michael Cray.

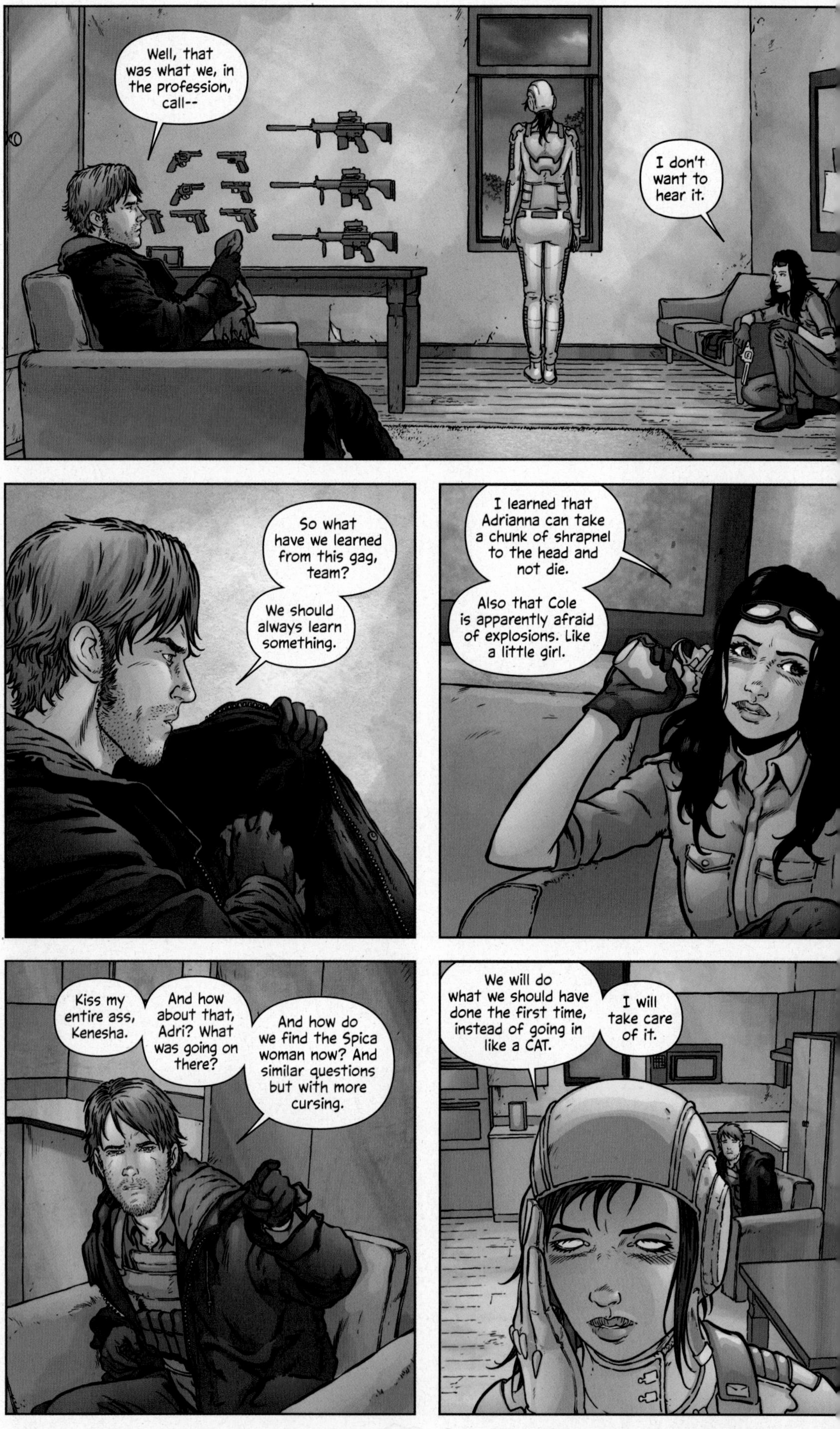
Well, that was what we, in the profession, call--
I don't want to hear it.
So what have we learned from this gag, team?
We should always learn something.
I learned that Adrianna can take a chunk of shrapnel to the head and not die.
Also that Cole is apparently afraid of explosions. Like a little girl.
Kiss my entire ass, Kenesha.
And how about that, Adri? What was going on there?
And how do we find the Spica woman now? And similar questions but with more cursing.
We will do what we should have done the first time, instead of going in like a CAT.
I will take care of it.

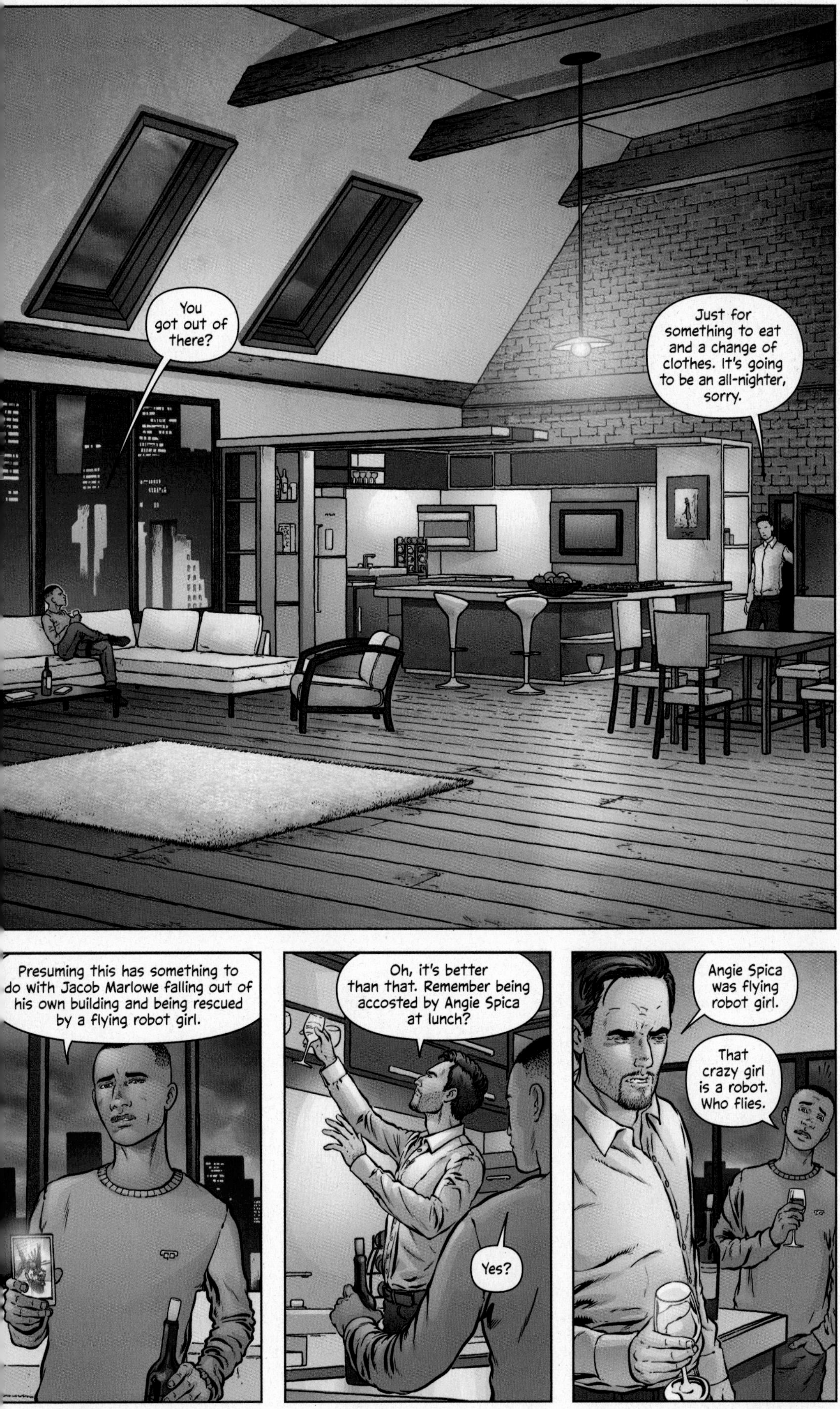

You got out of there?
Just for something to eat and a change of clothes. It's going to be an all-nighter, sorry.
Presuming this has something to do with Jacob Marlowe falling out of his own building and being rescued by a flying robot girl.
Oh, it's better than that. Remember being accosted by Angie Spica at lunch?
Yes?
Angie Spica was flying robot girl.
That crazy girl is a robot. Who flies.

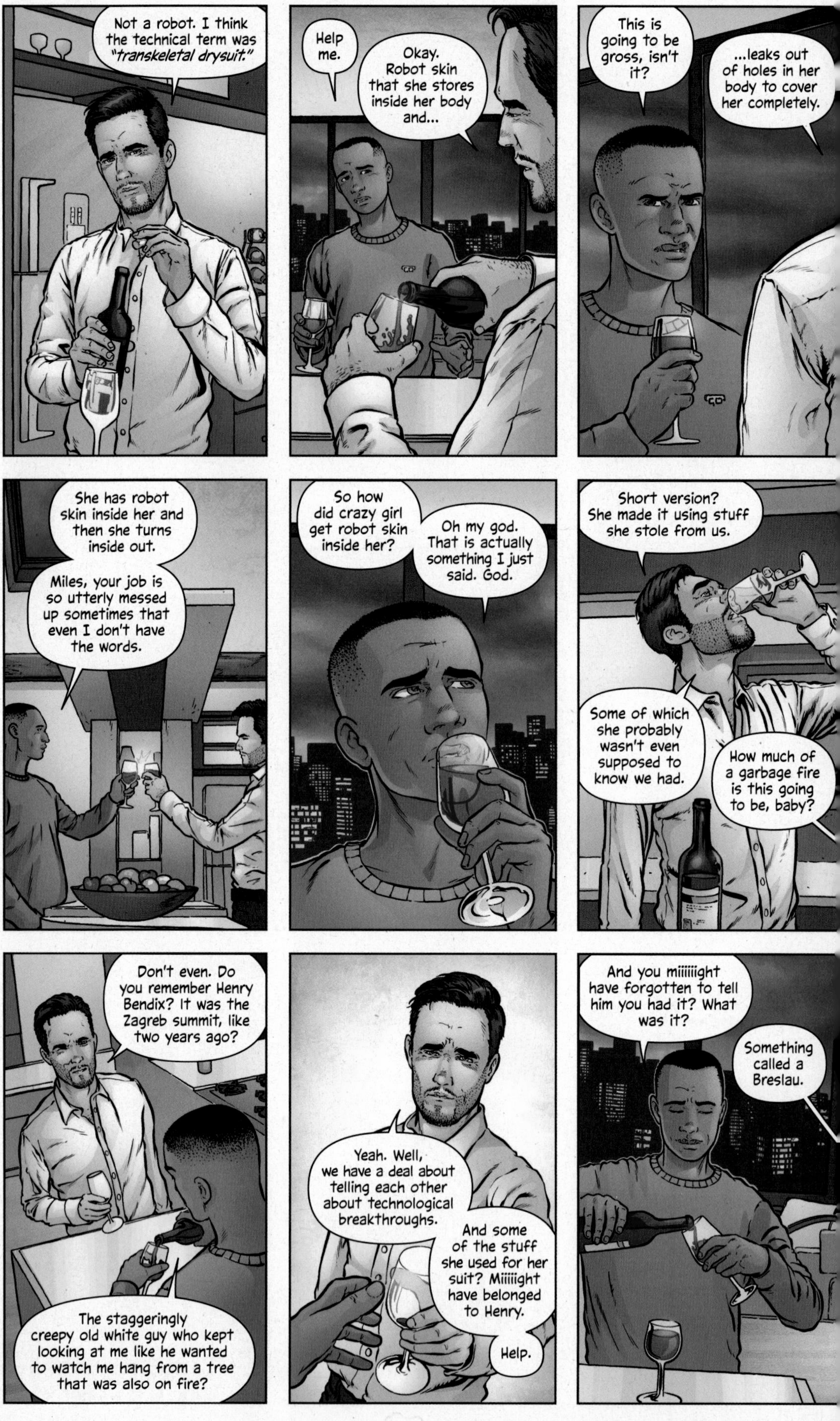
Not a robot. I think the technical term was *"transkeletal drysuit."*
Help me.
Okay. Robot skin that she stores inside her body and...
This is going to be gross, isn't it?
...leaks out of holes in her body to cover her completely.
She has robot skin inside her and then she turns inside out.
Miles, your job is so utterly messed up sometimes that even I don't have the words.
So how did crazy girl get robot skin inside her?
Oh my god. That is actually something I just said. God.
Short version? She made it using stuff she stole from us.
Some of which she probably wasn't even supposed to know we had.
How much of a garbage fire is this going to be, baby?
Don't even. Do you remember Henry Bendix? It was the Zagreb summit, like two years ago?
The staggeringly creepy old white guy who kept looking at me like he wanted to watch me hang from a tree that was also on fire?
Yeah. Well, we have a deal about telling each other about technological breakthroughs.
And some of the stuff she used for her suit? Miiiiight have belonged to Henry.
Help.
And you miiiiight have forgotten to tell him you had it? What was it?
Something called a Breslau.

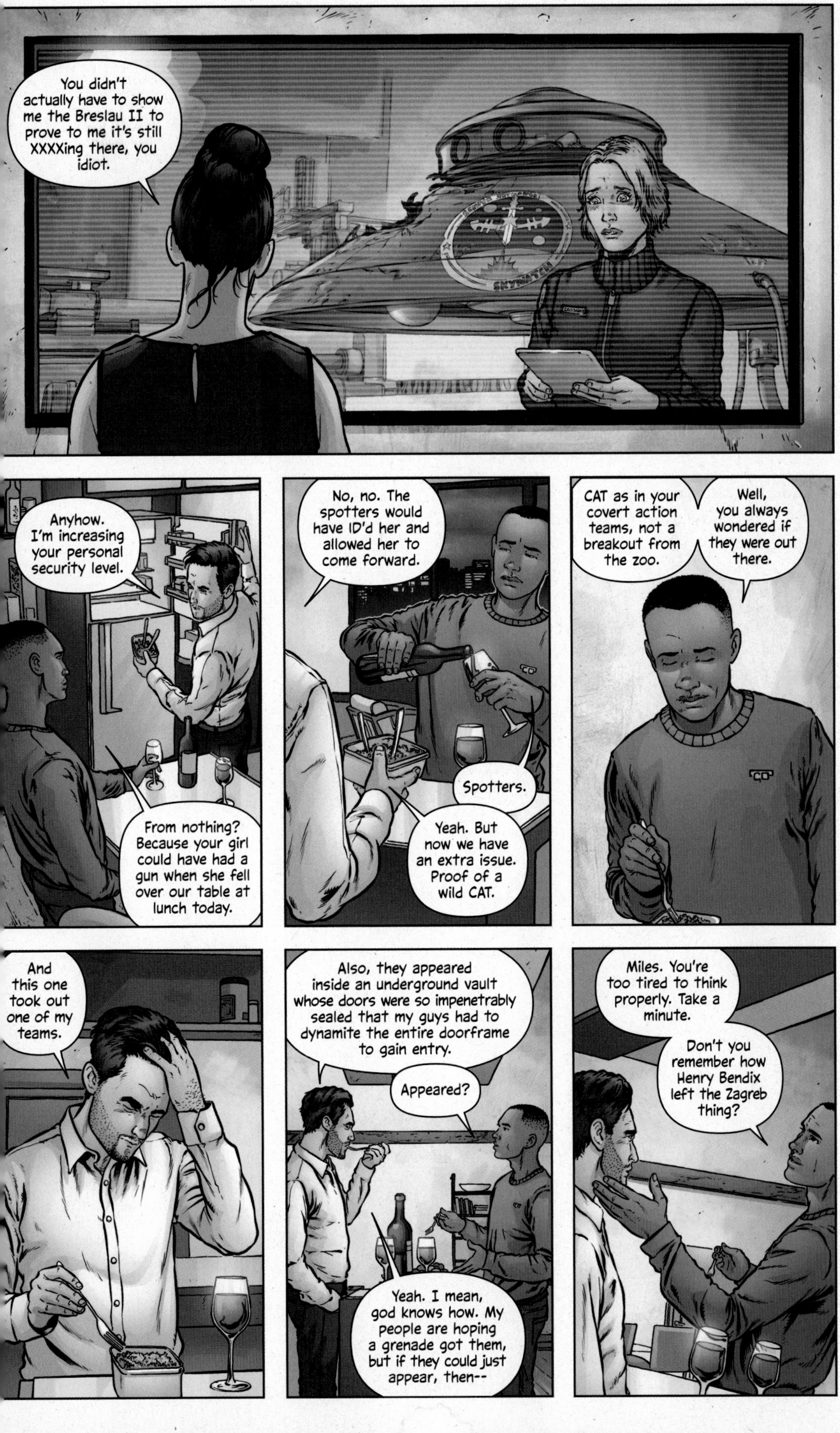
You didn't actually have to show me the Breslau II to prove to me it's still XXXXing there, you idiot.
SKYWATCH
Anyhow. I'm increasing your personal security level.
From nothing? Because your girl could have had a gun when she fell over our table at lunch today.
No, no. The spotters would have ID'd her and allowed her to come forward.
Spotters.
Yeah. But now we have an extra issue. Proof of a wild CAT.
CAT as in your covert action teams, not a breakout from the zoo.
Well, you always wondered if they were out there.
And this one took out one of my teams.
Also, they appeared inside an underground vault whose doors were so impenetrably sealed that my guys had to dynamite the entire doorframe to gain entry.
Appeared?
Yeah. I mean, god knows how. My people are hoping a grenade got them, but if they could just appear, then--
Miles. You're too tired to think properly. Take a minute.
Don't you remember how Henry Bendix left the Zagreb thing?

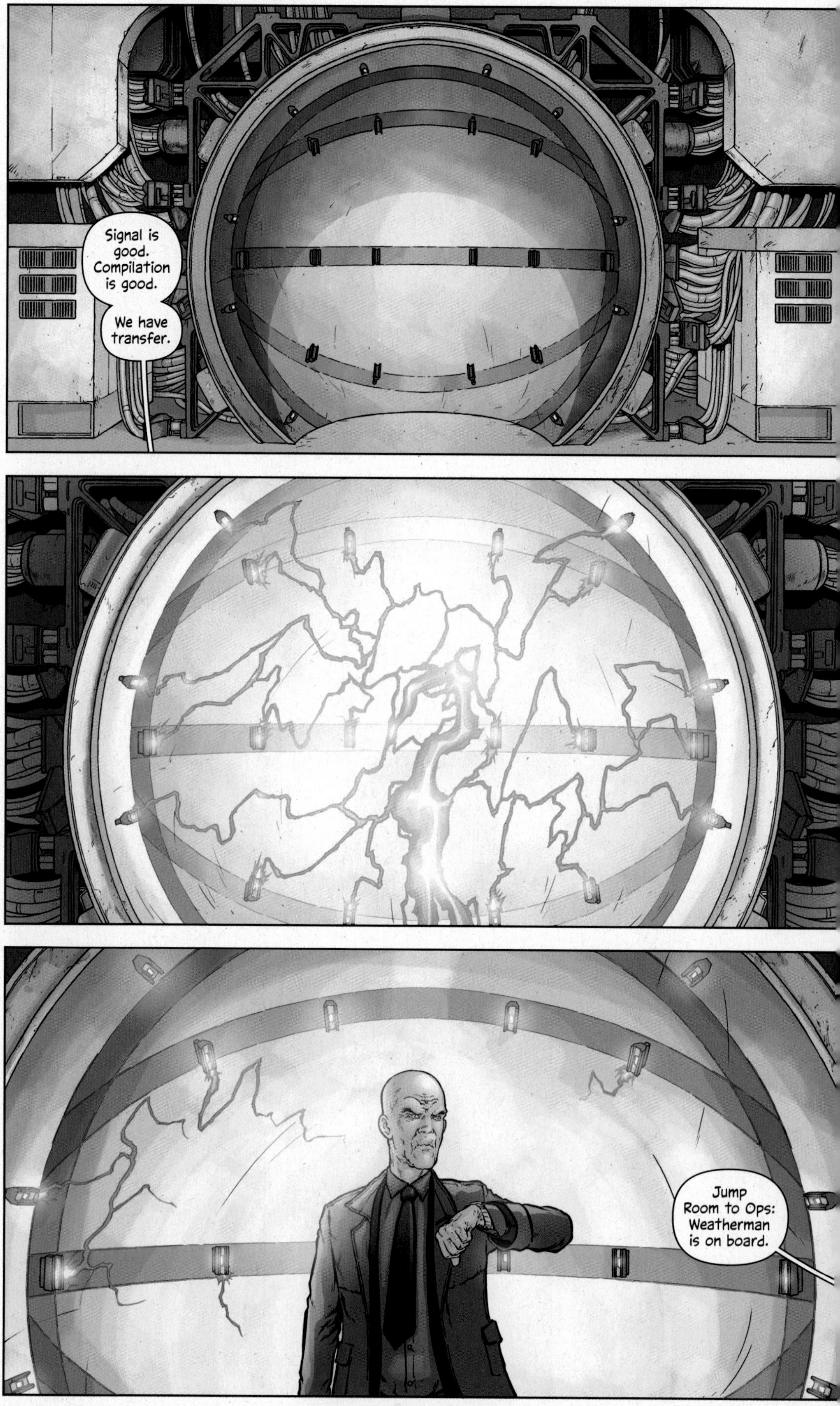
Signal is good. Compilation is good.
We have transfer.
Jump Room to Ops: Weatherman is on board.

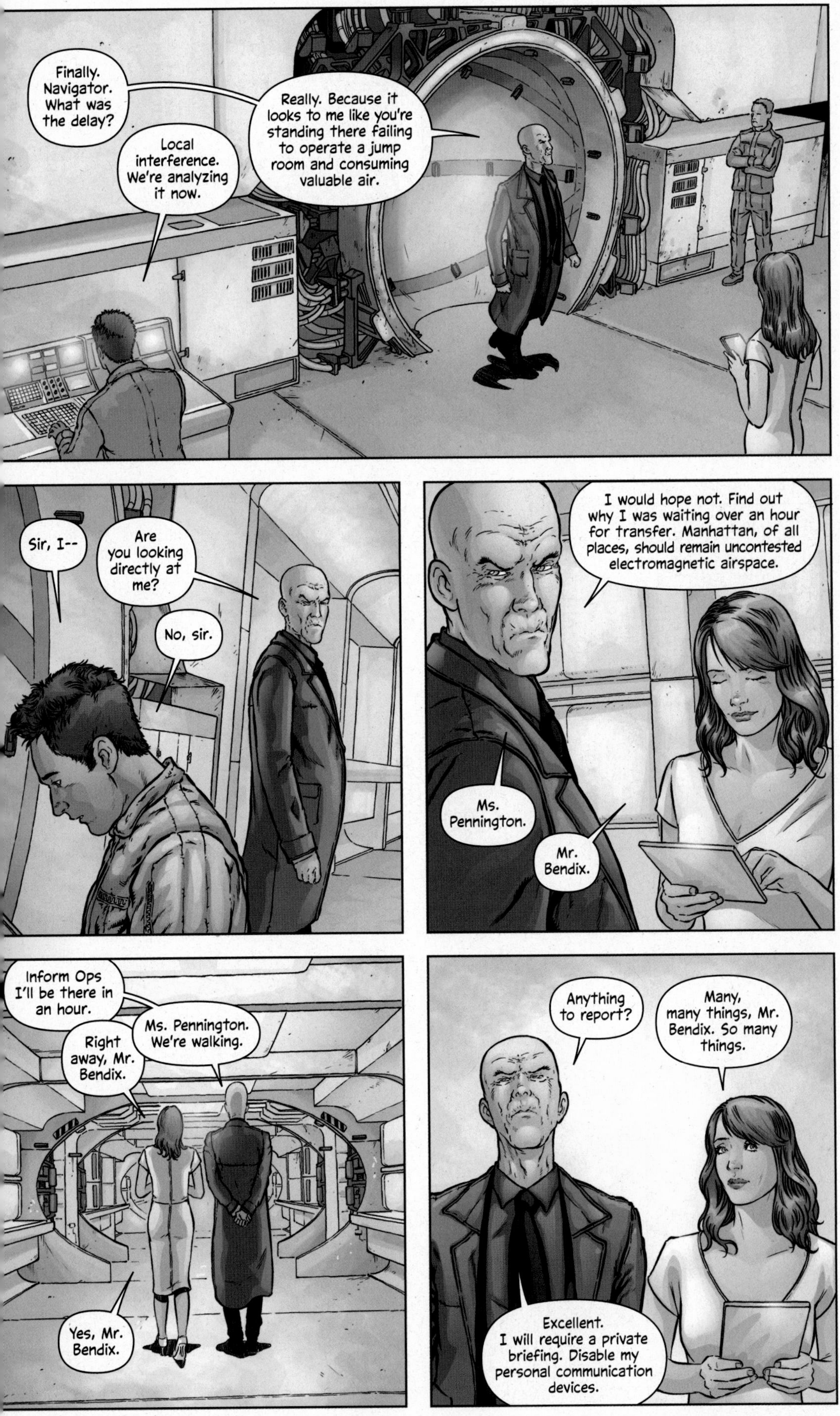
Finally. Navigator. What was the delay?
Local interference. We're analyzing it now.
Really. Because it looks to me like you're standing there failing to operate a jump room and consuming valuable air.
Sir, I--
Are you looking directly at me?
No, sir.
I would hope not. Find out why I was waiting over an hour for transfer. Manhattan, of all places, should remain uncontested electromagnetic airspace.
Ms. Pennington.
Mr. Bendix.
Inform Ops I'll be there in an hour.
Right away, Mr. Bendix.
Ms. Pennington. We're walking.
Yes, Mr. Bendix.
Anything to report?
Many, many things, Mr. Bendix. So many things.
Excellent. I will require a private briefing. Disable my personal communication devices.

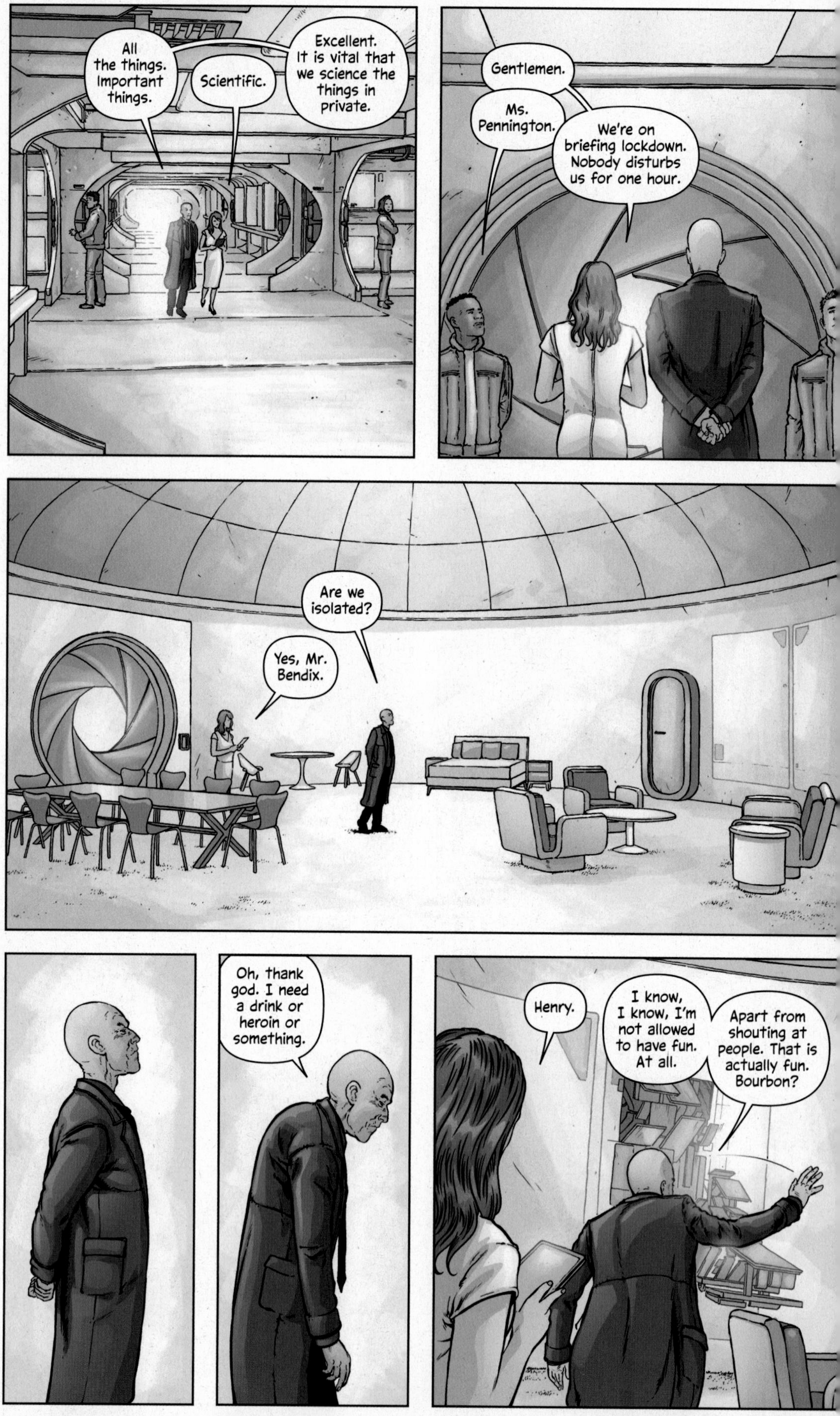
All the things. Important things.
Scientific.
Excellent. It is vital that we science the things in private.
Gentlemen.
Ms. Pennington.
We're on briefing lockdown. Nobody disturbs us for one hour.
Are we isolated?
Yes, Mr. Bendix.
Oh, thank god. I need a drink or heroin or something.
Henry.
I know, I know, I'm not allowed to have fun. At all.
Apart from shouting at people. That is actually fun. Bourbon?

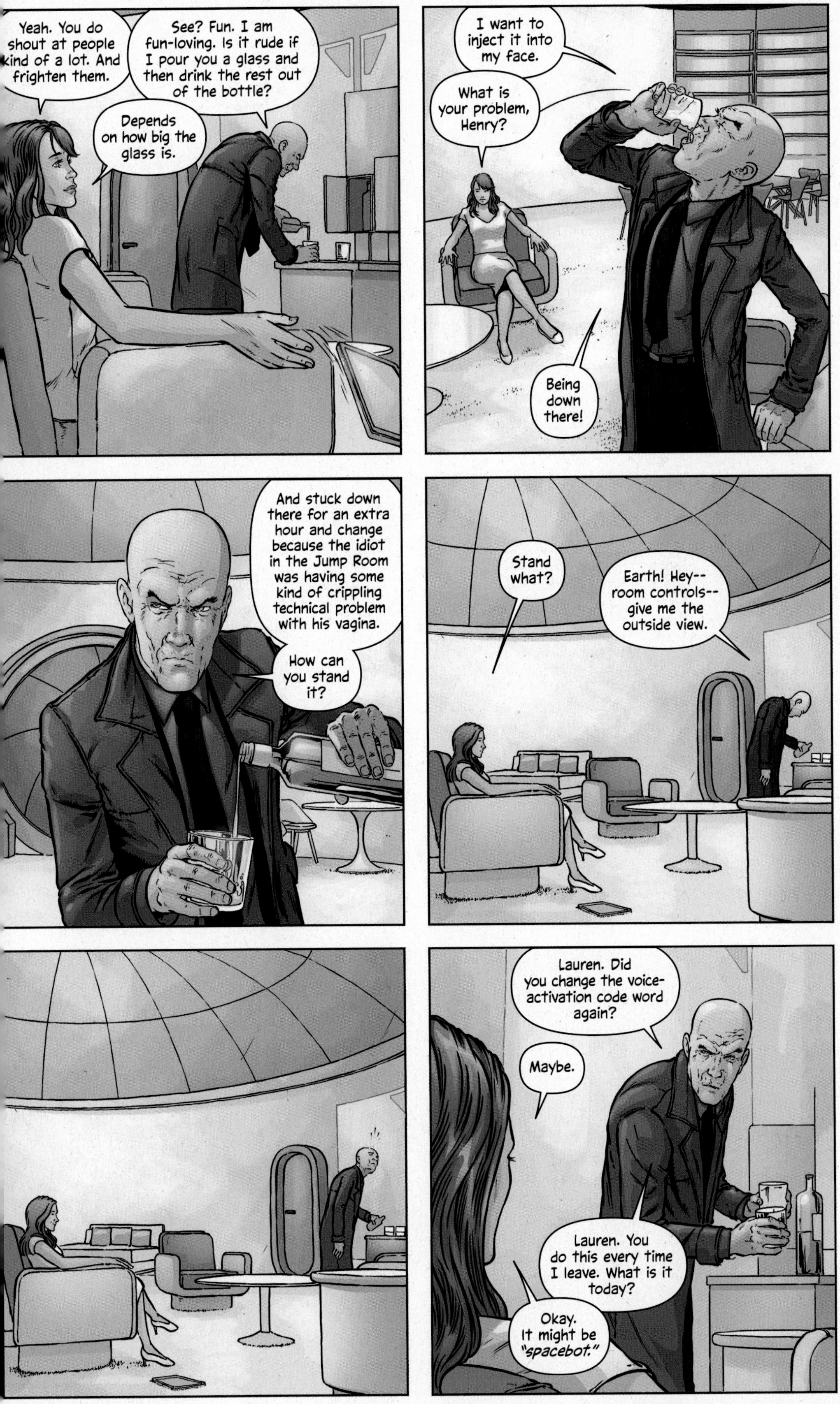

Yeah. You do shout at people kind of a lot. And frighten them.
See? Fun. I am fun-loving. Is it rude if I pour you a glass and then drink the rest out of the bottle?
Depends on how big the glass is.
I want to inject it into my face.
What is your problem, Henry?
Being down there!
And stuck down there for an extra hour and change because the idiot in the Jump Room was having some kind of crippling technical problem with his vagina.
How can you stand it?
Stand what?
Earth! Hey--room controls--give me the outside view.
Lauren. Did you change the voice-activation code word again?
Maybe.
Lauren. You do this every time I leave. What is it today?
Okay. It might be *"spacebot."*

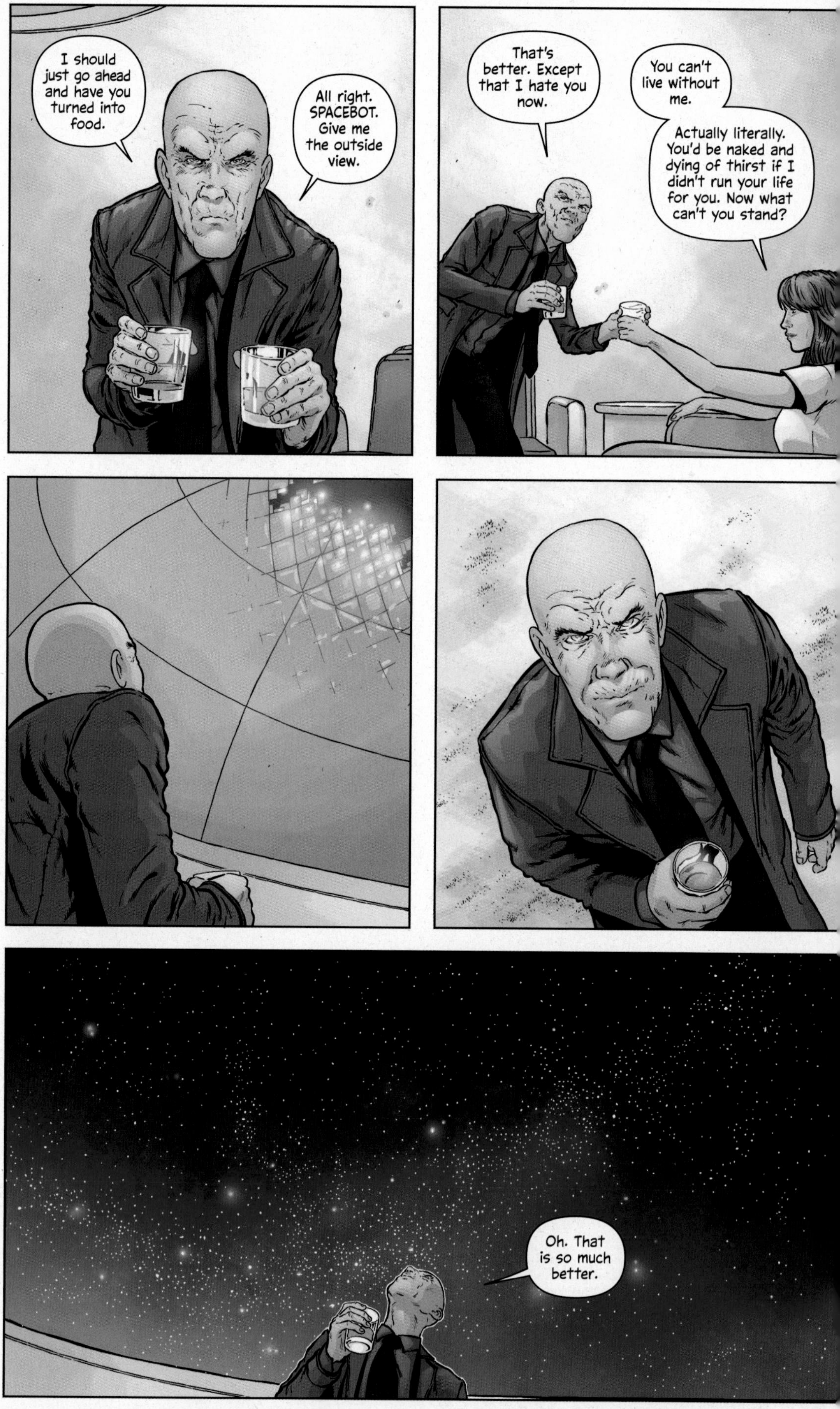
I should just go ahead and have you turned into food.
All right. SPACEBOT. Give me the outside view.
That's better. Except that I hate you now.
You can't live without me.
Actually literally. You'd be naked and dying of thirst if I didn't run your life for you. Now what can't you stand?
Oh. That is so much better.

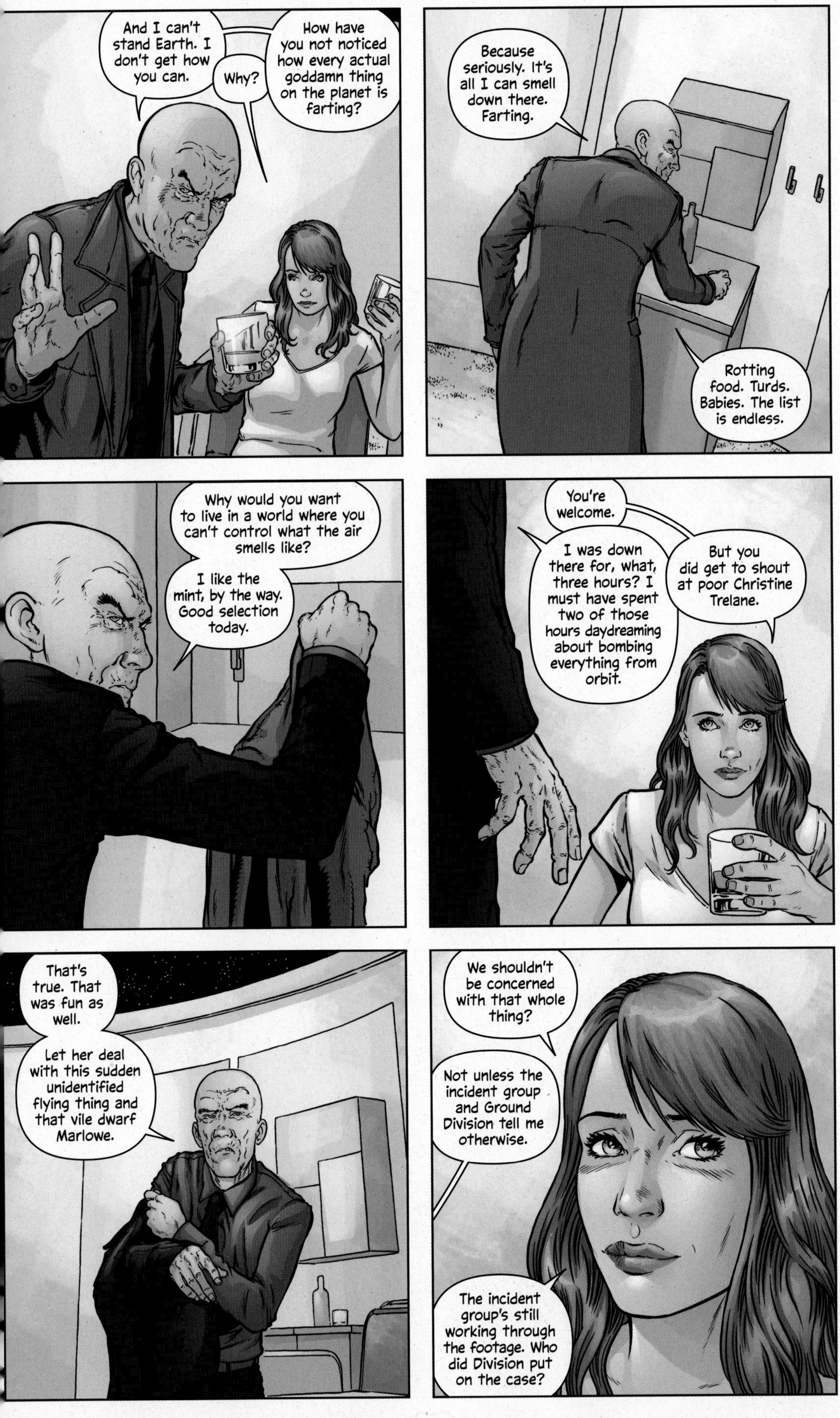
And I can't stand Earth. I don't get how you can.
Why?
How have you not noticed how every actual goddamn thing on the planet is farting?
Because seriously. It's all I can smell down there. Farting.
Rotting food. Turds. Babies. The list is endless.
Why would you want to live in a world where you can't control what the air smells like?
I like the mint, by the way. Good selection today.
You're welcome.
I was down there for, what, three hours? I must have spent two of those hours daydreaming about bombing everything from orbit.
But you did get to shout at poor Christine Trelane.
That's true. That was fun as well.
Let her deal with this sudden unidentified flying thing and that vile dwarf Marlowe.
We shouldn't be concerned with that whole thing?
Not unless the incident group and Ground Division tell me otherwise.
The incident group's still working through the footage. Who did Division put on the case?

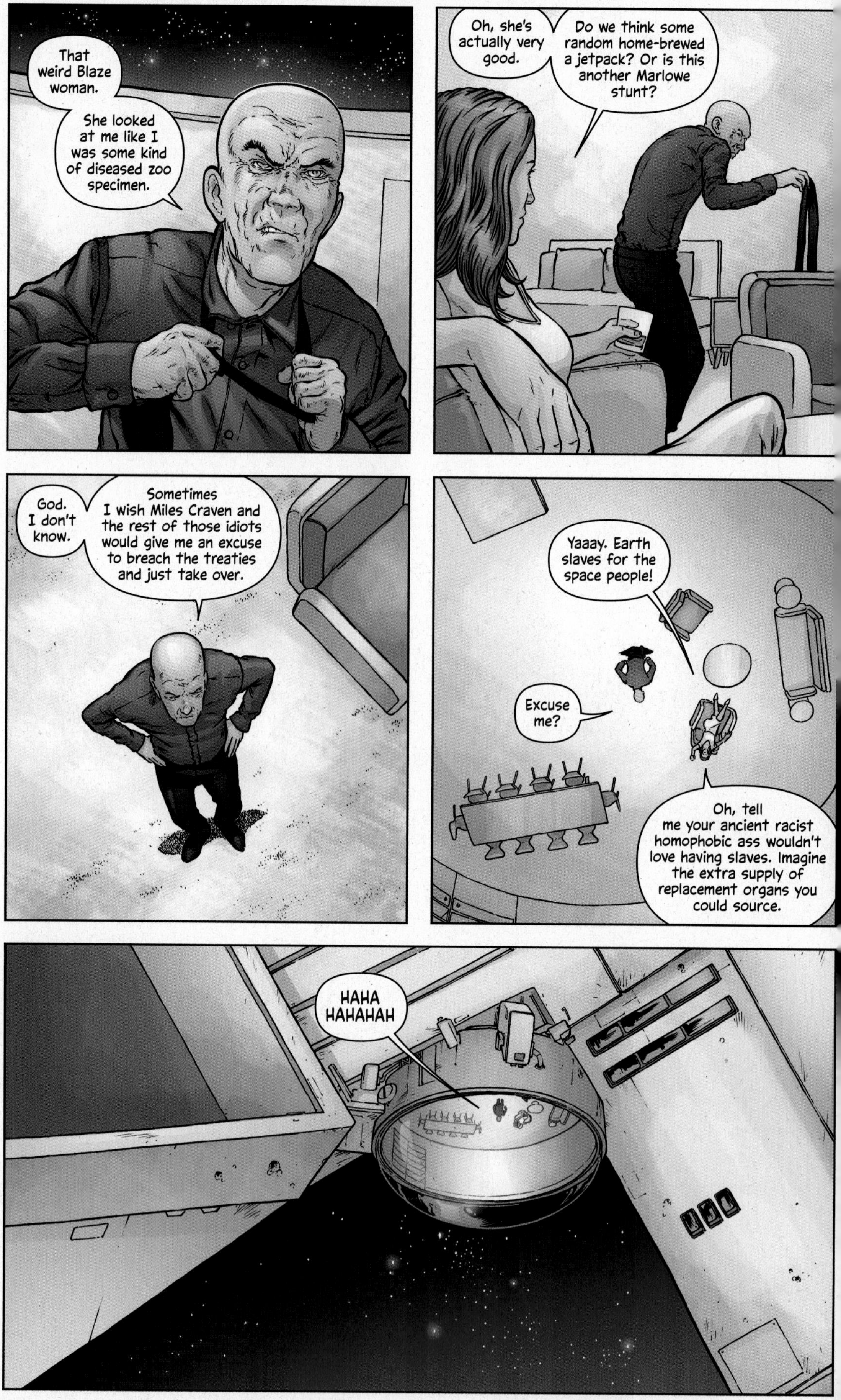

That weird Blaze woman.
She looked at me like I was some kind of diseased zoo specimen.
Oh, she's actually very good.
Do we think some random home-brewed a jetpack? Or is this another Marlowe stunt?
God. I don't know.
Sometimes I wish Miles Craven and the rest of those idiots would give me an excuse to breach the treaties and just take over.
Yaaay. Earth slaves for the space people!
Excuse me?
Oh, tell me your ancient racist homophobic ass wouldn't love having slaves. Imagine the extra supply of replacement organs you could source.
HAHA HAHAHAH

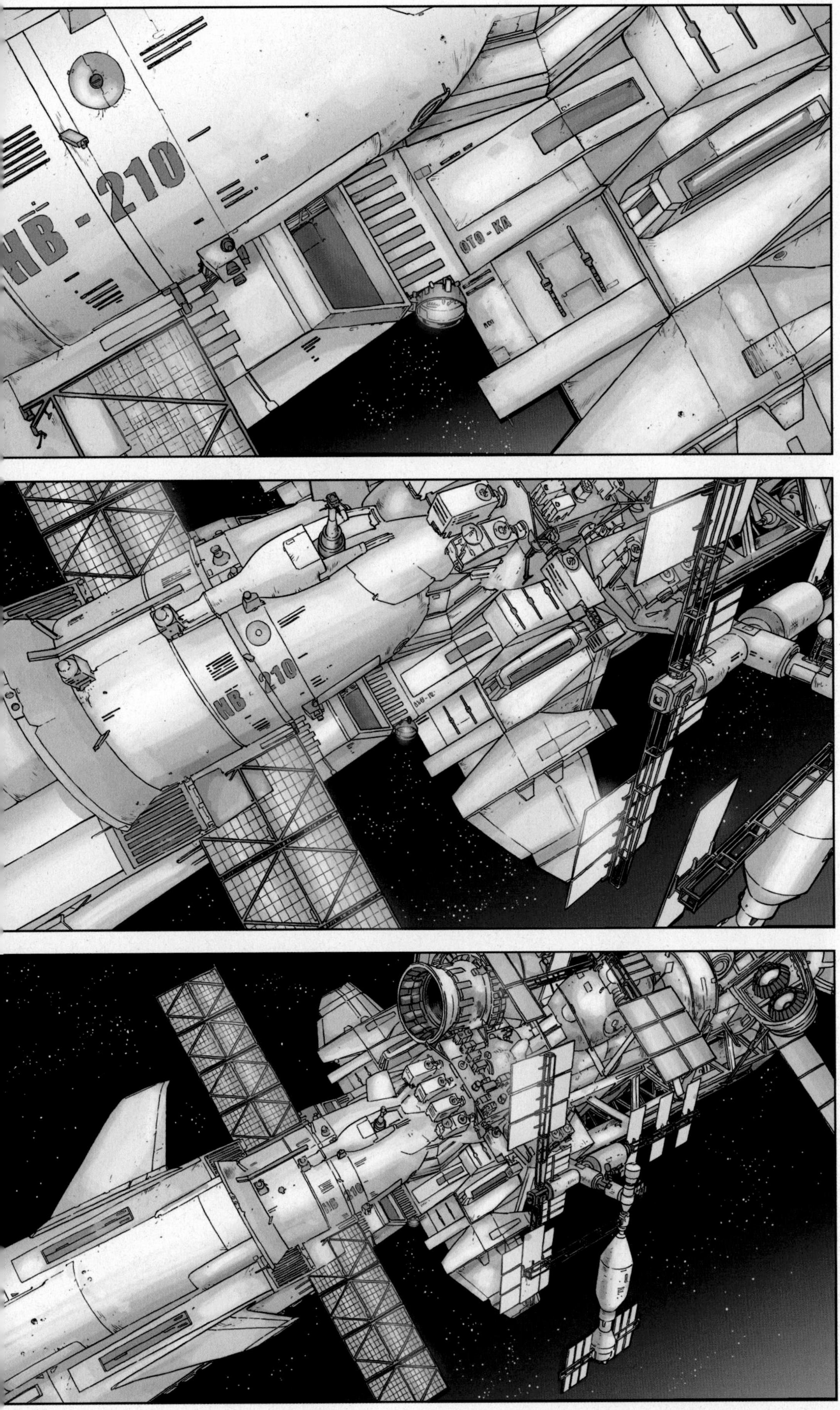
HB - 210
OTO - KA
HB 210
HB 210

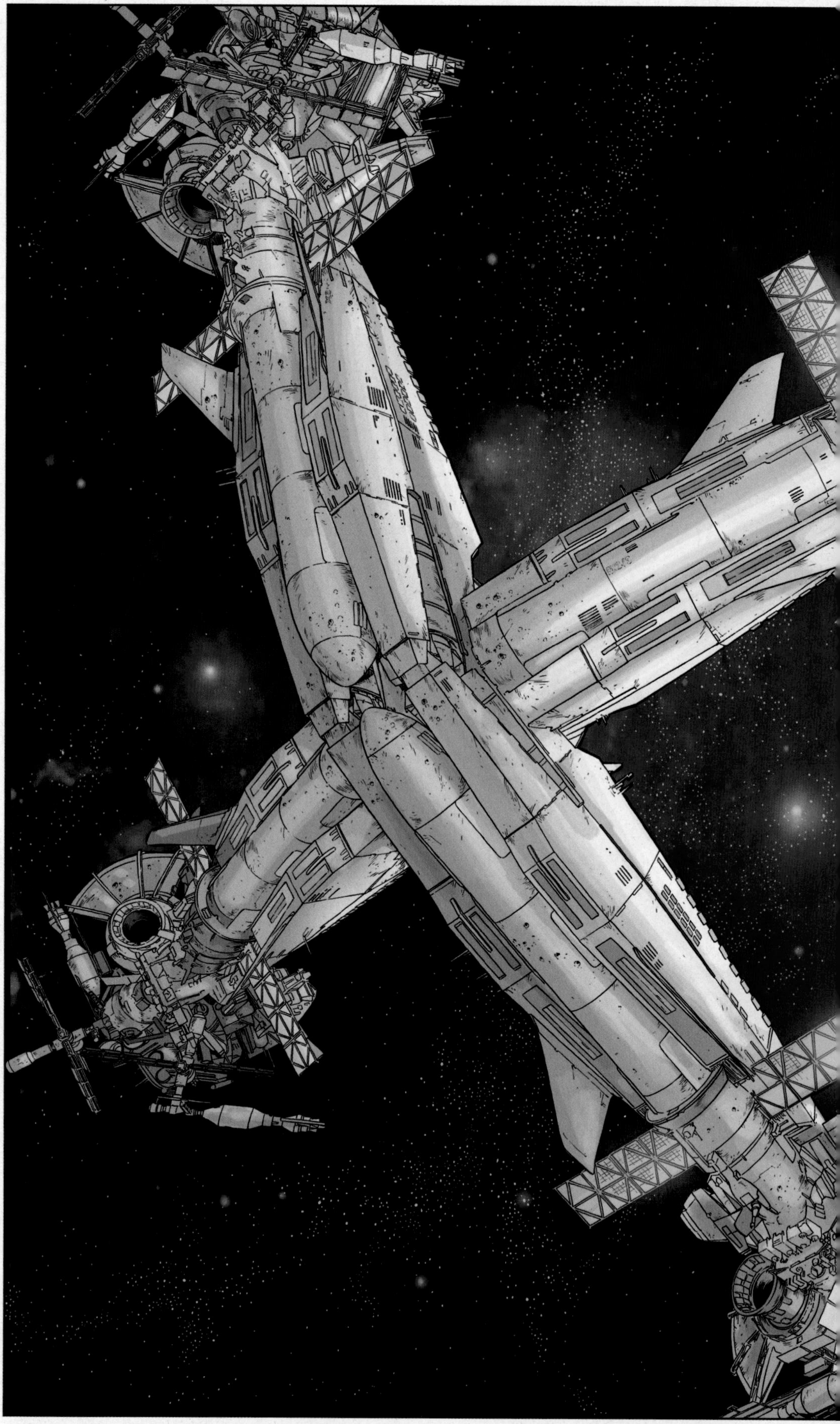

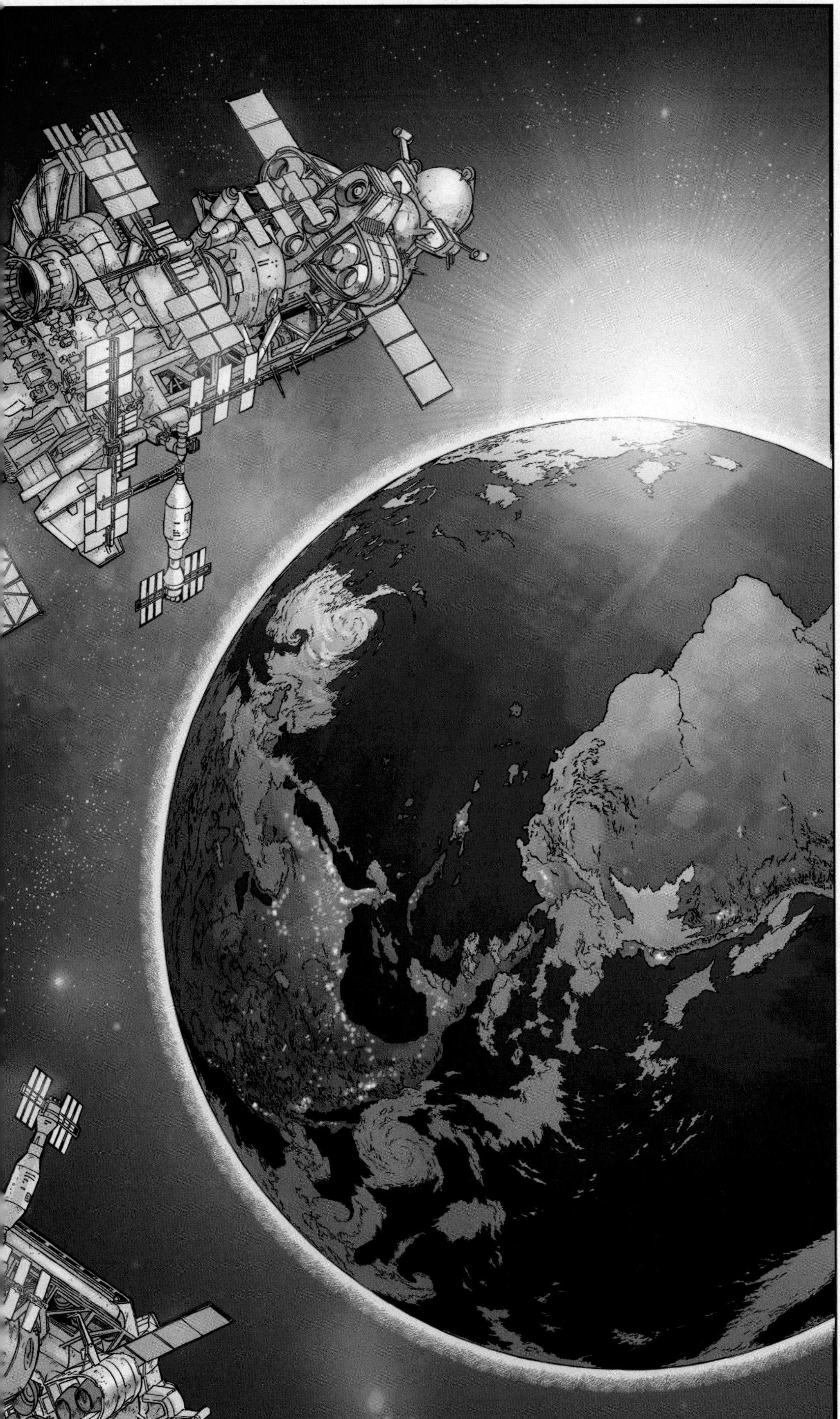

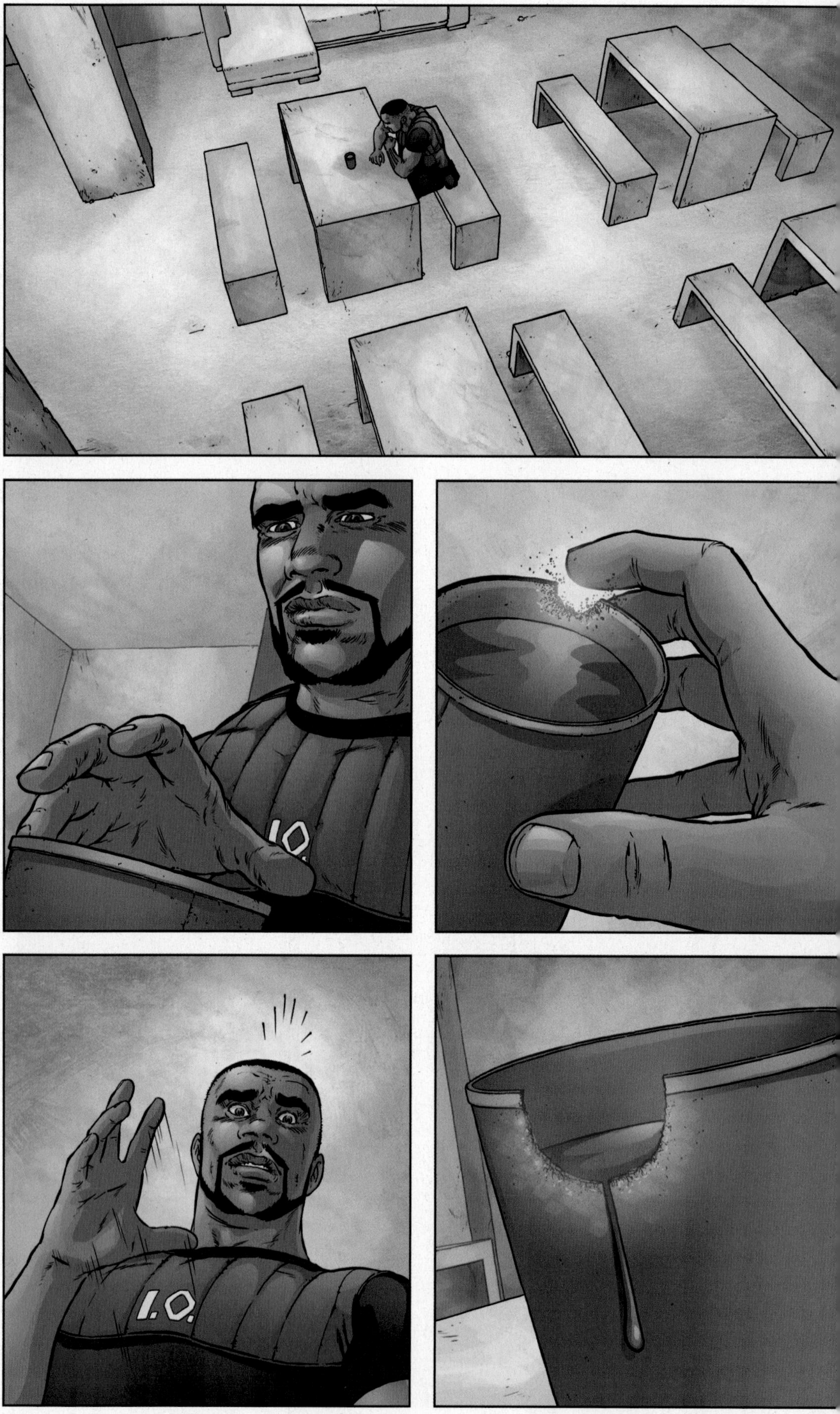
I.O.

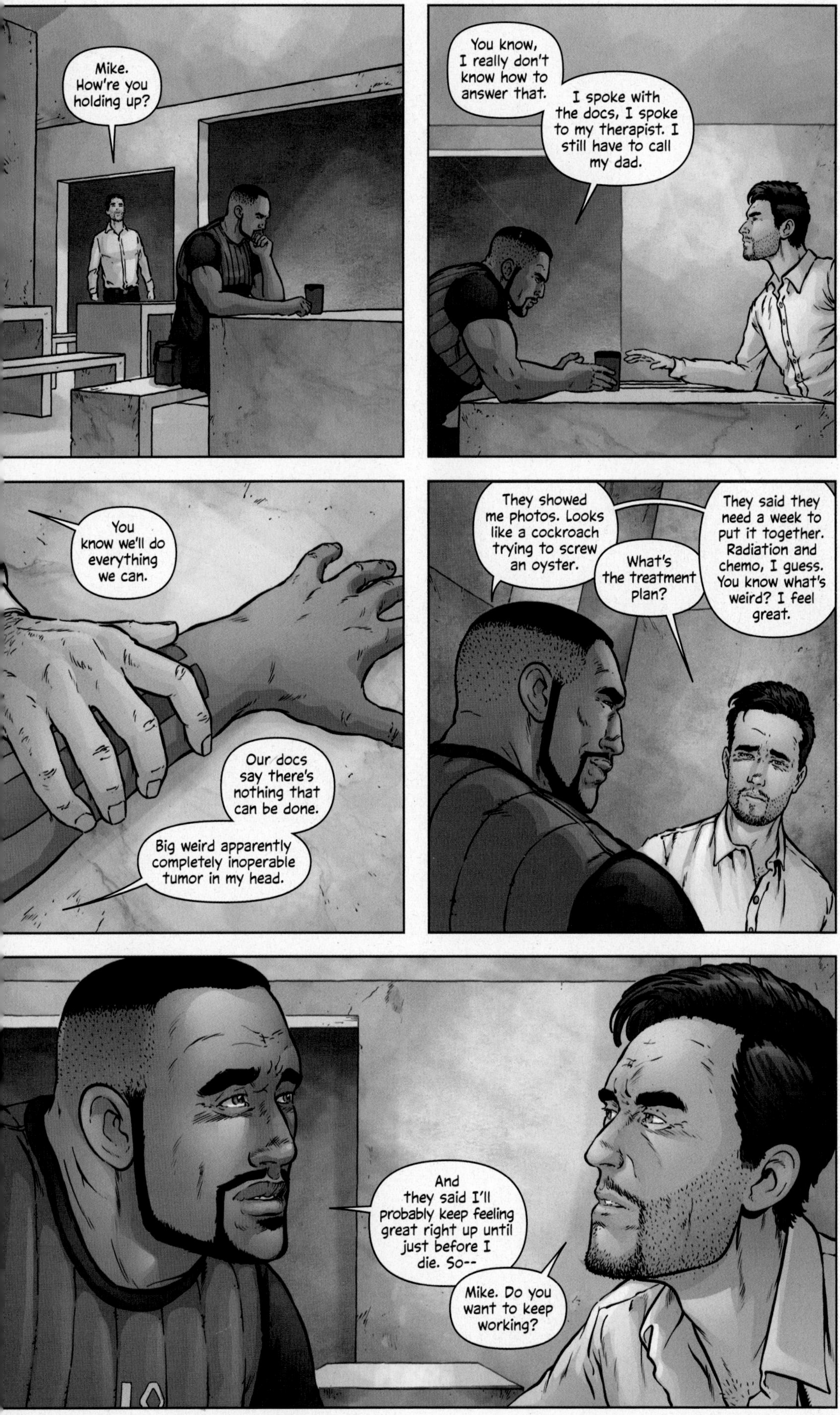
Mike. How're you holding up?
You know, I really don't know how to answer that.
I spoke with the docs, I spoke to my therapist. I still have to call my dad.
You know we'll do everything we can.
Our docs say there's nothing that can be done.
Big weird apparently completely inoperable tumor in my head.
They showed me photos. Looks like a cockroach trying to screw an oyster.
What's the treatment plan?
They said they need a week to put it together. Radiation and chemo, I guess. You know what's weird? I feel great.
And they said I'll probably keep feeling great right up until just before I die. So--
Mike. Do you want to keep working?

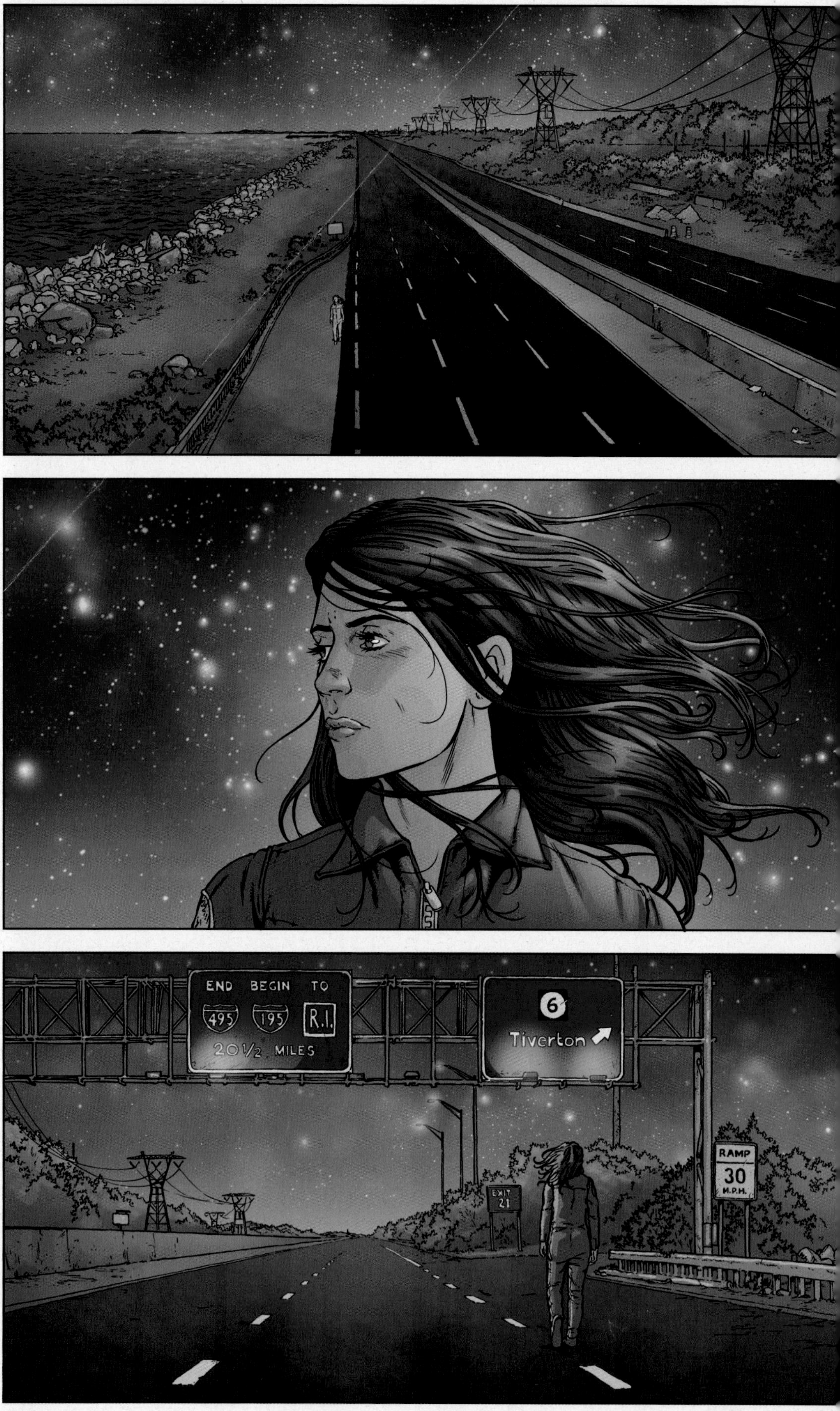
END BEGIN TO
495
195
R.I.
20½ MILES
6
Tiverton
EXIT
21
RAMP
30
M.P.H.

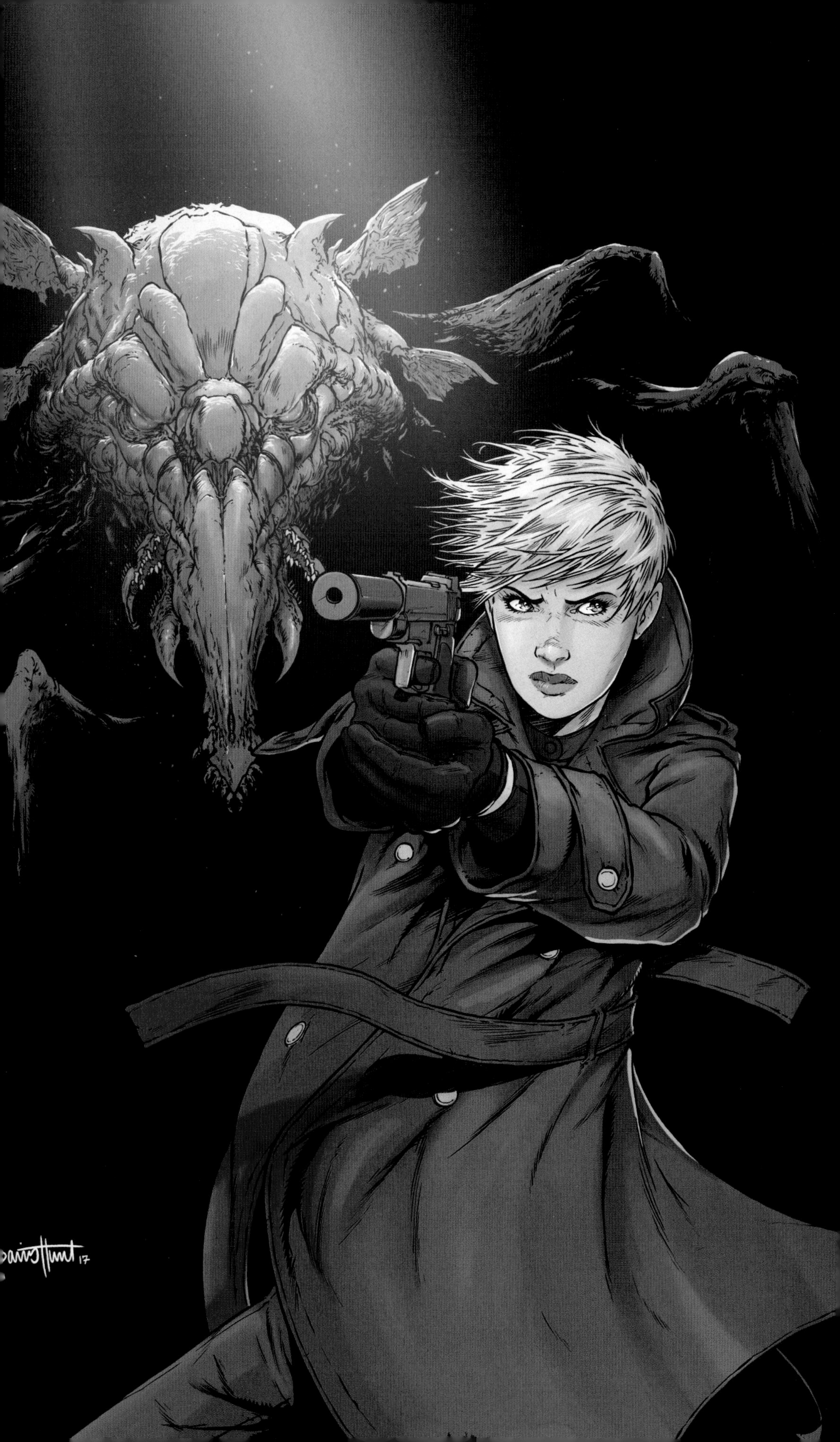

5

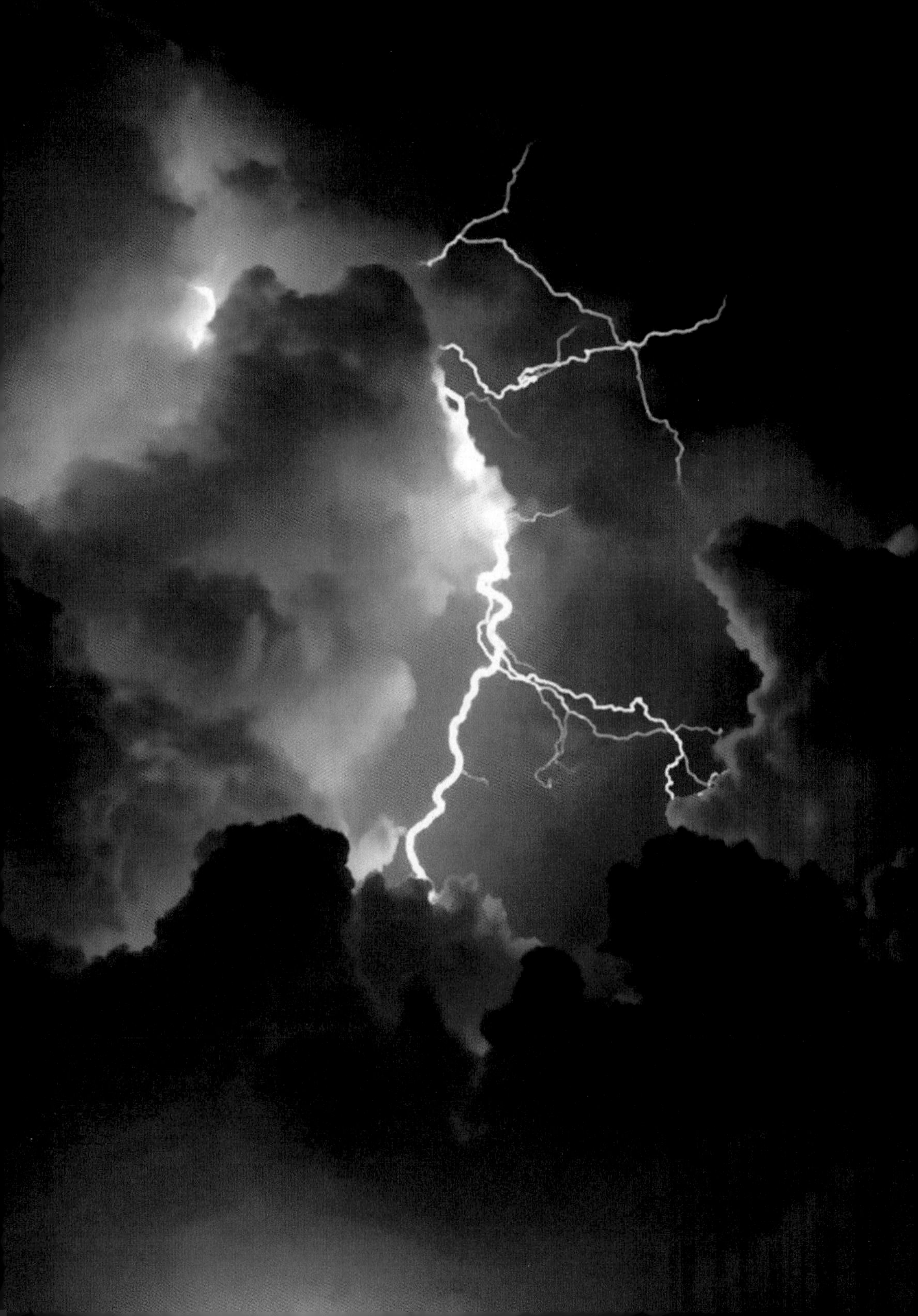

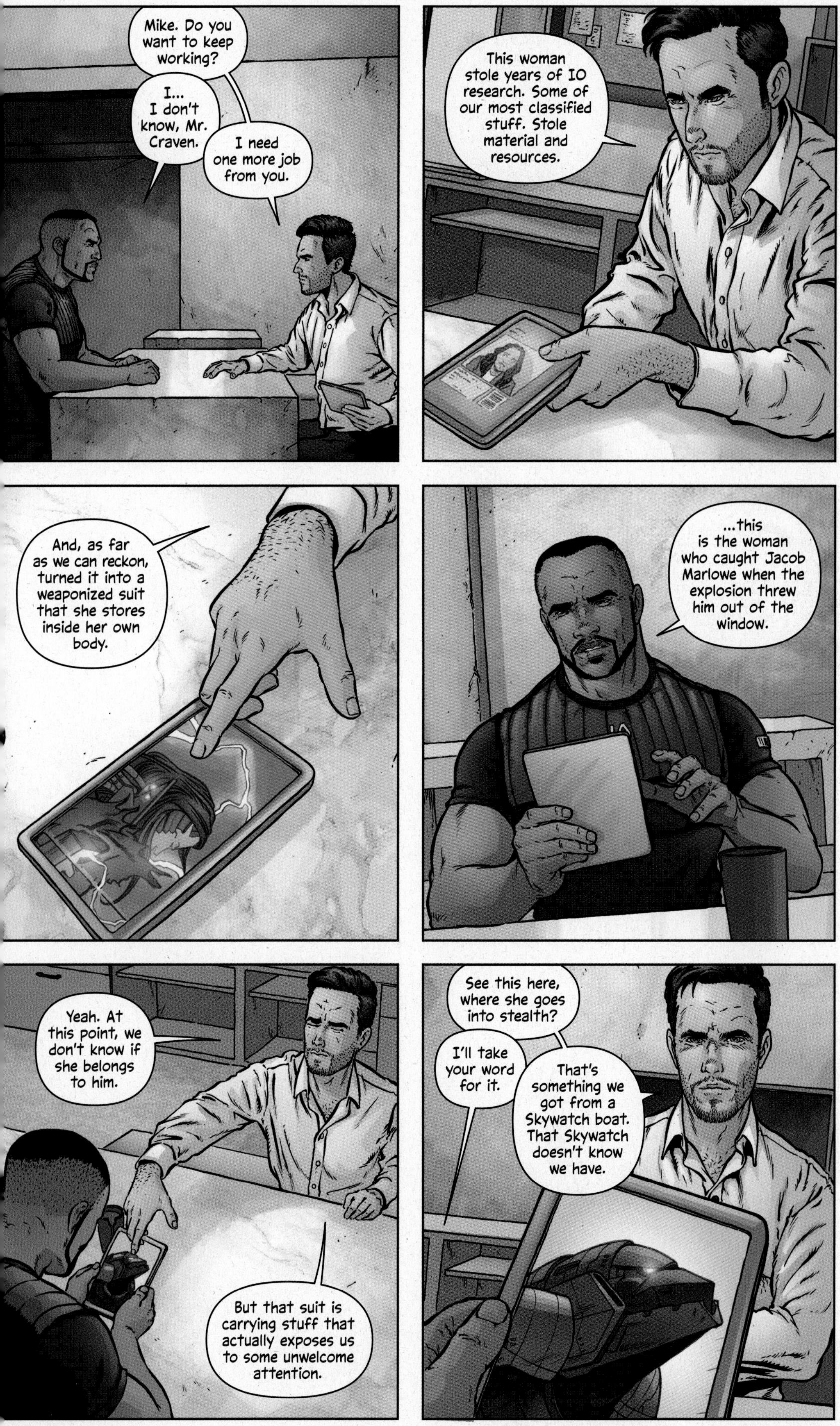
Mike. Do you want to keep working?
I... I don't know, Mr. Craven.
I need one more job from you.
This woman stole years of IO research. Some of our most classified stuff. Stole material and resources.
And, as far as we can reckon, turned it into a weaponized suit that she stores inside her own body.
...this is the woman who caught Jacob Marlowe when the explosion threw him out of the window.
Yeah. At this point, we don't know if she belongs to him.
But that suit is carrying stuff that actually exposes us to some unwelcome attention.
See this here, where she goes into stealth?
I'll take your word for it.
That's something we got from a Skywatch boat. That Skywatch doesn't know we have.

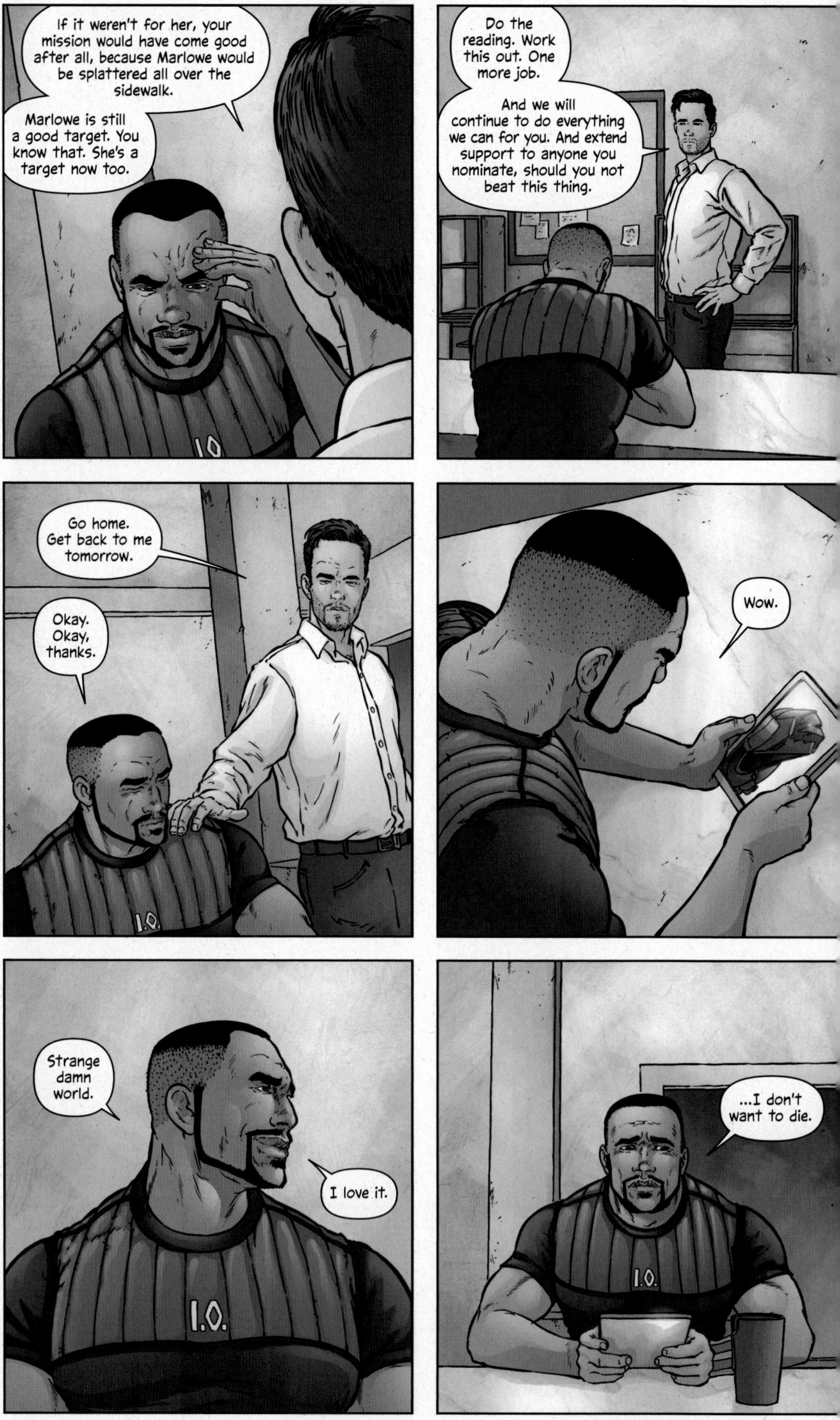
If it weren't for her, your mission would have come good after all, because Marlowe would be splattered all over the sidewalk.
Marlowe is still a good target. You know that. She's a target now too.
Do the reading. Work this out. One more job.
And we will continue to do everything we can for you. And extend support to anyone you nominate, should you not beat this thing.
Go home. Get back to me tomorrow.
Okay. Okay, thanks.
Wow.
Strange damn world.
I love it.
...I don't want to die.
I.O.
I.O.
I.O.
I.O.

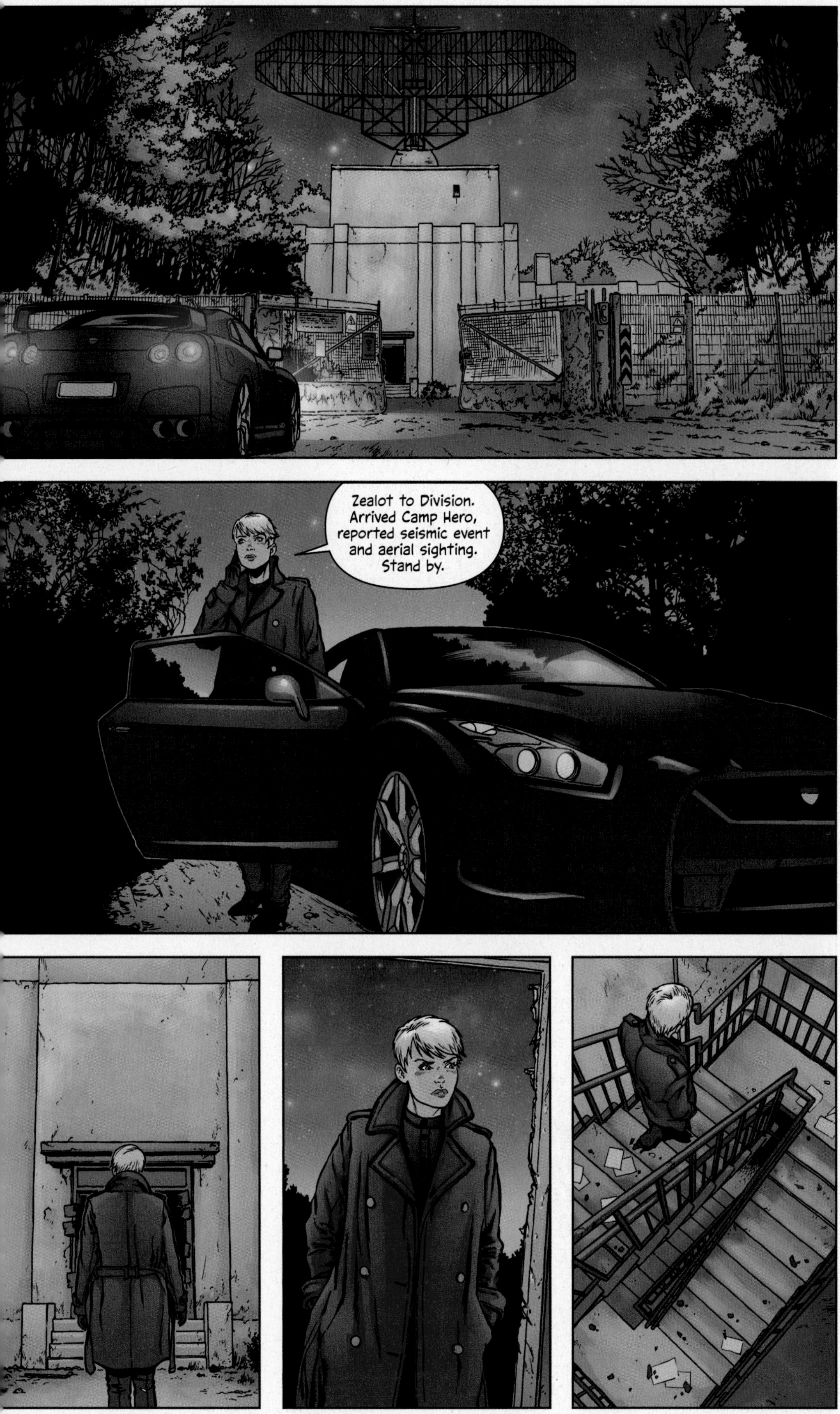
Zealot to Division. Arrived Camp Hero, reported seismic event and aerial sighting. Stand by.

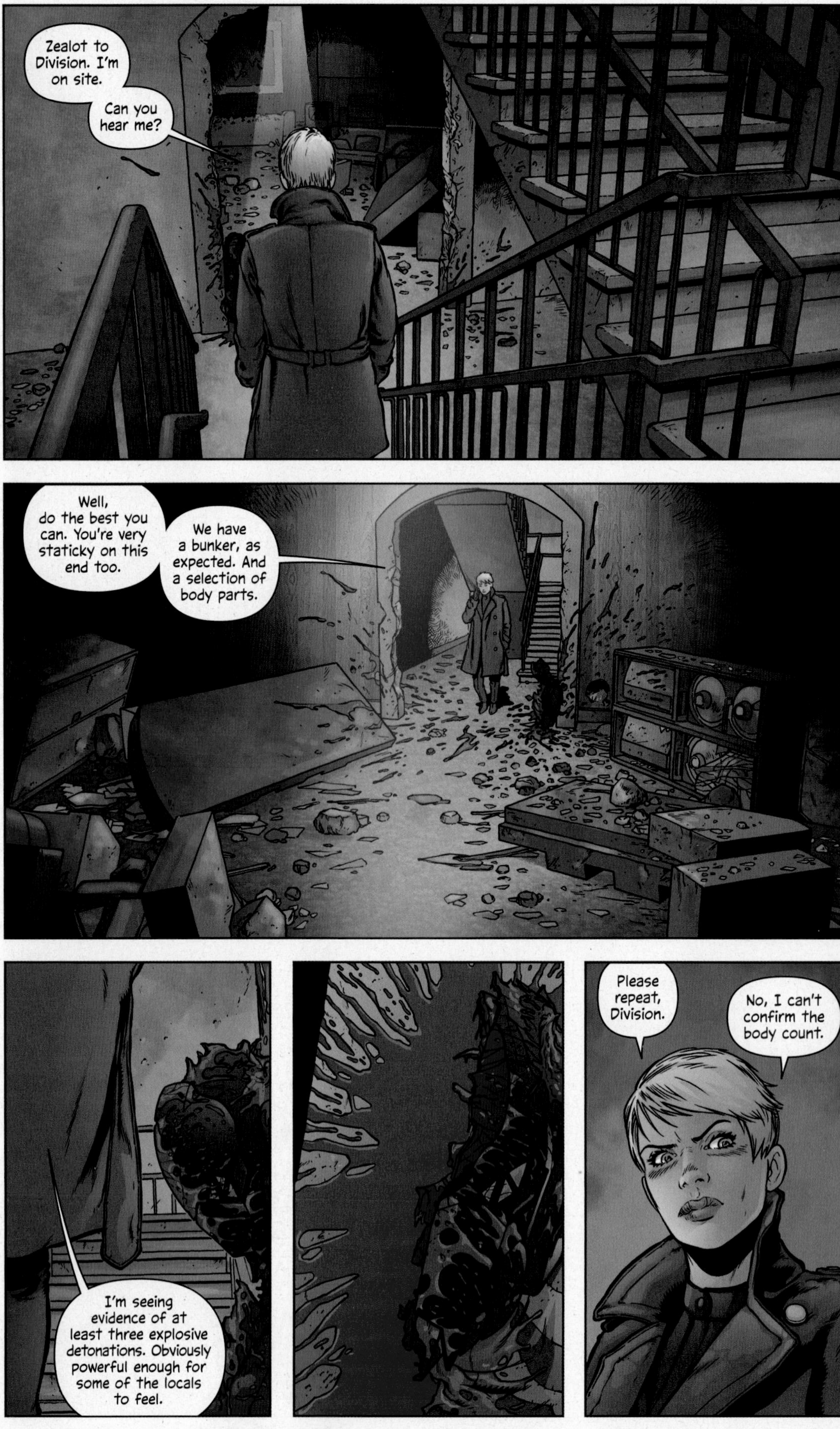
Zealot to Division. I'm on site.
Can you hear me?
Well, do the best you can. You're very staticky on this end too.
We have a bunker, as expected. And a selection of body parts.
I'm seeing evidence of at least three explosive detonations. Obviously powerful enough for some of the locals to feel.
Please repeat, Division.
No, I can't confirm the body count.

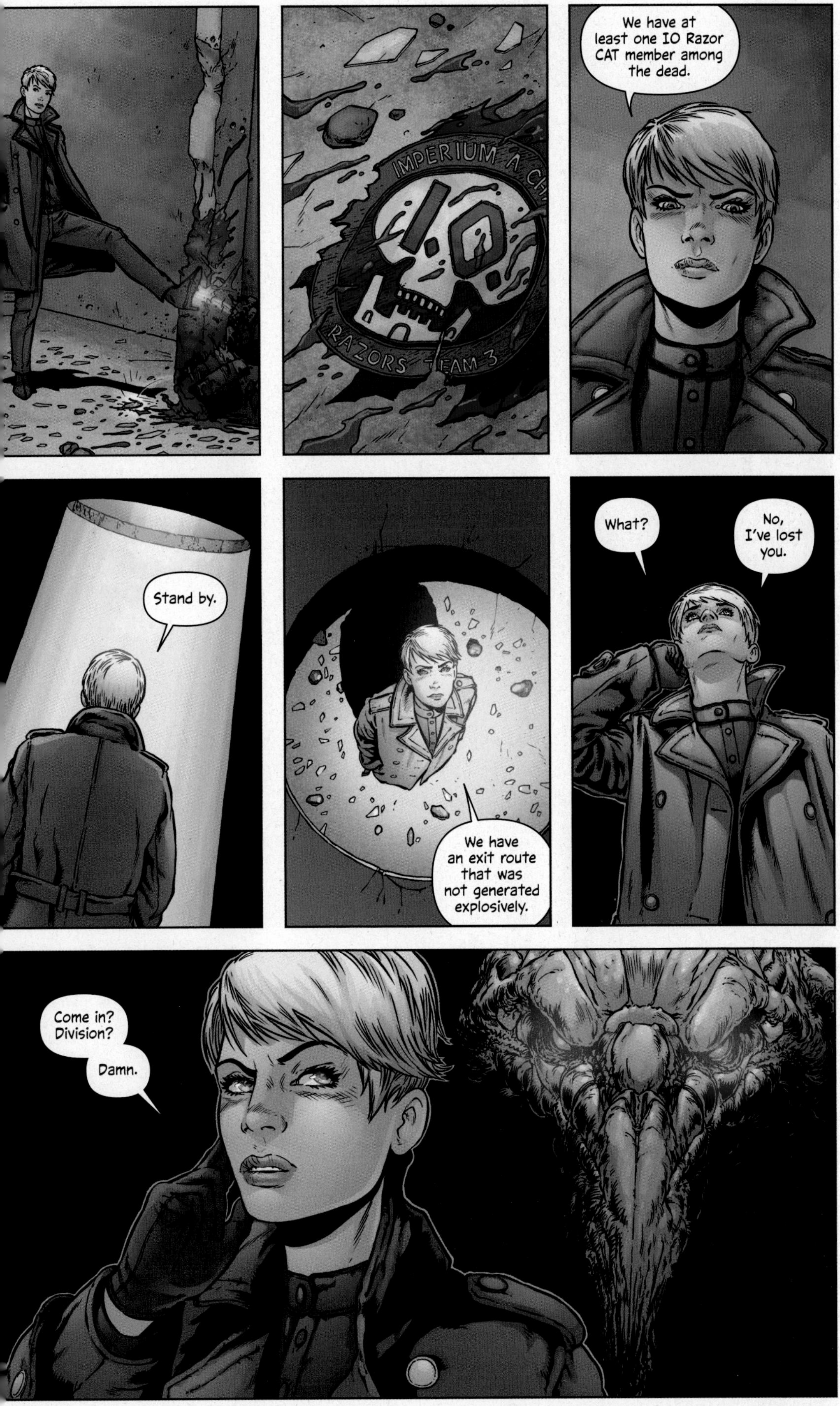
IMPERIUM A CH
I.O
RAZORS TEAM 3
We have at least one IO Razor CAT member among the dead.
Stand by.
We have an exit route that was not generated explosively.
What?
No, I've lost you.
Come in? Division?
Damn.

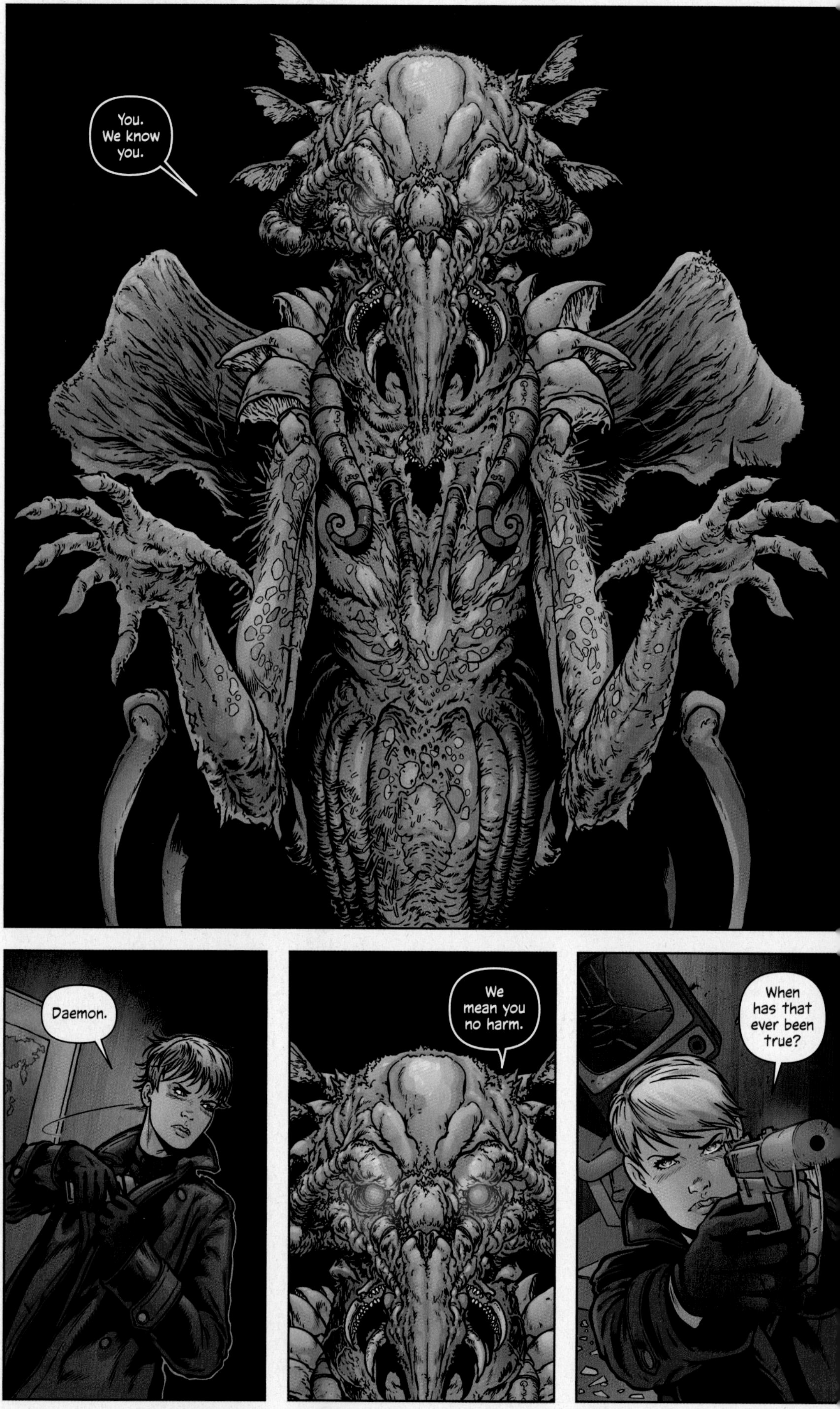
You. We know you.
Daemon.
We mean you no harm.
When has that ever been true?

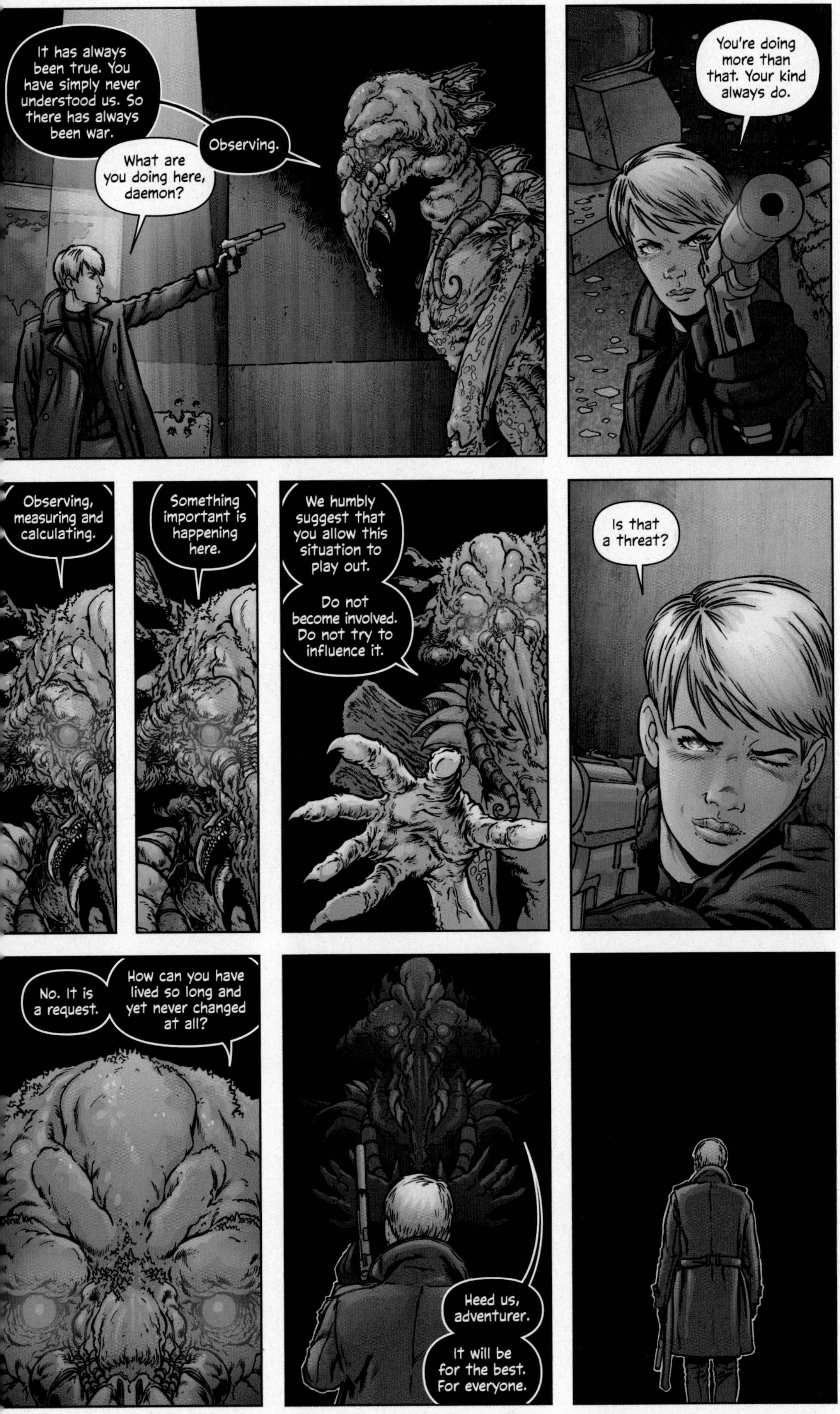
It has always been true. You have simply never understood us. So there has always been war.
What are you doing here, daemon?
Observing.
You're doing more than that. Your kind always do.
Observing, measuring and calculating.
Something important is happening here.
We humbly suggest that you allow this situation to play out.
Do not become involved. Do not try to influence it.
Is that a threat?
No. It is a request.
How can you have lived so long and yet never changed at all?
Heed us, adventurer.
It will be for the best. For everyone.

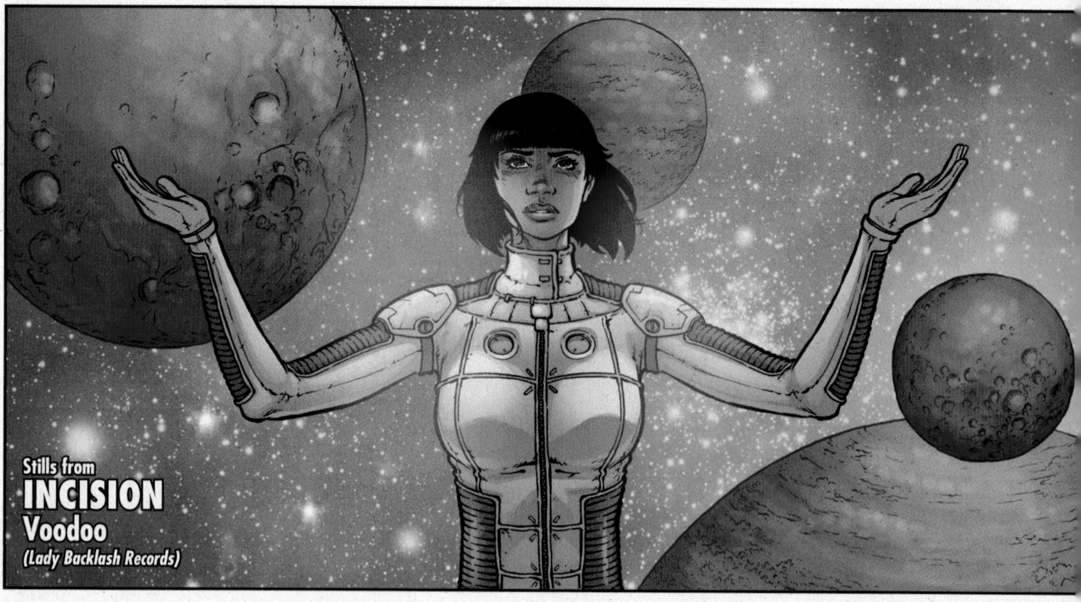
Stills from
INCISION
Voodoo
(Lady Backlash Records)

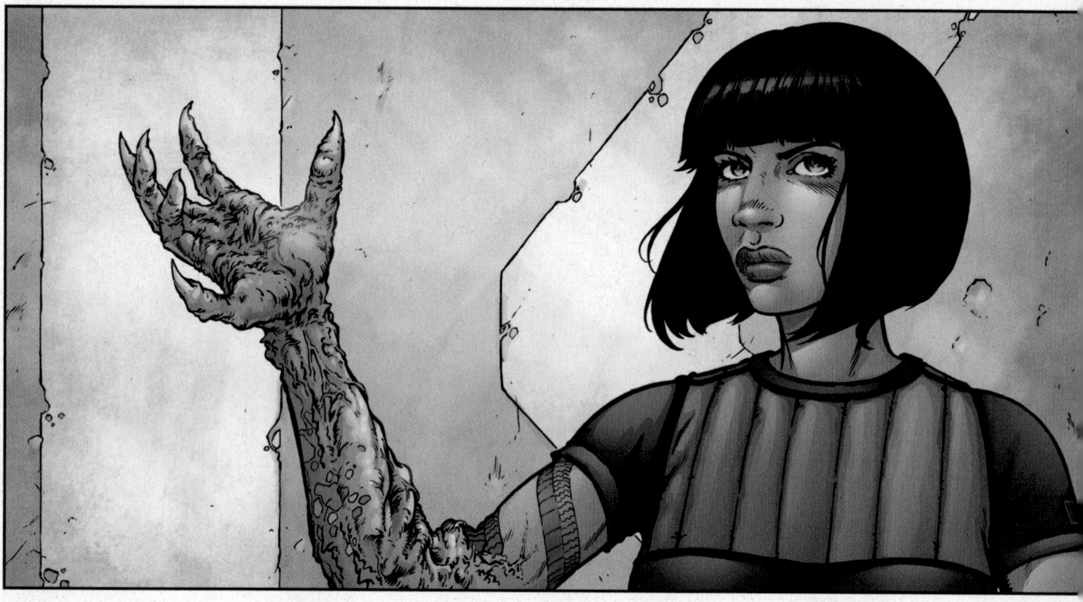

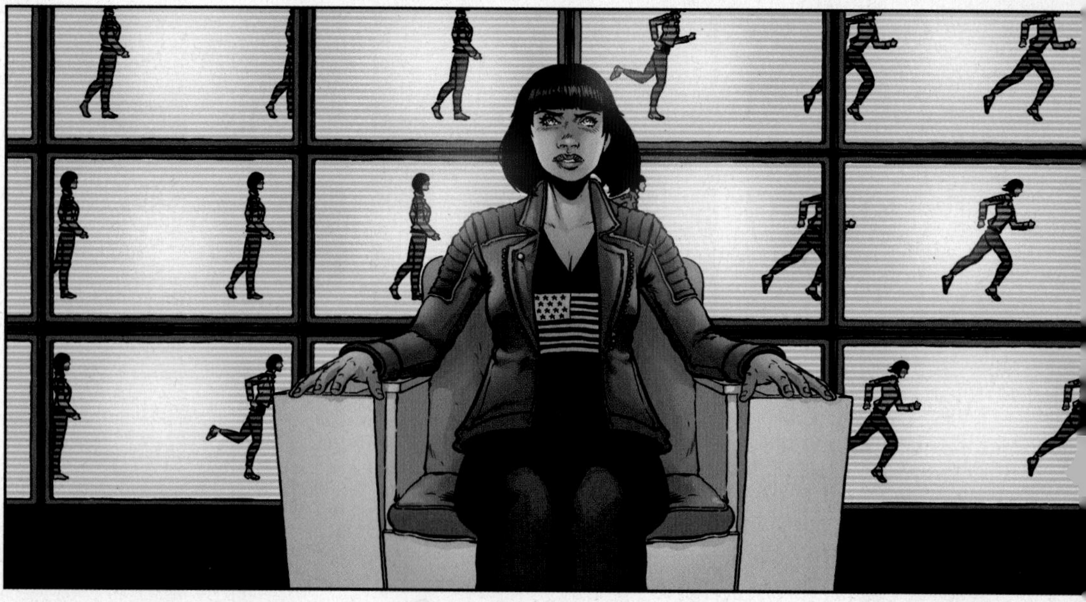

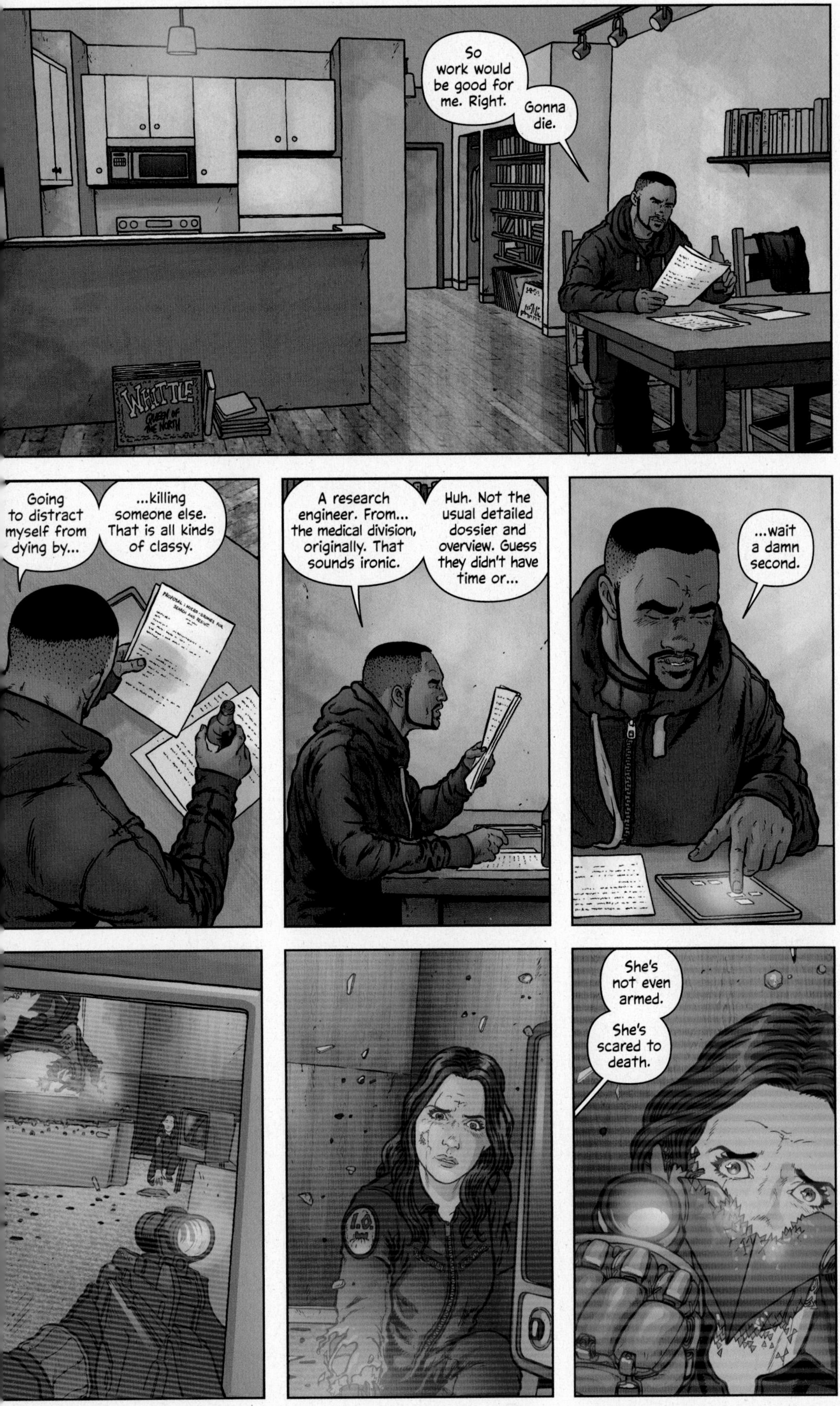
So work would be good for me. Right.
Gonna die.
Going to distract myself from dying by...
...killing someone else. That is all kinds of classy.
A research engineer. From... the medical division, originally. That sounds ironic.
Huh. Not the usual detailed dossier and overview. Guess they didn't have time or...
...wait a damn second.
She's not even armed.
She's scared to death.

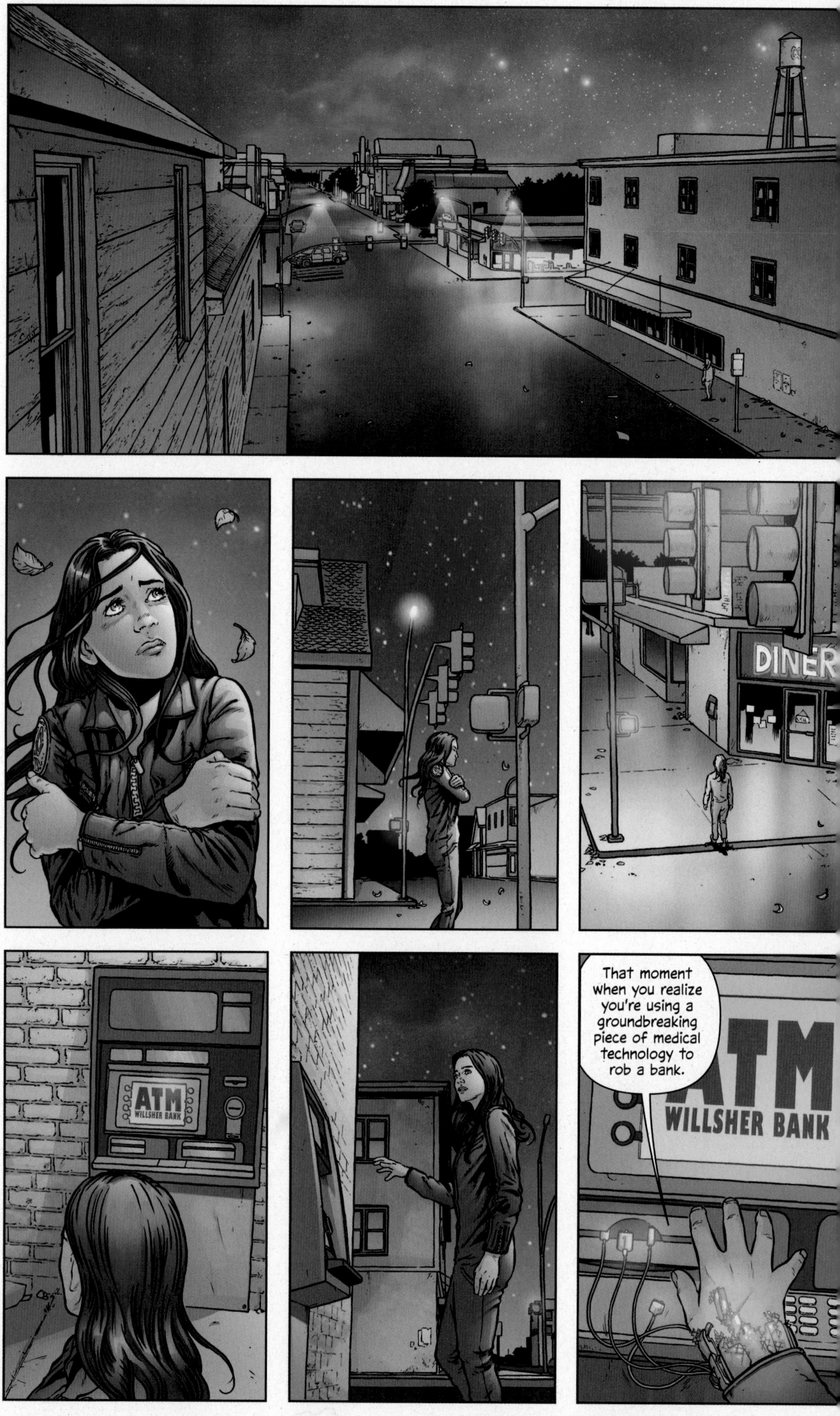
DINER
ATM
WILLSHER BANK
That moment when you realize you're using a groundbreaking piece of medical technology to rob a bank.
ATM
WILLSHER BANK

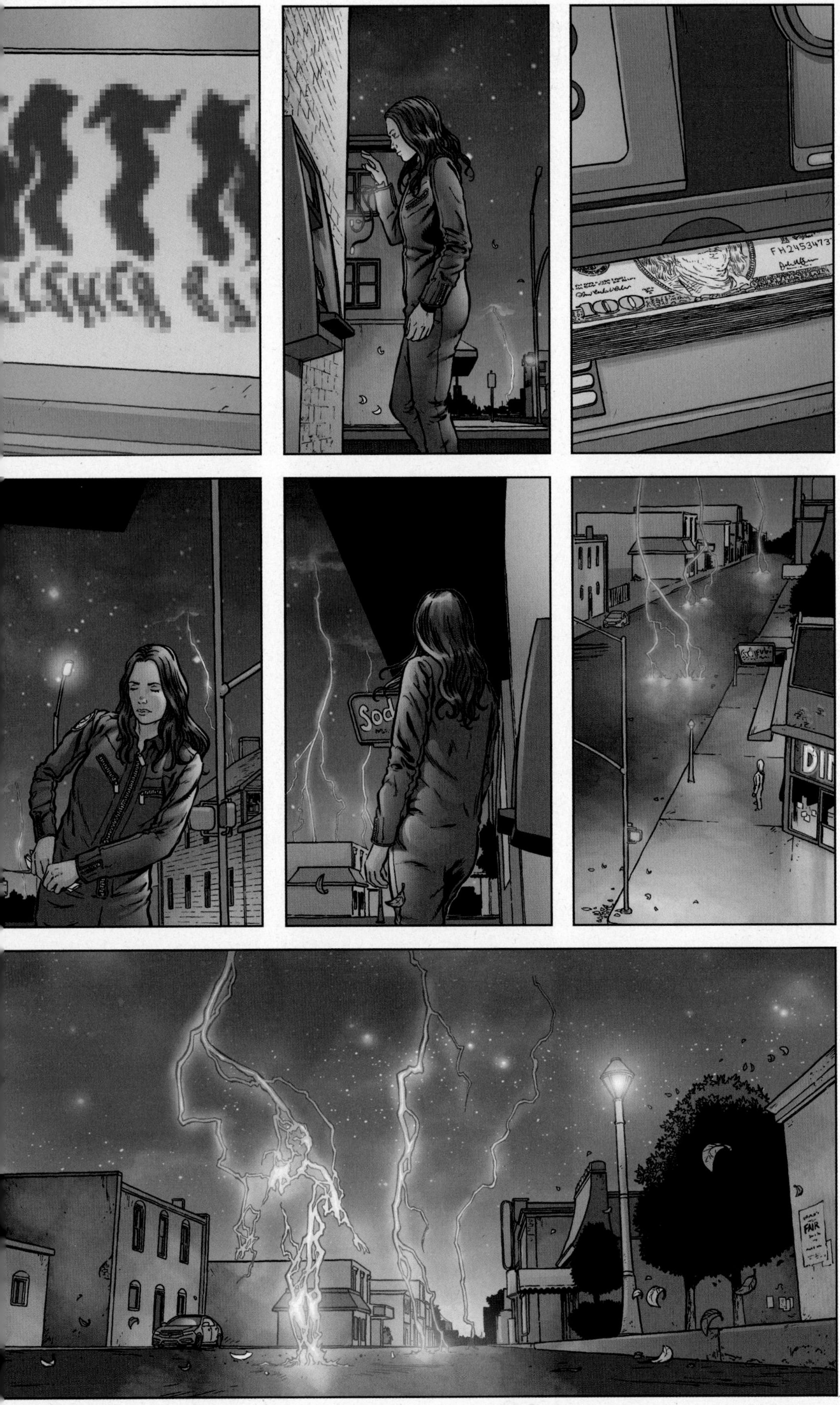
FAIR

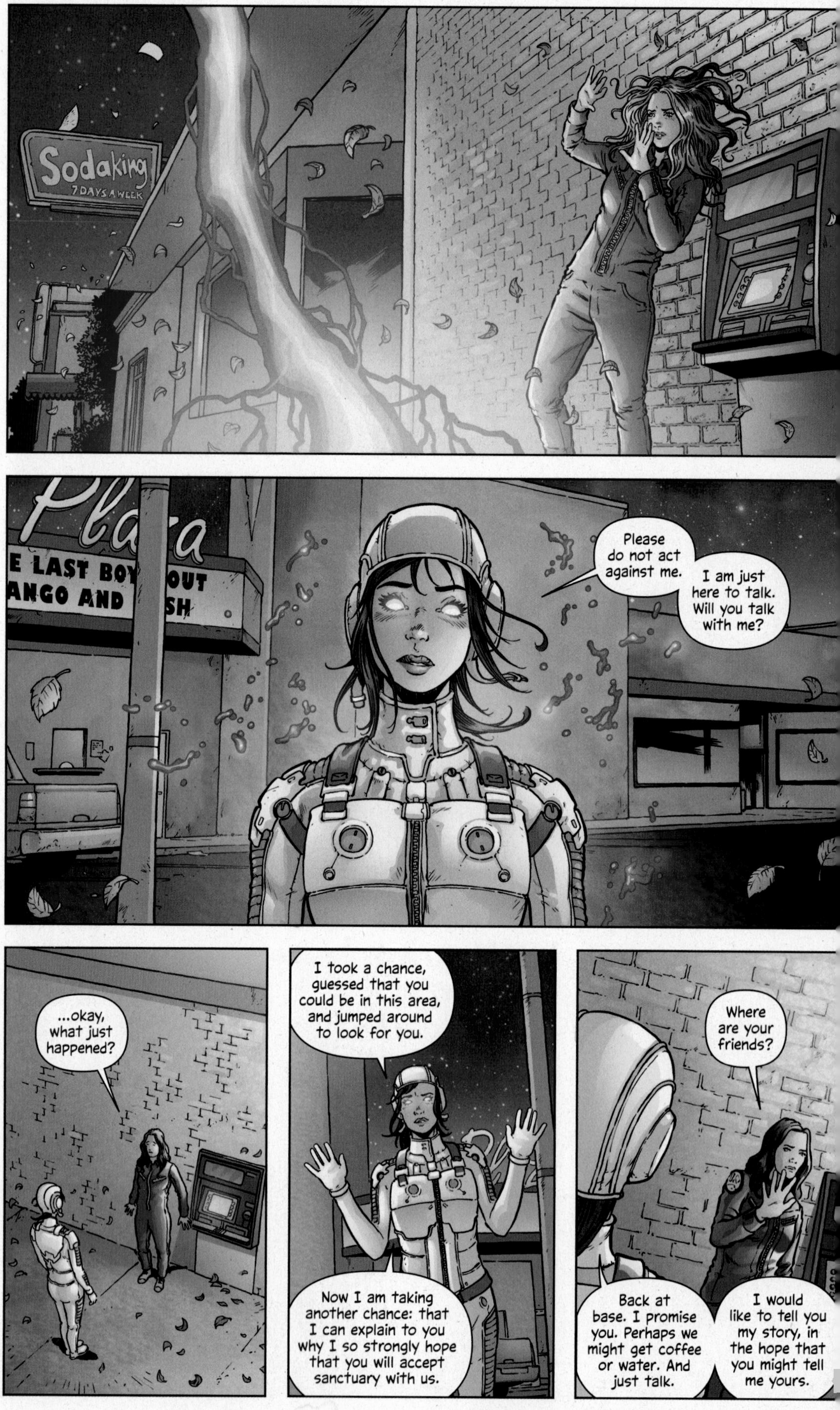
Sodaking
7 DAYS A WEEK
Plaza
E LAST BOY OUT
ANGO AND SH
Please do not act against me.
I am just here to talk. Will you talk with me?
...okay, what just happened?
I took a chance, guessed that you could be in this area, and jumped around to look for you.
Now I am taking another chance: that I can explain to you why I so strongly hope that you will accept sanctuary with us.
Where are your friends?
Back at base. I promise you. Perhaps we might get coffee or water. And just talk.
I would like to tell you my story, in the hope that you might tell me yours.

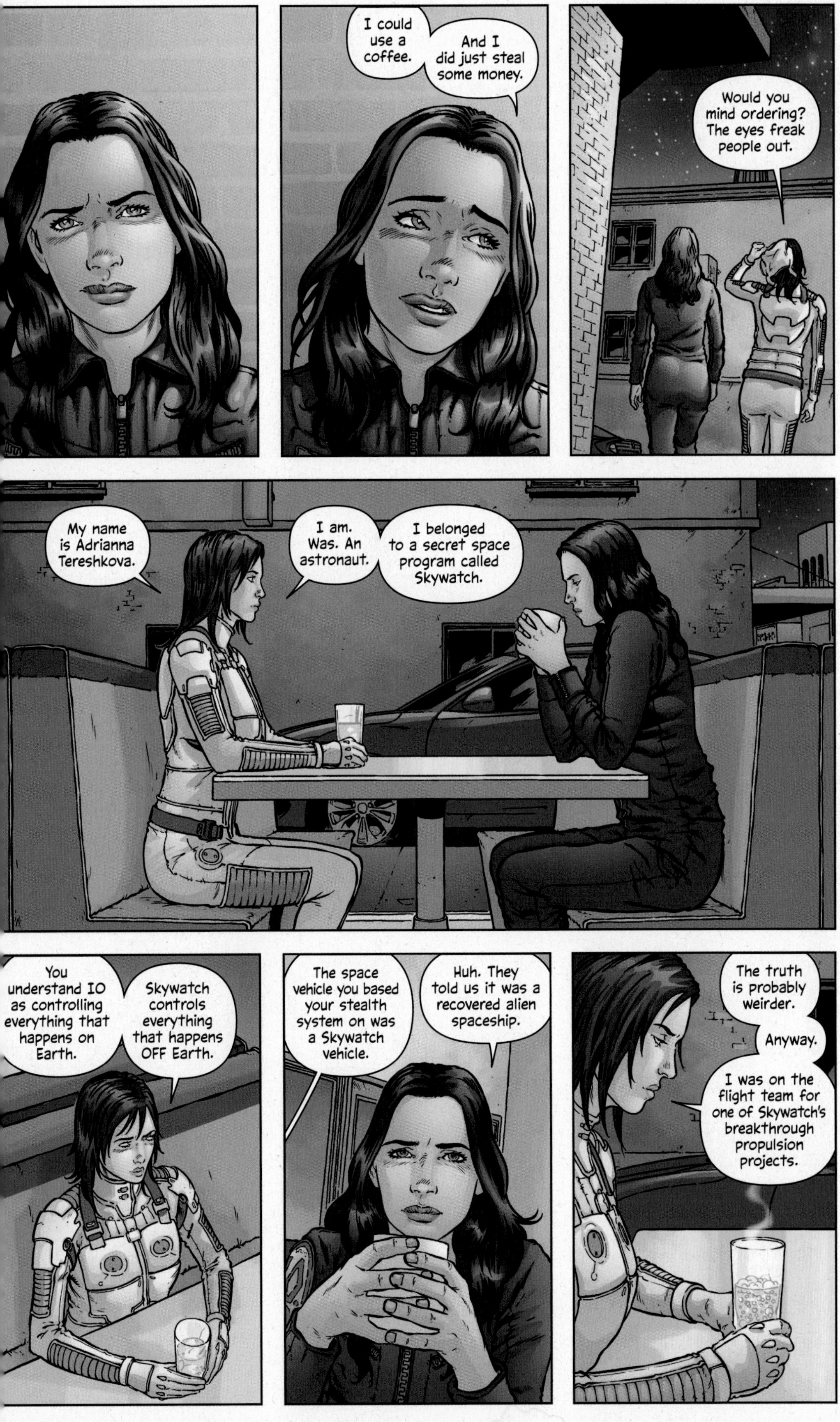
I could use a coffee.
And I did just steal some money.
Would you mind ordering? The eyes freak people out.
My name is Adrianna Tereshkova.
I am. Was. An astronaut.
I belonged to a secret space program called Skywatch.
You understand IO as controlling everything that happens on Earth.
Skywatch controls everything that happens OFF Earth.
The space vehicle you based your stealth system on was a Skywatch vehicle.
Huh. They told us it was a recovered alien spaceship.
The truth is probably weirder.
Anyway.
I was on the flight team for one of Skywatch's breakthrough propulsion projects.

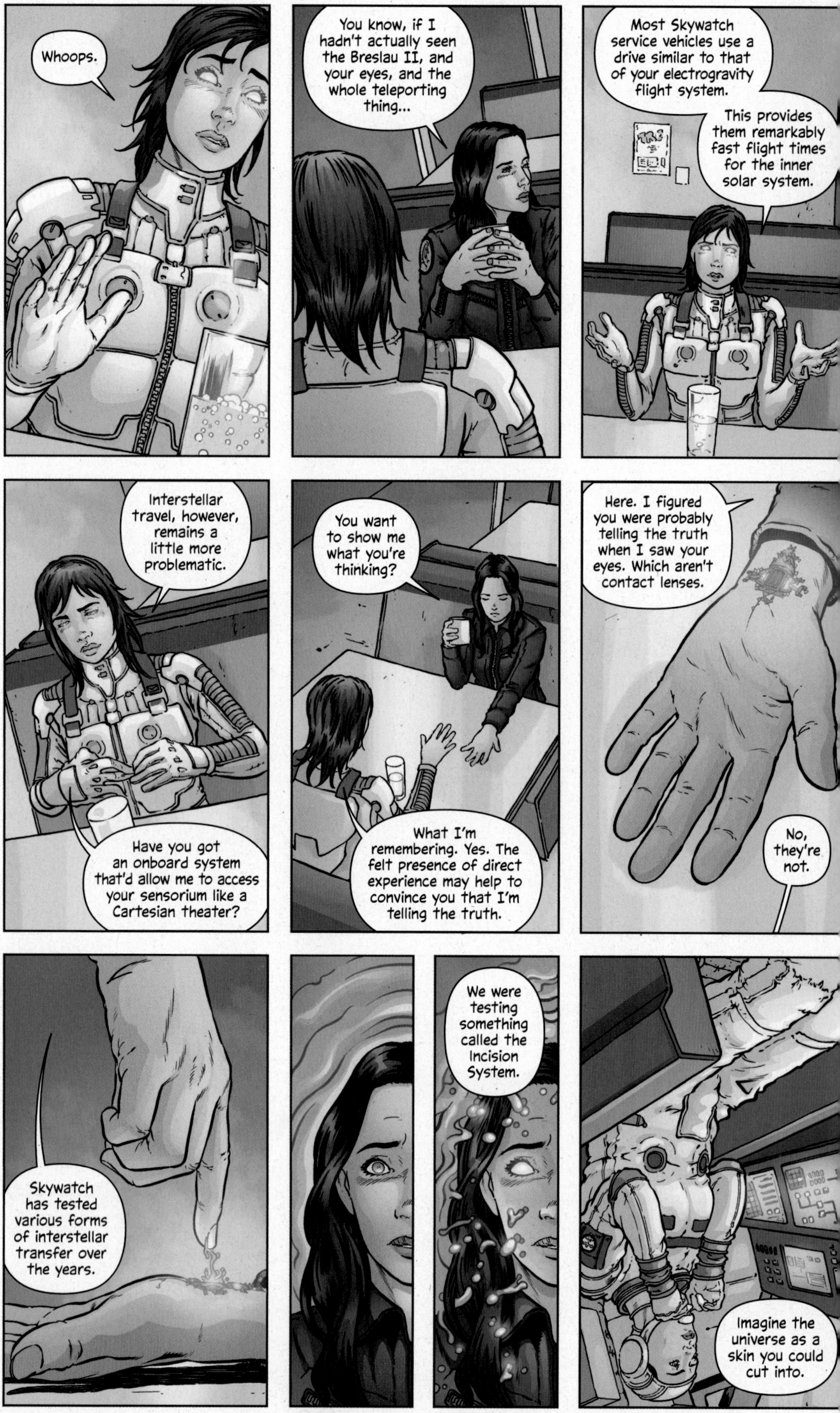
Whoops.
You know, if I hadn't actually seen the Breslau II, and your eyes, and the whole teleporting thing...
Most Skywatch service vehicles use a drive similar to that of your electrogravity flight system.
This provides them remarkably fast flight times for the inner solar system.
Interstellar travel, however, remains a little more problematic.
Have you got an onboard system that'd allow me to access your sensorium like a Cartesian theater?
You want to show me what you're thinking?
What I'm remembering. Yes. The felt presence of direct experience may help to convince you that I'm telling the truth.
Here. I figured you were probably telling the truth when I saw your eyes. Which aren't contact lenses.
No, they're not.
Skywatch has tested various forms of interstellar transfer over the years.
We were testing something called the Incision System.
Imagine the universe as a skin you could cut into.

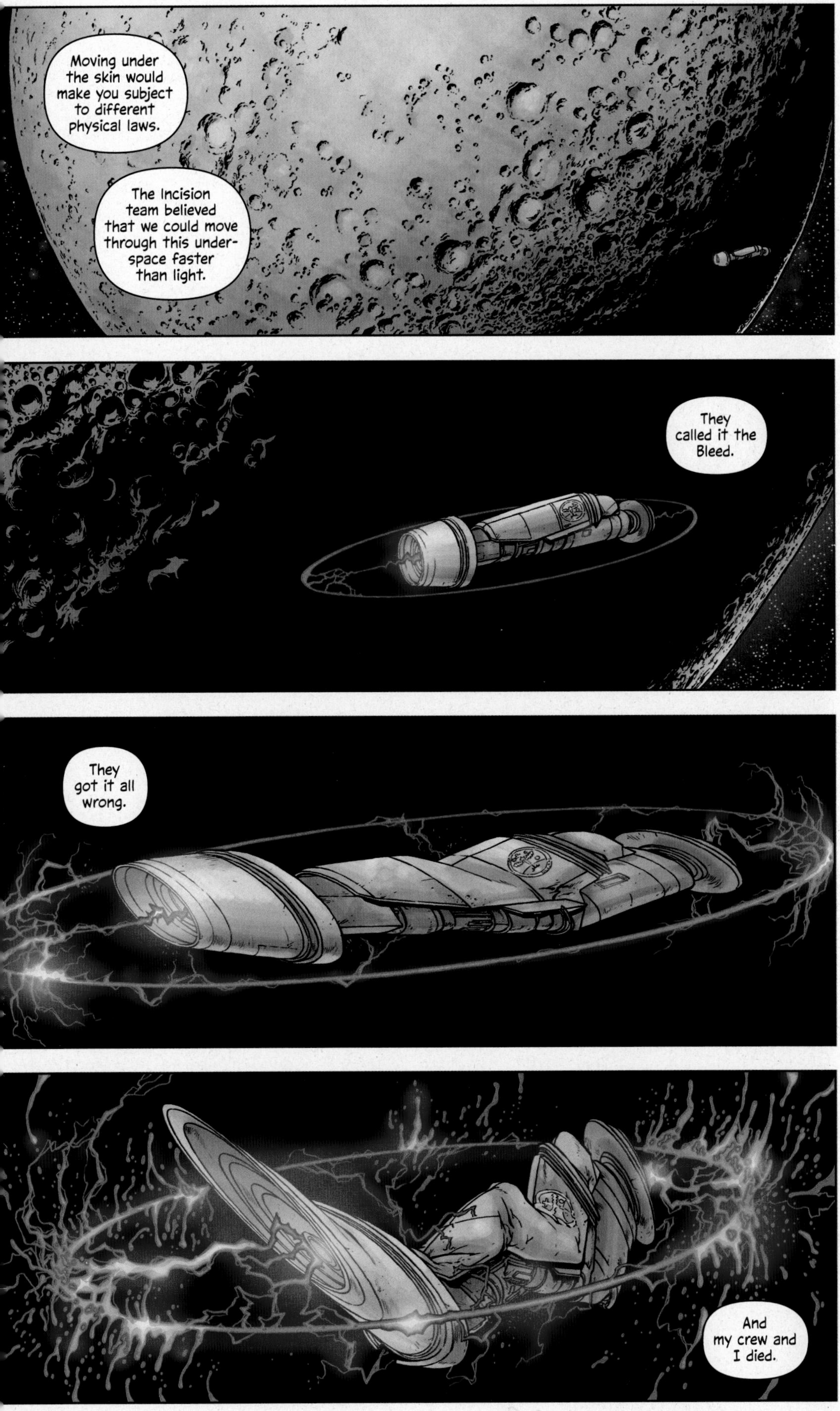
Moving under the skin would make you subject to different physical laws.
The Incision team believed that we could move through this under-space faster than light.
They called it the Bleed.
They got it all wrong.
And my crew and I died.

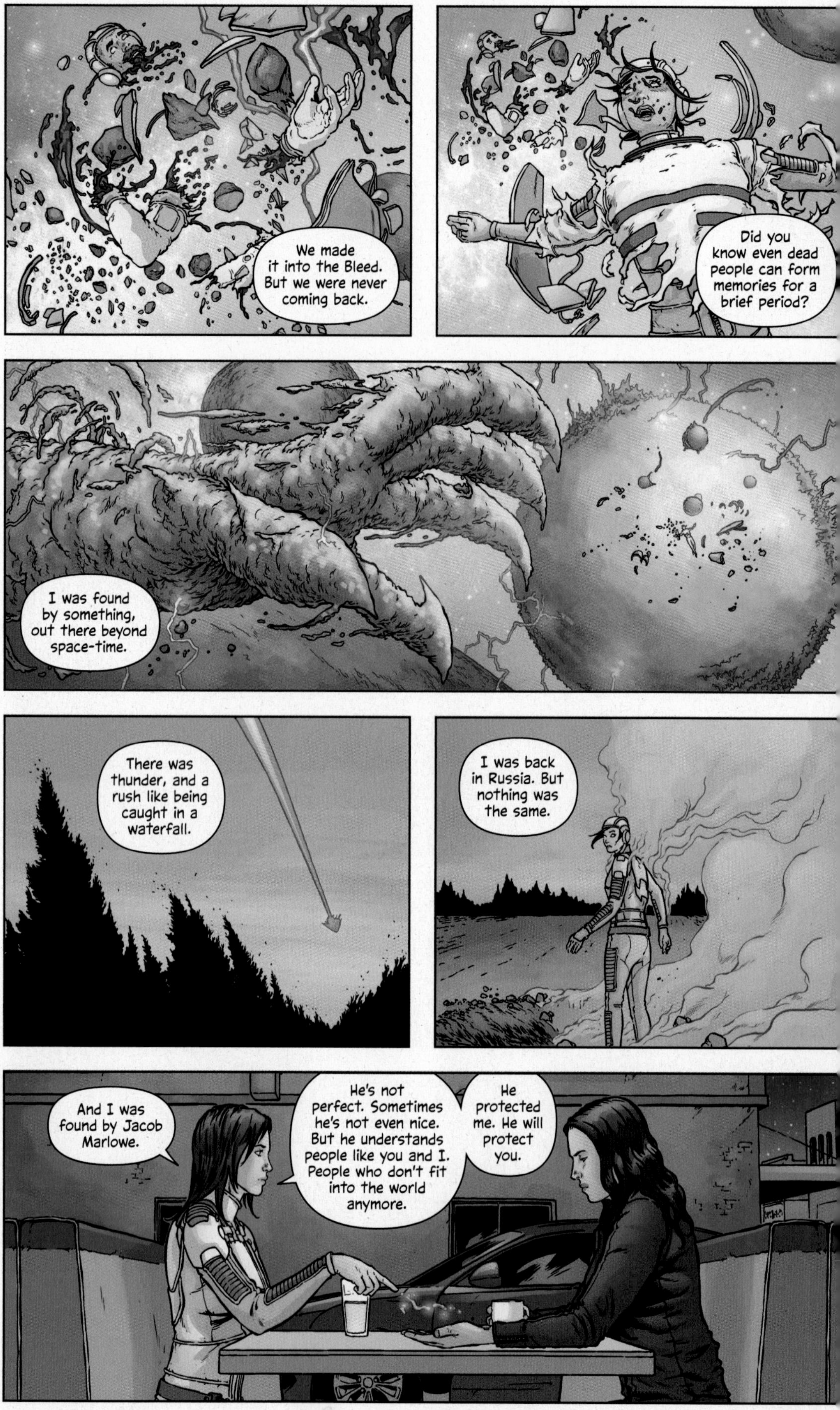
We made it into the Bleed. But we were never coming back.
Did you know even dead people can form memories for a brief period?
I was found by something, out there beyond space-time.
There was thunder, and a rush like being caught in a waterfall.
I was back in Russia. But nothing was the same.
And I was found by Jacob Marlowe.
He's not perfect. Sometimes he's not even nice. But he understands people like you and I. People who don't fit into the world anymore.
He protected me. He will protect you.

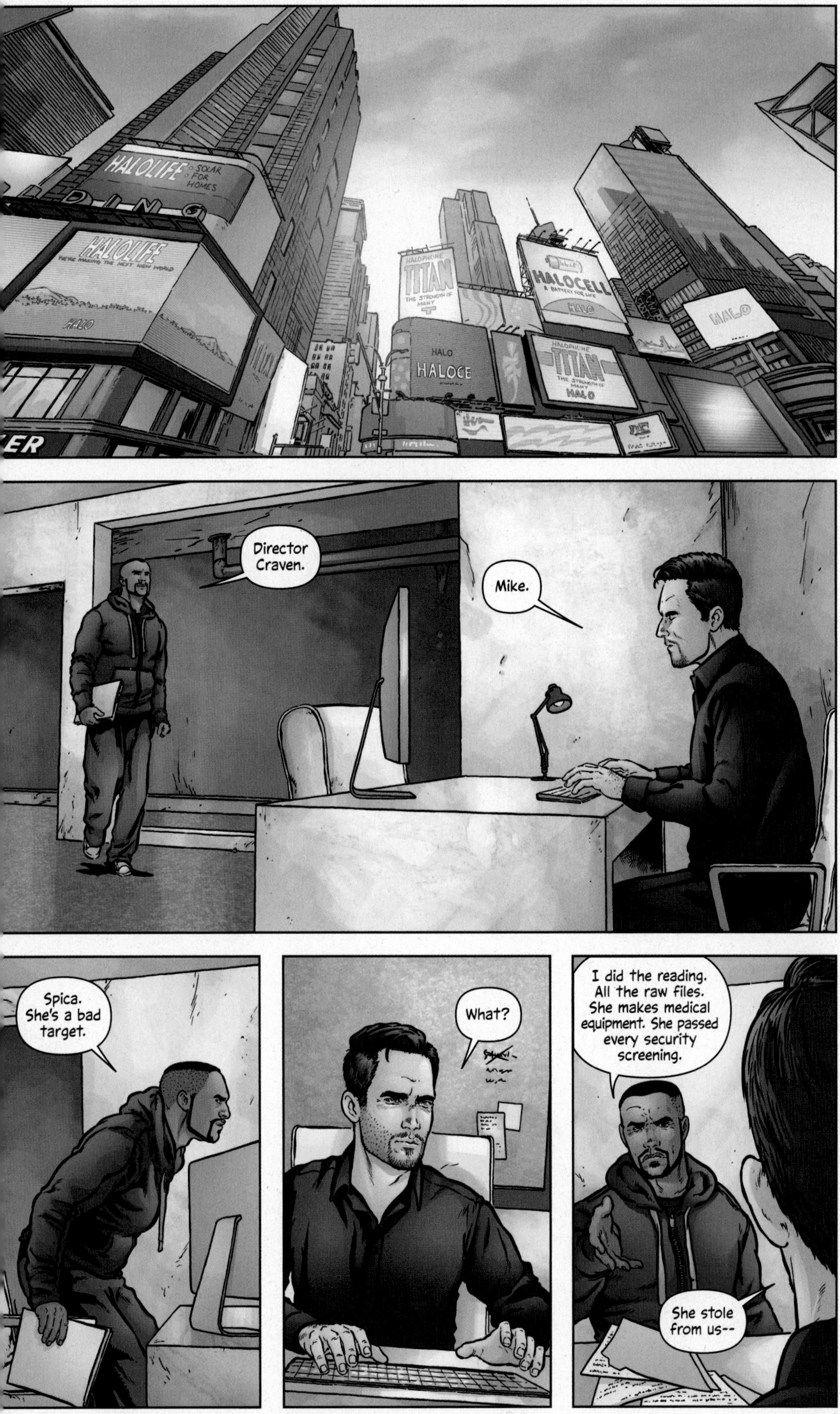
HALOLIFE
SOLAR FOR HOMES
HALOLIFE
WE'RE MAKING THE NEXT NEW WORLD
HALO
HALOPHONE
TITAN
THE STRENGTH OF MANY
HALOCELL
A BATTERY FOR LIFE
HALO
HALO
HALO
HALOCE
HALOPHONE
TITAN
THE STRENGTH OF MANY
HALO
Director Craven.
Mike.
Spica. She's a bad target.
What?
I did the reading. All the raw files. She makes medical equipment. She passed every security screening.
She stole from us--

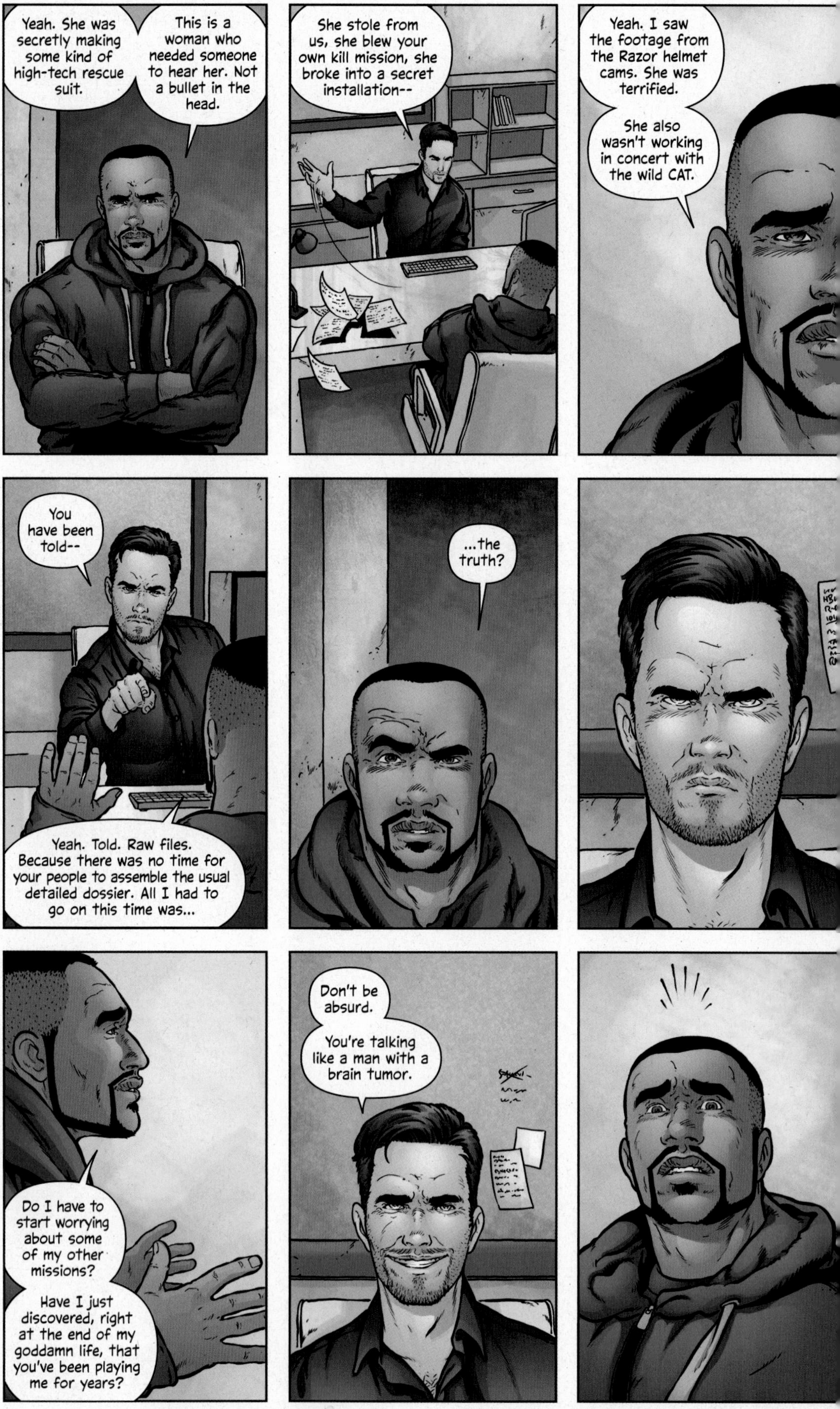
Yeah. She was secretly making some kind of high-tech rescue suit.
This is a woman who needed someone to hear her. Not a bullet in the head.
She stole from us, she blew your own kill mission, she broke into a secret installation--
Yeah. I saw the footage from the Razor helmet cams. She was terrified.
She also wasn't working in concert with the wild CAT.
You have been told--
Yeah. Told. Raw files. Because there was no time for your people to assemble the usual detailed dossier. All I had to go on this time was...
...the truth?
Do I have to start worrying about some of my other missions?
Have I just discovered, right at the end of my goddamn life, that you've been playing me for years?
Don't be absurd.
You're talking like a man with a brain tumor.

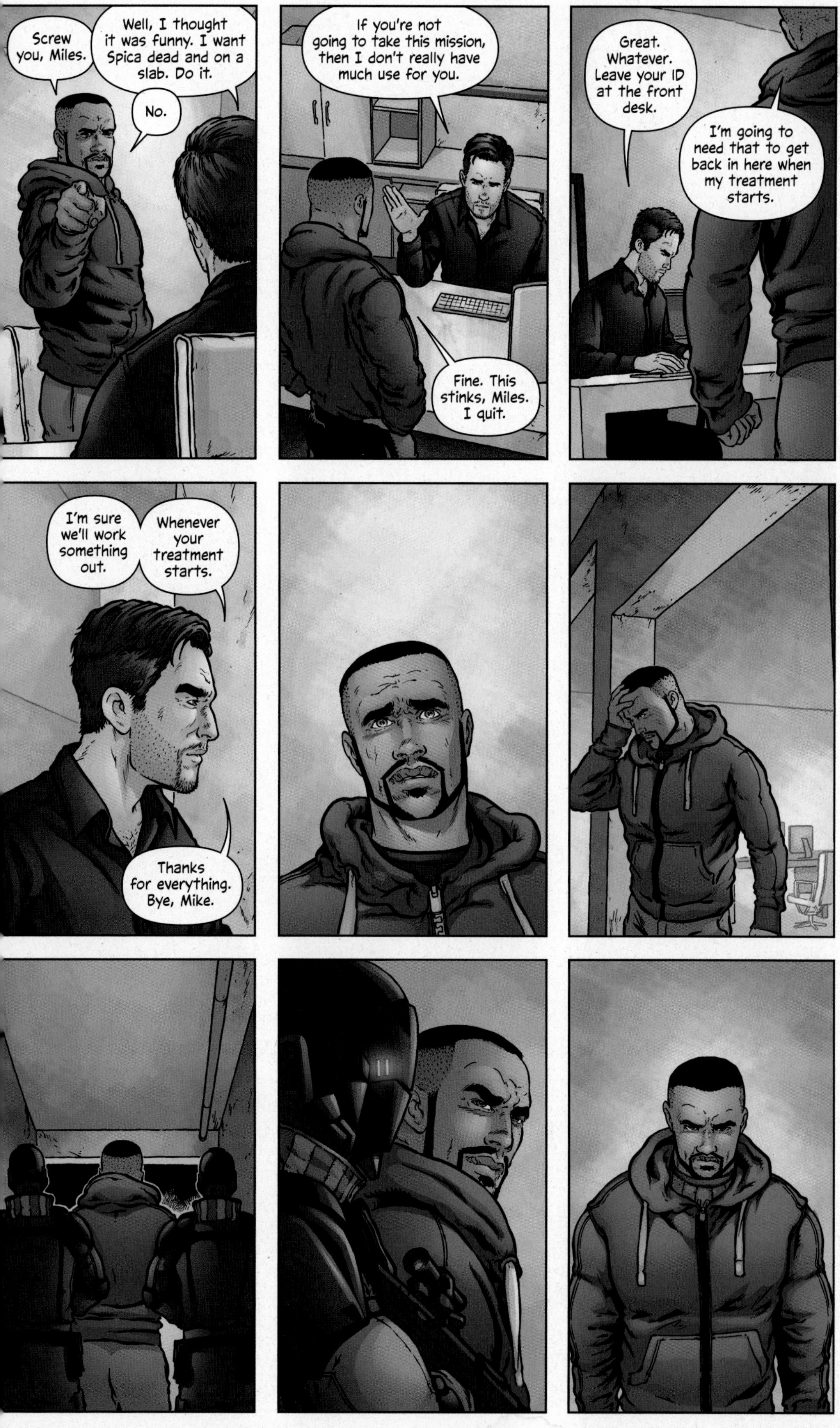
Screw you, Miles.
Well, I thought it was funny. I want Spica dead and on a slab. Do it.
No.
If you're not going to take this mission, then I don't really have much use for you.
Fine. This stinks, Miles. I quit.
Great. Whatever. Leave your ID at the front desk.
I'm going to need that to get back in here when my treatment starts.
I'm sure we'll work something out.
Whenever your treatment starts.
Thanks for everything. Bye, Mike.

--and I said to him, my little Mikey ain't going to be like that, talking the talk but pistol-whipping his own tailor, Jesus--

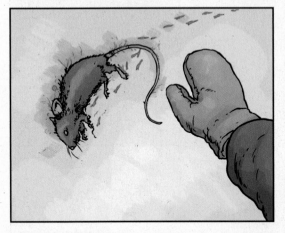

--said leave him ALONE--

all RIGHT all RIGHT--

--all of it. I want to see everything there is.

You're not going to hurt me, are you, Mike?

Never in hell. You don't deserve that. Ever.

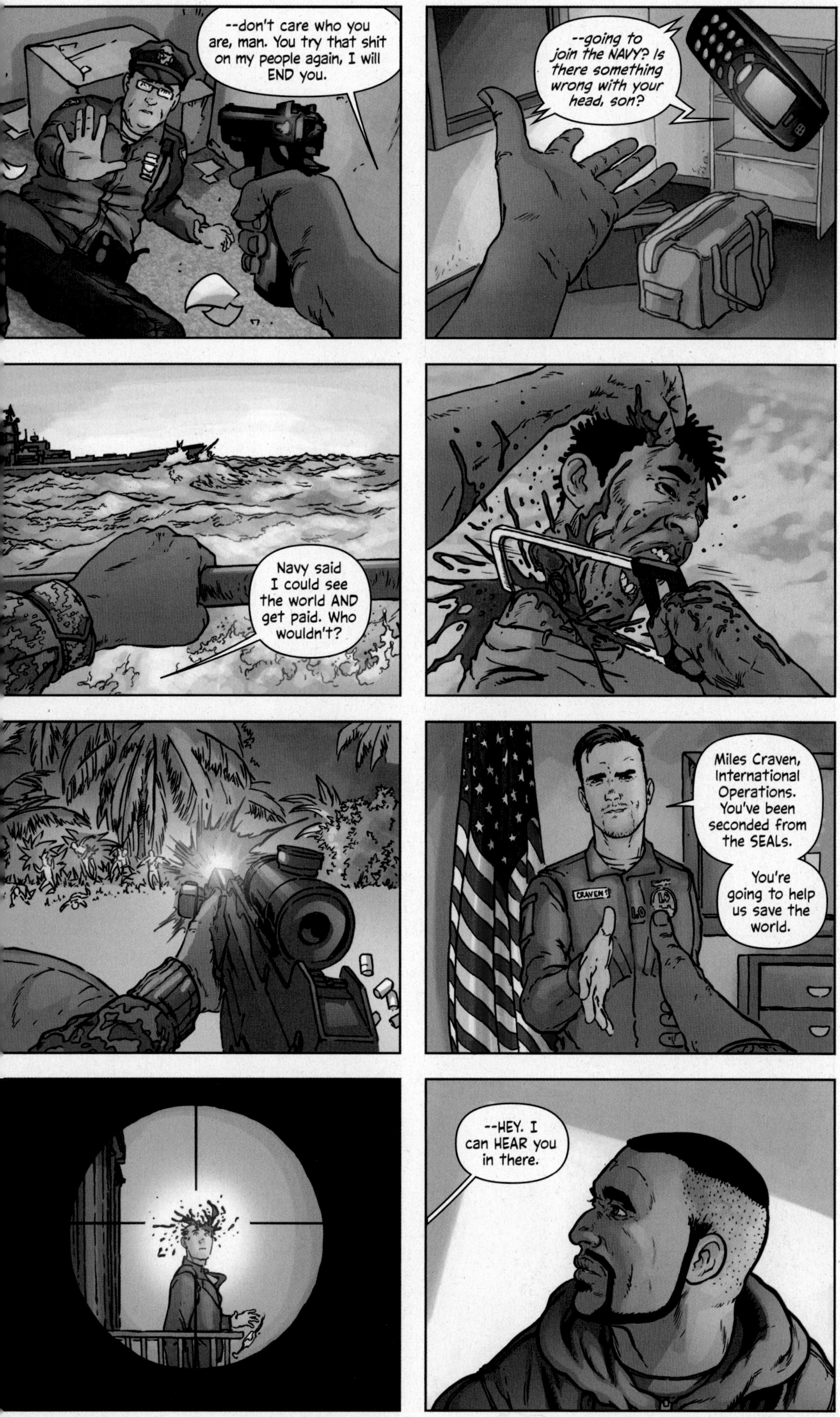
--don't care who you are, man. You try that shit on my people again, I will END you.
--going to join the NAVY? Is there something wrong with your head, son?
Navy said I could see the world AND get paid. Who wouldn't?
Miles Craven, International Operations. You've been seconded from the SEALs.
You're going to help us save the world.
CRAVEN
--HEY. I can HEAR you in there.

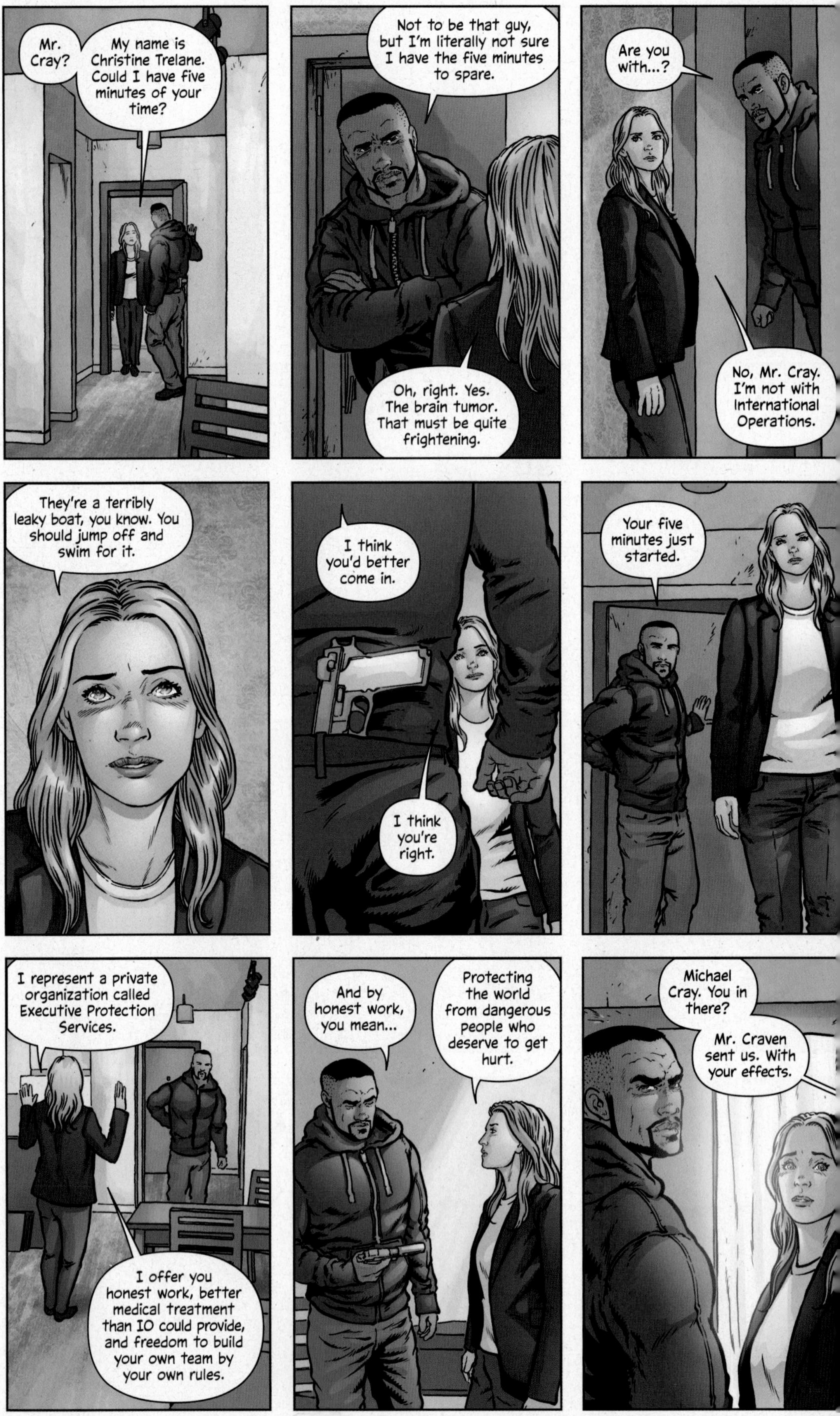
Mr. Cray?
My name is Christine Trelane. Could I have five minutes of your time?
Not to be that guy, but I'm literally not sure I have the five minutes to spare.
Oh, right. Yes. The brain tumor. That must be quite frightening.
Are you with...?
No, Mr. Cray. I'm not with International Operations.
They're a terribly leaky boat, you know. You should jump off and swim for it.
I think you'd better come in.
I think you're right.
Your five minutes just started.
I represent a private organization called Executive Protection Services.
I offer you honest work, better medical treatment than IO could provide, and freedom to build your own team by your own rules.
And by honest work, you mean...
Protecting the world from dangerous people who deserve to get hurt.
Michael Cray. You in there?
Mr. Craven sent us. With your effects.

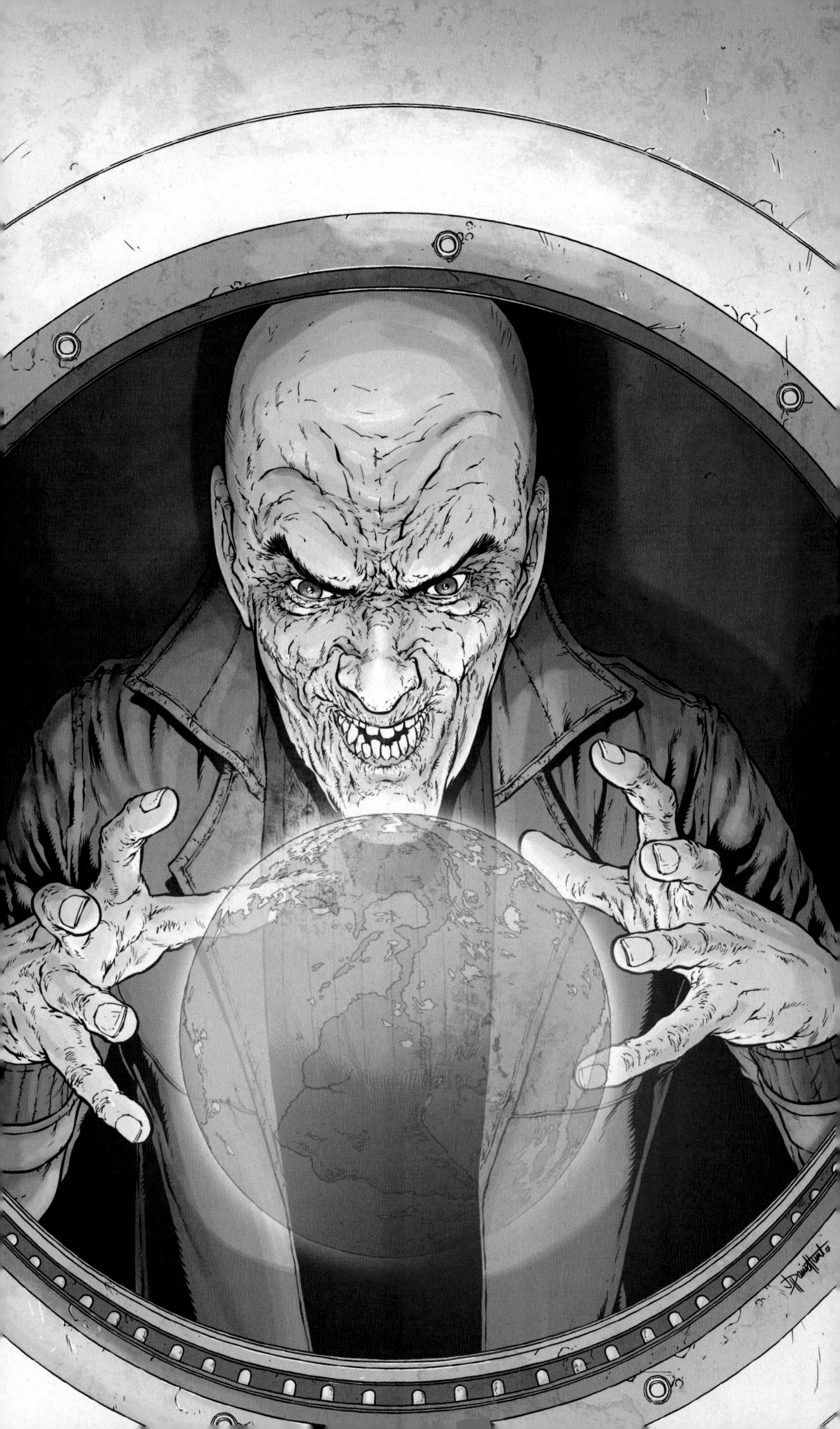

6

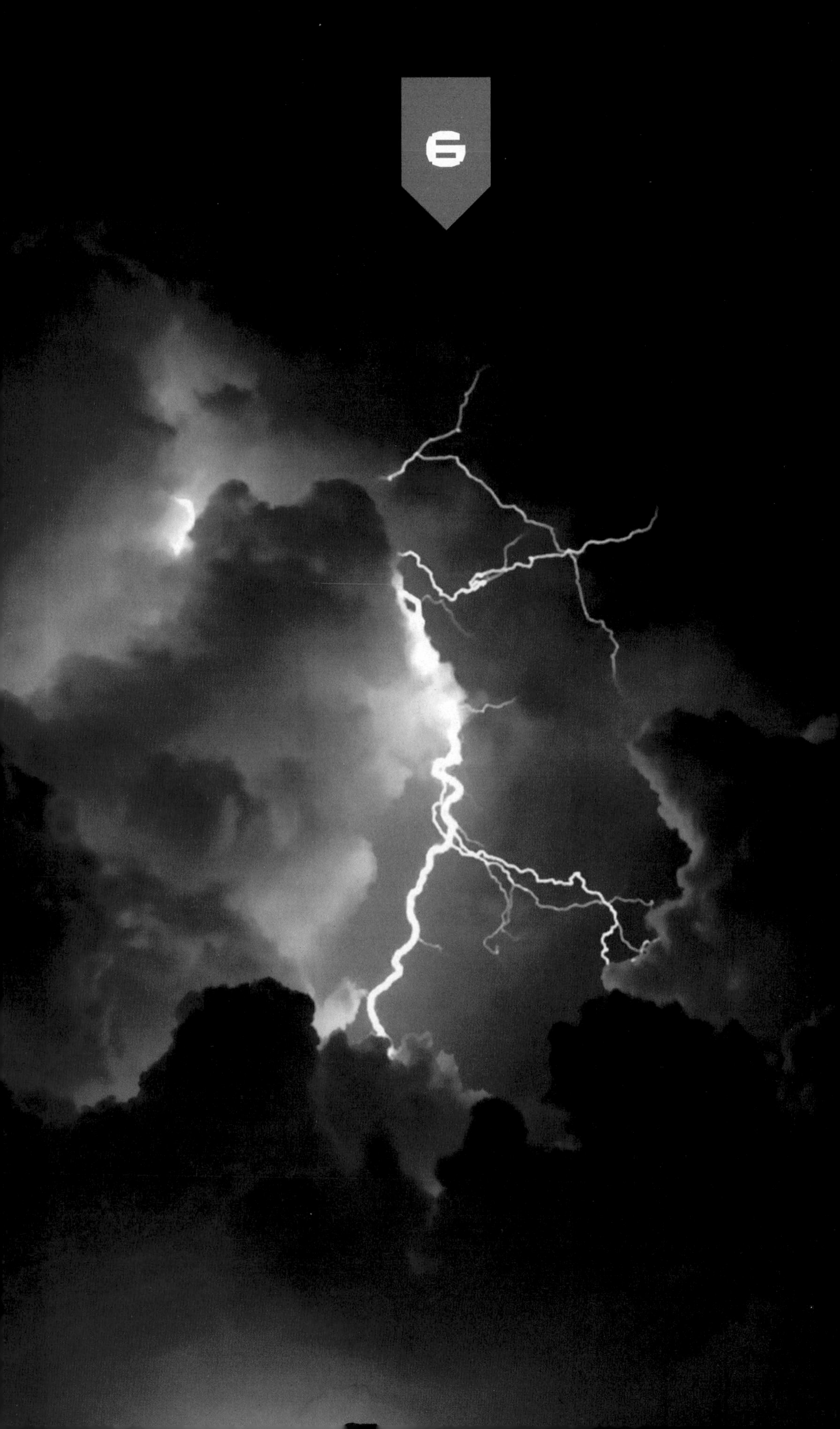

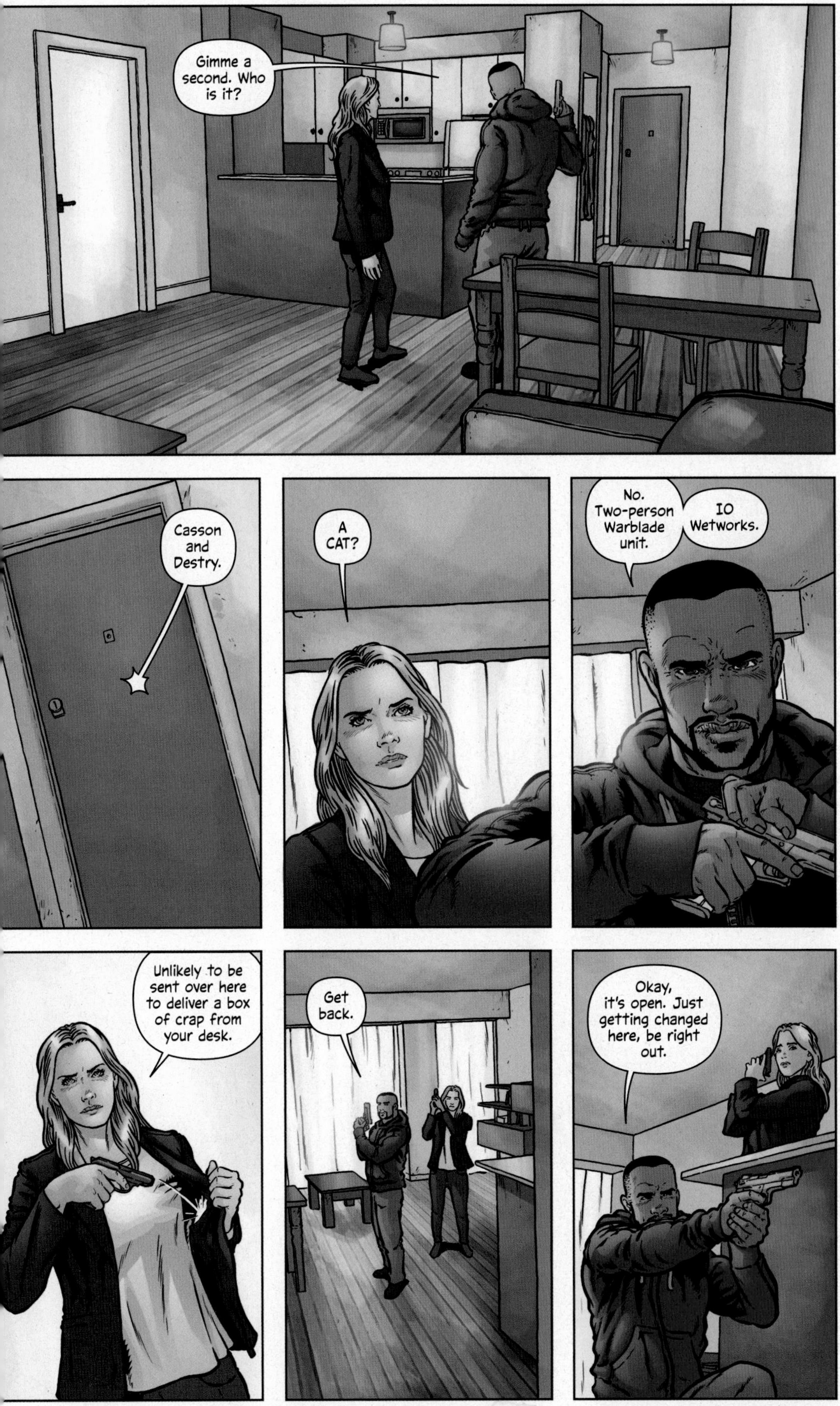
Gimme a second. Who is it?
Casson and Destry.
A CAT?
No. Two-person Warblade unit.
IO Wetworks.
Unlikely to be sent over here to deliver a box of crap from your desk.
Get back.
Okay, it's open. Just getting changed here, be right out.

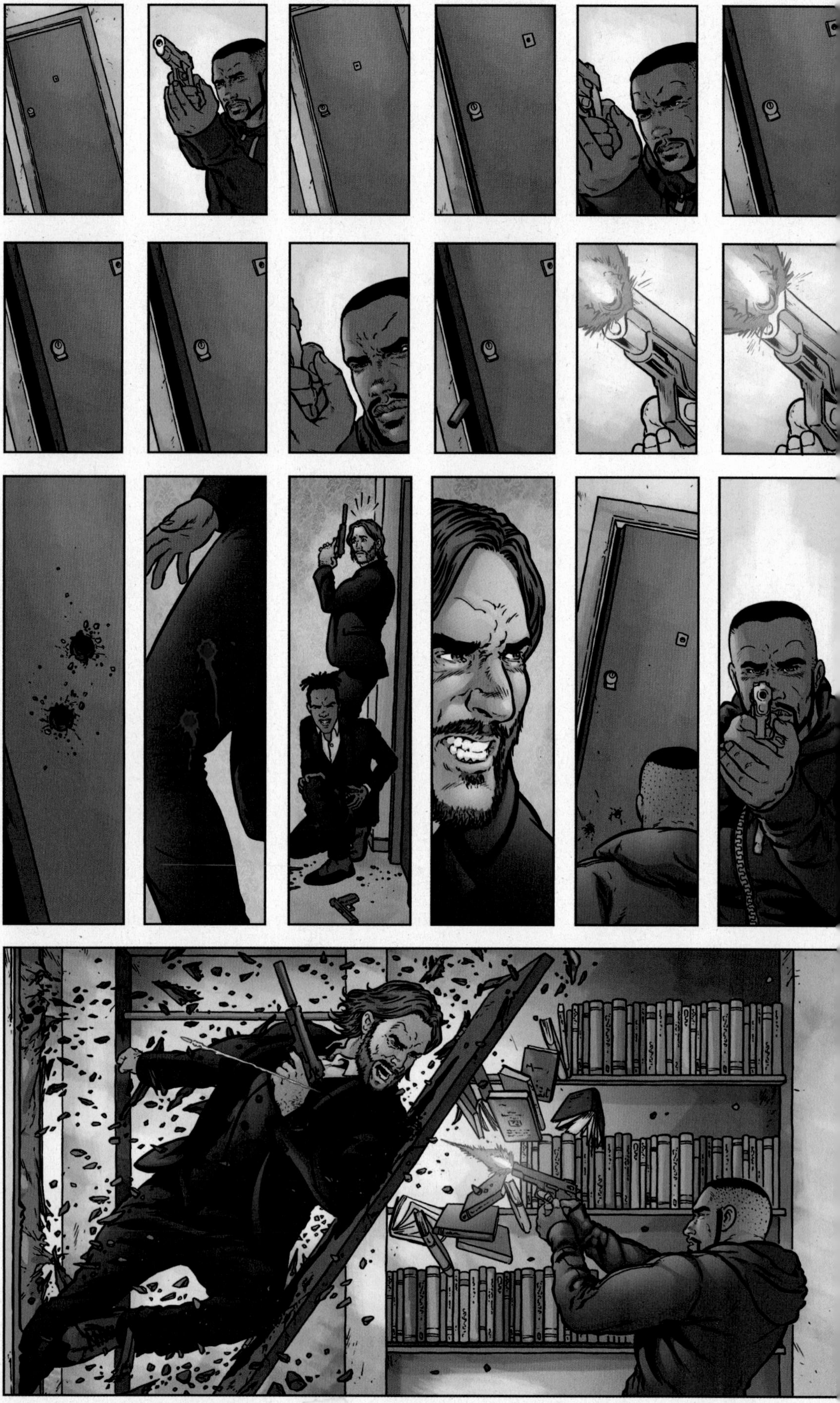

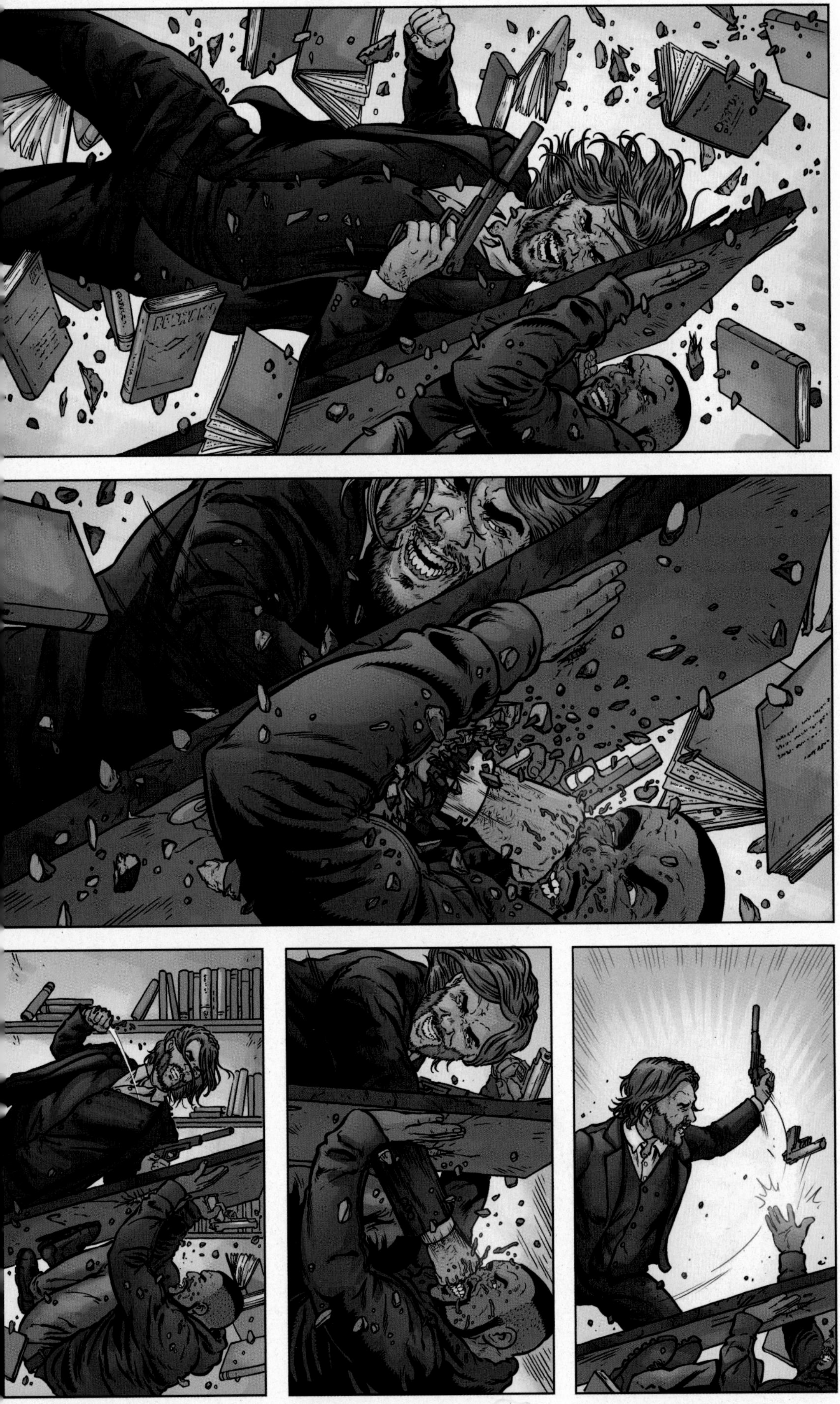

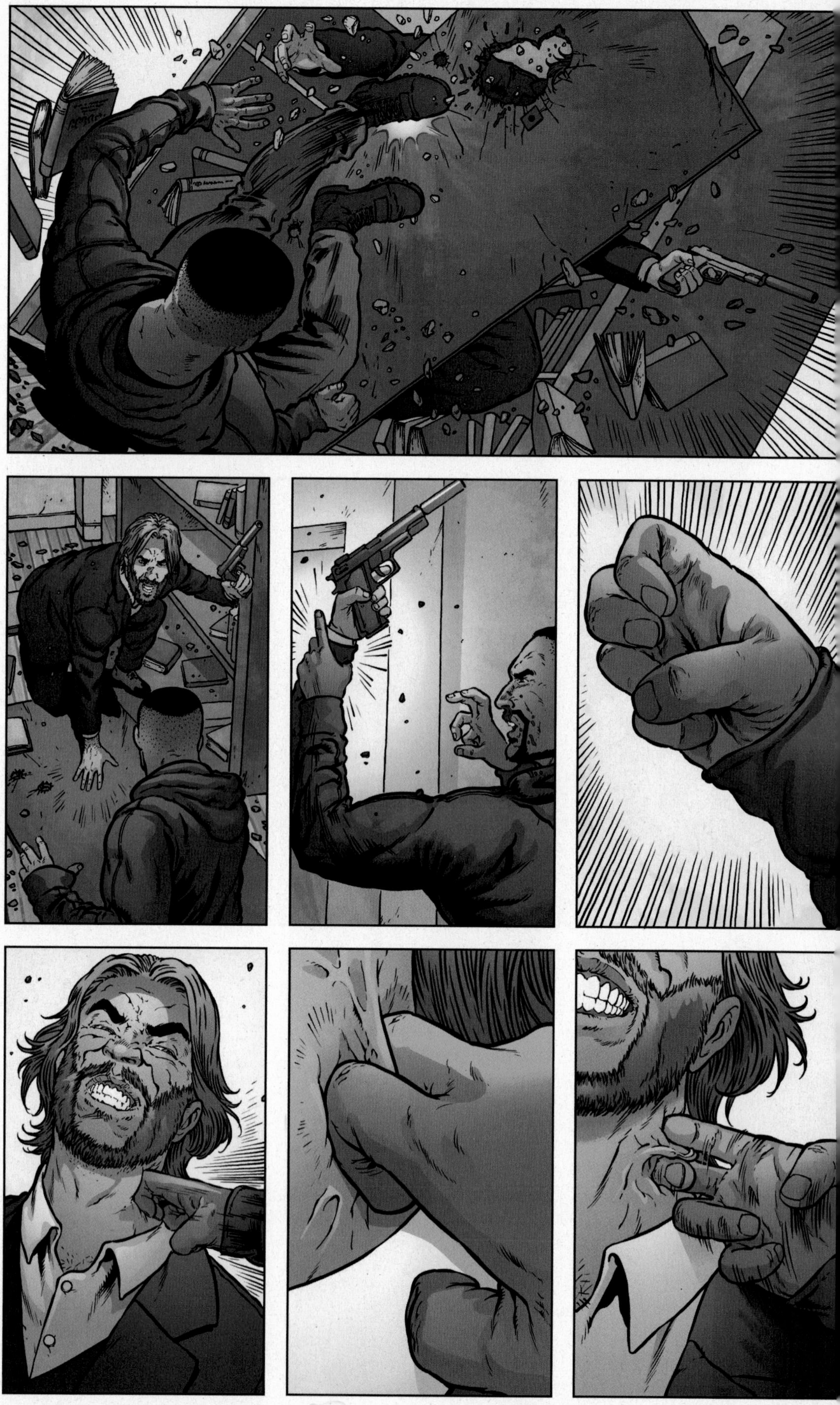

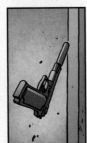

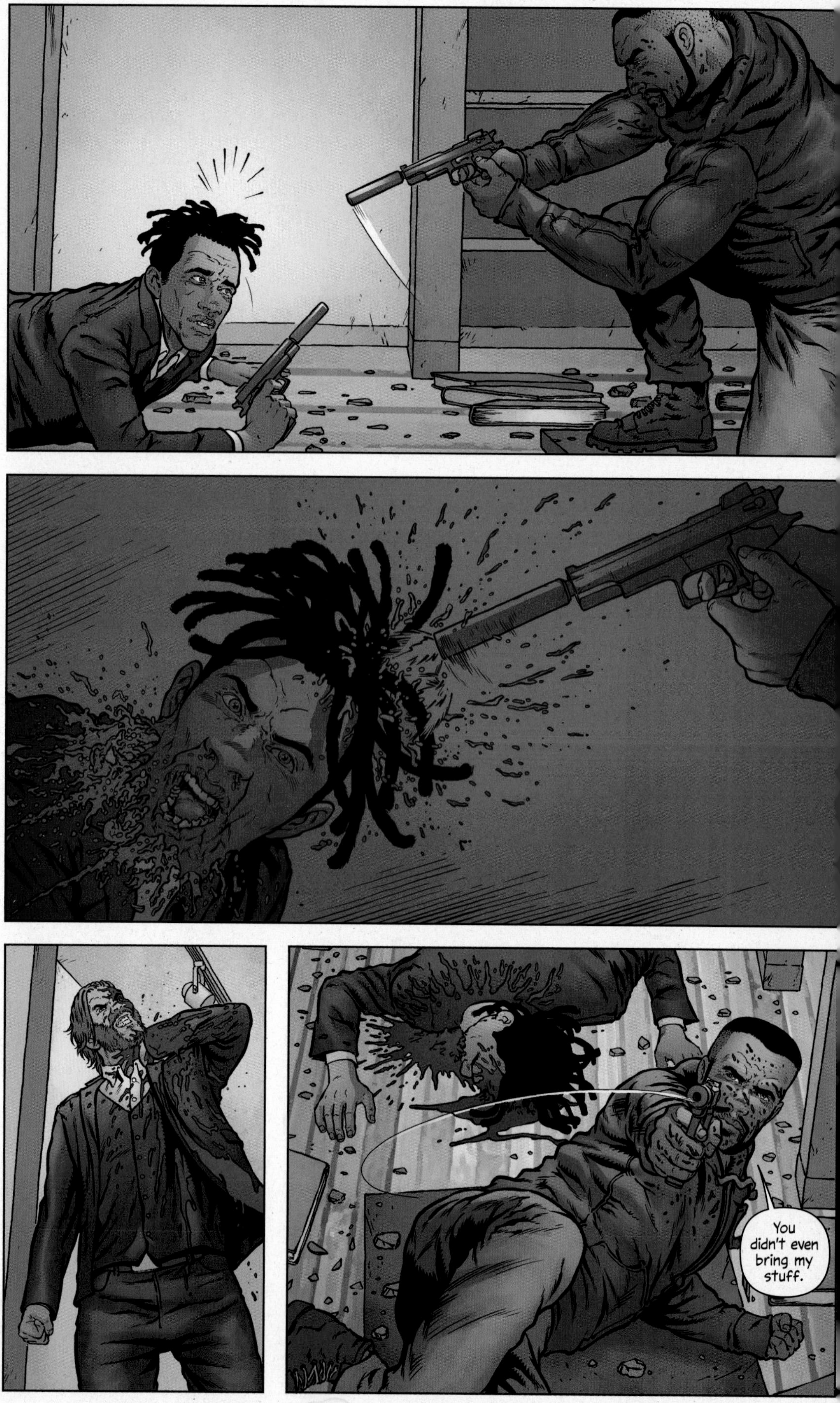
You didn't even bring my stuff.

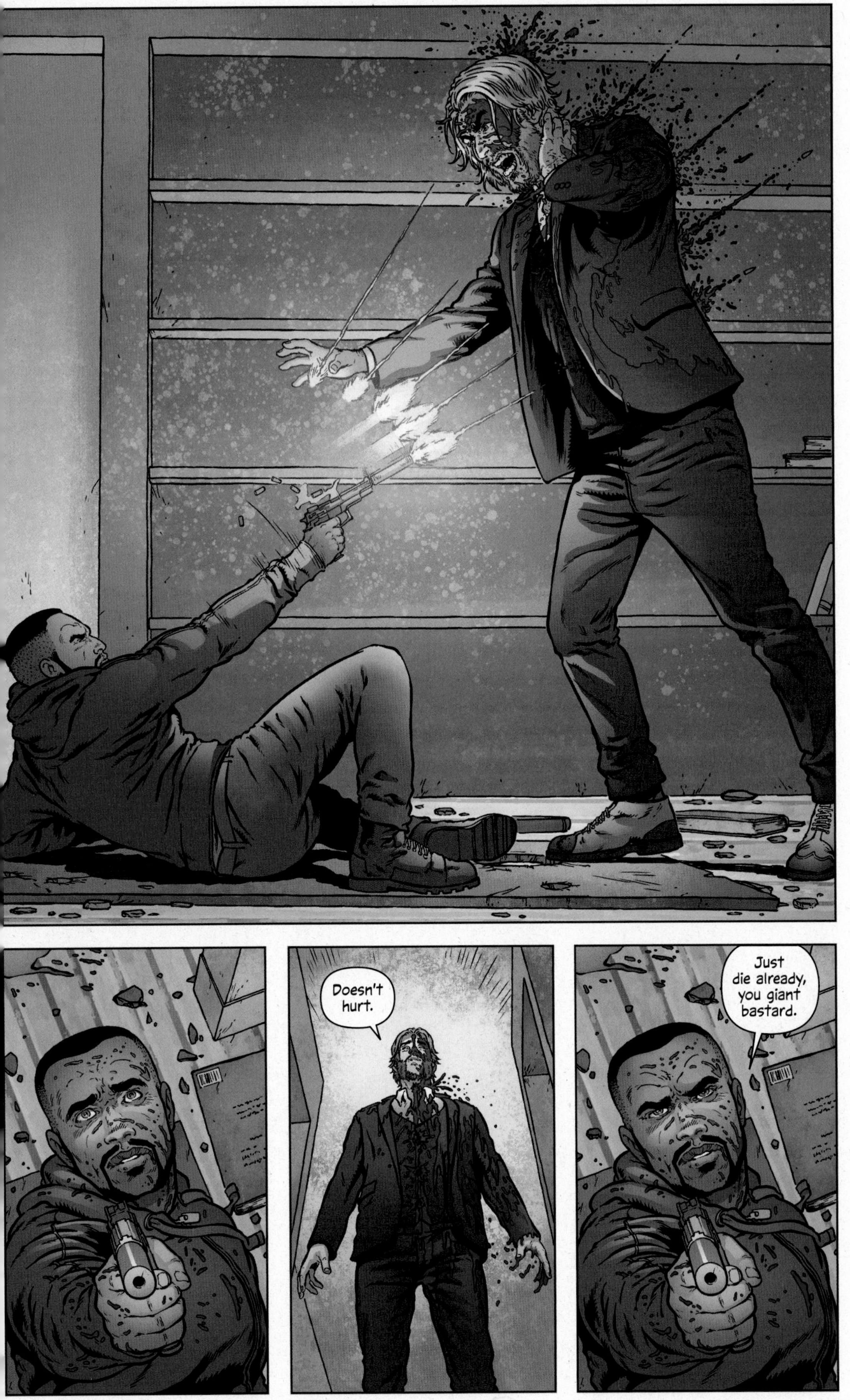
Doesn't hurt.
Just die already, you giant bastard.

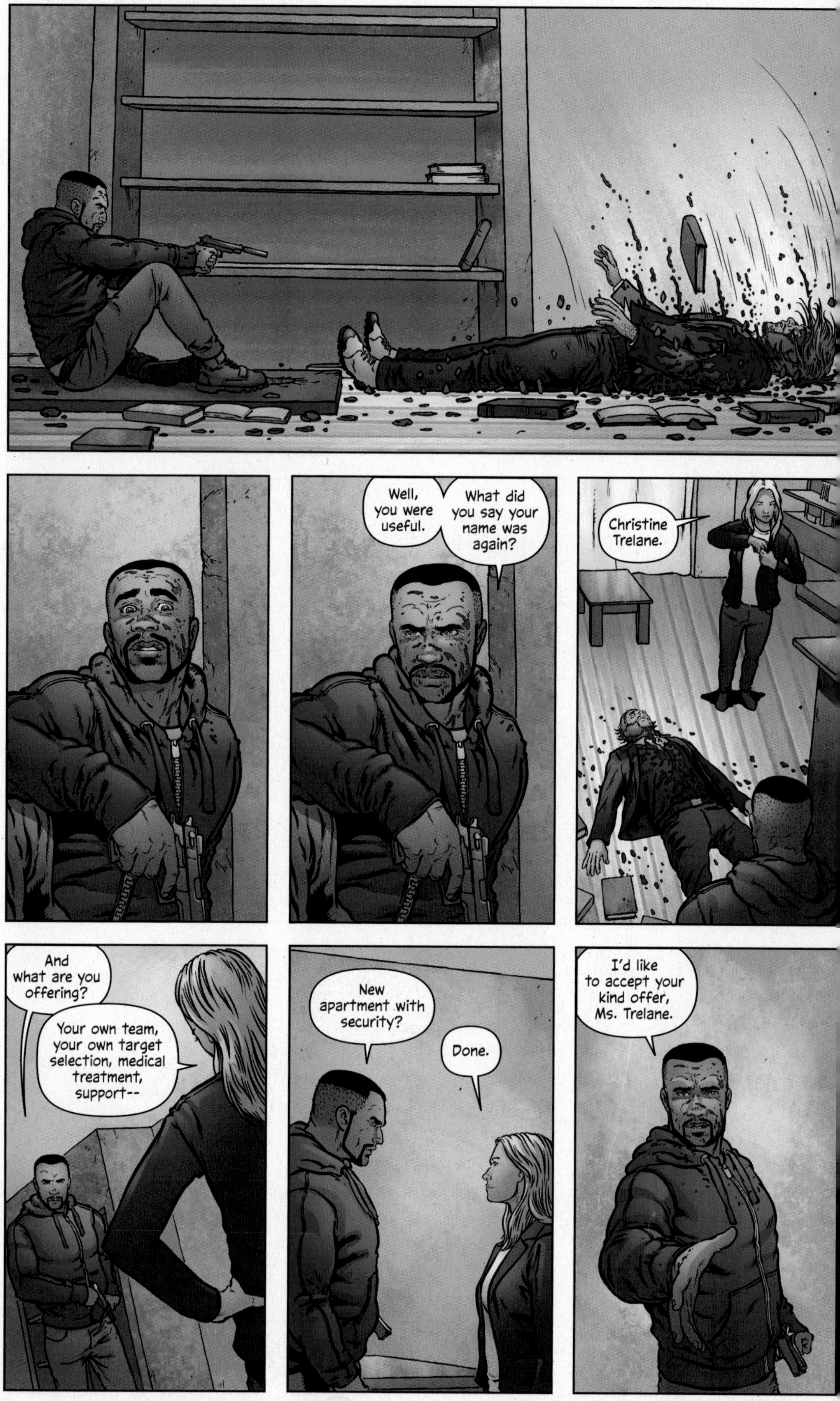
Well, you were useful.
What did you say your name was again?
Christine Trelane.
And what are you offering?
Your own team, your own target selection, medical treatment, support--
New apartment with security?
Done.
I'd like to accept your kind offer, Ms. Trelane.

Well, that was awful.
Where are we? Secret headquarters? Volcano base? Space station?
Brooklyn.

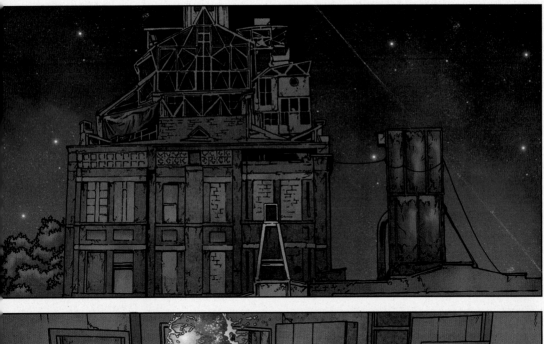

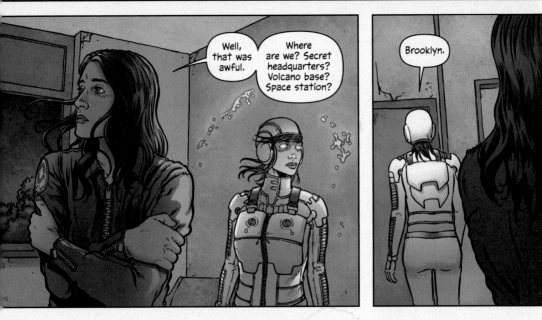

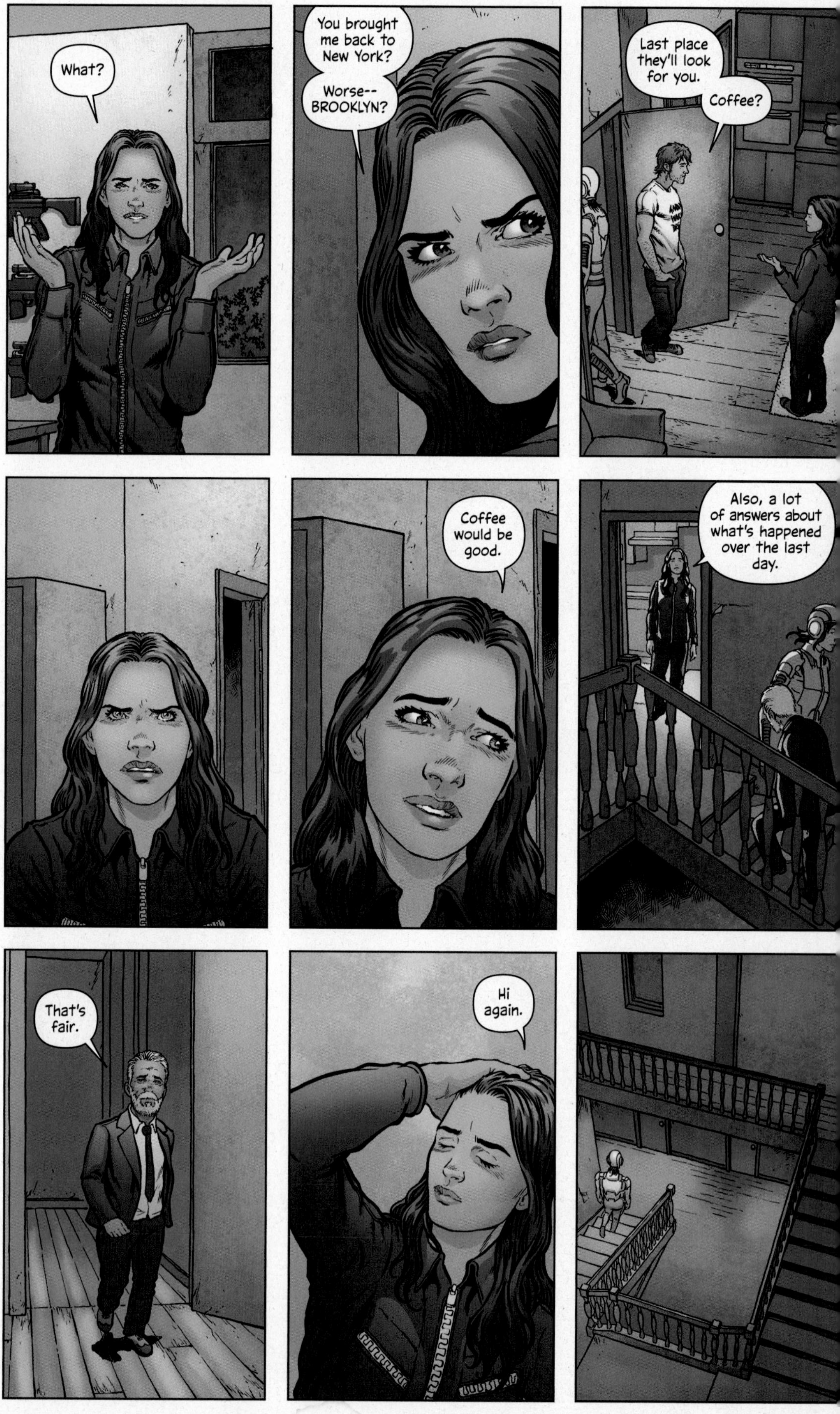
What?
You brought me back to New York?
Worse-- BROOKLYN?
Last place they'll look for you.
Coffee?
Coffee would be good.
Also, a lot of answers about what's happened over the last day.
That's fair.
Hi again.

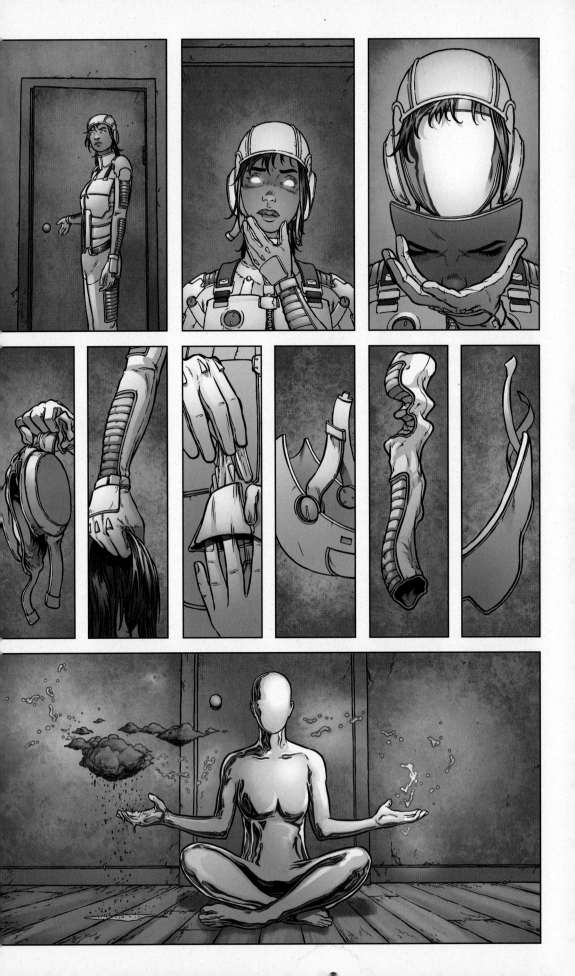

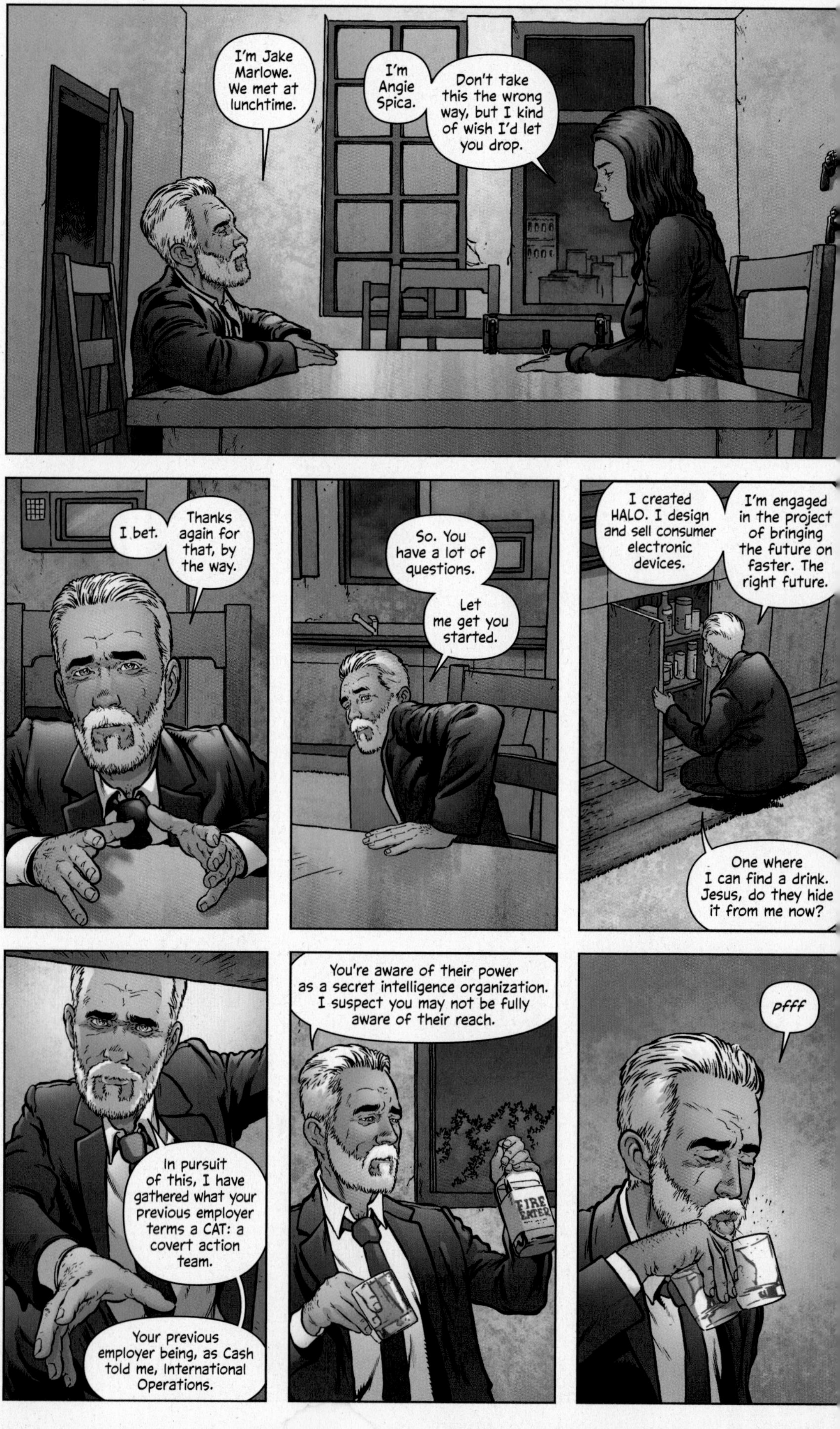

I'm Jake Marlowe. We met at lunchtime.
I'm Angie Spica.
Don't take this the wrong way, but I kind of wish I'd let you drop.
I bet.
Thanks again for that, by the way.
So. You have a lot of questions.
Let me get you started.
I created HALO. I design and sell consumer electronic devices.
I'm engaged in the project of bringing the future on faster. The right future.
One where I can find a drink. Jesus, do they hide it from me now?
In pursuit of this, I have gathered what your previous employer terms a CAT: a covert action team.
Your previous employer being, as Cash told me, International Operations.
You're aware of their power as a secret intelligence organization. I suspect you may not be fully aware of their reach.
FIRE EATER
pfff

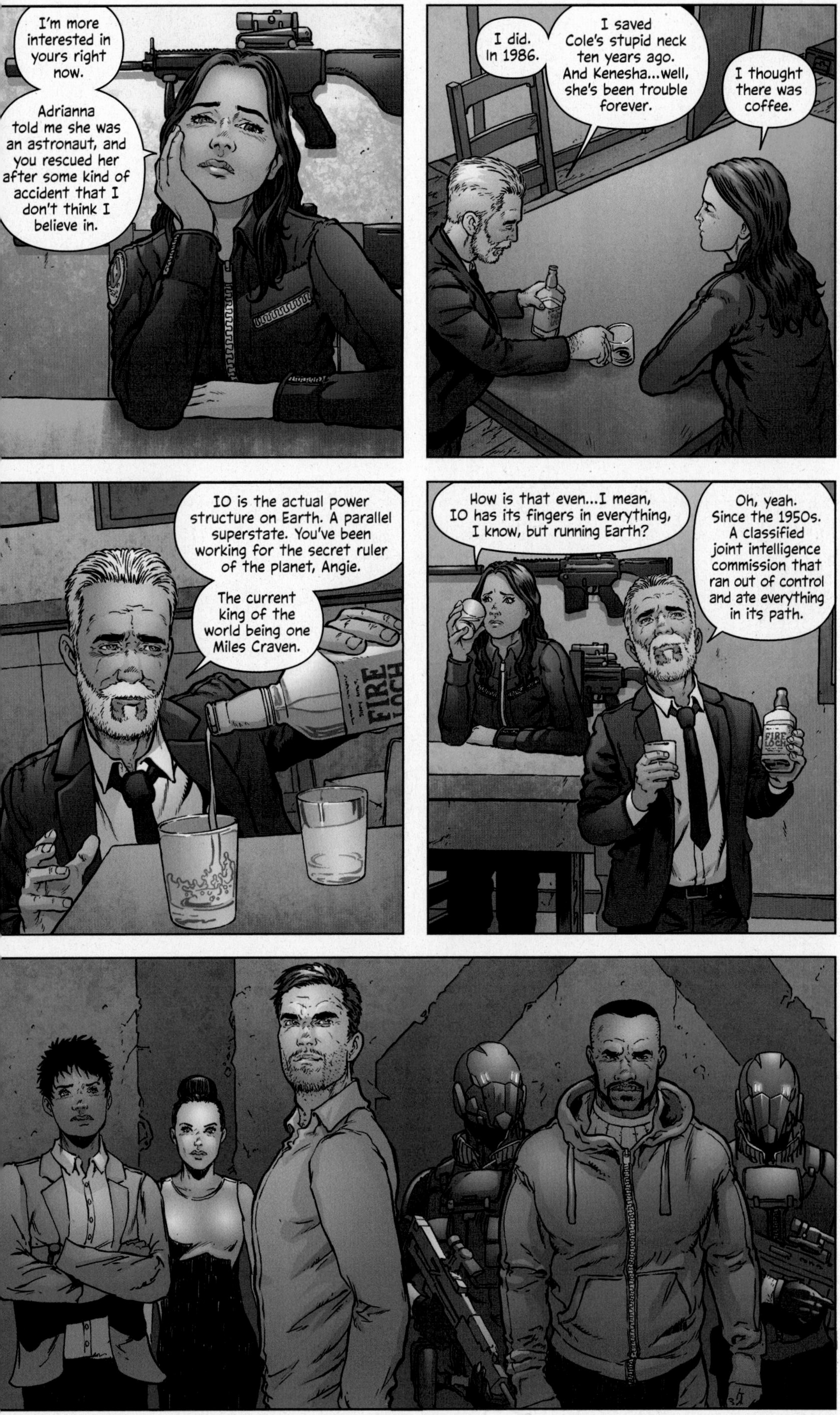
I'm more interested in yours right now.
Adrianna told me she was an astronaut, and you rescued her after some kind of accident that I don't think I believe in.
I did. In 1986.
I saved Cole's stupid neck ten years ago. And Kenesha...well, she's been trouble forever.
I thought there was coffee.
IO is the actual power structure on Earth. A parallel superstate. You've been working for the secret ruler of the planet, Angie.
The current king of the world being one Miles Craven.
FIRE LOCH
How is that even...I mean, IO has its fingers in everything, I know, but running Earth?
Oh, yeah. Since the 1950s. A classified joint intelligence commission that ran out of control and ate everything in its path.
FIRE LOCH

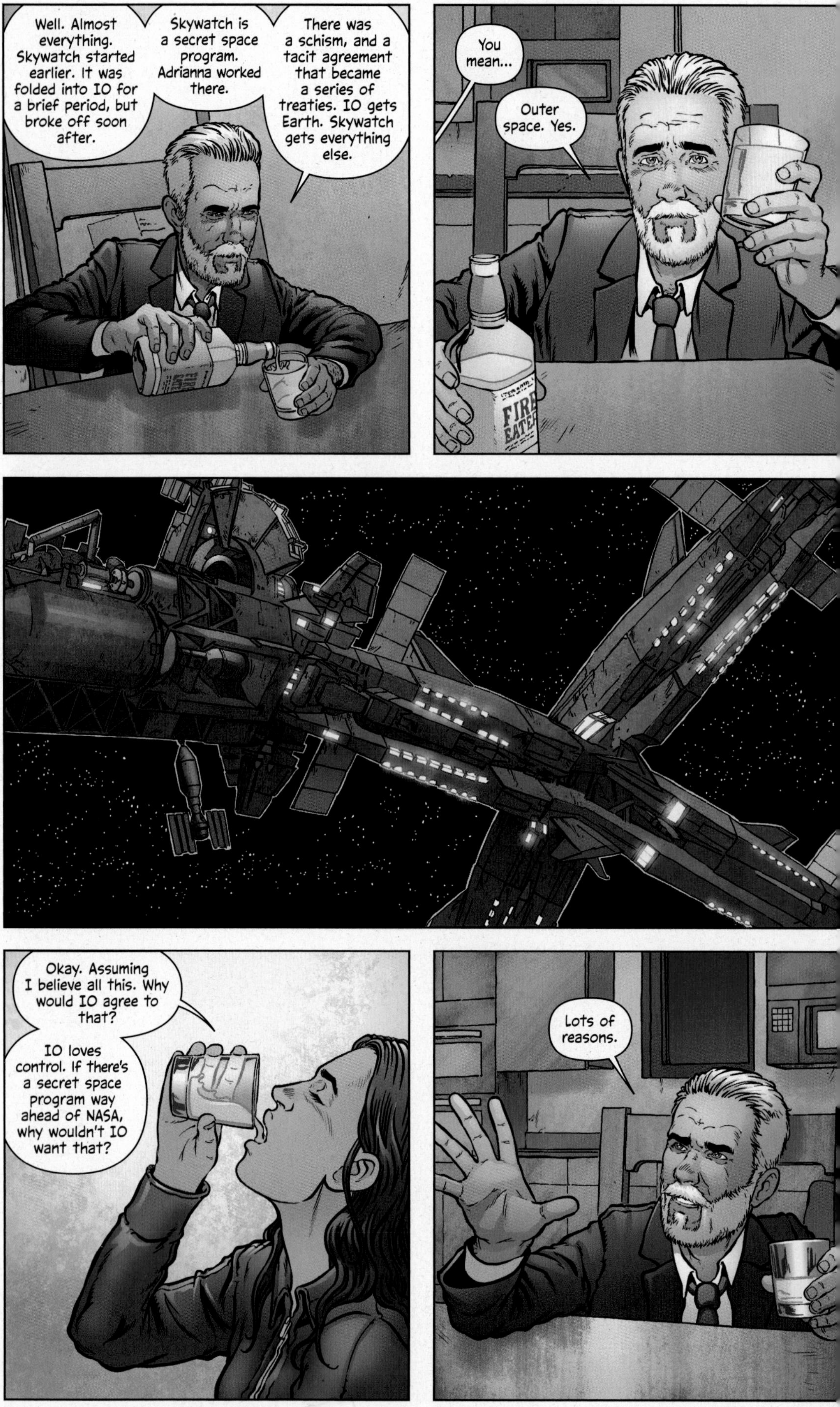

Well. Almost everything. Skywatch started earlier. It was folded into IO for a brief period, but broke off soon after.
Skywatch is a secret space program. Adrianna worked there.
There was a schism, and a tacit agreement that became a series of treaties. IO gets Earth. Skywatch gets everything else.
You mean...
Outer space. Yes.
FIRE EATER
Okay. Assuming I believe all this. Why would IO agree to that?
IO loves control. If there's a secret space program way ahead of NASA, why wouldn't IO want that?
Lots of reasons.

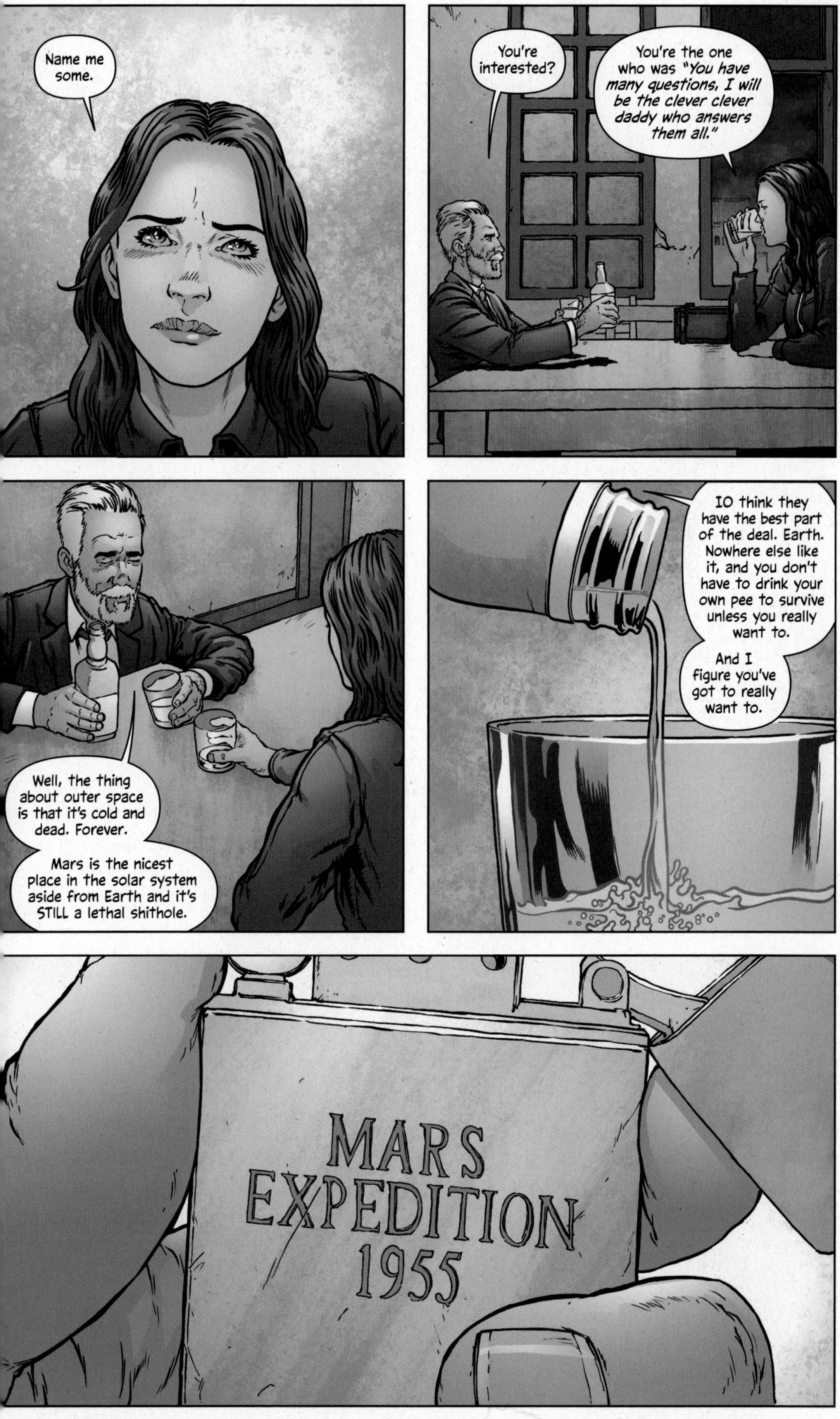
Name me some.
You're interested?
You're the one who was "You have many questions, I will be the clever clever daddy who answers them all."
Well, the thing about outer space is that it's cold and dead. Forever.
Mars is the nicest place in the solar system aside from Earth and it's STILL a lethal shithole.
IO think they have the best part of the deal. Earth. Nowhere else like it, and you don't have to drink your own pee to survive unless you really want to.
And I figure you've got to really want to.
MARS EXPEDITION 1955

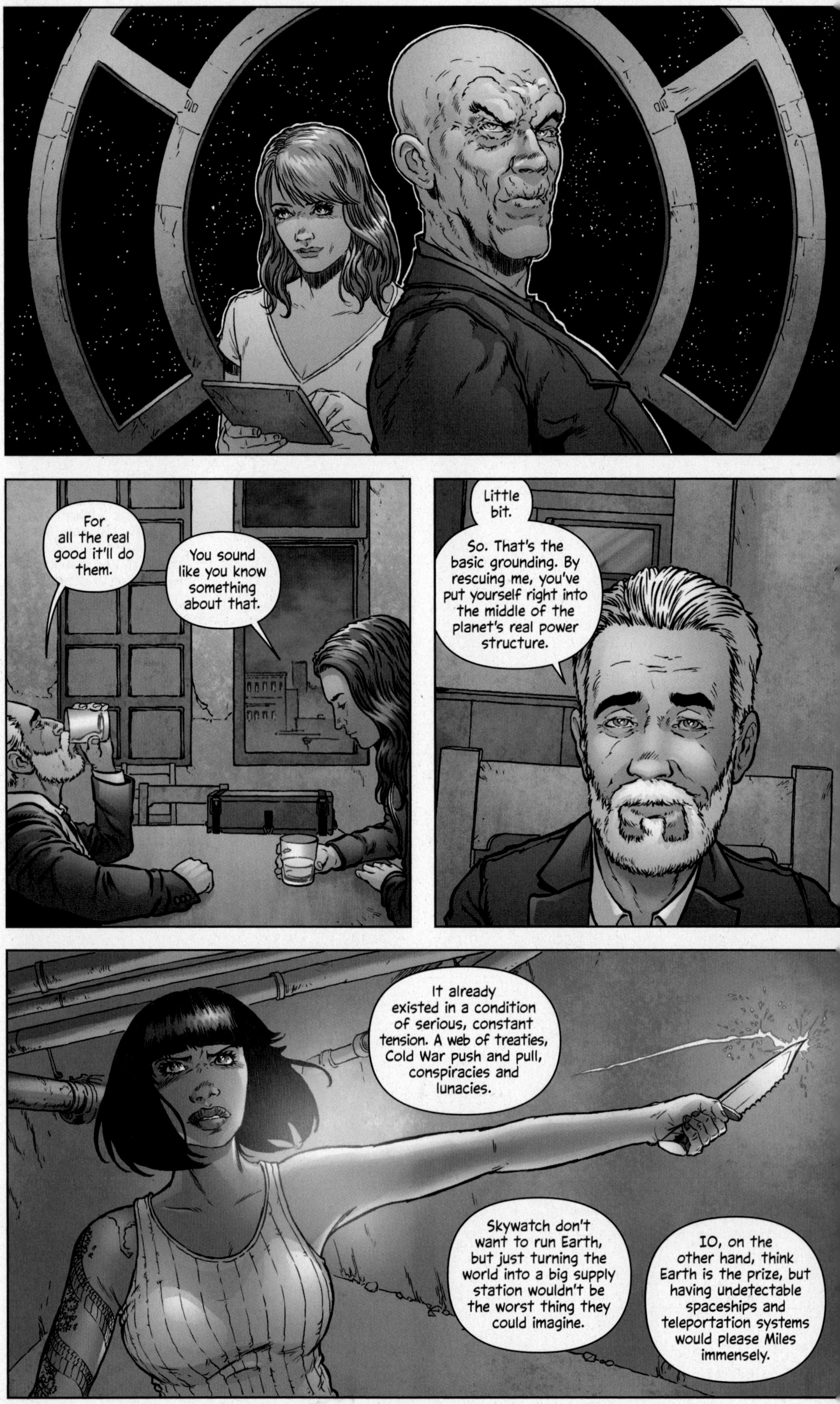
For all the real good it'll do them.
You sound like you know something about that.
Little bit.
So. That's the basic grounding. By rescuing me, you've put yourself right into the middle of the planet's real power structure.
It already existed in a condition of serious, constant tension. A web of treaties, Cold War push and pull, conspiracies and lunacies.
Skywatch don't want to run Earth, but just turning the world into a big supply station wouldn't be the worst thing they could imagine.
IO, on the other hand, think Earth is the prize, but having undetectable spaceships and teleportation systems would please Miles immensely.

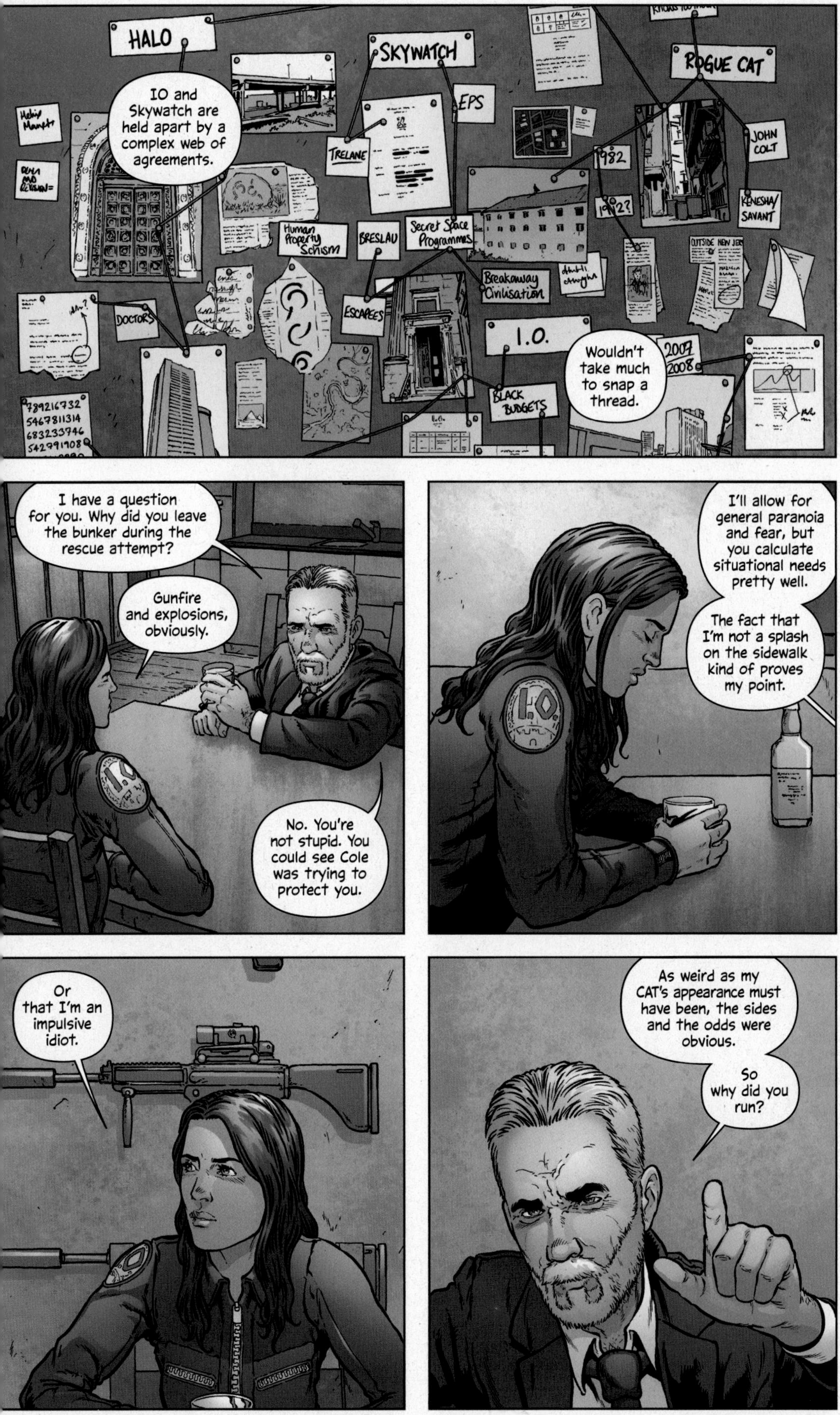
HALO
SKYWATCH
ROGUE CAT
IO and Skywatch are held apart by a complex web of agreements.
EPS
TRELANE
JOHN COLT
1982
1992?
KENESHA/SAVANT
Human Property Schism
BRESLAU
Secret Space Programmes
Breakaway Civilisation
DOCTORS
ESCAPEES
OUTSIDE NEW JERS
I.O.
Wouldn't take much to snap a thread.
2007
2008
BLACK BUDGETS
789216732
5467811314
683233746
542791908
I have a question for you. Why did you leave the bunker during the rescue attempt?
Gunfire and explosions, obviously.
No. You're not stupid. You could see Cole was trying to protect you.
I'll allow for general paranoia and fear, but you calculate situational needs pretty well.
The fact that I'm not a splash on the sidewalk kind of proves my point.
Or that I'm an impulsive idiot.
As weird as my CAT's appearance must have been, the sides and the odds were obvious.
So why did you run?

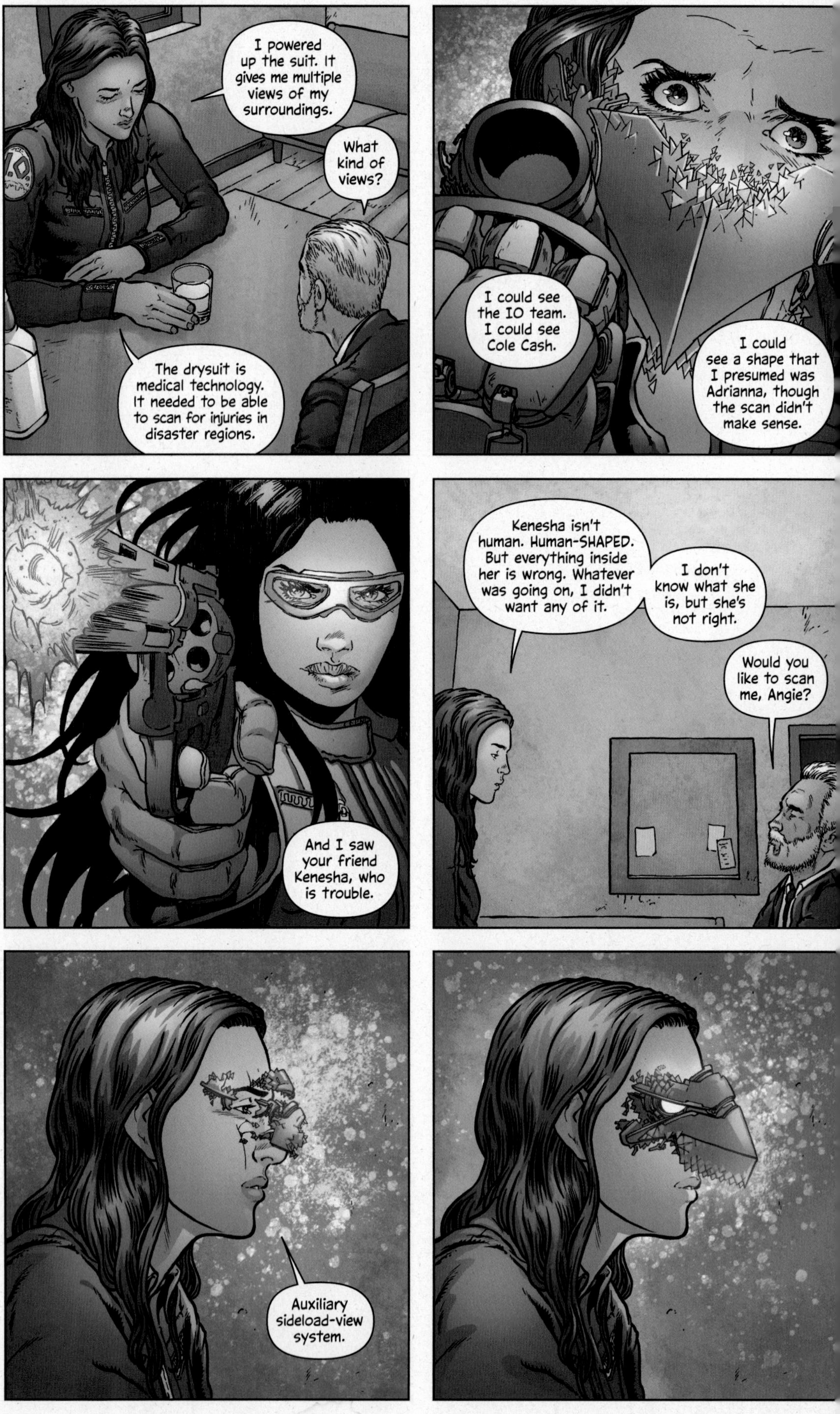

I powered up the suit. It gives me multiple views of my surroundings.
What kind of views?
The drysuit is medical technology. It needed to be able to scan for injuries in disaster regions.
I could see the IO team. I could see Cole Cash.
I could see a shape that I presumed was Adrianna, though the scan didn't make sense.
And I saw your friend Kenesha, who is trouble.
Kenesha isn't human. Human-SHAPED. But everything inside her is wrong. Whatever was going on, I didn't want any of it.
I don't know what she is, but she's not right.
Would you like to scan me, Angie?
Auxiliary sideload-view system.

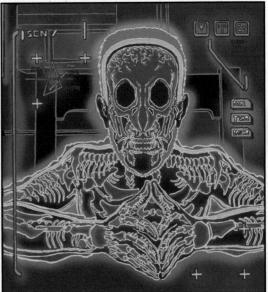

So.

I'm not ill. I wasn't in a terrible accident. I am not hiding 85 deformities in a noble or deluded attempt to save your eyesight.

I'm not from around here.

This house is where the people who don't belong in the world live.

We are fighting two different secret ruling structures, and any number of smaller operations, to try and fix this world that we don't belong in.

Would you like to stay with us and help?

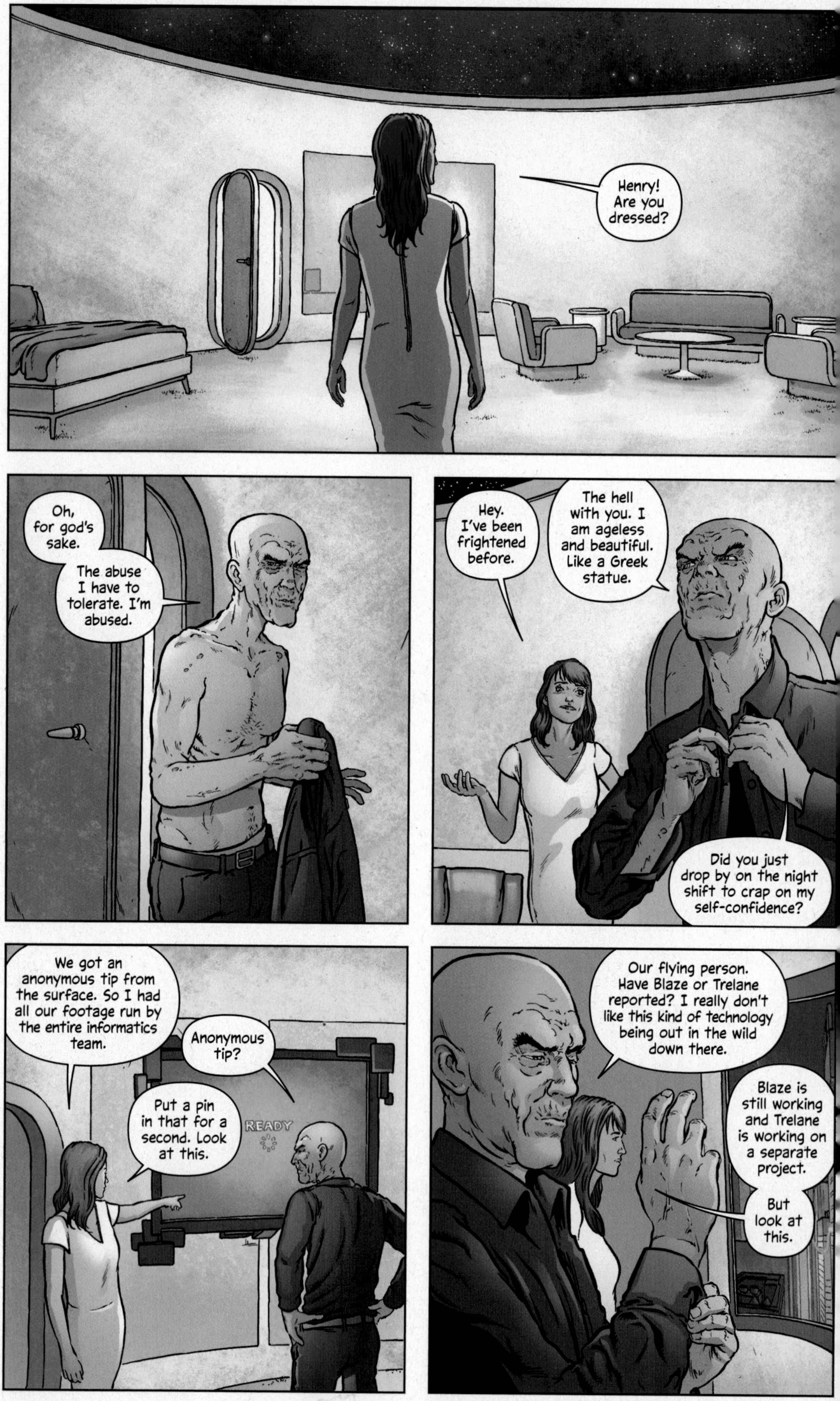

Henry! Are you dressed?
Oh, for god's sake.
The abuse I have to tolerate. I'm abused.
Hey. I've been frightened before.
The hell with you. I am ageless and beautiful. Like a Greek statue.
Did you just drop by on the night shift to crap on my self-confidence?
We got an anonymous tip from the surface. So I had all our footage run by the entire informatics team.
Anonymous tip?
Put a pin in that for a second. Look at this.
READY
Our flying person. Have Blaze or Trelane reported? I really don't like this kind of technology being out in the wild down there.
Blaze is still working and Trelane is working on a separate project.
But look at this.

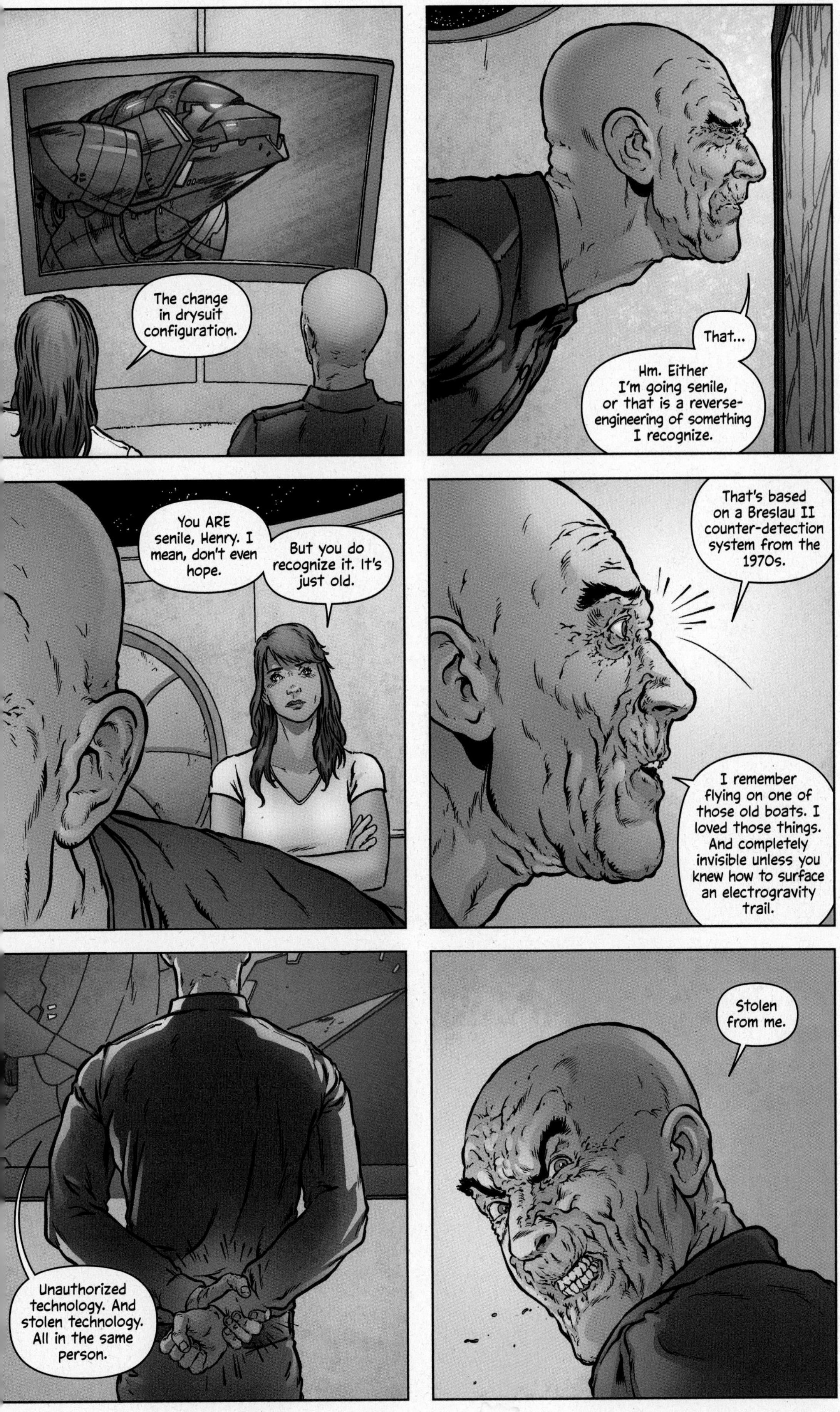
The change in drysuit configuration.
That...
Hm. Either I'm going senile, or that is a reverse-engineering of something I recognize.
You ARE senile, Henry. I mean, don't even hope.
But you do recognize it. It's just old.
That's based on a Breslau II counter-detection system from the 1970s.
I remember flying on one of those old boats. I loved those things. And completely invisible unless you knew how to surface an electrogravity trail.
Unauthorized technology. And stolen technology. All in the same person.
Stolen from me.

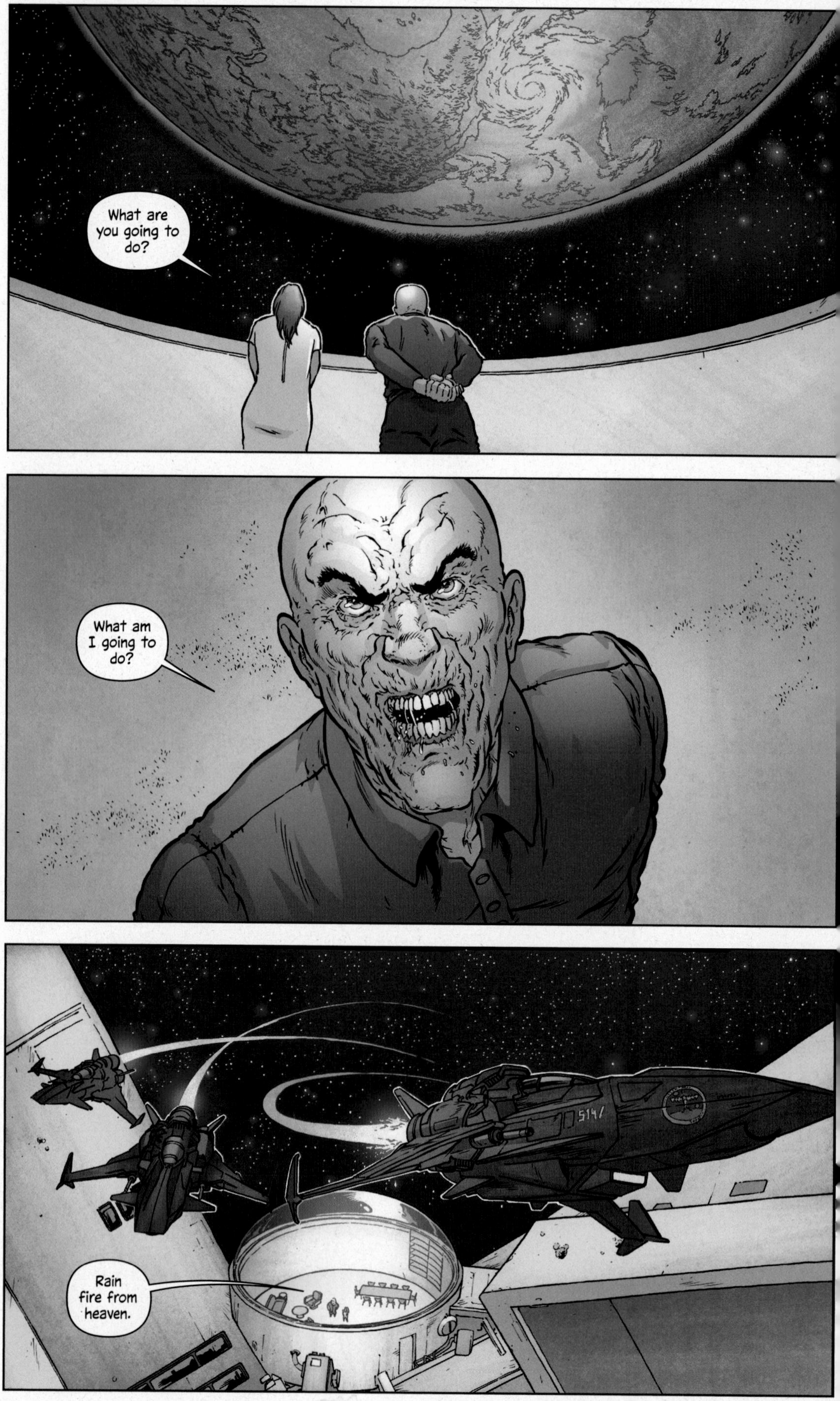
What are you going to do?
What am I going to do?
Rain fire from heaven.

DECLASSIFIED FORECAST

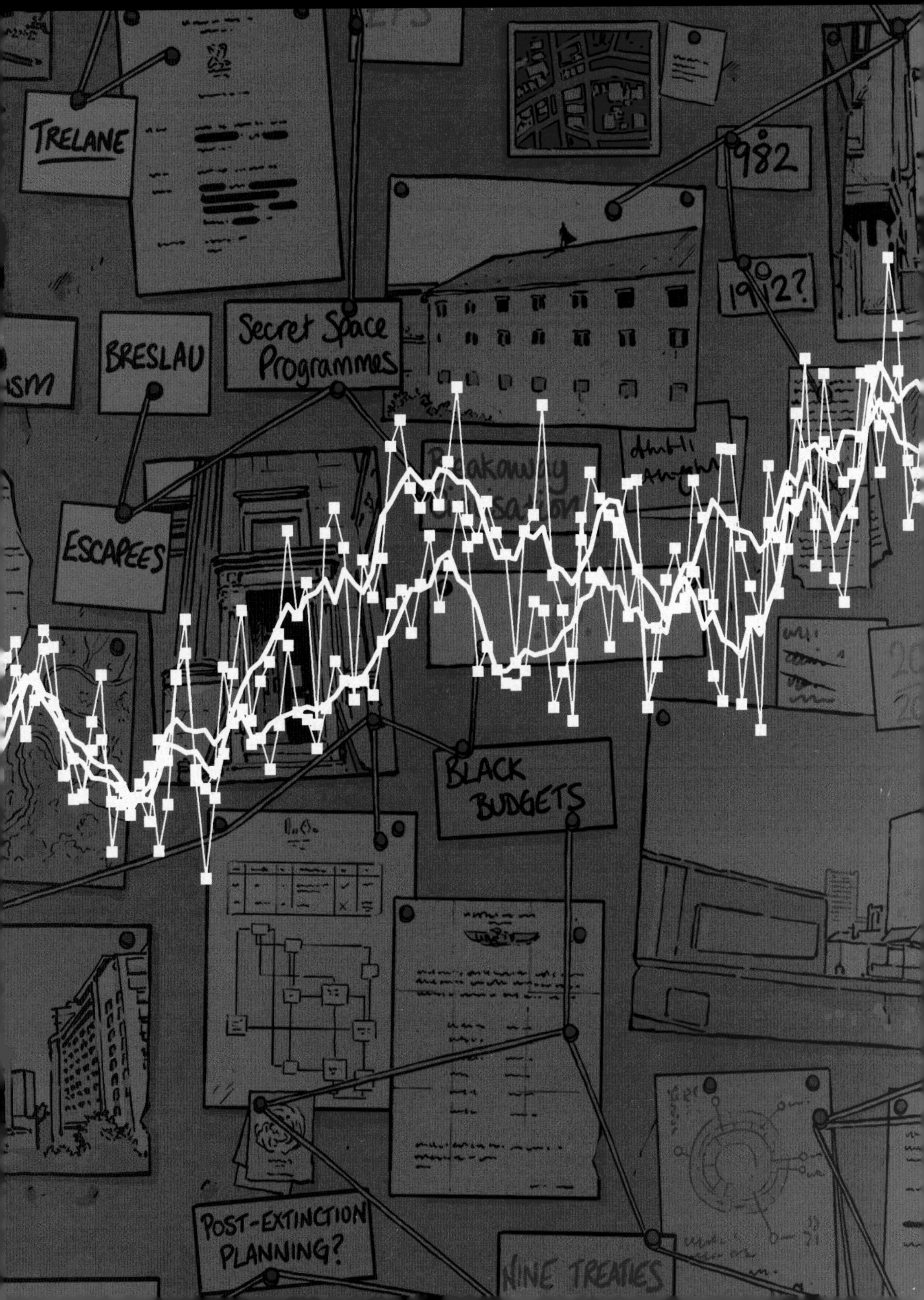
TRELANE
1982
1912?
BRESLAU
Secret Space Programmes
ESCAPEES
BLACK BUDGETS
POST-EXTINCTION PLANNING?
NINE TREATIES

THE WILD STORM #1 by TULA LOTAY

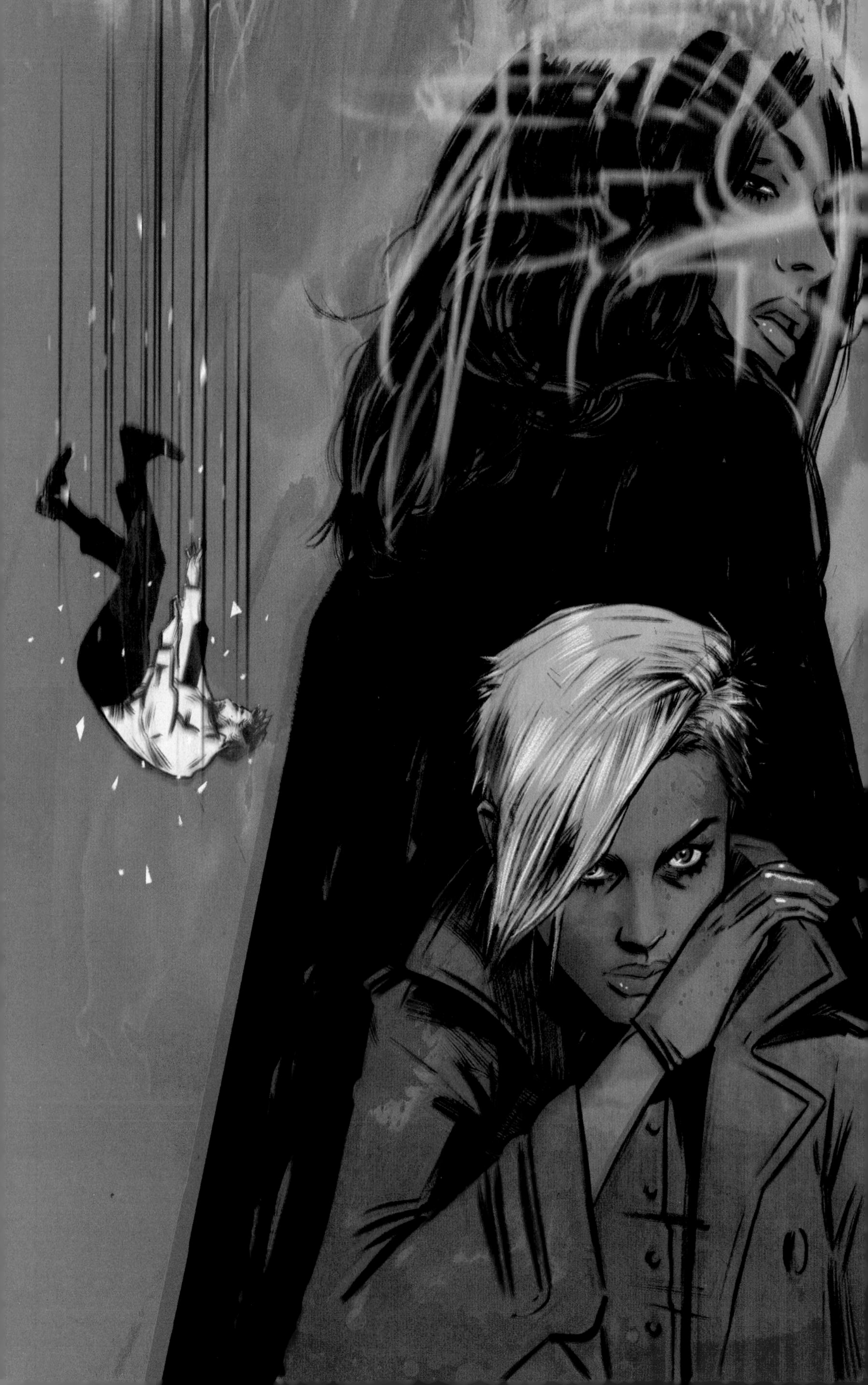

THE WILD STORM #1 by JIM LEE,
SCOTT WILLIAMS and ALEX SINCLAIR

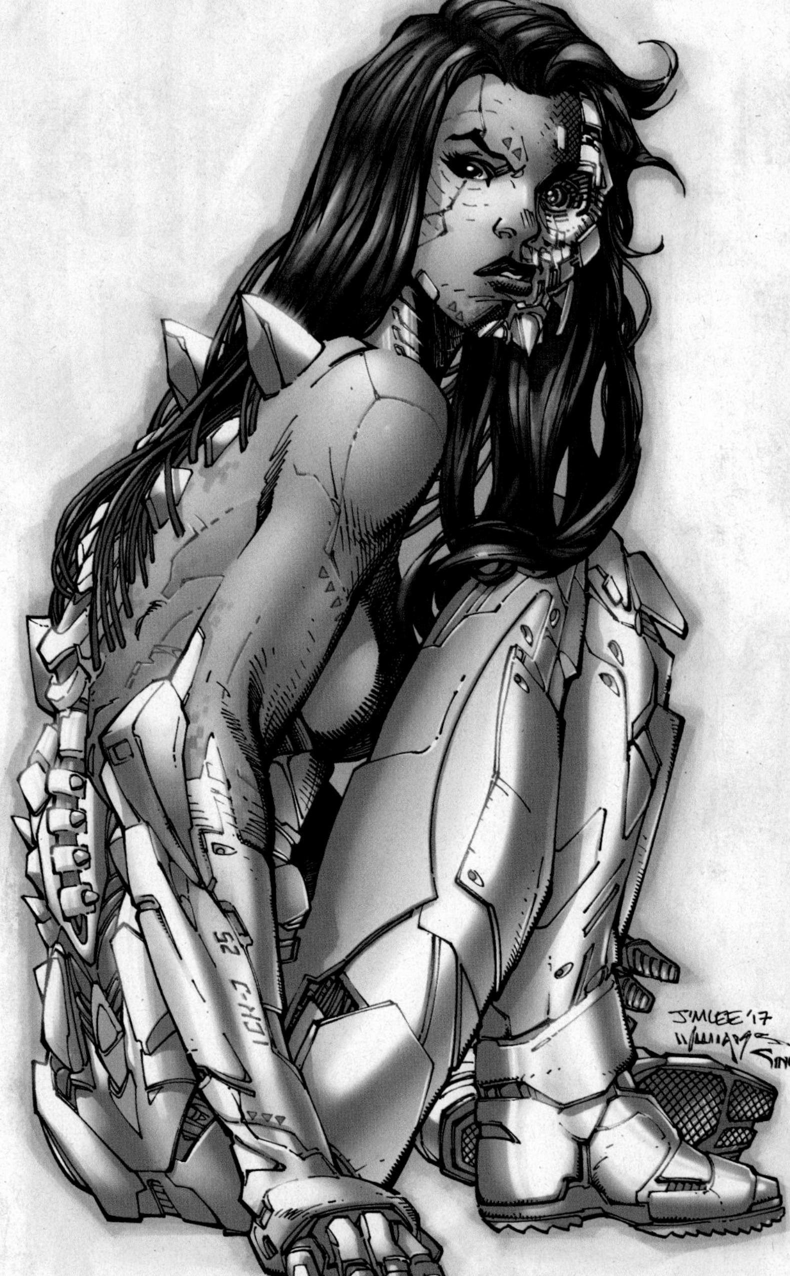
ICK-J 25

THE WILD STORM #2 by AFUA RICHARDSON

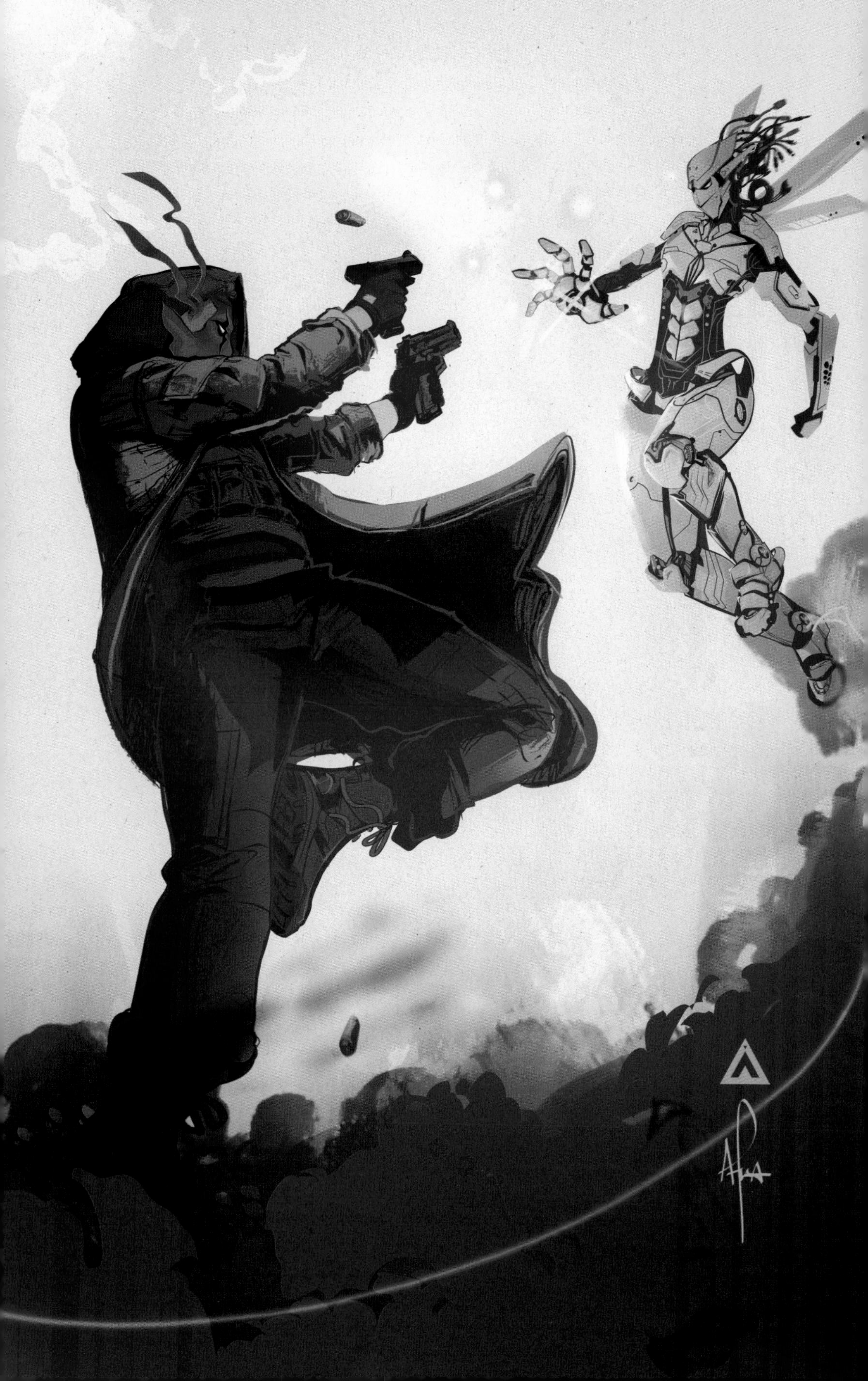
Afua

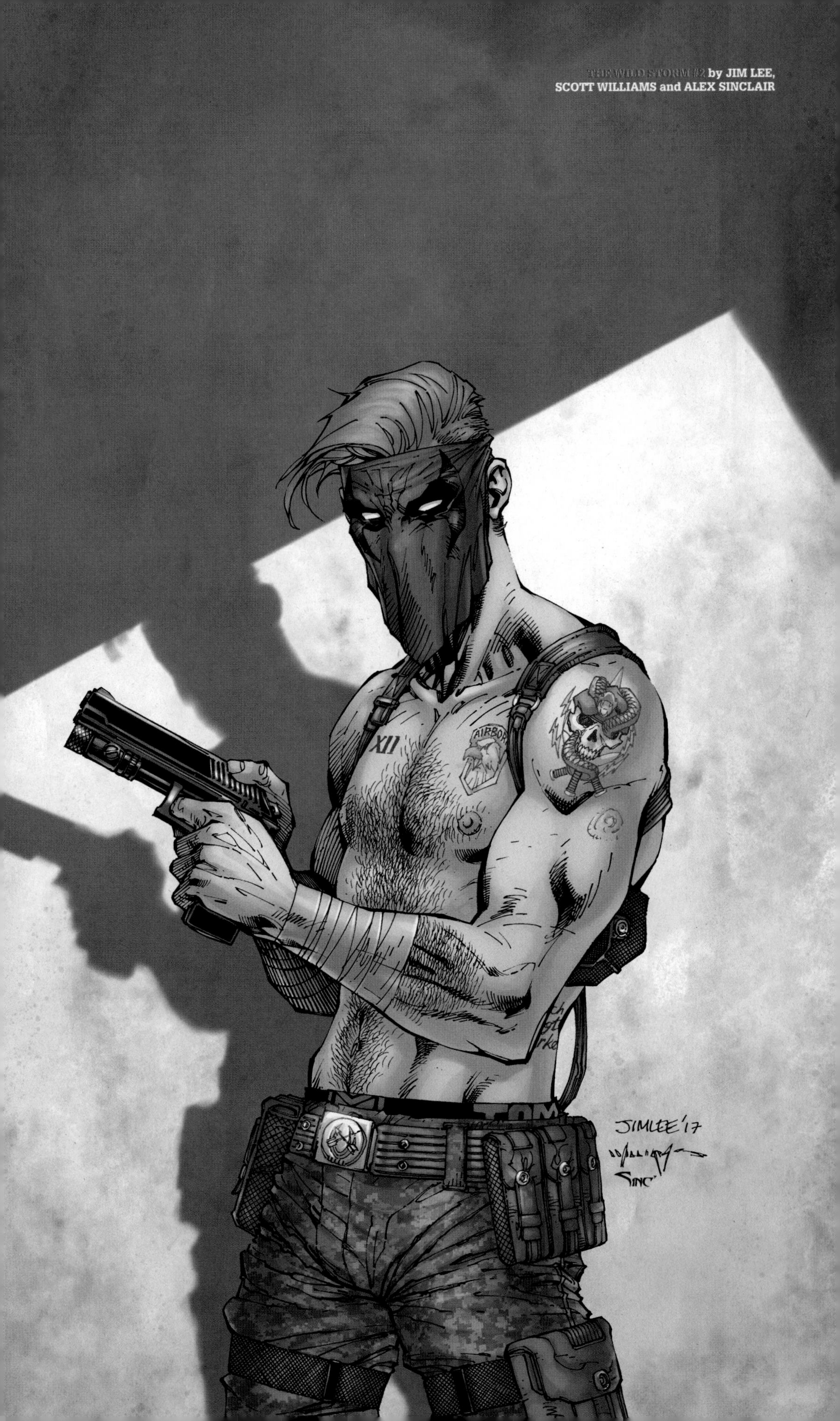
JIMLEE'17

THE WILD STORM #2 by JIM LEE,
SCOTT WILLIAMS and ALEX SINCLAIR

THE WILD STORM #3 by JAMIE McKELVIE

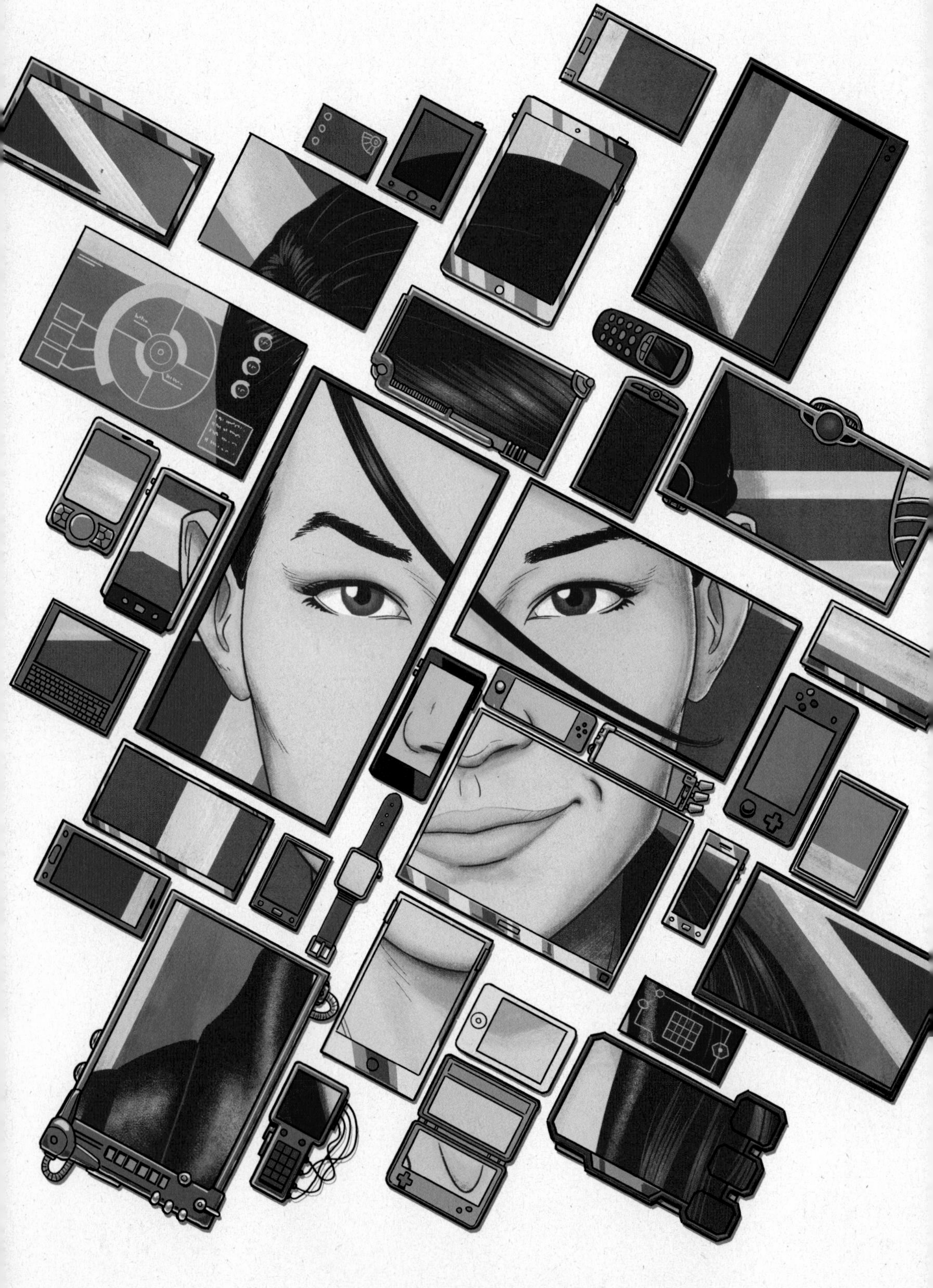

THE WILD STORM #3 by JIM LEE,
SCOTT WILLIAMS and ALEX SINCLAIR

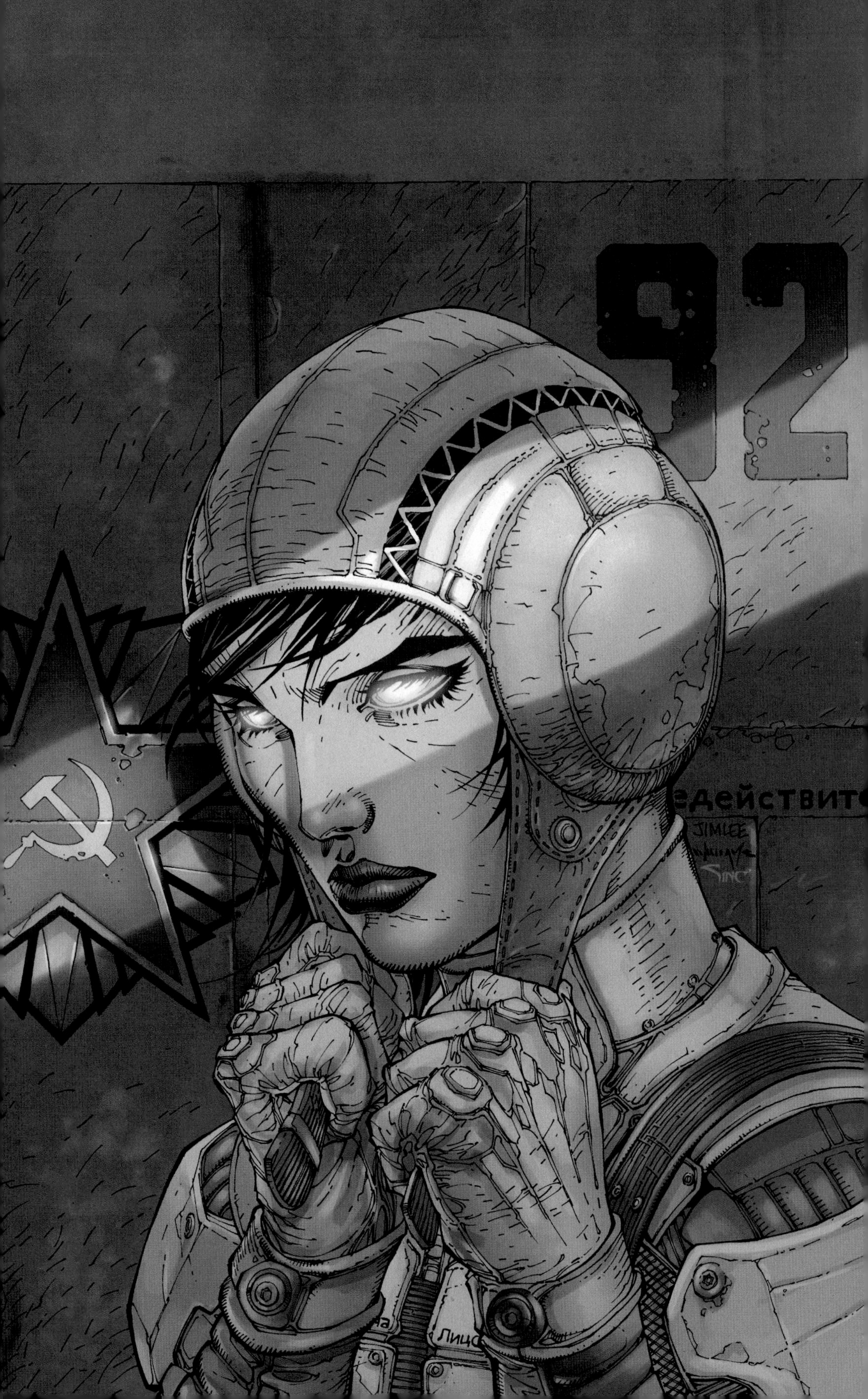
92
JIMLEE

THE WILD STORM #4 by **JASON HOWARD**

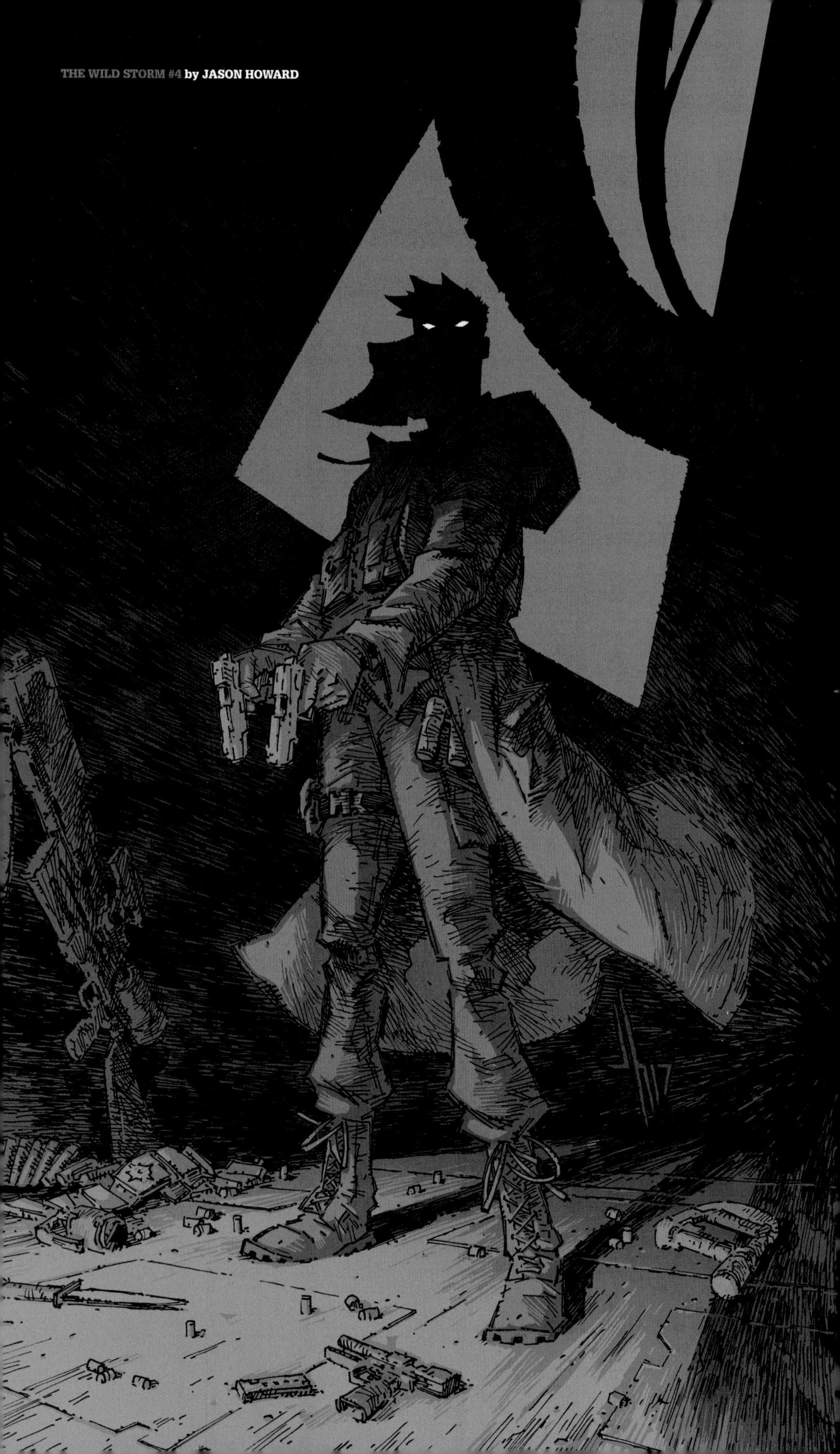

THE WILD STORM #4 by JIM LEE,
SCOTT WILLIAMS and ALEX SINCLAIR

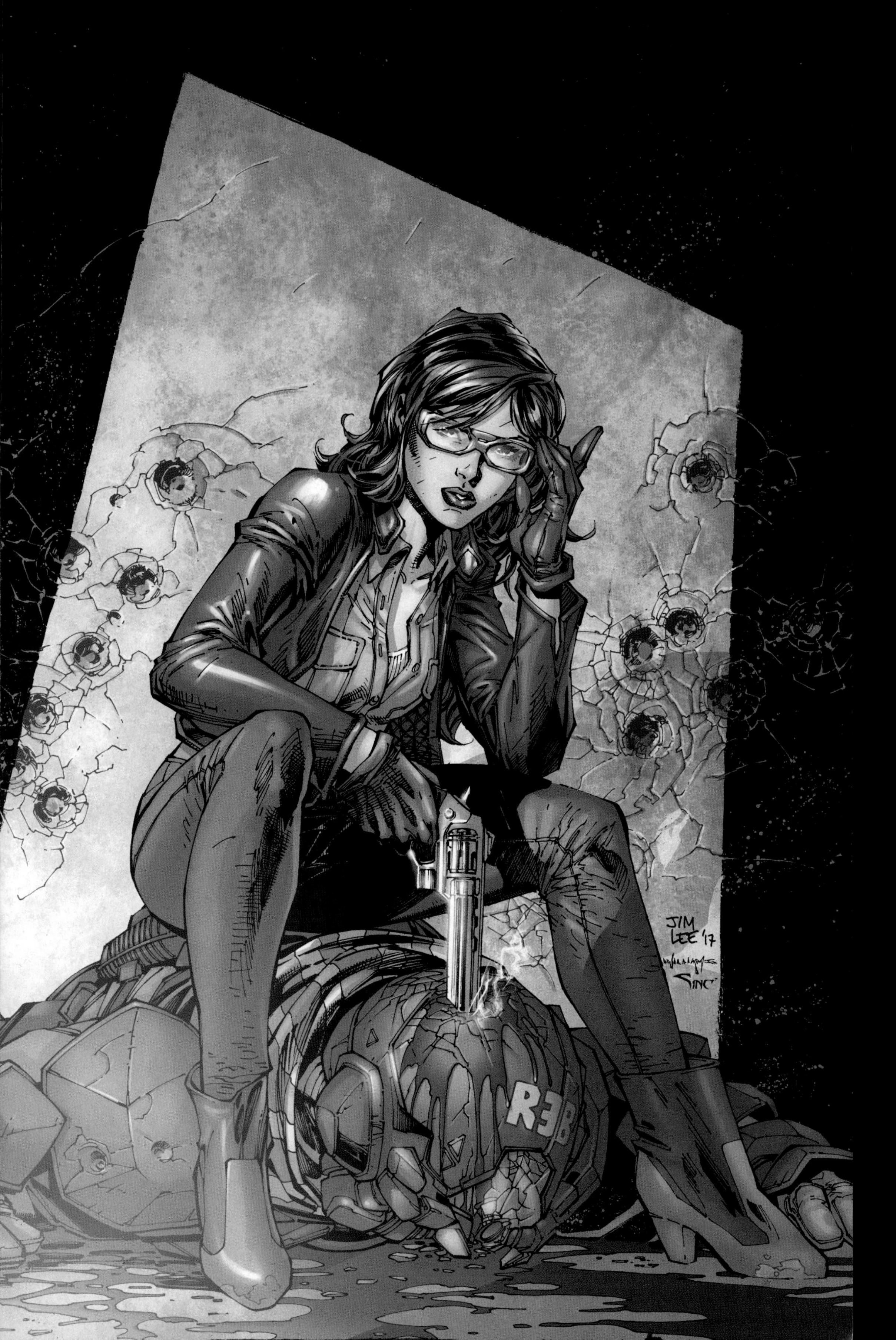
JIM LEE '17
R3B

THE WILD STORM #5 by DECLAN SHALVEY
and JORDIE BELLAIRE

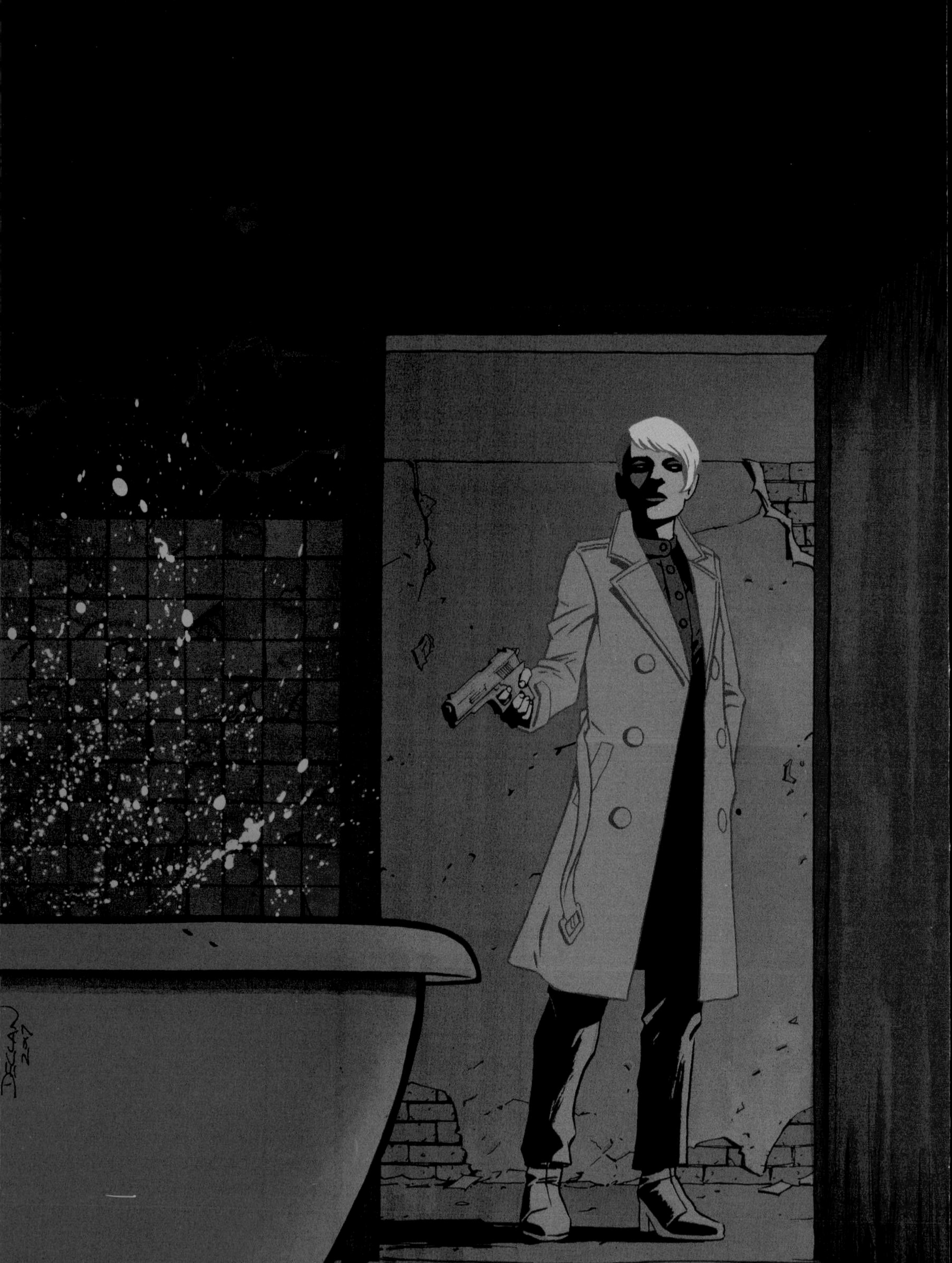
DECLAN 2017

THE WILD STORM #5 by JIM LEE,
SCOTT WILLIAMS and ALEX SINCLAIR

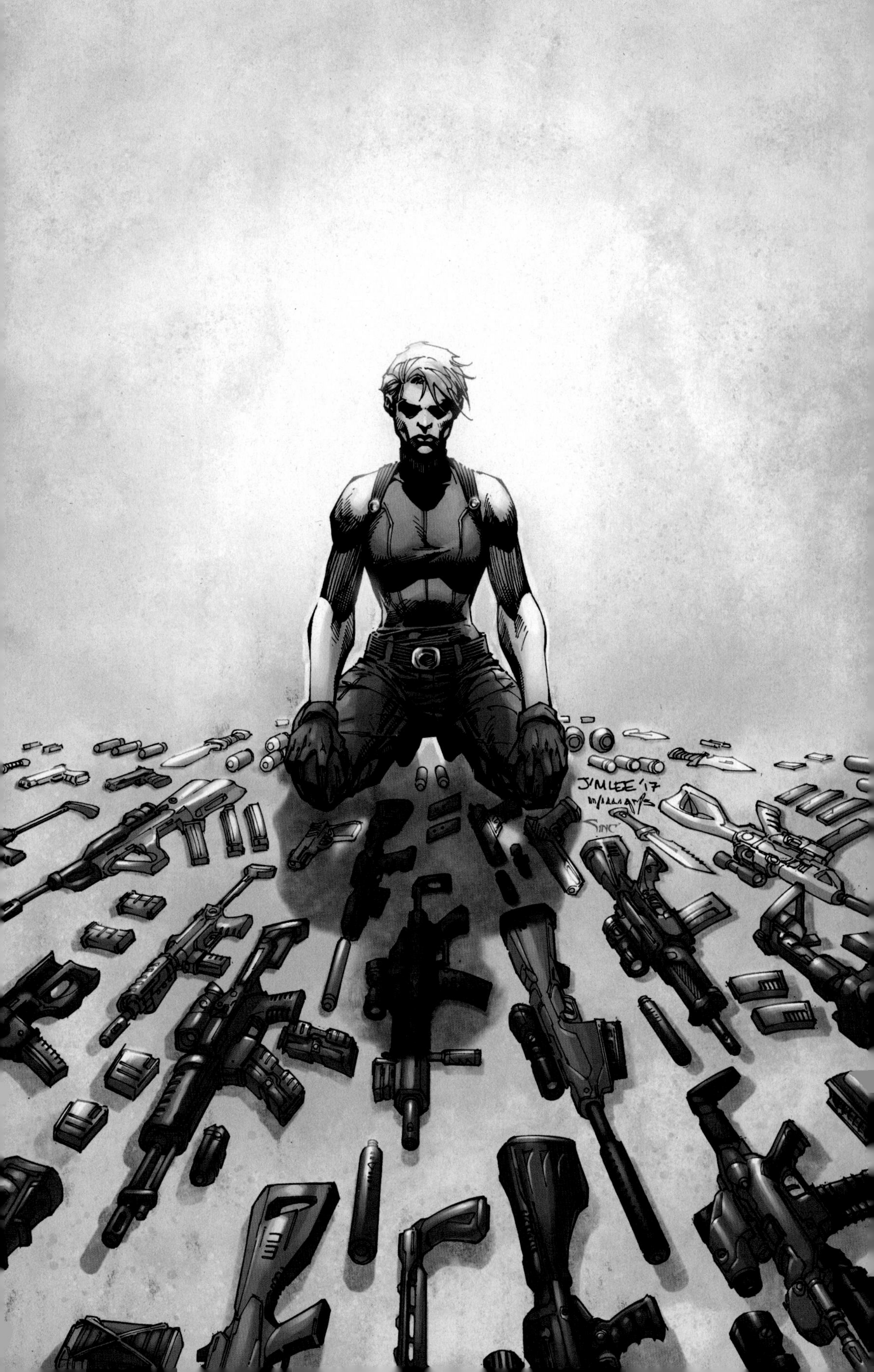
JIM LEE '17

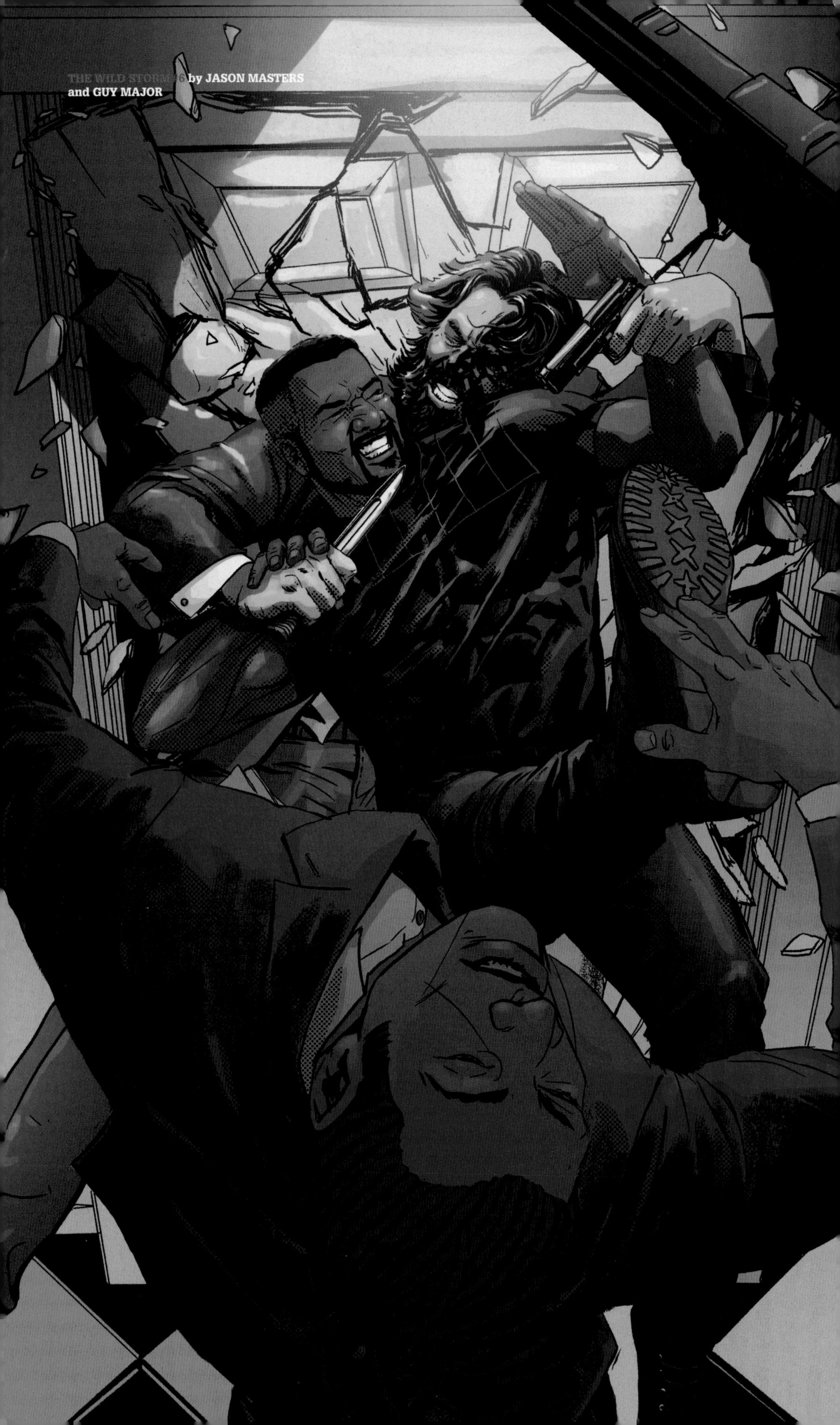

THE WILD STORM #6 by JASON MASTERS
and GUY MAJOR

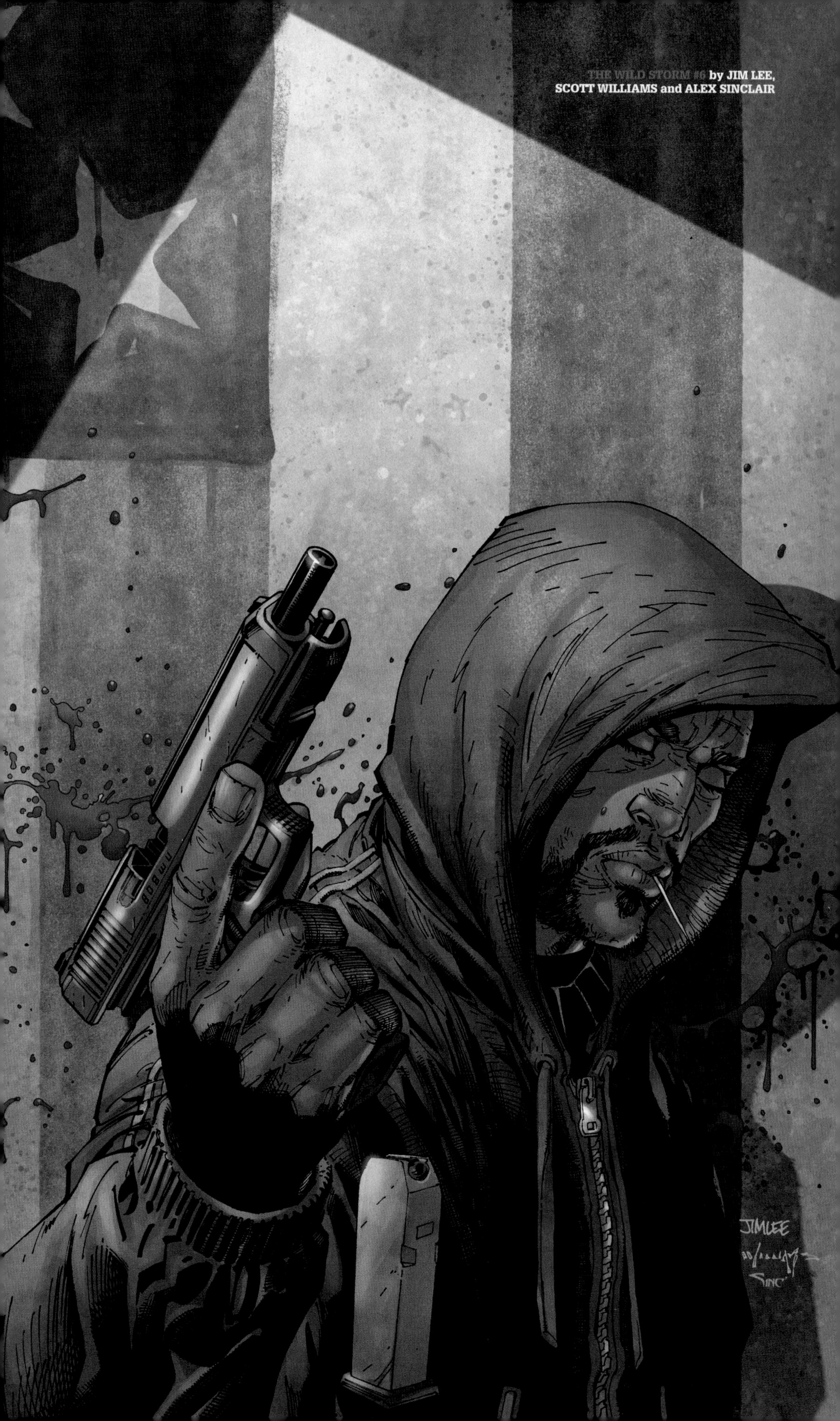

THE WILD STORM #6 by JIM LEE,
SCOTT WILLIAMS and ALEX SINCLAIR

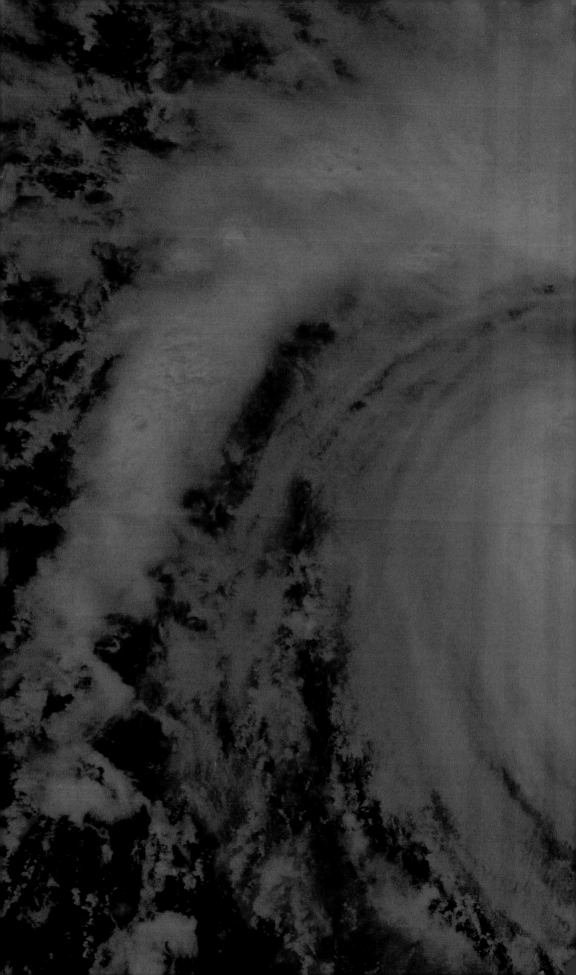

STORM WARNING

Q. What made you come back to **WildStorm**?

A. I was abducted. Please help. I'm sending this message out through an advertisement in the hope that Jim Lee won't see it and therefore won't give me the hose again.

I'm in a bunker under a building in Burbank. **Please help me.**

Warren Ellis

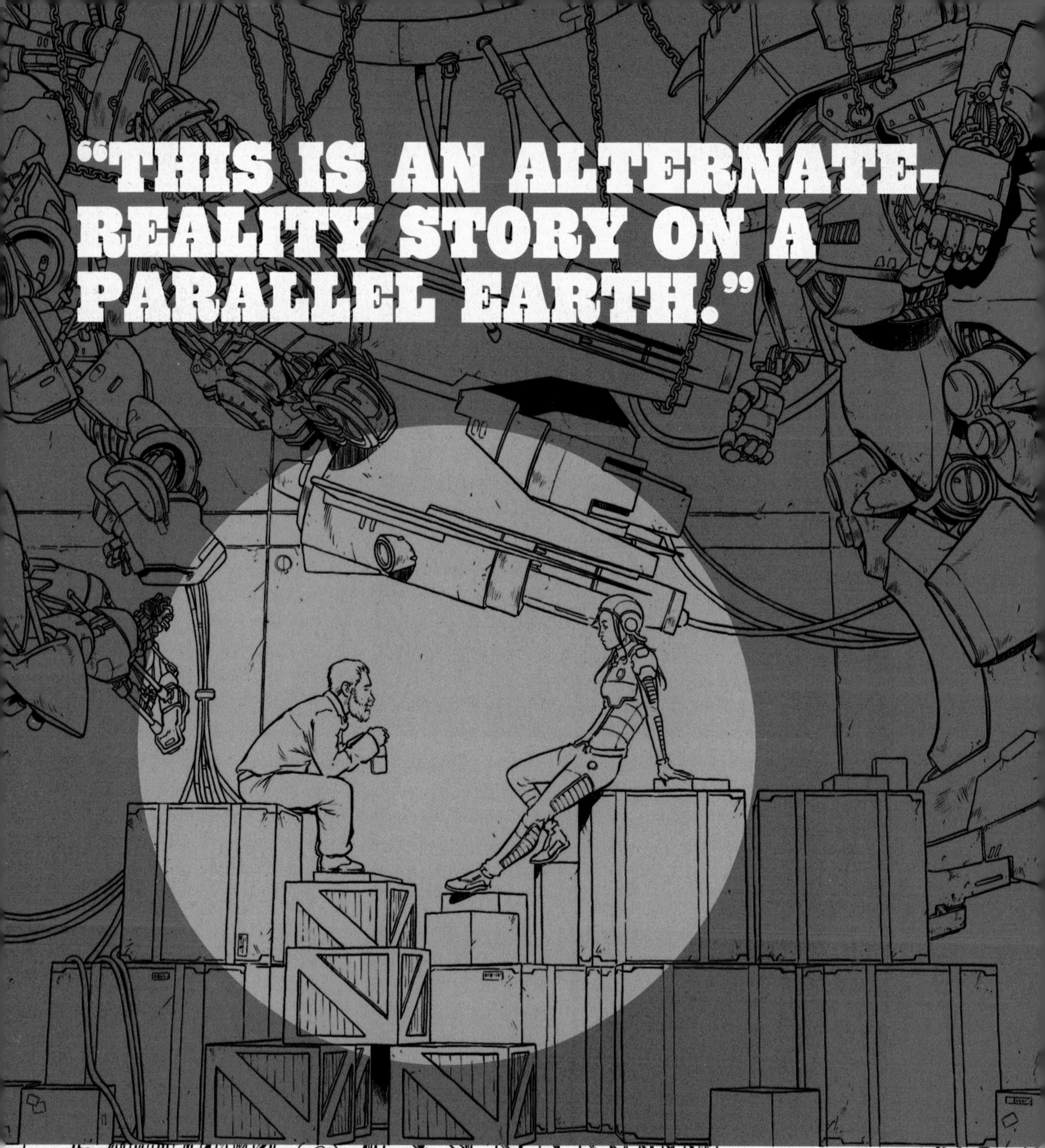
"THIS IS AN ALTERNATE-REALITY STORY ON A PARALLEL EARTH."

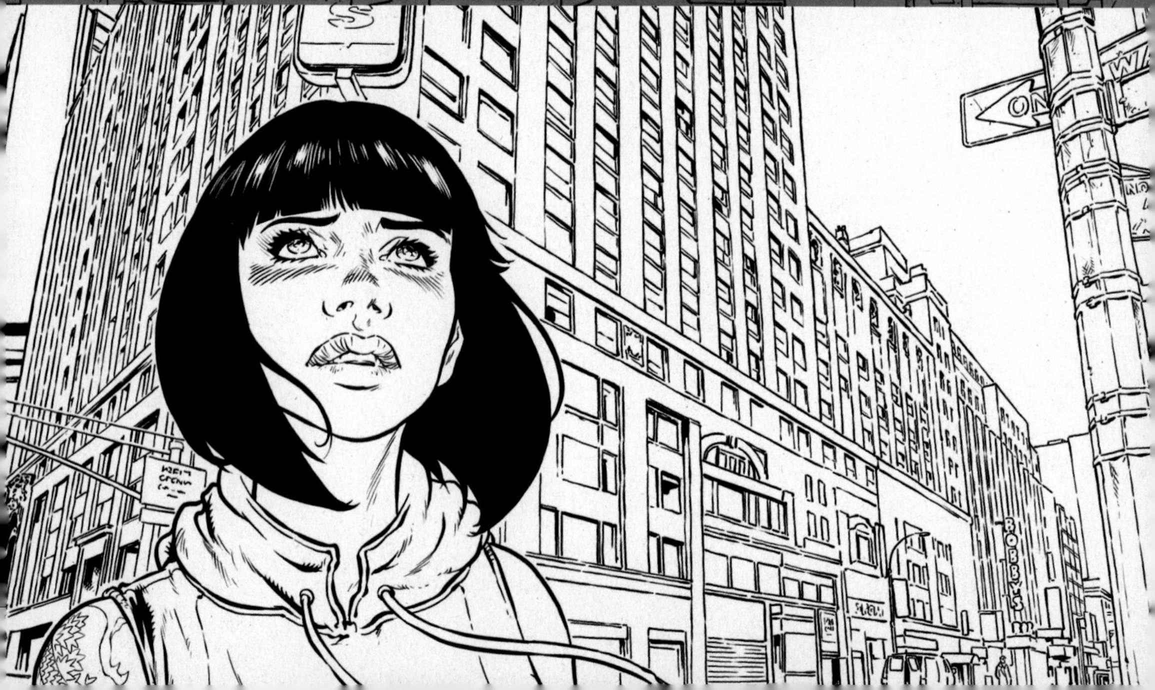
BOBBY'S

WARREN ELLIS

Photograph by Ellen J. Rogers

THE WILD STORM WORKBOOK

BEGINNINGS

Let me start with Jim Lee's original note:

We would love to have you come on board and do what you do best with the entire WildStorm line as a separate independent launch from the DC Universe. If you wrote one title and curated the others...well, that would be just ideal. Having a visionary like yourself at the creative helm would be amazing.

It could be a staggered launch over several months so each book could get the proper support and breathing room to find its widest audience, but in the end, the idea would be to work with you to figure out what's best for the line.

This note has been my throughline for everything that follows. Also, the use of the word "visionary" indicates that DC is in trouble.

I am generating four titles (and a surprise or two) on a staggered launch. The launch is perhaps a little more staggered than the above might indicate, but I am very wary of front-loading an entire line in a matter of a few months. This is, as you also see from Jim's note, an independent launch, separate from the DCU. There will be hooks into the DCU here and there, but this is an alternate-reality story on a parallel Earth.

What I've landed on is this. Four books over two years. And, on the first month of year three, one book will become another.

I have a scheme.

CORE CONCEPTS OF THE ORIGINAL LINE

I started by making a list of what I considered to be the central ideas behind the original WildStorm books. Aliens on Earth. Black ops and intel. Scientific experiments on people. Hybridization. Secret power structures. Funnily enough, I was doing this at the same time the X-FILES reboot was approaching broadcast. I tend to look at this list as pretty much everything Jim and his friends thought was cool in 1991. It's kind of hard to disagree with. I did a

ton of research and reading to see what the current state of these things were in the parapolitics literature. And, you know... still pretty cool. There's loads to work with here.

So what I can do here is assemble all the stuff that Jim and his friends loved enough to make a line of comics about, update it, and build it out from the start into a new linear shape. You'll recognize all the pieces in what follows. It seems to me that finding the pure tone of the original work is as worth a shot as anything.

THE INTENT OF A REVIVAL

Or, put another way—what is the point of a revival? What does bringing WildStorm back actually give to the world? What does it have to say about the world in 2017?

We're more paranoid about secret power structures in the world than ever before. And we're even hungrier for big mad stories and fantasies, because our suspension of disbelief is complex — we want the epic stories, but we want them to give us a new view of the world we're in, too.

I keep coming back to two metaphors for all this. In one sense, it's like building out a cinematic universe. In another, I find myself making references to *Game of Thrones*. Both of these things seem to apply—in the first instance, clear and linear worldbuilding that spins out new projects. In the other, a rich and complex story that creates a broad fabric of a story

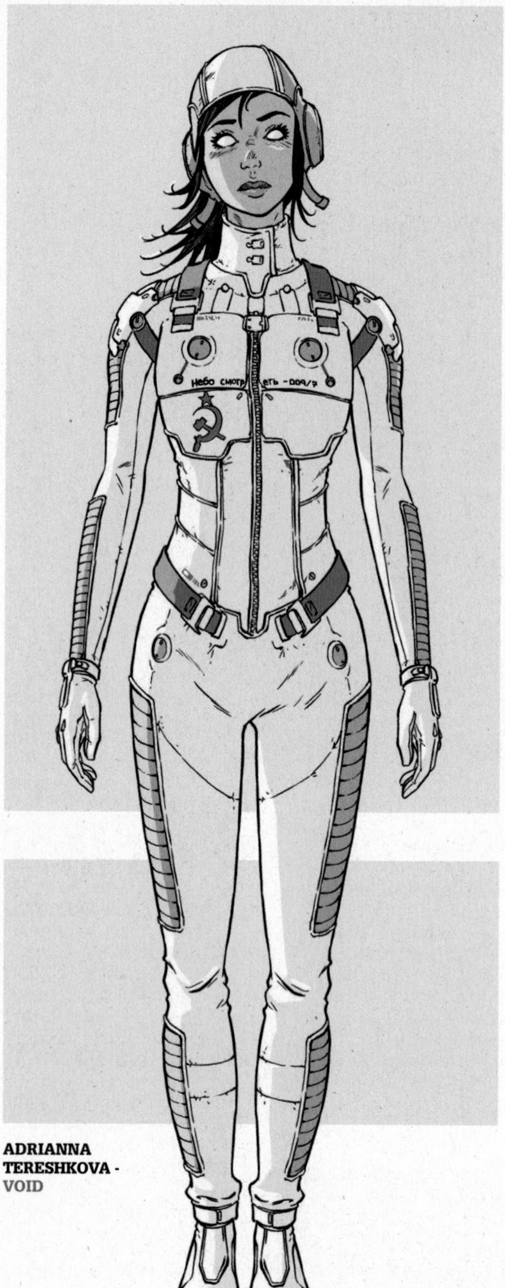

ADRIANNA TERESHKOVA - VOID

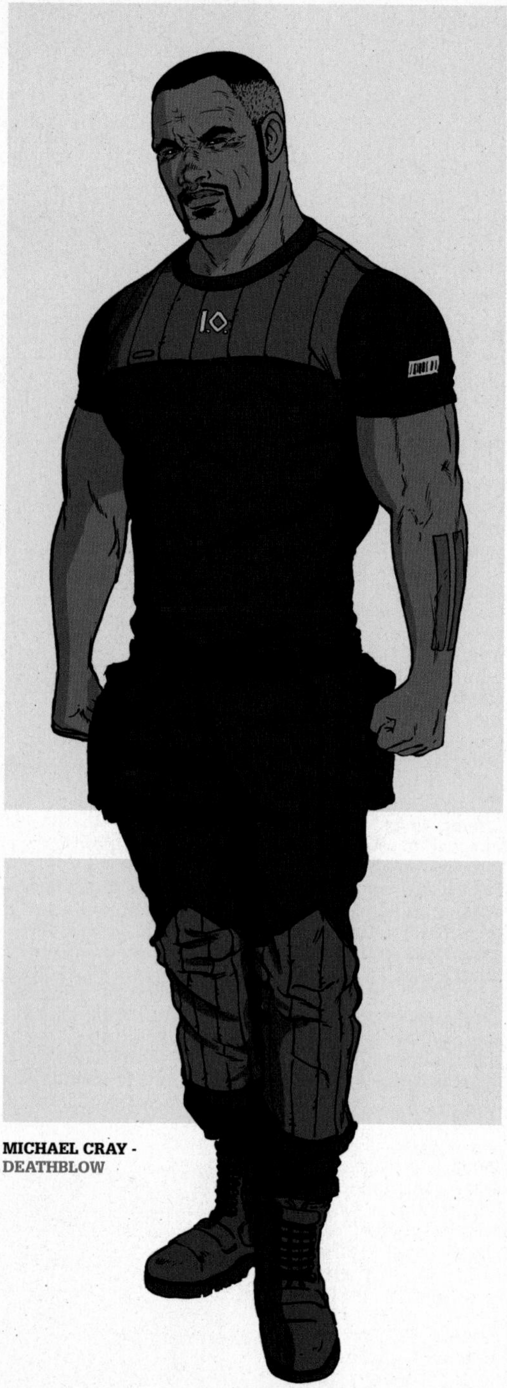

MICHAEL CRAY - DEATHBLOW

universe. This, in particular, is the goal of the first and main book of the first two years, which I'm calling THE WILD STORM.

THE WILD STORM is, essentially, about one act of selflessness destabilizing and revealing a shadow world of hidden government and secret power. The entire story reels out from that one act. It's a covert history of terrible things. There's a line from an old song that I like. "The past is steeped in shame, but tomorrow's fair game." The line through the first two years to the top of year three is into the dark and out again to something aspirational.

And it does get dark. This is a story of the human response to secret power structures and ancient conspiracies. The proper WildStorm stuff. And it has layers. Over the two years, we start with what looks like a covert intelligence org armed with breakthrough science and carte blanche at war with a worldchanging corporation. Then we reveal more. Drill down. Literally, in one case. We start with a world we know and strip it down to reveal its true nature.

In gathering all the central WildStorm concepts into one place, as it were, we're introducing a structured world as rich as that of *Game of Thrones*. Instead of great houses, we have covert organisations, secret societies, secret space programmes, ancient cults. Instead of house sigils, we have

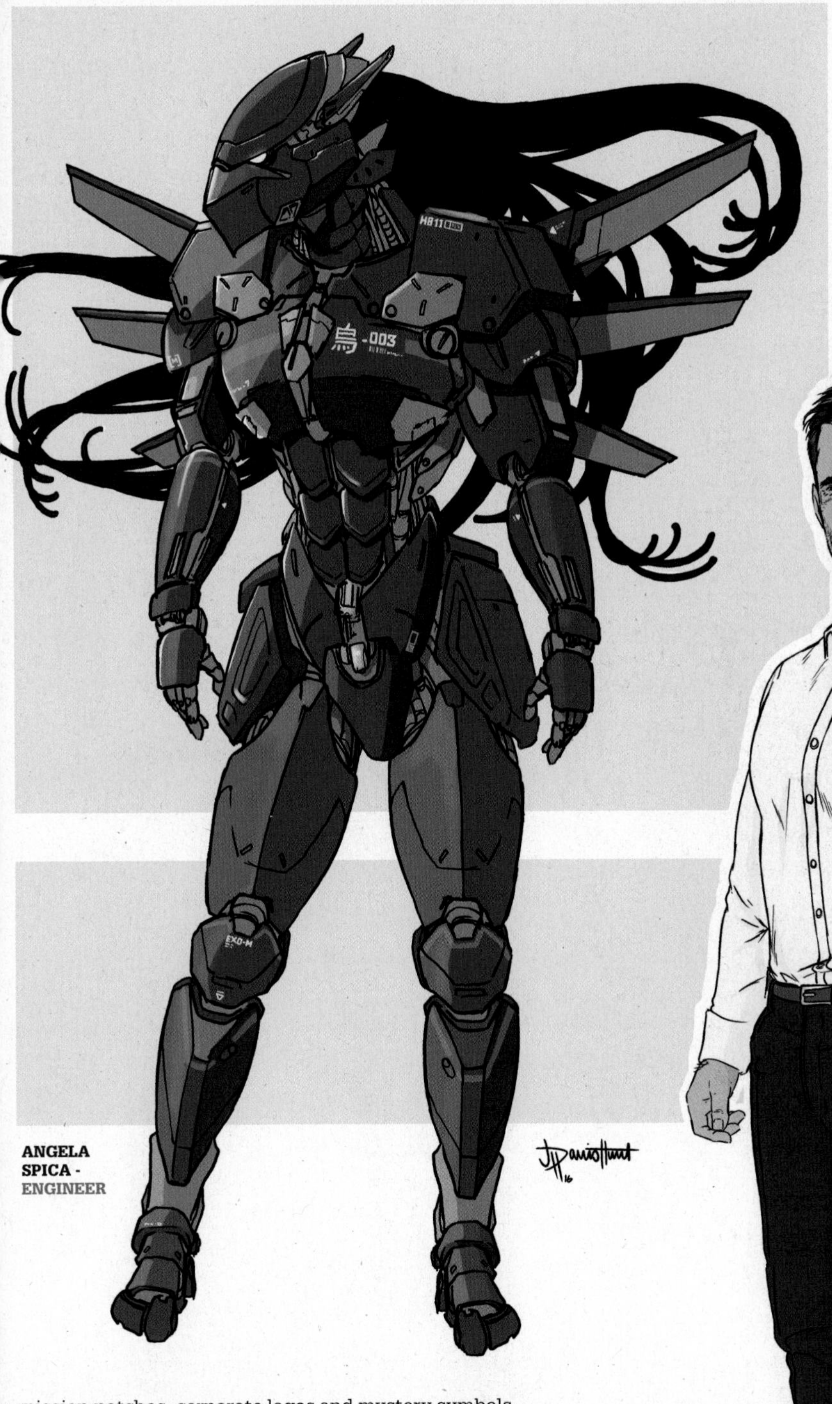

ANGELA SPICA - ENGINEER

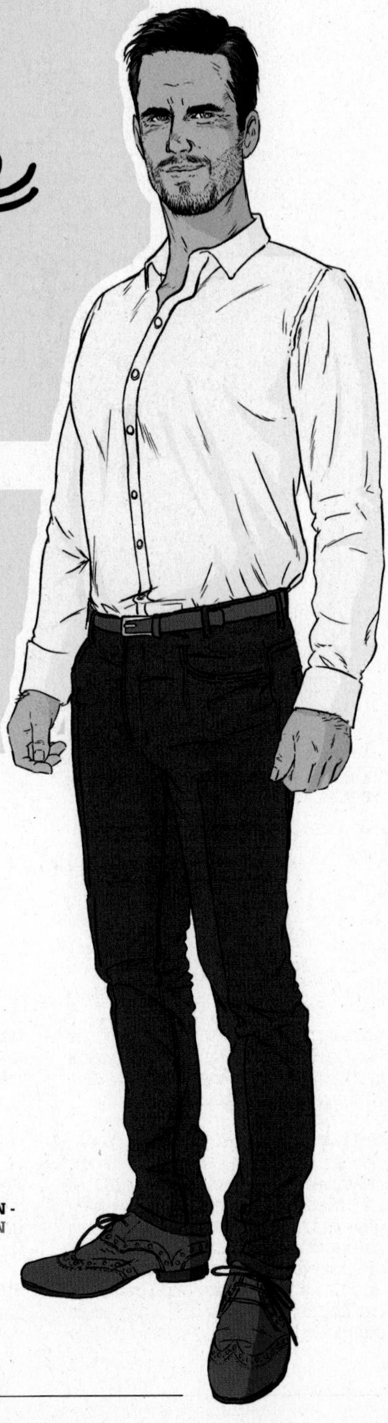

MILES CRAVEN - MILES CRAVEN

mission patches, corporate logos and mystery symbols.

What we bring to market is a new world that we always kind of suspected was there, and then show it to be even weirder and nastier than we hoped. Even as we peel more layers off it, there is a shape to it, teams to root for, mavericks to fear for, villains to hate or enjoy. New territories, new maps.

CORE CONCEPTS OF A REVIVAL

The really very short version, I swear:

International Operations (IO) is a renegade covert intelligence organization fighting its own war for

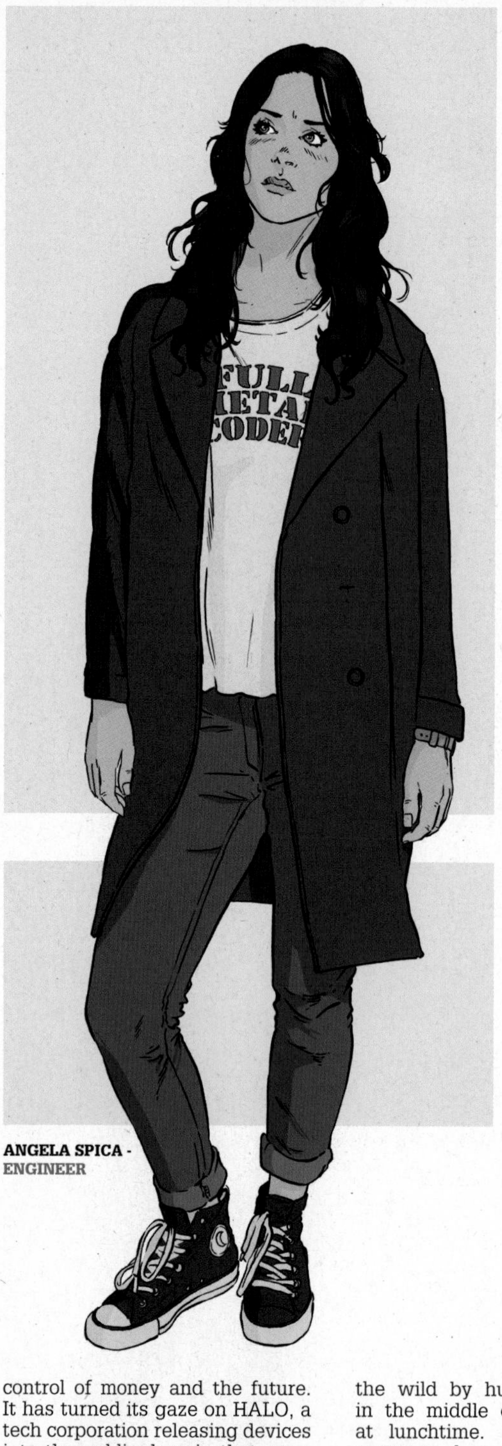

ANGELA SPICA -
ENGINEER

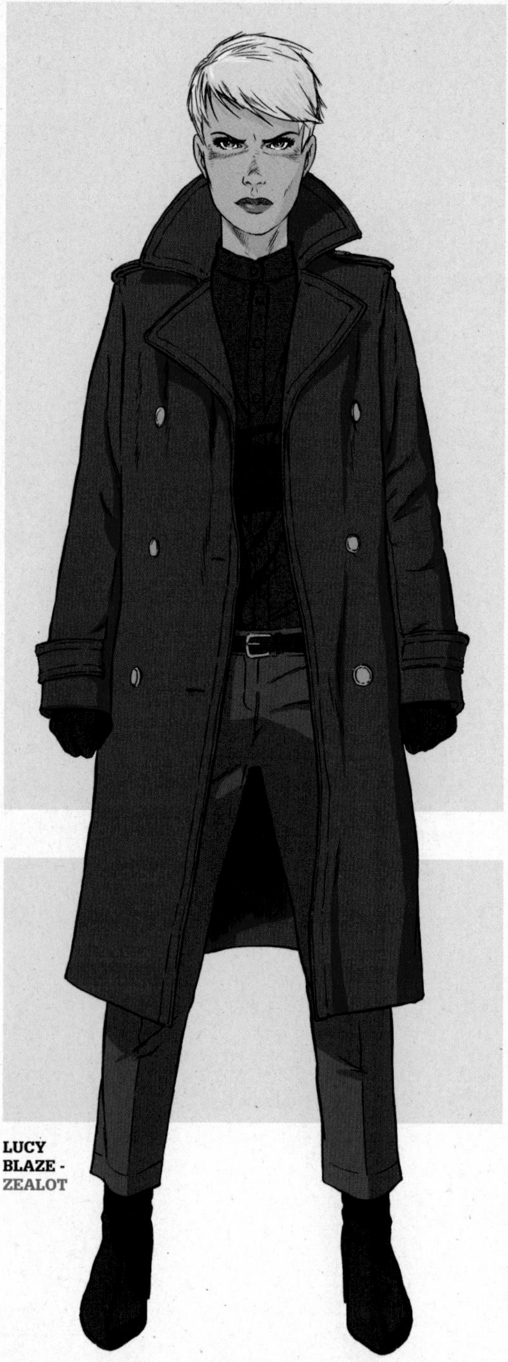

LUCY
BLAZE -
ZEALOT

control of money and the future. It has turned its gaze on HALO, a tech corporation releasing devices into the public domain that are a little too far ahead of their time and a little too economically destabilizing. They attempt an assassination of its director, Jacob Marlowe, using IO killer Michael Cray. Marlowe's life is saved by an IO engineer, Angela Spica, who's been redirecting funds and resources to construct a transkeletal multifunction drysuit: a full-body shell device that lives in her bones. The bleeding edge of secret IO tech, witnessed in the wild by hundreds of people in the middle of New York City at lunchtime. In 2017. Where everyone has cameras on their phones.

The apple cart is tipped over.

IO puts a Covert Action Team (CAT) into the field to find and end Angela Spica. They are intercepted by another CAT—one that IO has no files on. A Wild CAT.

GROUPS AND SOCIETIES

All of these need a mission patch or other identifying symbols. Did you know that most "secret missions" in America get their own mission patch? And they're all insane pieces of design? Go search for Trevor Paglen's curation work sometime.

IO

International Operations: deep black, unchecked, American intelligence organisation. It maintains the façade of being funded through U.S. government black budgets, but it's essentially a rogue actor at this point. Notable

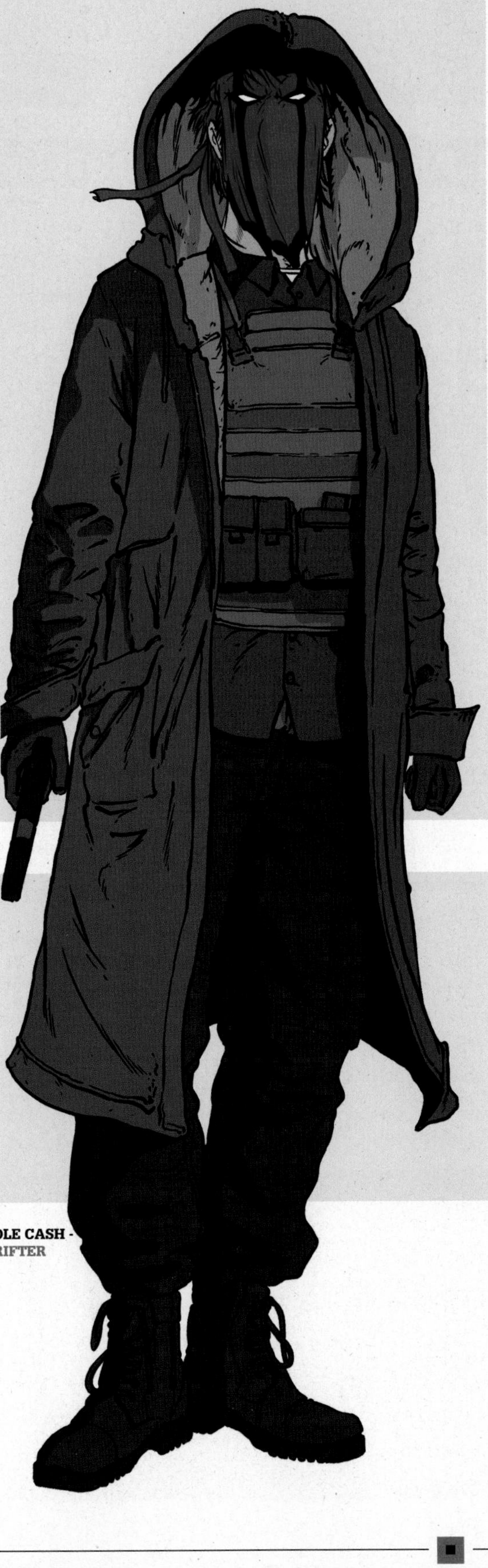

COLE CASH -
GRIFTER

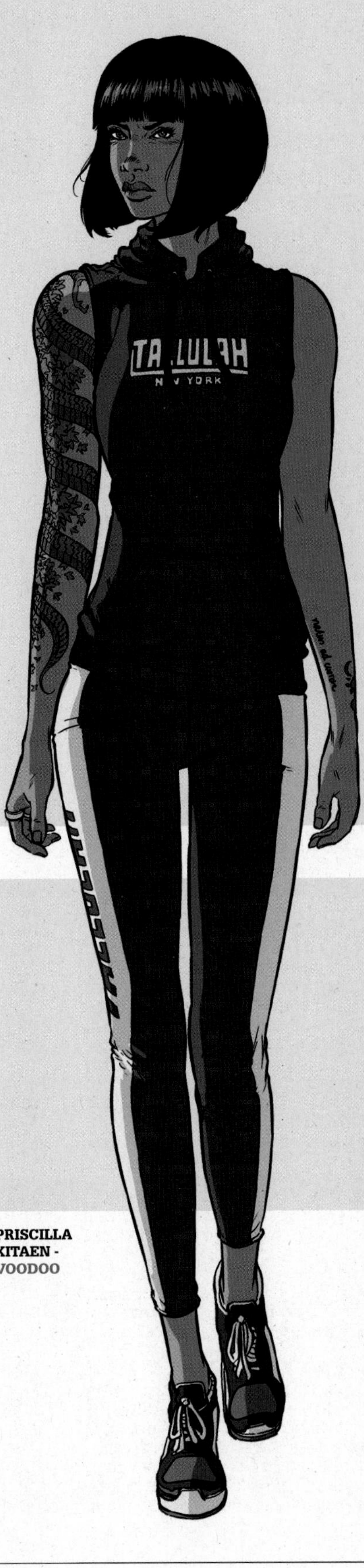

PRISCILLA KITAEN -
VOODOO

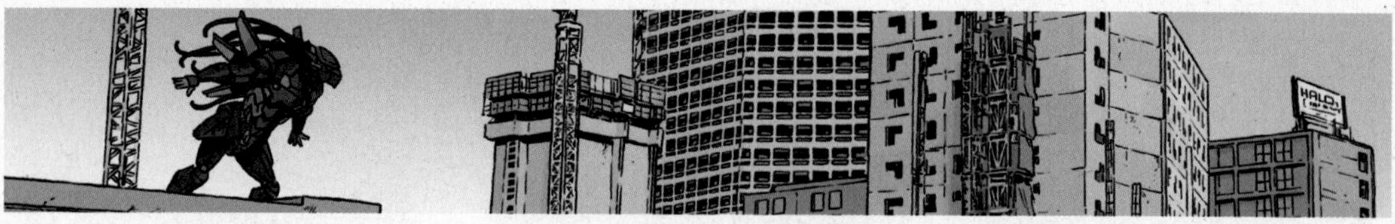

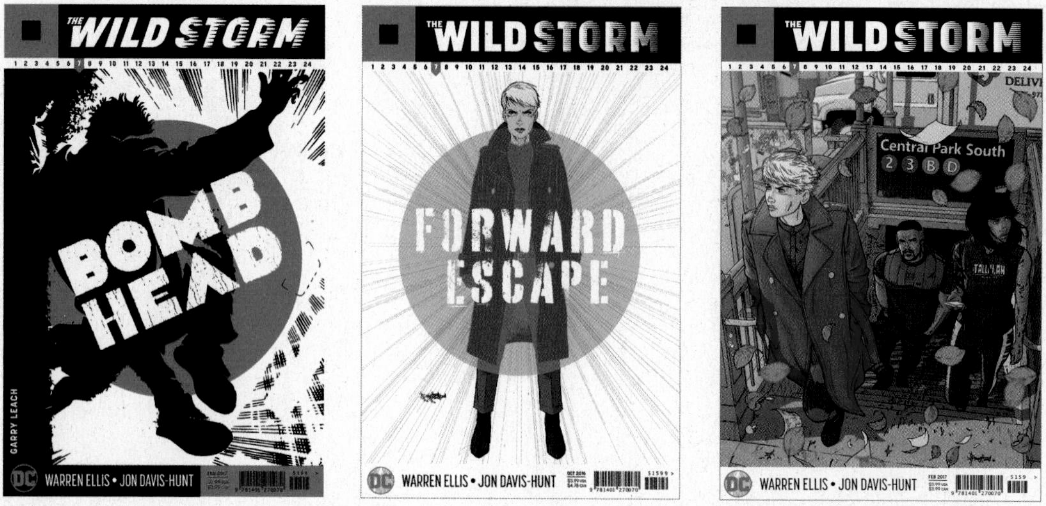
THE WILD STORM
BOMB HEAD
GARRY LEACH
WARREN ELLIS • JON DAVIS-HUNT
THE WILD STORM
FORWARD ESCAPE
WARREN ELLIS • JON DAVIS-HUNT
THE WILD STORM
Central Park South
2 3 B D
WARREN ELLIS • JON DAVIS-HUNT

Three initial trade dress concepts designed by Steve Cook. The red and black square is based on a maritime alert signal, warning of an approaching storm. Illustrations by Jon Davis-Hunt.

for its four-body strike units, known as CATs—Covert Action Teams. They think they have the run of the world.

HALO

A groundbreaking technological corporation: Apple plus Tesla plus science fiction. Run by the charismatic little person Jacob Marlowe as, publicly, an aspirational brand, and privately as what Marlowe calls "The Main Project"—a plan to change the world. He is folding [REDACTED] and hidden breakthrough human science into retail technology. The Main Project is to uplift human society: he's waited [REDACTED] years to raise humanity into [REDACTED] without seriously distorting their development, and now is the time, before the planet reaches the tight spot in the Gaian bottleneck.

SKYWATCH

A secret space programme.

DESIGN

When Jim launched WildStorm, the look was best-in-class for commercial superhero comics—computer-assisted colour, pinsharp printing, great paper. We can't replicate that, and, frankly, I can't think of a technological way to top it. So let's try something else.

Stripped-down, stark and authentic.

Strongly typographic logos. Basing all the series logos on the same base font would give the line a subtle sense of visual cohesion. I understand Steve Cook is at DC these days, and he has a background in book design and music design, and I'm pretty sure we'd speak the same language on this.

Stripped-down—monochrome covers, even? Certainly nothing splashy—straight-up images of the cast, no more than three of them at any one time. Record covers, essentially.

We will also need a WildStorm mark, which I would like to be as neutral as, say, the BBC mark, a font-based piece, probably of the same family as whatever we start the series logos with.

No broken-out subheaders on the covers. (I realise DC has reasons to use them, but I don't feel like they have a place here.) ■

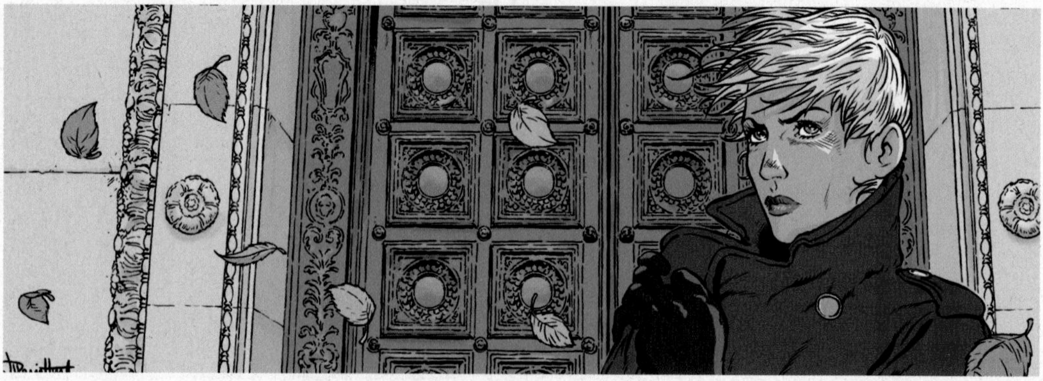

ROUGH LAYOUTS BY JON DAVIS-HUNT FOR

THE WILD STORM

1

THE WILD STORM 01 – PAGE #01.

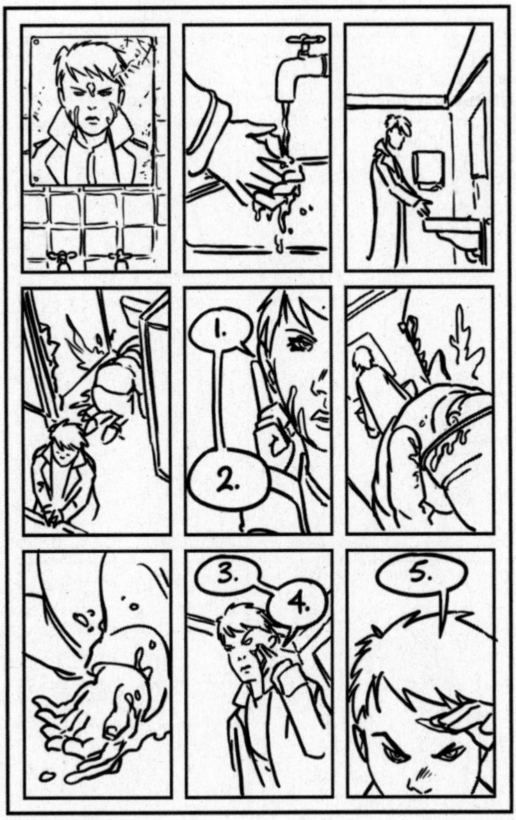

THE WILD STORM 01 – PAGE #02.

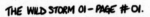

THE WILD STORM 01 - PAGE # 03.

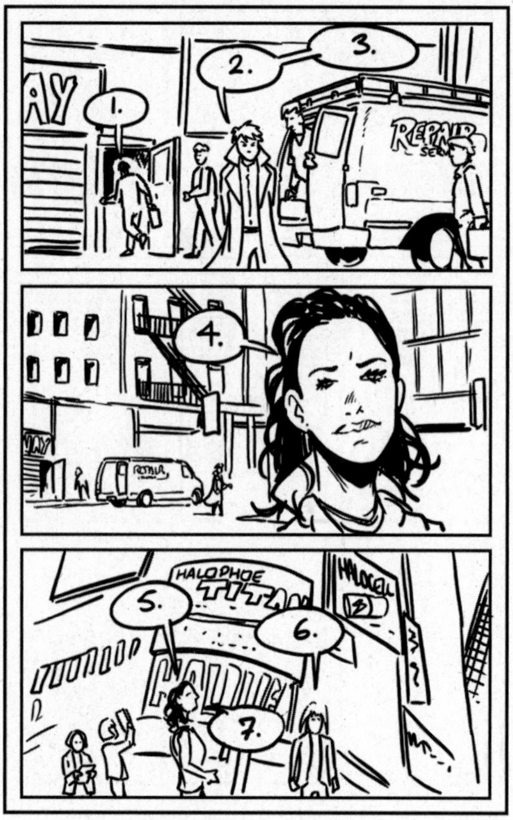
REPAIR

THE WILDSTORM 01 - PAGE #4.

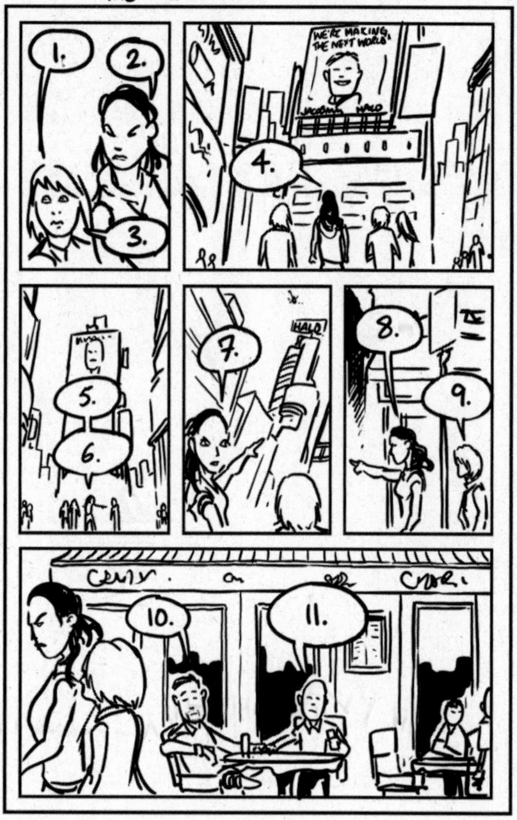
WE'RE MAKING THE NEXT WORLD
HALO

THE WILD STORM 01 - PAGE # 05.

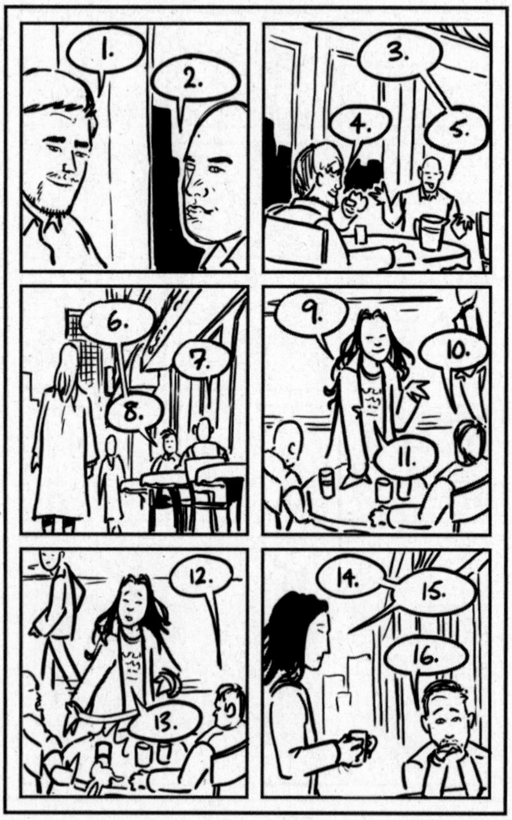

THE WILD STORM 01 - PAGE # 06.

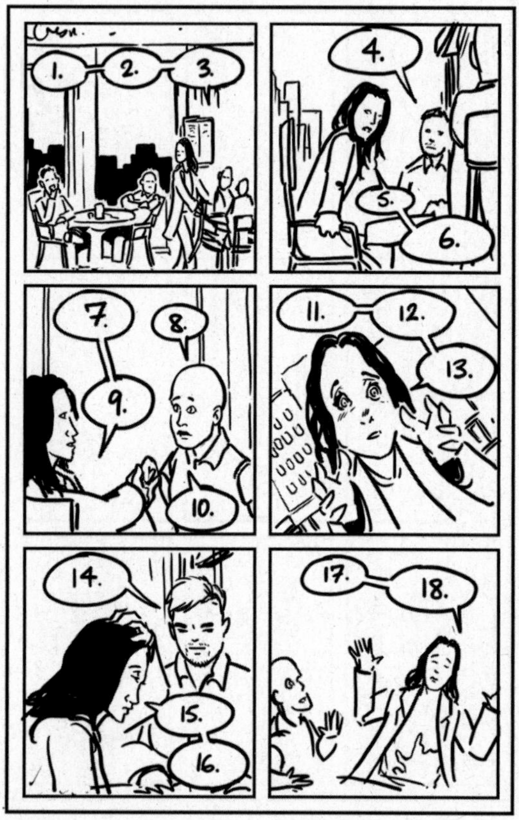

THE WILD STORM 01 – PAGE # 7.

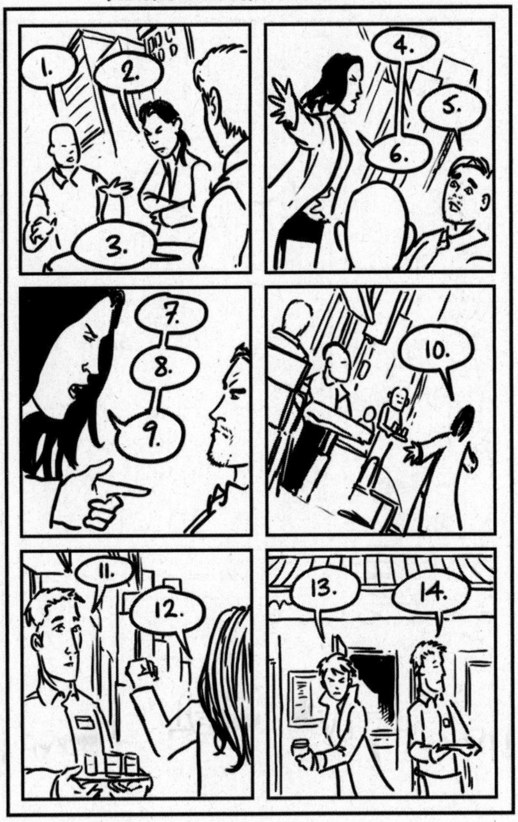
1.
2.
3.
4.
5.
6.
7.
8.
9.
10.
11.
12.
13.
14.

THE WILD STORM 01 – PAGE # 08.

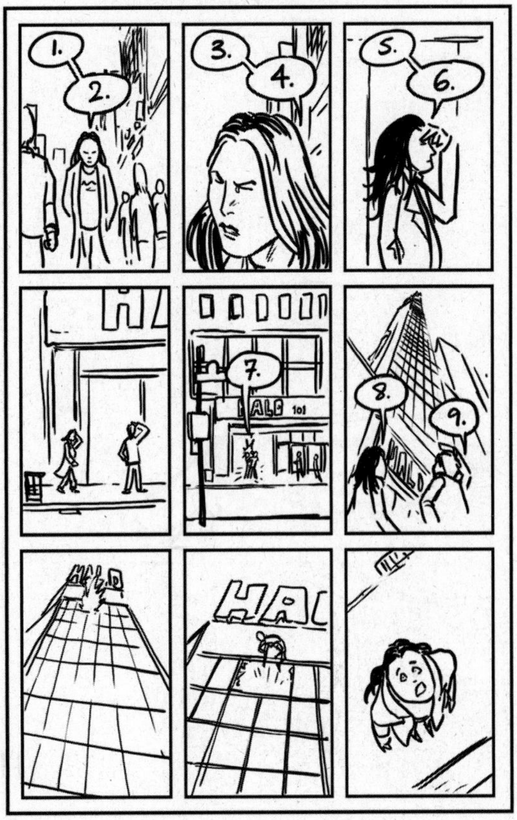
1.
2.
3.
4.
5.
6.
HALO 101
7.
8.
9.

THE WILD STORM 01 – PAGE # 09.

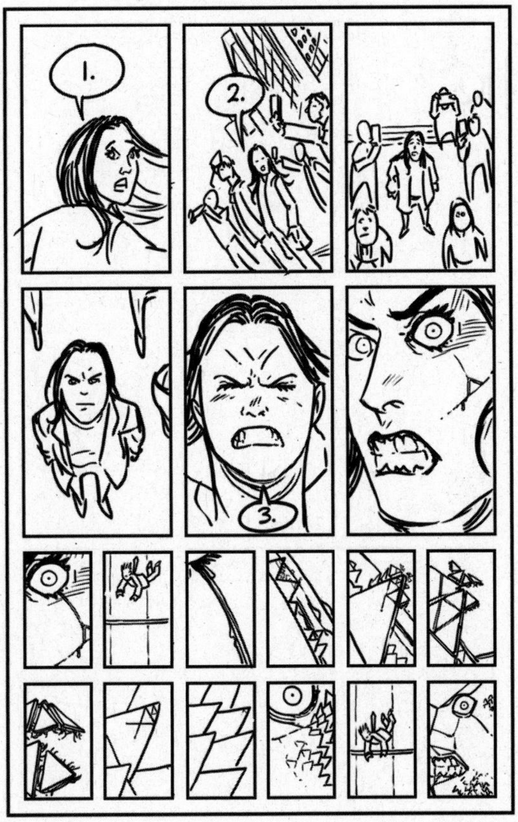
1.
2.
3.

THE WILD STORM 01 – PAGE # 10.

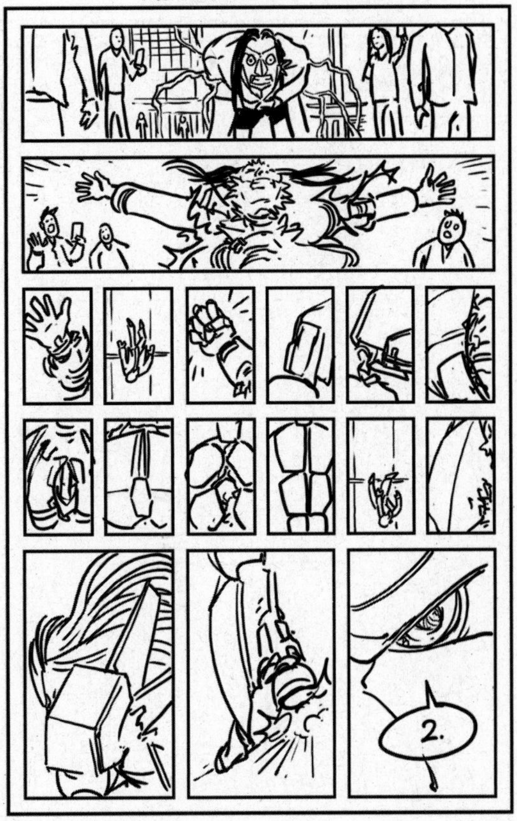
2.

THE WILD STORM 01 – PAGE # 11.

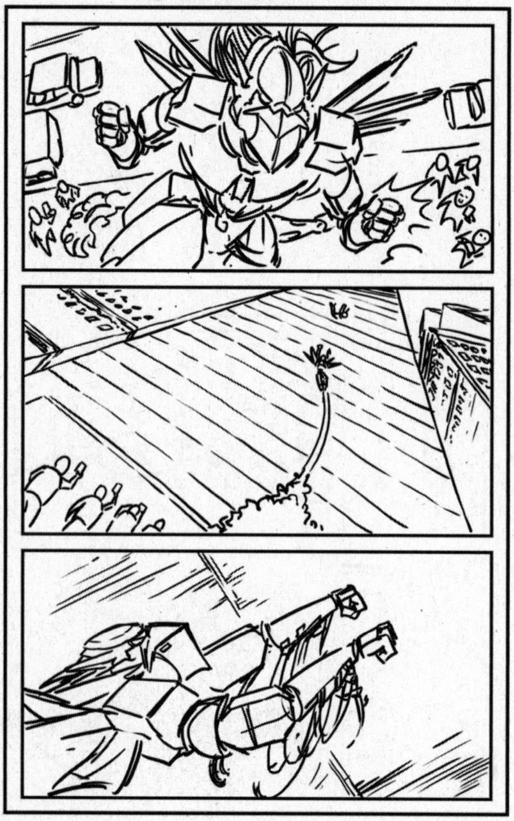

THE WILD STORM 01 – PAGE # 12.

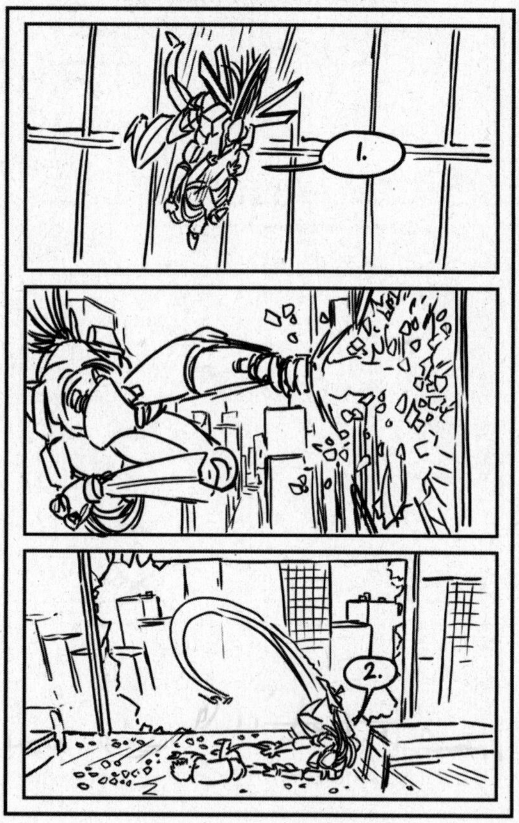
1.
2.

THE WILD STORM 01 – PAGE # 13.

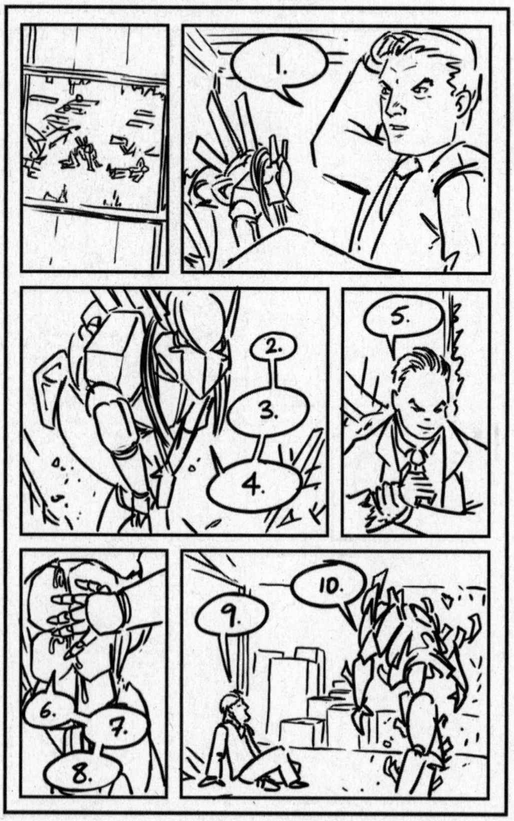
1.
2.
3.
4.
5.
6.
7.
8.
9.
10.

THE WILDSTORM 01 – PAGE # 14.

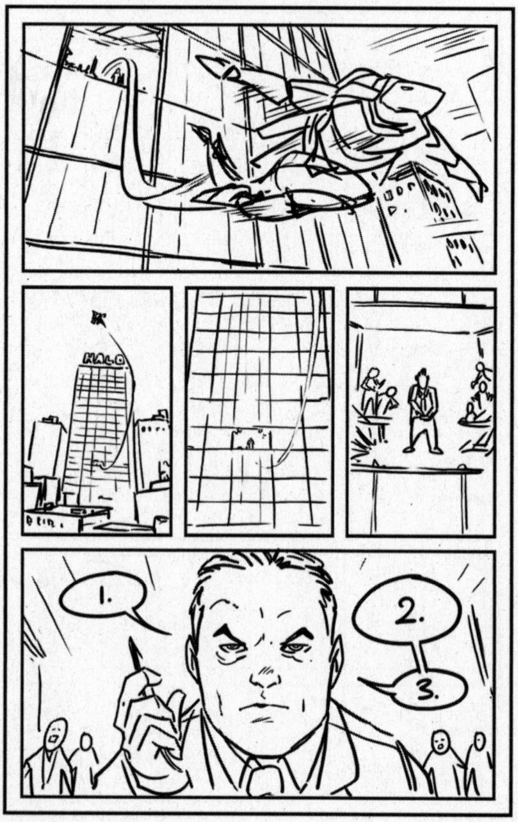
HALO
1.
2.
3.

THE WILD STORM 01 – PAGE 15.

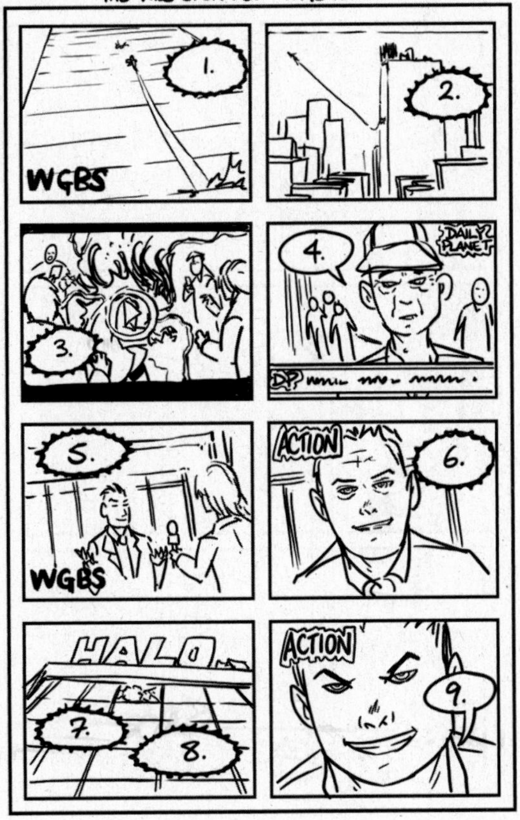
1.
2.
WGBS
3.
4.
DAILY PLANET
DP
5.
WGBS
ACTION
6.
HALO
7.
8.
ACTION
9.

THE WILD STORM 01 – PAGE 16.

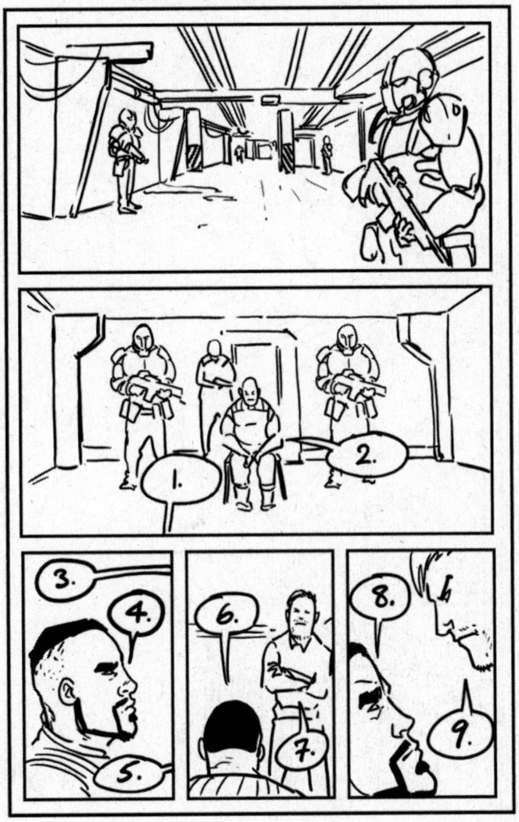
1.
2.
3.
4.
5.
6.
7.
8.
9.

THE WILD STORM 01 – PAGE #17

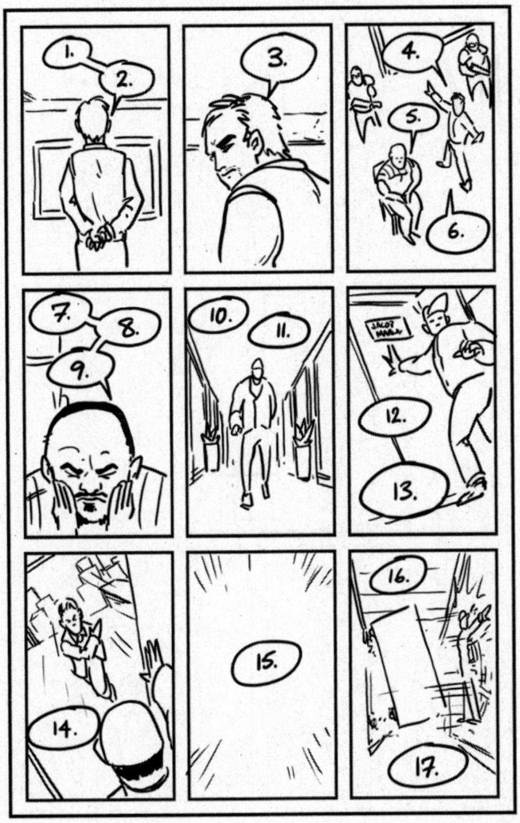
1.
2.
3.
4.
5.
6.
7.
8.
9.
10.
11.
12.
13.
14.
15.
16.
17.

THE WILD STORM 01 – PAGE # 18.

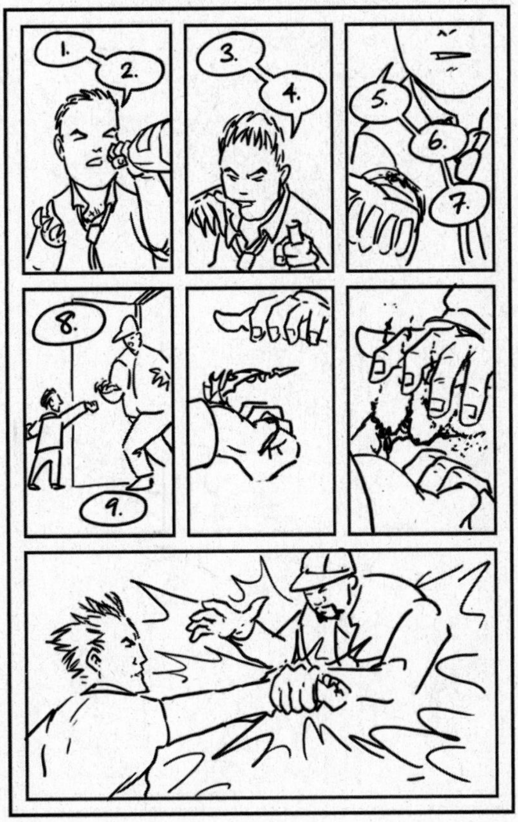
1.
2.
3.
4.
5.
6.
7.
8.
9.

THE WILD STORM 01 – PAGE # 19.

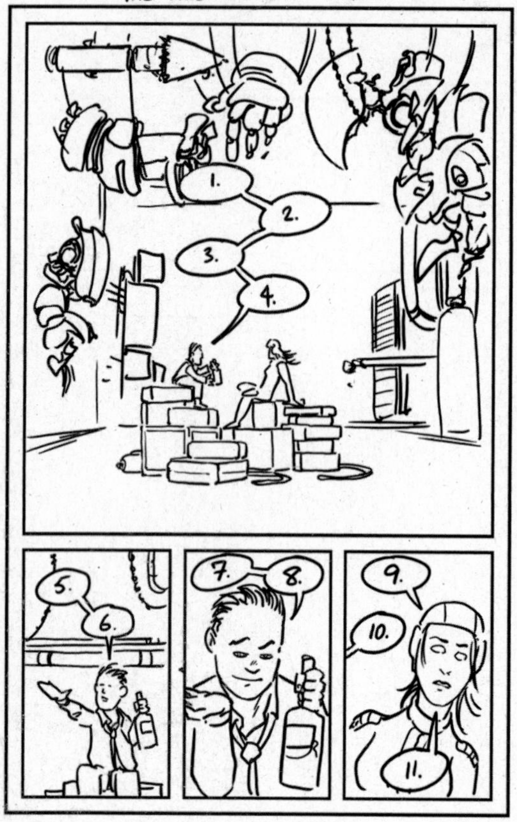

THE WILD STORM 01 – PANELS # 20.

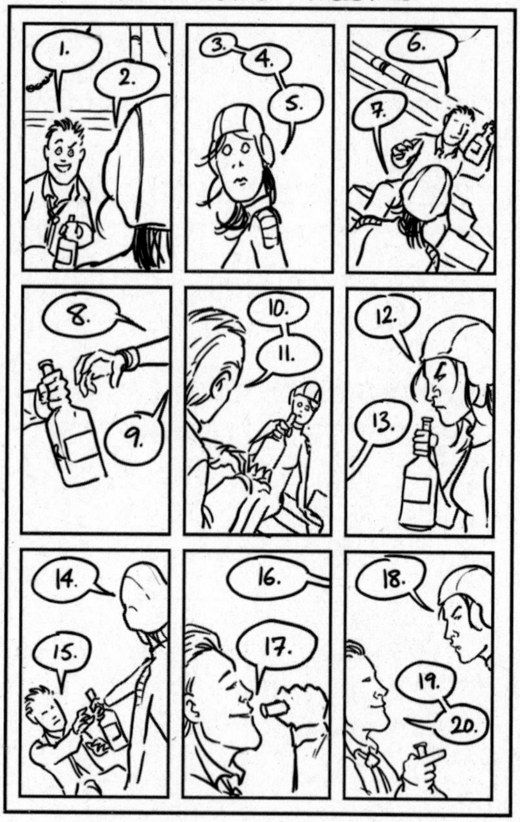

THE WILD STORM 01 – PAGE # 21.

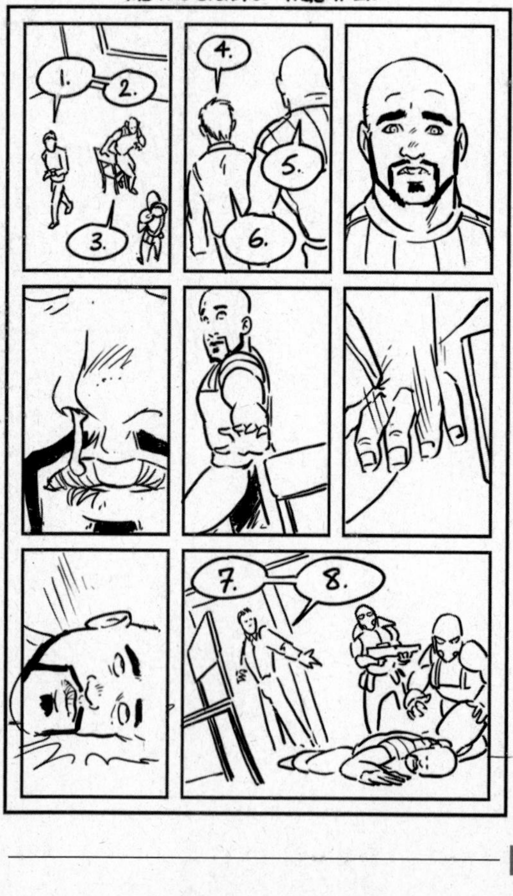

THE WILD STORM 01 – PAGE # 22.

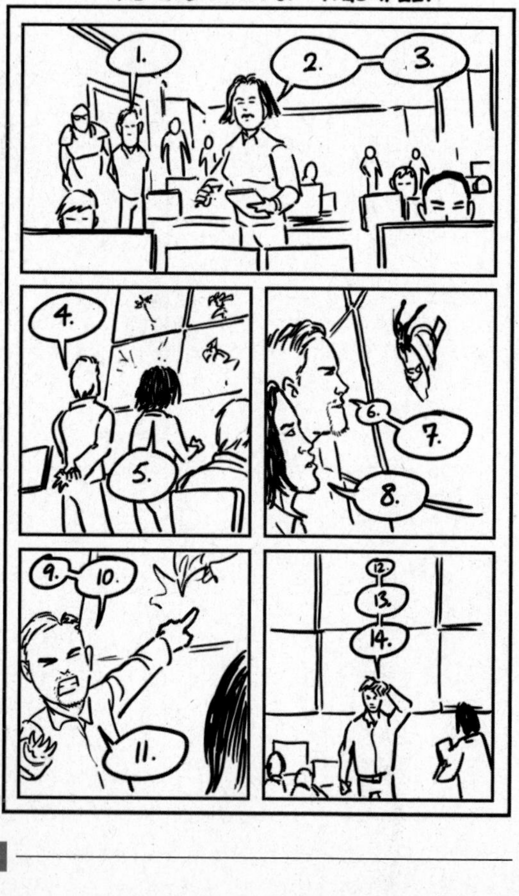